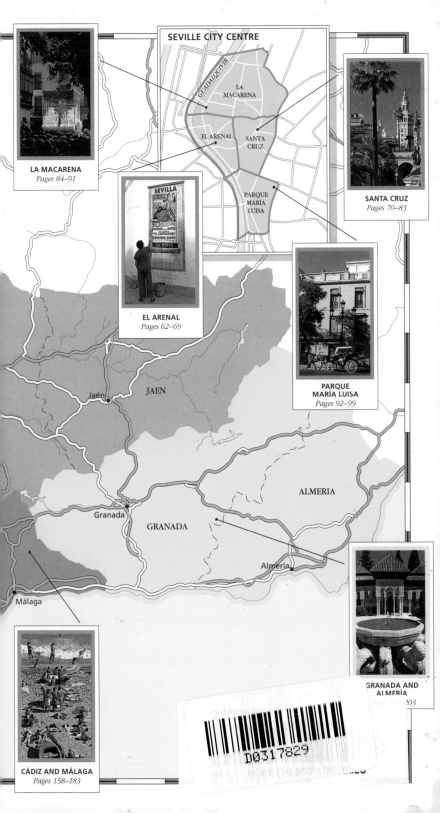

SEVILLE CITY CENTRE

GUADALQUIVIR

LA MACARENA

EL ARENAL

SANTA CRUZ

PARQUE MARIA LUISA

LA MACARENA
Pages 84–91

SANTA CRUZ
Pages 70–83

EL ARENAL
Pages 62–69

PARQUE MARÍA LUISA
Pages 92–99

JAEN

Jaén

ALMERIA

Granada

GRANADA

Almería

Málaga

GRANADA AND ALMERÍA
?03

CÁDIZ AND MÁLAGA
Pages 158–183

D0317829

EYEWITNESS TRAVEL

SEVILLE
& ANDALUSIA

DK

LONDON, NEW YORK,
MELBOURNE, MUNICH AND DELHI
www.dk.com

PROJECT EDITOR Anna Streiffert
ART EDITOR Robert Purnell
EDITORS Marcus Hardy, Jane Oliver
DESIGNERS Malcolm Parchment, Katie Peacock
PICTURE RESEARCH Monica Allende, Naomi Peck
DTP DESIGNERS Samantha Borland, Sarah Martin

MAIN CONTRIBUTORS
David Baird, Martin Symington, Nigel Tisdall

PHOTOGRAPHERS
Neil Lukas, John Miller, Linda Whitwam

ILLUSTRATORS
Richard Draper, Isidoro González-Adalid Cabezas
(Acanto Arquitectura y Urbanismo S.L.), Steven Gyapay,
Claire Littlejohn, Maltings, Chris Orr, John Woodcock

Reproduced by Colourscan (Singapore)
Printed and bound by L. Rex Printing Co. Ltd., China

First published in Great Britain in 1996
by Dorling Kindersley Limited
80 Strand, London WC2R 0RL

Reprinted with revisions 1997, 1998, 1999,
2000, 2001, 2002, 2003, 2004, 2006, 2008, 2010

Copyright © 1996, 2010 Dorling Kindersley Limited, London
A Penguin Company

A CIP CATALOGUE RECORD IS AVAILABLE FROM THE BRITISH LIBRARY.

ISBN 978-1-4053-5310-6

Front cover main image: Torre del Oro, Seville

MIX
From responsible
sources
FSC   FSC™C018179
www.fsc.org

**The information in this
DK Eyewitness Travel Guide is checked regularly.**
Every effort has been made to ensure that this book is as up-to-date
as possible at the time of going to press. Some details, however,
such as telephone numbers, opening hours, prices, gallery hanging
arrangements and travel information, are liable to change. The
publishers cannot accept responsibility for any consequences arising
from the use of this book, nor for any material on third party
websites, and cannot guarantee that any website address in this
book will be a suitable source of travel information. We value the
views and suggestions of our readers very highly. Please write to:
Publisher, DK Eyewitness Travel Guides,
Dorling Kindersley, 80 Strand, London, Great Britain WC2R 0RL.

Previous pages: Torre del Oro in Seville by night

CONTENTS

**Bible illustration in Moorish style
dating from the 10th century**

INTRODUCING
SEVILLE AND
ANDALUSIA

**Horse and carriage at Plaza de
España, Parque María Luisa**

Zahara de la Sierra, one of Andalusia's traditional *pueblos blancos* (white towns)

The Generalife

HOW TO USE THIS GUIDE

This guide helps you to get the most from your stay in Seville and Andalusia. It provides both expert recommendations and detailed practical information. *Introducing Seville and Andalusia* maps the region and sets it in its historical and cultural context. *Seville Area by Area* and *Andalusia Area by Area* describe the important sights, with maps, pictures and detailed illustrations. Suggestions on what to eat and drink, accommodation, shopping and entertainment are in *Travellers' Needs*, and the *Survival Guide* has tips on everything from transport to using Spanish telephones.

SEVILLE AREA BY AREA

The centre of Seville has been divided into four sightseeing areas. *Across the River* makes up a fifth area. Each area has its own chapter, which opens with a list of the sights described. All the sights are numbered and plotted on an Area Map. The detailed information for each sight is presented in numerical order, thereby making it easy to locate within the chapter.

Sights at a Glance lists the chapter's sights by category: Churches, Museums and Galleries, Historic Buildings, Streets and Plazas, etc.

All pages relating to central Seville have red thumb tabs.

A locator map shows where you are in relation to other areas of the city centre.

1 Area Map
For easy reference, the sights are numbered and located on a map. The sights are also shown on the Street Finder *on pages 112–17.*

2 Street-by-Street Map
This gives a bird's-eye view of the heart of each sightseeing area.

A suggested route for a walk covers the more interesting streets in the area.

Stars indicate the sights that no visitor should miss.

3 Detailed information on each sight
All the sights in Seville are described individually. Addresses and practical information are provided. The key to the symbols used in the information block is shown on the back flap.

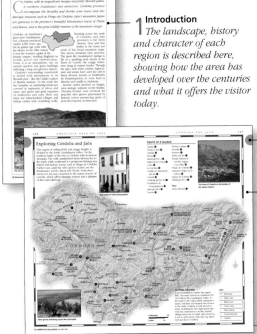

CORDOBA AND JAÉN

1 Introduction

The landscape, history and character of each region is described here, showing how the area has developed over the centuries and what it offers the visitor today.

ANDALUSIA AREA BY AREA

In this book, Andalusia has been divided into four distinct regions, each of which has a separate chapter. The most interesting sights to visit have been numbered on a Regional Map.

Each area of Andalusia has colour-coded thumb tabs.

2 Regional map

This shows the main road network and provides an illustrated overview of the whole region. All entries are numbered and there are also some useful tips on getting around the region by car, bus and train.

3 Detailed information on each entry

All the important towns and other places to visit are dealt with individually. They are listed in order, following the numbering given on the Regional Map. Within each town or city, there is detailed information on important buildings and other sights.

Features give information on topics of particular interest.

The Visitors' Checklist provides a summary of the practical information you need to plan your visit.

4 The top sights

These are given two or more full pages. Historic buildings are dissected to reveal their interiors; museums and galleries have colour-coded floorplans to help you locate the most interesting exhibits.

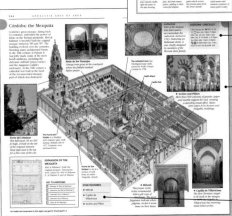

Stars indicate the best features and important works of art.

INTRODUCING SEVILLE AND ANDALUSIA

DISCOVERING SEVILLE AND ANDALUSIA

Andalusia is one of the largest regions of Spain, and easily the most varied. Stretching from the Atlantic Ocean to the Mediterranean, its landscapes take in wetlands rich in bird life, groves of olive trees, lush forests and snow-capped peaks. Most visitors head for the seaside resorts or focus

A wall shrine to the Virgin Mary in Cádiz

their sightseeing time on three cities famed for their art and architecture: Seville, Córdoba and Granada; however, there are many smaller, out-of-the-way places worth visiting. One of the great draws of Andalusia is the zest for life and sociability of its people, as witnessed in many spectacular fiestas.

The delightful Patio de las Doncellas in Seville's Real Alcázar

SEVILLE

- **Moorish Real Alcázar**
- **Cathedral and La Giralda**
- **Bars and bullfighting**
- **Flamboyant celebrations of Semana Santa**

Andalusia's capital, a lively city on the Guadalquivir River, combines the glories of Moorish and Christian Spain in the unmistakable Giralda belltower, originally a minaret, attached to its cathedral *(see pp78–9)* and in the lavishly decorated royal palace of the **Real Alcázar** *(see pp82–3)*. Visitors also flock to see the quaint whitewashed streets and squares of the **Santa Cruz quarter** *(see pp72–3)* and to sample Seville's immense number and variety of bars. When there is a bullfight on, they join the locals in the **Plaza de Toros de la**

Maestranza *(see p68)*, Seville's world-famous bull ring. As appealing as the many monuments and museums is the city's appetite for spectacle and living life to its fullest: in spring, the exuberant processions of **Holy Week** (Semana Santa) *(see p38)* are followed by the gaudy revelry of the **April Fair** *(see p38)*.

HUELVA & SEVILLE

- **Roman ruins of Itálica**
- **The Moorish stronghold of Carmona**
- **Doñana National Park**
- **The Columbus connection**

Seville makes the perfect base for exploring the sights in the province of the same name and in neighbouring Huelva. The ruins of the Roman town of **Itálica** *(see p132)* and the splendid old

hilltop town of **Carmona** *(see p132)*, developed by the Arabs on Roman foundations, can both be visited within half-day trips.

The outstanding attraction of western Andalusia is the **Doñana National Park** *(see pp130–31)*, an area of fragile coastal wetlands that is rich in both flora and fauna. Reserve a place on the official guided tour in a 4x4 bus; you will be sure to see plenty of Doñana's abundant birdlife.

The westerly province of Huelva, nudging up to Portugal, is best known for its associations with Christopher Columbus, who set sail from here in search of the New World. The **Monasteria de la Rábida** *(see p127)* is something of a shrine to his memory. Inland, the **Sierra de Aracena** *(see p126)* has great scenery for walking or horse riding; it also produces some of Spain's finest dry-cured hams.

A horse in the Doñana National Park, in western Andalusia

◁ Painting of the Feria de Abril in Seville by Dominguez Becquer (1885)

Palacio Jabalquinto, in the pretty hilltop town of Baeza

CÓRDOBA AND JAÉN

- **The Great Mosque of Córdoba**
- **Córdoba's Jewish Quarter**
- **Renaissance towns**
- **Splendid Baroque churches and mansions**

Córdoba *(see pp140–146)* is a city that requires a leisurely visit, not least to allow time to appreciate the scale of the **Mezquita** *(see pp144–5)*, its extraordinary mosque/cathedral built between the 8th and 10th centuries. Its interior is made up of elegant columns and arches. Beside the Mezquita is the city's former Jewish quarter, a warren of enchanting medieval streets and secretive patios.

The countryside of both Córdoba and Jaén provinces is characterized by endless lines of olive trees, which produce high-quality extra virgin oils. Take the time to explore the many interesting small towns. **Priego de Córdoba** *(see p150)* is a handsome assembly of Baroque architecture, and it also boasts a beautiful medieval quarter. **Jaén** is filled with castles, churches and mansions built during the Renaissance. Two towns sitting on adjacent hilltops are a particular delight to stroll around: **Úbeda** *(see pp154–5)* and its smaller neighbour **Baeza** *(see pp152–3)*.

CÁDIZ AND MÁLAGA

- **Clifftop Ronda**
- **The sherry triangle**
- **Popular beaches along the Costa del Sol**
- **Vibrant Tangier**

The famous *pueblos blancos* (white towns) of southern Spain – picturesque clusters of houses sheltering beneath an ancient castle – are the trademark of the hills between the Atlantic and the southern Mediterranean coasts. Outstanding among them is **Ronda** *(see pp176–7)*, which stands on the lip of a cliff and is cut in half by a deep gorge.

Wine lovers will find plenty of interest in and around **Jerez de la Frontera** *(see p162)*, the centre of production for sherry and other fortified wines. Just south on the coast, the narrow alleyways and harbour views of **Cádiz** *(see pp164–7)*, Europe's oldest city, are a delight to explore.

The **Costa del Sol** *(see p182)*, especially the stretch between Málaga and Estepona, is where you will find the best beaches, family attractions and nightlife. A highlight is the luxurious resort of Marbella.

Only 45 minutes from Tarifa by ferry, **Tangier** *(see p170)*, which is uniquely neither African, European nor Moroccan but a heady mix of all three, has been a favoured haunt of artists and writers for decades. The exotic charms of its bazaars and mosques still attract fascinated visitors.

The exclusive yacht harbour at Marbella's Puerto Banus

GRANADA AND ALMERÍA

- **The Alhambra**
- **The rolling Alpujarras**
- **Desert landscapes**

The exquisitely ornate palace-fortress of the **Alhambra** *(see pp194–5)*, which looks down over Granada from a hilltop, is not to be missed. South of Granada, over the other side of the **Sierra Nevada** *(see p197)* – site of Europe's southernmost ski resort – are the picturesque valleys of the **Alpujarras** *(see pp198–9)*. The hills are dotted with quaint villages.

The arid, easterly province of Almería gets fewer visitors than other parts of Andalusia, but has some magnificent scenery, especially the dramatic cliffs and headlands of Cabo de Gata *(see p202)*. Tabernas is in the only desert in Europe and has often served as a back-drop for westerns and other films.

The beautiful architecture of the ancient Alhambra Palace in Granada

Putting Seville and Andalusia on the Map

Andalusia is Spain's southernmost region, bordered by
Extremadura and Castilla-La Mancha to the north and
Murcia to the northwest. Its long coastline faces the Atlantic
to the west and the Mediterranean to the south and east.
One of Spain's largest regions, it covers an area of 87,267 sq
km (33,693 sq miles) and has a
population of 6.8 million.
Seville is the pro-
vince's capital.

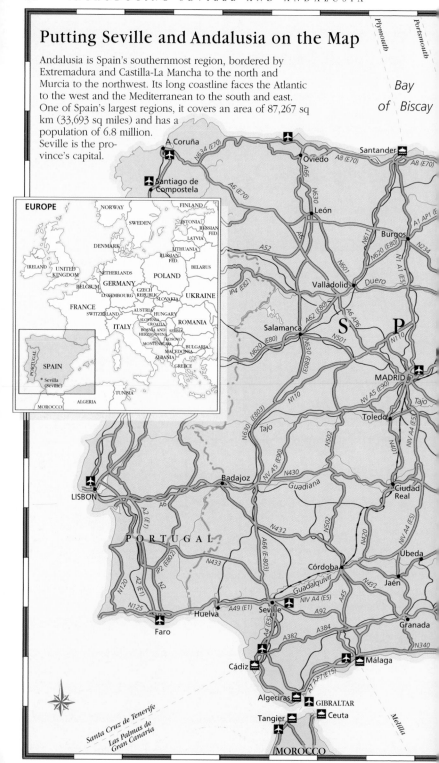

EUROPE

NORWAY · FINLAND · SWEDEN · ESTONIA · LATVIA · RUSSIAN FED. · LITHUANIA · DENMARK · IRELAND · UNITED KINGDOM · NETHERLANDS · GERMANY · POLAND · BELARUS · RUSSIAN FED. · BELGIUM · LUXEMBOURG · CZECH REPUBLIC · SLOVAKIA · UKRAINE · FRANCE · SWITZERLAND · AUSTRIA · HUNGARY · SLOVENIA · ROMANIA · CROATIA · BOSNIA AND HERZEGOVINA · SERBIA · MONTENEGRO · KOSOVO · BULGARIA · ITALY · MACEDONIA · ALBANIA · GREECE · PORTUGAL · SPAIN · Sevilla (Seville) · TUNISIA · MOROCCO · ALGERIA

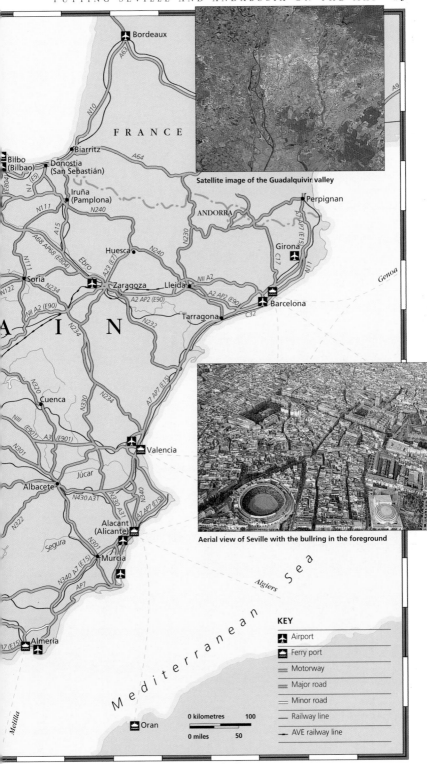

Satellite image of the Guadalquivir valley

Aerial view of Seville with the bullring in the foreground

KEY

✈	Airport
⛴	Ferry port
—	Motorway
—	Major road
—	Minor road
—	Railway line
→	AVE railway line

0 kilometres	100
0 miles	50

Seville City Centre and Greater Seville

Seville city centre is a compact maze of old, narrow streets, with most sights within walking distance. A couple of wide, busy avenues cut through the centre, dividing it into separate areas. This book focuses on these areas, starting with the historic neighbourhoods on each side of Avenida de la Constitución. To the west, along the river, is El Arenal with the Plaza de Toros; and to the east lies the old Jewish quarter of Santa Cruz, dominated by the massive cathedral and the Reales Alcázares. In the north lies La Macarena with its many churches, while the Parque María Luisa stretches out beyond the Universidad, south of the historic centre.

El Arenal: Teatro de la Maestranza and Torre del Oro

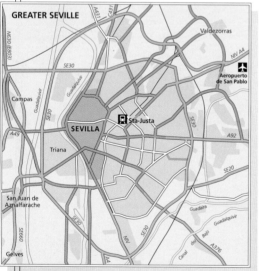

Greater Seville

West of the Guadalquivir river lies the site of Expo '92 and the picturesque Triana quarter. Sprawling industrial zones and modern residential areas surround the town centre.

Parque María Luisa: the Plaza de España, built for the 1929 Exposition

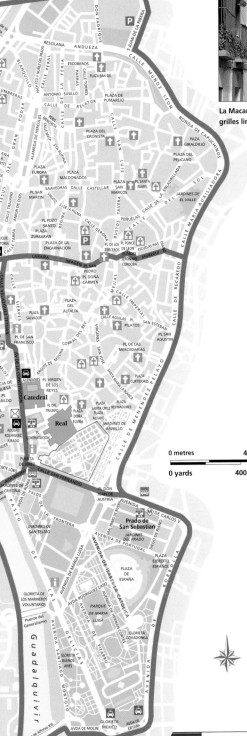

La Macarena: Sevillian façades with window grilles lining Calle Santa Clara

Santa Cruz: Horses and carriages at Plaza del Triunfo by the cathedral

KEY

◼	Major sight
◼	Seville city centre
◼	Built-up area
☐	Greater Seville
✈	Airport
🚆	Railway station
🚌	Bus terminus
🚍	Coach terminus
🚊	Metro-Centro tram stop
Ⓜ	Metro station
🚢	River boat boarding point
🚖	Taxi rank
P	Parking
ℹ	Tourist information
✚	Hospital with casualty unit
🚓	Police station
✝	Church
✝	Convent or monastery
⊠	Post office
▬	Motorway
▬	Major road
▬	Minor road
—	Railway

0 metres 400

0 yards 400

A PORTRAIT OF ANDALUSIA

Andalusia is where all Spain's stereotypes appear to have come together. Bullfighters, flamenco dancers, white villages and harsh sierras are all there in abundance. But they form only part of an intricate tapestry. Beneath the surface, expect to find many contradictions. Wherever you travel, particularly when you escape from the tourist-engulfed coast, you will come across the unexpected, whether it is a local fiesta *or a breathtaking view.*

Until the 1950s Andalusia had changed scarcely at all since the middle of the 19th century, when the English traveller, Richard Ford, described it as "a land bottled for antiquarians" – almost a feudal society, with attendant rigid social strata.

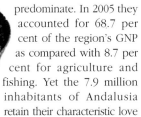

A basket of newly-harvested olives

Today, four-lane highways stretch where not so long ago there were only dirt tracks. Children whose parents are illiterate play with computers and plan their university careers. Agriculture is still important, but there are also factories turning out cars and aircraft. As in most other European countries, the service industries, tourism especially, predominate. In 2005 they accounted for 68.7 per cent of the region's GNP as compared with 8.7 per cent for agriculture and fishing. Yet the 7.9 million inhabitants of Andalusia retain their characteristic love of talk and folklore, their indifference to time and their abundant hospitality.

THE MOORISH LEGACY

The Andalusian character is complex because it reflects a complex history. Successive invaders, including the Phoenicians, Romans, Visigoths and Moors, have all left their indelible mark. Although the Christian rulers of Spain ejected both Jews and Moors

Musicians, singers and dancers continuing a flamenco tradition that dates from the 18th century *(see p28)*

◁ Bullfighters *(see pp26–7)* in traditional costumes, preparing for the *corrida* from their kingdom, they could not remove their influences on the country – let alone on Andalusia. Look at the face of an Andalusian man or woman and you will catch a glimpse of North Africa. Centuries of Moorish occupation *(see pp46–7)* and the inevitable mingling of blood have created a race and culture different from any in Europe.

As you travel around the region, you will find much physical evidence of the Moorish legacy: in the splendour of the Alhambra *(see pp 194–5)* and the Mezquita *(see pp144–5)* in Córdoba, and in ruined fortresses and elaborate tilework. Workshops across the region still practise crafts handed down from great Moorish kingdoms. Many of the irrigation networks in use today follow those laid out by the Moors, who built *norias* (waterwheels), *aljibes*

Sevillanos enjoying a pre-dinner drink and some tapas (see pp224–5)

(tanks for collecting the rain), *albercas* (cisterns), and *acequias* (irrigation channels).

As these words show, the Moors also left a strong linguistic legacy, not only of agricultural terms, but also of words for foods – *naranja* (orange), for example, and *aceituna* (olive).

Moorish influence may also account for Andalusians' love of poetry and fine language. It is no coincidence that Spain's finest poets, including among them Nobel prize winners, come from this region.

PEOPLE AND CULTURE

Sevillanos work hard to sustain their reputation for flamboyance and hedonism. A 13th-century Moorish commentator noted that

Moorish-style stucco work

they were "the most frivolous and most given to playing the fool". Living up to that image is a full-time occupation, but the visitor should not be deceived by the exuberant façade. One surprising aspect of both Seville and Andalusia is that although the society may appear open and extrovert, it is, in fact, one that also values privacy.

The Andalusian concept of time can also be perplexing. Progressive business types may try to adjust to the rigorous demands of Europe, but in general, northern Europeans' obsession with time is an object of mirth here. The moment is to be enjoyed and tomorrow will look after itself. A concert will often begin well after the advertised time, and lunch can feasibly take place at any time between 1pm and 4:30pm.

Penitents parading a monstrance, Semana Santa *(see p38)*

Barren, remote countryside, one of the many faces of Andalusia's varied landscape (see pp20–21)

Attitudes to women in Andalusia are changing, as elsewhere in western Europe, though southern Spain's tradition for *machismo* means that there is still some way to go. The number of women, for example, who work outside the home is still lower than in other countries of the West. Although many women have a job in their twenties, they still give up work when they marry in order to have children and look after the house.

Paradoxically, the mother is an almost sacred figure in Andalusia, where family ties are written in blood. Although new affluence and a steady movement to the cities is now beginning to erode old values, Andalusia remains a traditional rural society with a distinct emphasis on personal relationships.

Sevillian lady in the traditional Semana Santa costume (see p38)

Catholicism is Spain's dominant religion, and adoration of the Virgin is a striking feature of Andalusia. Apart from a purely religious devotion, she is also subject to a peculiar admiration from the male population. A man who never attends Mass may be ecstatic about the Virgin of his local church; when she emerges from the church in procession, he feels fiercely possessive of her. If you try to think of the gorgeously robed figure as a pagan earth mother or fertility goddess, the phenomenon is much easier to understand.

As a society, Andalusia is unafraid of its emotions, which are almost always near the surface. There is no shame in the singing of a *saeta*, the "arrow" of praise launched at the Virgin in Semana Santa (Holy Week), nor is there any ambivalence in the matador's desire to kill his antagonist, the bull. The quintessence of this is flamenco; the pain and passion of its songs reflect not just the sufferings and yearnings of gypsies and the poor, but also Andalusia's soul.

Decorative tilework in the Palacio de Viana (see p143)

Nun with convent jams

The Landscape of Andalusia

Prickly pear, a native of the Americas

Each year, several million visitors are drawn to the high-rise resorts along Andalusia's Mediterranean coast. Away from these, however, are empty, windswept Atlantic shores and expansive areas of wetland wilderness. Inland there are rugged mountain ranges clothed with forests of pine, cork and wild olive. Also typical of the landscape are the undulating hills awash with vines, cereals and olive trees. Of Andalusia's total land area, some 17 per cent has been designated national parks or nature reserves in order to protect the region's unique abundance of animal and plant life.

The fertile plains *of the Guadalquivir valley are watered by the river and have been the bread basket of Andalusia since Moorish times. Fields of cereals alternate with straight lines of citrus trees.*

0 kilometres   50

0 miles   25

SIERRA DE ARACENA

SIERRA

MOR

Córdoba

Río Guadalquivir

Río Genil

Sevilla

Huelva

Embalse del Guadalhorce

Río Guadalete

Río Guadalhorce

Málaga

Cádiz

SERRANÍA DE RONDA

The Atlantic beaches, *where pine trees grow behind the sand dunes, are less developed than the Mediterranean costas. Fishing fleets from Cádiz and Huelva operate offshore.*

The Río Guadalquivir runs through the wetlands of Coto Doñana (see pp130–31) before finally entering the Atlantic Ocean.

The Costa del Sol and the rest of the Mediterranean coast are mainly characterized by arid cliffs draped in bougainvillea and other subtropical shrubs. The beaches below are either pebbly or of greyish sand.

KEY

	Desert
	Marshland
	Forest
	Cultivated land
♠	Olive groves
⚘	Vineyards
⬮	Citrus cultivation

Craggy mountains *around Ronda encompass the nature reserve of Sierra de Grazalema. The area is home to a diverse wildlife, including griffon vultures and three species of eagle, and a forest of the rare Spanish fir.*

Endless olive groves *give the landscape in the provinces of Córdoba and, in particular, Jaén a distinct, crisscrossed pattern. These long-living trees are of great importance to the local economy, for their oil (see p148) as well as their beautiful wood.*

Vast forests, mainly of Corsican pine, cover the craggy sierras of Cazorla, Segura and Las Villas *(see p156)* in one of Spain's largest nature reserves.

Embalse del Tranco de Beas

SIERRA DE CAZORLA

Jaén

SIERRA DE SEGURA

Embalse de Negratín

mbalse de ájar

Granada

Pico Veleta ▲ 3398m

▲ Mulhacén 3482m

SIERRA NEVADA

SIERRA DE LOS FILABRES

Almería

Vegetables and exotic fruits are grown all year round in greenhouses covering many hectares around El Ejido. The soil of Almería is otherwise unproductive.

The Sierra Nevada, *Spain's highest mountain range, reaches 3,482 m (11,420 ft) at the peak of Mulhacén. Although only 40 km (25 miles) from the Mediterranean beaches, some areas are snow-capped all year round. The skiing season starts in December and lasts until spring. In summer the area is perfect for hiking and climbing.*

ANDALUSIAN WILDLIFE

Southern Spain is blessed with some of the richest and most varied flora and fauna in Europe, including some species which are unique to the area. The best time to appreciate this is in spring when wild flowers bloom and migratory birds stop en route from Africa to northern Europe.

Cork oak *grows mainly in the province of Cádiz. Its prized bark is stripped every ten years.*

The Cazorla violet, *which can only be found in Sierra de Cazorla (see p157), flowers in May.*

A mouflon *is a nimble and agile wild sheep that was introduced to mountainous areas in the 1970s.*

Flamingos *gather in great flocks in the wetlands of Coto Doñana and the Río Odiel delta in Huelva.*

Moorish Architecture

The first significant period of Moorish architecture arrived with the Cordoban Caliphate. The Mezquita was extended lavishly during this period and possesses all the enduring features of the Moorish style: arches, stucco work and ornamental use of calligraphy. Later, the Almohads imported a purer Islamic style, which can be seen at La Giralda *(see p78)*. The Nasrids built the superbly crafted Alhambra in Granada, while the *mudéjares (see p24)* used their skill to create beautiful Moorish-style buildings such as the Palacio Pedro I, part of Seville's Real Alcázar. *(see also pp46–9)*.

Reflections *in water combined with an overall play of light were central to Moorish architecture.*

Moorish domes *were often unadorned on the outside. Inside, however, an intricate lattice of stone ribs supported the dome's weight. Like this one in the Mezquita* (see pp144–5), *they were inlaid with multi-coloured mosaics featuring flower or animal motifs.*

Defensive walls

Moorish gardens were often arranged around gently rippling pools and channels.

DEVELOPMENT OF MOORISH ARCHITECTURE

Pre-Caliphal era 710–929	Caliphal era 929–1031	Almoravid and Almohad era 1091–1248	Nasrid era 1238–1492
	1031–91 Taifa period *(see p46)*		**c.1350** Alhambra palace

700	800	900	1000	1100	1200	1300	1400
	785 Mezquita in Córdoba begun			**1184** La Giralda in Seville begun		**c.1350** Palacio Pedro I	
			936 Medina Azahara near Córdoba begun		**Mudéjar era,** after **c.1215**		

Azulejos (see p76) *were used for wall decorations. Patterns became increasingly geometric, as on these tiles in the Palacio Pedro I (p82).*

MOORISH ARCHES

The Moorish arch was developed from the horseshoe arch that the Visigoths used in the construction of churches. The Moors modified it and used it as the basis of great architectural endeavours, such as the Mezquita. Subsequent arches show more sophisticated ornamentation and the slow demise of the basic horseshoe shape.

Caliphal arch, Medina Azahara *(see p138)*

Almohad arch, Patio del Yeso *(see p83)*

Mudéjar arch, Salón de Embajadores *(see p83)*

Nasrid arch, the Alhambra *(see p195)*

MOORISH PALACE

The palaces of the Moors were designed with gracious living, culture and learning in mind. The imagined palace here shows how space, light, water and ornamentation were combined to harmonious effect.

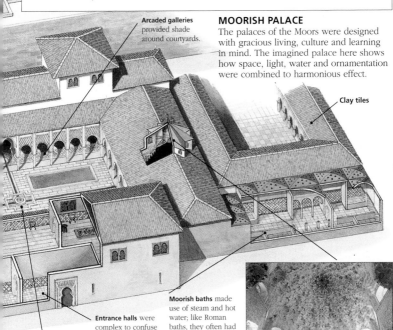

Arcaded galleries provided shade around courtyards.

Clay tiles

Entrance halls were complex to confuse unwanted visitors.

Moorish baths made use of steam and hot water; like Roman baths, they often had underfloor heating.

Water *cooled the Moors' elegant courtyards and served a contemplative purpose. Often, as here in the Patio de los Leones (see p195), water had to be pumped from a source far below.*

Elaborate stucco work *typifies the Nasrid style of architecture. The Sala de los Abencerrajes (see p195) in the Alhambra was built using only the simplest materials, but it is nevertheless widely regarded as one of the most outstanding monuments of the period of the Moorish occupation.*

Post-Moorish Architecture

The Christian reconquest was followed by the building of new churches and palaces, many by *mudéjares (see p48)*. Later, prejudice against the Moors grew as Christians began to assert their faith. Gothic styles from northern Europe filtered into Andalusia, though Mudéjar influences survived into the 18th century. In the 16th century, Andalusia was the centre of the Spanish Renaissance; and a uniquely Spanish interpretation of the Baroque emerged in the 18th century.

Mudéjar tower, Iglesia de Santa Ana *(see p192)*

THE RECONQUEST (MID-13TH TO LATE 15TH CENTURY)

Moorish craftsmen working on Christian buildings created a hybrid Christian Islamic style known as Mudéjar. Mid-13th-century churches, such as the ones built in Seville and Córdoba, show a varying degree of Moorish influence, but the Palacio Pedro I in the Real Alcázar *(see pp82–3)* is almost exclusively Moorish in style. By the early 15th century, pure Gothic styles, which are best exemplified by Seville Cathedral *(see pp78–9)*, were widespread. After the fall of Granada in 1492 *(see p48)*, a late Gothic style, called Isabelline, developed.

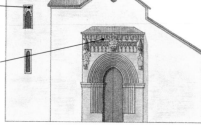

Bell towers were often added later; this one is a Baroque addition.

Windows are framed by Islamic-style, marble columns.

The Iglesia de San Marcos (see p90) *is a typical example of a Christian church built at the time of the Reconquest. Mudéjar features include the portal and minaret-like tower.*

Window openings become progressively narrower towards ground level.

Islamic-style decoration on the main entrance is characteristic of many Mudéjar churches.

Mudéjar portal, Nuestra Señora de la O *(see p162)*

Classical arches, a motif of the transitional Isabelline style, look forward to Renaissance architecture.

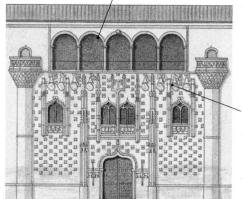

Gothic window, Seville Cathedral

Heavily worked stone reliefs, as decoration on façades of buildings, have their roots in the Gothic style.

The Palacio Jabalquinto (see p152) *has a highly ornate façade. Its coats of arms and heraldic symbols, typical of Isabelline buildings, reveal a strong desire to establish a national style.*

THE RENAISSANCE (16TH CENTURY)

Early Renaissance architecture was termed Plateresque because its fine detailing resembled ornate silverwork. (*Platero* means silversmith.) The façade of the Ayuntamiento *(see p74)* in Seville is the best example of Plateresque in Andalusia. A High Renaissance style is typified by the Palacio Carlos V. The end of the 16th century saw the rise of the austere Herreran style, named after Juan de Herrera, who drafted the initial plans of the Archivo de Indias *(see p80)*.

Plateresque detail on Seville's Ayuntamiento

Courtyard, with Herreran proportions, in the Archivo de Indias

Stone roundels were used as decoration; the central ones would bear the emperor's coat of arms.

Classical pediments adorn the windows.

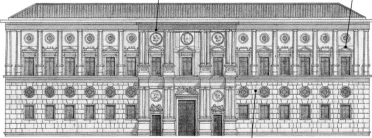

The Palacio Carlos V, *begun in 1526, is located in the heart of the Alhambra* (see p195). *Its elegant, grandiose style reflects Carlos V's power as Holy Roman Emperor.*

Rusticated stonework gives the lower level a solid appearance.

BAROQUE (17TH AND 18TH CENTURIES)

Early Spanish Baroque tended to be austere. The 18th century, however, gave rise to the Churrigueresque, named after the Churriguera family of architects. Although the family's own style was fairly restrained, it had many flamboyant imitations. Priego de Córdoba *(see p150)* is a showcase of the Baroque; La Cartuja *(p191)* in Granada contains a Baroque sacristy.

Flamboyant Baroque sacristy of La Cartuja, Granada

Palacio del Marqués de la Gomera, Osuna *(p133)*

Baroque pinnacles were carved individually from stone.

Repeated string courses define the church's storeys and contribute to the complex decoration of the façade.

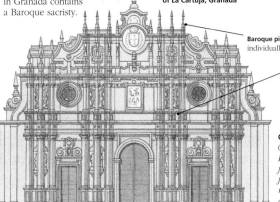

Guadix Cathedral (see p198) *comprises a Renaissance building fronted by a Baroque façade. Such a combination of styles is very common in Andalusia.*

The Art of Bullfighting

Poster for a bullfight

Bullfighting is a sacrificial ritual in which men (and some women) pit themselves against an animal bred for the ring. In this "authentic religious drama", as poet García Lorca described it, the spectator experiences vicariously the fear and exaltation of the matador. Some Spaniards oppose it on the grounds of cruelty, but it remains as popular as ever in Andalusia.

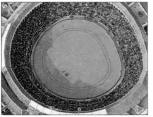

Maestranza Bullring, Seville
This is regarded, with Las Ventas in Madrid, as one of the top venues for bullfighting in Spain.

Bull Breeding
Well treated at the ranch, the toro bravo (fighting bull) is bred specially for aggressiveness and courage.

The matador wears a *traje de luces* (suit of light), a colourful silk outfit embroidered with gold sequins.

The passes are made with a *muleta*, a scarlet cape stiffened along one side.

FIESTA!

Bullfighting is an essential and highly popular part of many *fiestas* in Spain. An enthusiastic and very knowledge-able audience, often in traditional dress, fills the arenas from the start of the season in April until its end in October (*see pp38–9*).

Fiesta wear

THE BULLFIGHT

The *corrida* (bullfight) has three stages, called *tercios*. In the first one, the *tercio de varas*, the matador and *picadores* (horsemen with lances) are aided by *peones* (assistants). In the *tercio de banderillas*, *banderilleros* stick pairs of darts in the bull's back. In the *tercio de muleta* the matador makes a series of passes at the bull with a *muleta* (cape). He then executes the kill, the *estocada*, with a sword.

The matador *plays the bull with a capa (red cape) in the* tercio de varas *in order to gauge its intelligence and speed.* Peones *then draw it towards the* picadores.

Today, horses are heavily padded

Picadores *goad the bull with steel-pointed lances, testing its bravery as it charges their horses. The lances weaken the animal's shoulder muscles.*

THE BULLRING

The *corrida* audience sits in the *tendidos* (stalls) or in the *palcos* (balcony), where the *presidencia* (president's box) is. Opposite are the *puerta de cuadrillas*, through which the matador and team arrive, and the *arrastre de toros* (exit for bulls). Before entering the ring, the matadors wait in a corridor *(callejón)* behind the *barreras* and *burladeros* (ring-side barriers). Horses are kept in the *patio de caballos* and the bulls wait in the *corrales*.

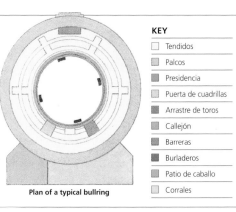

Plan of a typical bullring

KEY

☐	Tendidos
☐	Palcos
☐	Presidencia
☐	Puerta de cuadrillas
☐	Arrastre de toros
☐	Callejón
☐	Barreras
☐	Burladeros
☐	Patio de caballo
☐	Corrales

Banderillas, barbed darts, are thrust into the bull's already weakened back muscles.

Manolete

Regarded as one of the greatest matadors ever, Manolete was gored to death by the bull Islero at Linares, Jaén, in 1947.

The bull may go free if it shows courage – spectators wave white handkerchiefs, asking the *corrida* president to let it leave the ring alive.

Julian López (El Juli)

El Juli debuted at the age of 16. He is renowned for his fierce courage and his flair with the capa *and the* muleta.

Banderilleros *enter to provoke the wounded bull in the* tercio de banderillas, *gauging its reaction to punishment by sticking pairs of* banderillas *in its back.*

The bull weighs about 500 kg (1,100 lb)

The matador *makes passes with the cape in the* tercio de muleta, *then lowers it to make the bull bow its head, and thrusts in the sword for the kill.*

The estocada recibiendo *is a difficult kill that is rarely seen. The matador awaits the bull's charge rather than moving forwards to meet it.*

Flamenco, the Soul of Andalusia

Seville feria
poster 1953

More than just a dance, flamenco is a forceful artistic expression of the sorrows and joys of life. Although it has interpreters all over Spain and even the world, it is a uniquely Andalusian art form, traditionally performed by gypsies. There are many styles of *cante* (song) from different parts of Andalusia, but no strict choreography – dancers improvise from basic movements, following the rhythm of the guitar and their feelings. Flamenco was neglected in the 1960s and '70s, but serious interest has once again returned. Recent years have seen a revival of traditional styles and the development of exciting new forms.

Sevillanas, *a folk dance that is strongly influenced by flamenco, is danced by Andalusians in their bars and homes (see p244).*

At a tablao (flamenco club) there will be at least four people on stage, including the hand clapper.

The origins of flamenco *are hard to trace. Gypsies may have been the main creators of the art, mixing their own Indian-influenced culture with existing Moorish and Andalusian folklore, and with Jewish and Christian music. There were gypsies in Andalusia by the early Middle Ages, but only in the 18th century did flamenco begin to develop into its present form.*

THE SPANISH GUITAR

The guitar has a major role in flamenco, traditionally accompanying the singer. The flamenco guitar developed from the modern classical guitar, which evolved in Spain in the 19th century. Flamenco guitars have a lighter, shallower construction and a thickened plate below the soundhole, used to tap rhythms. Today, flamenco guitarists often perform solo. One of the greatest, Paco de Lucía, began by accompanying singers and dancers, but made his debut as a soloist in 1968. His slick, inventive style, which combines traditional playing with Latin, jazz and rock elements, has influenced many musicians outside the realm of flamenco, such as the group Ketama, who play flamenco-blues.

Classical
guitar

**Paco de Lucía playing
flamenco guitar**

Singing is an integral part of flamenco, and the singer often performs solo. Camarón de la Isla (1952–92), a gypsy born near Cádiz, is among the most famous contemporary cantaores *(flamenco singers). He began as a singer of* cante jondo *(literally, "deep songs"), from which he developed his own, rock-influenced style. He has inspired many singers.*

WHERE TO ENJOY FLAMENCO

Flamenco festivals pp34–9, p244
Flamenco guitar pp34–7, p244
Flamenco in Sacromonte p193
Flamenco singing pp34–7, p244
Flamenco tablaos p244
Flamenco dress p239

Eva Yerbabuena is a bailaora *(female dancer) renowned for her amazing footwork and intensity. Sara Baras is another dancer famous for her personal style. Both lead their own acclaimed flamenco companies. Other international flamenco stars include Juana Amaya.*

The proud yet graceful posture of the *bailaora* seems to suggest a restrained passion.

A harsh, vibrating voice is typical of the singer.

Traditional polka-dot dress

The bailaor *(male dancer) plays a less important role than the* bailaora. *However, many have achieved fame, including Antonio Canales. He has introduced a new beat through his original foot movements.*

THE FLAMENCO TABLAO

These days it is rare to come across spontaneous dancing at a *tablao*, but if dancers and singers are inspired, an impressive show usually results. Artists performing with *duende* ("magic spirit") will hear appreciative *olés* from the audience.

FLAMENCO RHYTHM

The unmistakable rhythm of flamenco is created by the guitar. Just as important, however, is the beat created by hand-clapping and by the dancer's feet in high-heeled shoes. The *baila-oras* may also beat a rhythm with castanets; Lucero Tena (born in 1939) became famous for her solos on castanets. Graceful hand movements are used to express the dancer's feelings of the moment – whether pain, sorrow or happiness. Hand and body movements are choreographed, but styles vary from person to person.

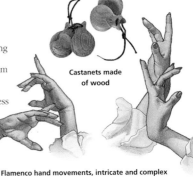

Castanets made of wood

Flamenco hand movements, intricate and complex

The Land of Sherry

The Phoenicians introduced the vine to the Jerez region 3,000 years ago. Later, Greeks, then Romans, exported wine from these gentle hills bordering the Atlantic. However, the foundations of the modern sherry trade were laid by British merchants who settled here after the Reconquest *(see pp48–9)*.

González Byass logo

They discovered that the chalky soil, climate and local grapes produced fine wines, particularly if fortified with grape spirit.

The connection persists today with companies such as John Harvey still in British ownership.

Preparing soil to catch the winter rain

Grapes thriving in the chalky soil near Jerez

- SANLÚCAR DE BARRAMEDA
- JEREZ DE LA FRONTERA
- Rota
- *Rio Guadalete*
- EL PUERTO DE SANTA MARÍA
- CÁDIZ
- Puerto Real
- San Fernando
- Chiclana de la Frontera

SHERRY REGIONS

Sherry is produced at *bodegas*, or wineries, in the towns of Jerez de la Frontera, Sanlúcar de Barrameda and El Puerto de Santa María. It is also produced in smaller centres such as Rota and Chiclana de la Frontera.

0 kilometres   10

0 miles   5

KEY

☐	Sanlúcar de Barrameda
☐	Jerez de la Frontera
☐	El Puerto de Santa María
–	Delimited sherry-producing region

DIFFERENT TYPES OF SHERRY

Three months after pressing, and before the fortification process, all sherry is classified as one of five principal types.

Fino *is by far the favoured style in Andalusia. Dry, fresh, light and crisp, it is excellent as an apéritif or with tapas. It should always be served chilled.*

Manzanilla *is similar to fino, but comes exclusively from Sanlúcar. Light, dry and delicate, it has a highly distinctive, salty tang.*

Amontillado *is fino aged in the barrel. The "dying" flor (yeast) imparts a strong, earthy taste. Some brands are dry, others slightly sweetened.*

Oloroso *(which in Spanish means fragrant) is a full, ruddy-coloured sherry, with a rich, nutty aroma. It is sometimes sweetened.*

Cream *sherry is a full, dark, rich blend of oloroso with Pedro Ximénez grapes. As the sweetest type, it is often drunk as a dessert wine.*

HOW SHERRY IS MADE

Sherry is mixed from two principal grape varieties: Palomino, which produces a drier, more delicate sherry; and Pedro Ximénez, which is made into a fuller, sweeter sherry type.

Grape-drying *is only required for Pedro Ximénez grapes. They are laid on* esparto *mats to shrivel in the sun, concentrating the sugar before they are pressed.*

Grape-picking *takes place during the first three weeks in September. Palomino grapes are taken as quickly as possible to the presses to ensure freshness.*

Crusher and de-stemmer

Grape-pressing *and de-stalking, in cylindrical stainless steel vats, is usually done at night to avoid the searing Andalusian heat.*

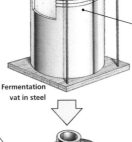

Fermentation vat in steel

Flor, *a yeast, may form on the exposed surface of young wine in the fermentation vat, preventing oxidization and adding a delicate taste. If* flor *develops, the wine is a* fino.

Fortification *is the addition of pure grape spirit, raising the level of alcohol from around 11 per cent by volume to around 18 per cent for* olorosos, *and 15.5 per cent for* finos.

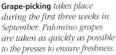

The solera system

The youngest solera contains new wine.

Sherry for bottling is taken from the oldest solera at the bottom row.

The solera system *assures that the qualities of a sherry remain constant. The wine from the youngest solera is mixed with the older below, taking on its character. The oldest solera contains a tiny proportion of very old wine.*

The finished product

Beach Life and Leisure in Andalusia

Painted fishing boat, Costa del Sol

Thanks to its subtropical climate with an average of 300 days' sunshine a year, the coastline of Andalusia – in particular the Costa del Sol – has become one of the most favoured playgrounds for those looking for fun and relaxation. In the 1950s, there was nothing more than a handful of fishing villages (*see p183*). Now the area attracts several million tourists a year who are well catered for by the vast array of hotels and apartments along the coast. The varied coastline lends itself perfectly to the whole gamut of water sports (*see p246*), while just inland golf courses have become a major feature of the landscape (*see p246*). Some of the most popular golf courses are shown on this map, together with a selection of the beaches most worth a visit.

Sunbathing on one of Marbella's beaches, Costa del Sol

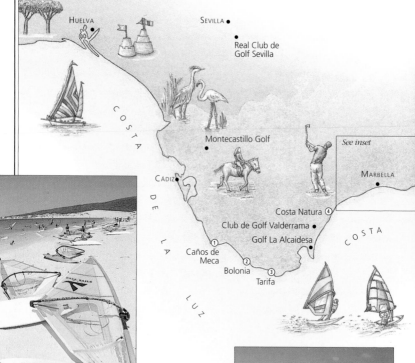

HUELVA

SEVILLA ●

● Real Club de Golf Sevilla

COSTA

Montecastillo Golf

CÁDIZ ●

DE

LA

See inset

MARBELLA

Costa Natura ④

Club de Golf Valderrama ●

Golf La Alcaidesa

COSTA

Caños de Meca ①

Bolonia ②

Tarifa ③

LUZ

Costa de la Luz *in western Andalusia is a stretch of largely unspoiled beaches, refreshingly free from crowds and tower blocks. Atlantic winds make it a windsurfer's paradise.*

Costa Tropical *is punctuated by pretty coves, ideal for scuba diving. The water is warmer and clearer than on Costa de la Luz, while the sand is coarse and stony.*

0 kilometres   50

0 miles   25

ANDALUSIA'S BEST BEACHES

Caños de Meca ①
Charming white, sandy beach sheltered by cliffs and sand dunes.

Bolonia ②
Picturesque beach with Roman ruins close by.

Tarifa ③
Sweeping white sands, and winds and waves perfect for skilled windsurfers.

Costa Natura ④
Popular nudist beach just outside Estepona.

Babaloo Beach ⑤
Trendy spot just off Puerto Banús. Gym and jetskiing.

Victor's Beach ⑥
A classic Marbella beach for stylish barbecue parties.

Don Carlos ⑦
Perhaps Marbella's best beach, shared by the exclusive Don Carlos beach club.

Cabopino/Las Dunas ⑧
Nudist beach and sand dunes beside modern marina. Not too crowded.

Rincón de la Victoria ⑨
Nice unspoiled family beach area just east of Málaga.

La Herradura ⑩
A stony but picturesque bay west of Almuñécar.

Playa de los Genoveses ⑪
One of the unspoilt beaches between Cabo de Gata and the village of San José.

Playa Agua Amarga ⑫
Excellent sand beach in secluded fishing hamlet turned exclusive resort.

Costa de Almería is famous for its picturesque fishing villages, and rocky landscapes which come to life in the breathtaking sunsets. Beaches tend to have escaped overdevelopment, in particular those in the nature reserve of Cabo de Gata, such as San José, here.

Agua Amarga ⑫

Playa de los Genoveses ⑪

ALMERÍA

MÁLAGA ⑨
Rincón de la Victoria

La Herradura ⑩

COSTA TROPICAL

COSTA DE ALMERÍA

DEL SOL

COSTA DEL SOL

Apart from the crowds of holiday-makers, half a million foreign residents have chosen to live on the Costa del Sol. Complementing the luxury and high life of Marbella are a number of popular beaches and more than 30 of Europe's finest golf courses, including the prestigious Club de Golf Valderrama, host of the 1997 Ryder Cup tournament.

MÁLAGA ●

Club de Campo de Málaga ●

TORREMOLINOS ●

Golf Torrequebrado ●

Club Milas Golf ●
La Cala Golf ●

Club de Golf Las Brisas ●

Club Dama de Noche ●

Guadalmina Golf ●

Monte Mayor ●
Golf

Babaloo Beach ⑤

MARBELLA ⑥
Victor's Beach

● Golf Rio Real
⑦ ● Marbella Golf
Don Carlos

⑧
Cabopino and Las Dunas

Player on the green at the high-profile Marbella Golf

ANDALUSIA THROUGH THE YEAR

Festivals and cultural events fill Andalusia's calendar. Every town and village has an annual *feria* (fair) featuring parades, dancing, fairs, fireworks and bullfights. These are held from April to October throughout Andalusia. There are also numerous *fiestas*, all exuberant occasions when religious devotion mixes with *joie de vivre*. Spring is an ideal time to visit; the countryside is at its most beautiful, the climate is mild and *ferias* and *fiestas*

**Poster for 1903
Seville *feria***

celebrate the ending of winter. Summer brings heat to the interior and crowds to the *costas*. Autumn is greeted with more *fiestas* and heralds the opening of music and theatre seasons. In winter, jazz, pop and classical concerts can be enjoyed in the cities. The first snow on the Sierra Nevada marks the start of the skiing season. Note that dates for all events, especially *fiestas*, may change from year to year; check with the tourist board *(see p255)*.

Feria del Caballo, held in Jerez de la Frontera in May

Almond trees in blossom on the lush hillsides of Andalusia

SPRING

Few parts of the world can match the beauty of spring in Andalusia. After winter rains, the hills and plains are green and lush, and water cascades along riverbeds and irrigation channels. Country roads are a riot of wild flowers; almond blossom covers the hillsides and strawberries are harvested. Popular festivals abound, many of them religious, though often linked with pagan ceremonies marking the end of winter.

MARCH

Cristo de la Expiración *(Friday, nine days before Palm Sunday)*, Orgiva *(see p198)*. One of Andalusia's most ear-splitting *fiestas*; shotguns are fired and rockets, gunpowder and firecrackers are set off.
Semana Santa *(Palm Sunday–Good Friday)*. Seville

celebrates this event spectacularly *(see p38)*, and there are processions in every town and village. On Holy Wednesday in Málaga *(see pp180–81)*, a prisoner is freed from jail and in gratitude joins in one of the processions. This tradition began two centuries ago, when prisoners, braving a plague, carried a holy image through the city's streets. In Baena *(see p147)*, the streets vibrate to the sound of thousands of drums.

APRIL

Fiesta de San Marcos *(25 April)*, Ohanes, Sierra Nevada. Accompanying the image of San Marcos through the streets are young men leading eight bulls. The bulls are persuaded to kneel before the saint.
Feria de Abril *(two weeks after Easter)*, Seville *(see p38)*.
Romería de Nuestra Señora de la Cabeza *(last Sunday in April)*, Andújar *(see p39)*. Major pilgrimage.

MAY

Día de la Cruz *(first week of May)*, Granada *(see pp190–96)* and Córdoba *(see p38)*.
Feria del Caballo *(first week of May)*, Jerez de la Frontera *(see p162)*. Horse fair.
Festival Internacional de Teatro y Danza *(throughout May)*, Seville. World-class companies perform in Teatro de la Maestranza *(see pp68–9)*.
Festival de los Patios *(second week in May)*, Córdoba *(see p38)*. Patios are on display.
Romería de San Isidro *(15 May)*. *Romerías* are held in many towns, including Nerja *(see p180)*, for San Isidro.
Concurso Nacional de Flamenco *(second week in May; every third year: 2010, 2013)*, Córdoba. National flamenco competition.
Feria de Mayo *(last week of May)*, Córdoba *(see p38)*.
Romería del Rocío *(late May or early June)*, El Rocío *(see p38)*.

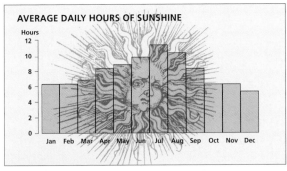

AVERAGE DAILY HOURS OF SUNSHINE

Hours

Sunshine Chart
Even in winter, few days in Andalusia are entirely without sunshine. From the spring, the sunshine starts to build up progressively, and by midsummer it can be dangerous to go out even for a short time without adequate skin protection.

Bullrunning during the Lunes de Toro *fiesta* in Grazalema

SUMMER

During the hot summer months, the *siesta* (afternoon nap) comes into its own. Many people finish work at lunch time and most of the entertainment takes place in the cool of evening. Foreign tourists flocking to the coasts are joined by thousands of Spaniards. Large pop concerts are held in coastal towns.

JUNE

Corpus Christi *(late May or early June)* is commemorated in Granada *(see p39)*. In Seville, the *seises*, young boys dressed in doublet and hose, dance before the cathedral altar. At Zahara, near Ronda, *(see p174)* houses and streets are decked out with greenery.

Día de San Juan *(23, 24 June)*. The evening of 23 June sees dancing, drinking and singing around bonfires on beaches across Andalusia in honour of

St John the Baptist. Lanjarón *(see p189)* celebrates with a water battle in its streets in the early hours of 24 June.

Romería de los Gitanos *(third Sunday in June)*, Cabra *(see p147)*. A procession made up of thousands of gypsies heads for a hilltop shrine.

Festival Internacional de Música y Danza *(mid-June–early July)*, Granada *(see pp190–96)*. Performers come to Granada from all over the world. Many events are held in the Alhambra *(see pp194–5)*.

JULY

Festival de la Guitarra *(first two weeks of July)*, Córdoba *(see pp140–46)*. Guitar festival presenting all musical styles, from classical to flamenco.

Fiesta de la Virgen del Carmen *(around 15 July)*. This Virgin is honoured in many coastal communities by regattas and other sporting events. In the evening, the Virgin's image is put aboard a fishing boat, which parades

across the sea accompanied by the crackle of fireworks.

Lunes de Toro *(Around 17 July)*, Grazalema *(see p174)*. Bullrunning daily for a week.

AUGUST

Fiestas Colombinas *(Around 3 August)*, Huelva *(see p127)*. A Latin American dance and music festival in celebration of Columbus's voyage. It is dedicated to a different Latin American country every year.

Fiestas Patronales de Santa María de la Palma *(15 August)*, Algeciras *(see p170)*. A saint's image is rescued from the sea. It is cleaned, before being carried in a procession of boats to a beach. Afterwards it is returned to the sea.

Fiestas de la Exaltación del Río Guadalquivir *(third week in August)*, Sanlúcar de Barrameda *(see p162)*. Horse races are held on the beach.

Feria de Málaga *(last two weeks in August, see p39)*.

Feria de Almería *(last week in August, see p39)*.

The Costa del Sol – popular with tourists and with the Spanish

AVERAGE MONTHLY RAINFALL

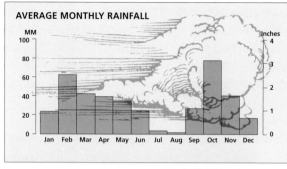

Rainfall Chart
Rain can be heavy in early spring, but summer is almost dry. Humidity and rainfall increase through September until October, when torrential rains can fall. In recent years, the rains have failed resulting in severe drought in the area.

Chirimoya harvest on the subtropical coast at Almuñécar *(see p189)*

AUTUMN

This is a most pleasant time to visit Andalusia. The weather is settled, but without the searing summer heat, and the holiday crowds are easing. Grape harvests are in full swing and being celebrated in towns and villages. The theatres start to open for drama and concerts. Along the subtropical coast of the Mediterranean, sweet potatoes and *chirimoyas* (custard apples) are harvested. Inland, mushrooms, freshly picked, figure on menus.

SEPTEMBER

Feria de Pedro Romero *(first two weeks in September)*, Ronda *(see pp176–7)*. This *fiesta* celebrates the founder of modern bullfighting *(see p177)*. All participants in the Corrida Goyesca, the highlight, wear costumes designed by Goya, a great bullfighting fan.

Fiestas Patronales de la Virgen de la Piedad *(6 September)*, Baza *(see p198)*. A bizarre *fiesta* in which a figure known as Cascamorras comes from neighbouring Guadix to try to steal a statue of the Virgin. Youths covered with oil taunt him and chase him out of town. He is sent back to Guadix empty-handed, where he receives further punishment for his failure.

Moros y Cristianos *fiesta*, Válor *(see p191)*

Moros y Cristianos *(15 September)*, Válor *(see p199)*. This *fiesta* features the recreation of Reconquest battles.
Fiesta de la Vendimia *(second or third week of September)*, La Palma del Condado *(see p129)*. A lively *fiesta* to bless the first grape juice.
Romería de San Miguel *(last Sunday of September)*, Torremolinos *(see p182)*. One of the largest *romerías* in Andalusia.
Bienal de Arte Flamenco *(last two weeks of September, even-numbered years)*, Seville. A fabulous opportunity for enthusiasts to see world-class flamenco artists, such as Cristina Hoyos.
Sevilla en Otoño *(September–November)*, Seville. A variety of cultural events, including dance, theatre and exhibitions, and, in addition, sports.

OCTOBER

Fiesta del Vino *(5–9 October)*, Cadiar *(see p199)*. A feature of this *fiesta* in the mountains of the Alpujarras is the construction of a fountain which gushes forth wine.
Festival Iberoamericano de Teatro *(last two weeks of October)*, Cádiz *(see pp164–5)*. Latin American theatre festival.

NOVEMBER

Festival Internacional de Jazz *(early November)*, Granada *(see pp190–96)* and Seville.
Festival de Cine Iberoamericano *(last two weeks of November)*, Huelva *(see p127)*. Latin American film festival.

Oil-covered youths chasing Cascamorras in Baza

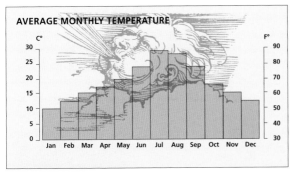

AVERAGE MONTHLY TEMPERATURE

Temperature Chart
Andalusia enjoys a warm Mediterranean climate throughout the year, although it can become cold at night. Temperatures rise from January to the summer months when, in some cities inland, they can far exceed the average for the region.

Medieval music at the Fiesta de los Verdiales in Málaga

They come to hear *pandas* (bands) compete in performing *verdiales*, wild, primitive music from Moorish times, played on medieval instruments.

WINTER

At this time of year the ripe olives are harvested in abundance. The restaurants serve venison, wild boar and partridge dishes as this is the hunting season. Skiers flock to the Sierra Nevada. Though winter is the rainy season and it is cold at night, many days have sunshine. By February, almond blossom and strawberries begin to appear again.

DECEMBER

La Inmaculada Concepción
(8 December), Seville. The *tuna*, groups of wandering minstrels, take to the streets around the Plaza del Triunfo and Santa Cruz *(see pp72–3)*.
Fiesta de los Verdiales *(28 December)*, Málaga *(see pp180–81)*. On Spain's equivalent of April Fool's Day, *El Día de los Santos Inocentes*, thousands of town and country folk gather at the Venta del Túnel, on the outskirts of Málaga.

JANUARY

Día de la Toma *(2 January)*, Granada *(see pp190–96)*. This *fiesta* recalls the ousting of the Moors in 1492 *(see p48)*. Queen Isabel's crown and King Fernando's sword are paraded through the streets, and the royal standard flies from the balcony of the Ayuntamiento.
Día de Reyes *(6 January)*. On the evening before this public holiday, the Three Kings arrive, splendidly dressed, to parade through town centres across Andalusia. They ride in small carriages that are drawn either by tractors or horses and, during processions, throw sweets to the excited children.
Certamen Internacional de Guitarra Clásica Andrés Segovia *(first week of January)*, Almuñécar *(see p189)*. Classical guitar competition in homage to the master.

FEBRUARY

Los Carnavales *(second or third week in February)*. Carnival is widely celebrated, most spectacularly in Cádiz *(see p39)* and the coastal town of Isla Cristina *(see p126)*.
Festival de Música Antigua *(February and March)*, Seville. Early music is performed on historic instruments.
Jerez Annual Flamenco Festival *(end February/early March)*, Jerez *(see p162)*. Flamenco performances and workshops.

PUBLIC HOLIDAYS

New Year's Day (1 Jan)
Epiphany (6 Jan)
Día de Andalucía (28 Feb)
Easter Thursday and Good Friday (variable)
Labour Day (1 May)
Assumption (15 Aug)
National Day (12 Oct)
All Saints' Day (1 Nov)
Constitution Day (6 Dec)
Immaculate Conception (8 Dec)
Christmas Day (25 Dec)

Ski station on the snow-covered slopes of the Sierra Nevada *(see p197)*

Fiestas in Andalusia

There is nothing quite like a Spanish *fiesta* or *feria,* and those of Andalusia are among the most colourful. *Fiestas* may commemorate an historic event or a change of season. More often they mark a religious occasion; Semana Santa (Holy Week), for example, is celebrated all over Andalusia. Feasting, dancing, singing, drinking – often right around the clock – are all integral to a *fiesta.* At a *feria* there will often be a decorated fairground, revellers dressed in traditional flamenco attire, and processions of horses and carriages. Throughout Andalusia you will also come across *romerías,* in which processions carry holy effigies through the countryside to a shrine.

Costume, Semana Santa, Córdoba

Horsemen and women in their finery at Seville's Feria de Abril

SEVILLE

Semana Santa, or Holy Week (Palm Sunday–Good Friday) is celebrated in flamboyant style in Seville. More than 100 *pasos* (floats bearing religious effigies) are carried through the streets of the city. They are accompanied by *nazarenos,* members of some 50 brotherhoods dating back to the 13th century, wearing long robes and tall pointed hoods. As the processions sway through the streets, appointed singers burst into *saetas,* shafts of song in praise of the Virgin. Emotion reaches fever-pitch in the early hours of Good Friday, when the Virgen de La Macarena is paraded, accompanied by 2,500 *nazarenos (see p89).*

During their Feria de Abril, the spring fair held around two weeks after Easter, the *sevillanos* go on a spree for a

week. Daily, from about 1pm, elegant horsemen and women wearing brightly coloured flamenco dresses show off their finery in a parade known as the *Paseo de Caballos.* At night, *casetas* (entertainment booths) throb to *sevillanas,* a popular dance

that has a flamenco accent (out of a thousand *casetas,* about a quarter are open to the public). There are bullfights in the Maestranza bullring *(see p68).*

HUELVA AND SEVILLA

One of Spain's most popular *fiestas,* the Romería del Rocío, is held during Pentecost. More than 70 brotherhoods trek to the shrine of El Rocío *(see p129)* amid Las Marismas, the marshlands at the mouth of the Guadalquivir. They are joined by pilgrims travelling on horseback, on foot or by car. All pay homage to the Virgen del Rocío, also called the White Dove or the Queen of the Marshes. There is drinking and dancing for several days and nights, until the early hours of Monday morning when the Virgin is brought out of the shrine. Young men from the nearby town of Almonte carry her through the crowds for up to 12 hours, fighting off anybody who tries to get near.

CORDOBA AND JAÉN

May is a nonstop *fiesta* in Córdoba *(see pp140–46).* The Día de la Cruz – the Day of the Cross – is held on the first three days of the month. Religious brotherhoods and neighbourhoods compete with each other to create the most colourful, flower-decorated crosses, which are set up in squares and at street corners. Following this is the Festival de los Patios (around 5–15 May), when the patios of the city's old quarter are thrown

Pilgrims taking part in the Romería del Rocío in Huelva province open for visitors to come and admire. Crowds go from patio to patio, at each one launching into flamenco dance or song.

During the last week of May, Córdoba holds its lively *feria*. It is as colourful as the Feria de Abril in Seville, but more accessible to strangers. This festival, with roots in Roman times, welcomes the spring.

The Romería de Nuestra Señora de la Cabeza takes place on the last Sunday in April at the Santuario de la Virgen de la Cabeza *(see p151)*, a remote shrine in the Sierra Morena. Over 250,000 people attend, some making the pilgrimage on foot or on horseback. At the site, flames shoot up day and night from a torch fed by candles lit by the faithful. Then the Virgin, known as La Morenita, is borne through the crowd to cries of *¡Guapa, guapa!* (beautiful, beautiful!).

Penitents at the Romería de Nuestra Señora de la Cabeza in April

CÁDIZ AND MÁLAGA

For two weeks in February, Los Carnavales (Carnival) is celebrated with more flair and abandon in Cádiz *(see p164)* than anywhere else in Andalusia. Some say it rivals the carnival in Río de Janeiro. Groups of singers practise for months in advance, composing outrageous satirical ditties that poke fun at anything from the current fashions to celebrities, especially politicians. Often sumptuously costumed, they perform their songs in the Falla Theatre in a competition lasting for several days. Then they take part in a parade. The whole city puts on fancy dress

Costumed revellers at the February Carnival (Los Carnavales) in Cádiz

and crowds of revellers throng the narrow streets of the city's old quarter, shouting, singing, dancing and drinking.

The Feria de Málaga in the middle of August each year, celebrates the capture of the city from the Moors by the Catholic Monarchs *(see p48)*. Eager to outdo Seville, Málaga *(see pp180–81)* puts on a fine show. The residents, famous for their ability to organize a good party, put on traditional costume and parade, along with decorated carriages and elegant horsefolk, through the city centre and the fairground. The entertainment goes on for a week nonstop, and top bullfighters perform at the city's bullring *(see p181)* in La Malagueta.

GRANADA AND ALMERIA

Corpus Christi, held in late May or early June, is one of the major events in Granada *(see pp190–96)*. On the day before Corpus a procession of bigheads (costumed caricatures with outsized heads) and giants parades through the city, led by the *tarasca*, a woman on a huge dragon. The next day, the *custodia*, or monstrance, is carried from the cathedral all through the streets. For a week afterwards there is bullfighting, flamenco and general revelry.

The *feria* in Almería *(see pp200–1)*, which is held at the end of August, is in honour of the Virgen del Mar. There are funfairs, processions, sporting events and bullfights. The city's Virgin dates back to 1502, when a coastguard on the lookout for Berber pirates found an image of the Virgin washed up on a beach.

Feria de Málaga, celebrating the capture of the city from the Moors

THE HISTORY OF SEVILLE AND ANDALUSIA

Andalusia's early history is an extraordinary tale of ancient cities – Cádiz (see pp164–5), founded in 1100 BC, is the oldest city in Europe – and waves of settlers, each one contributing new ideas and customs.

Hominids first inhabited the region about one million years ago. *Homo sapiens* had arrived by 25,000 BC, and by the Iron Age a strong Iberian culture had emerged. Later, trade and

Stone carving of an Iberian warrior

cultural links developed first with the Phoenicians, then with the Greeks and Carthaginians. These ties and the abundance of natural raw materials, such as iron, gold and copper ore, made this part of Iberia one of the wealthiest areas of the Mediterranean.

Attracted by its riches, the Romans made their first forays into southern Spain in 206 BC. They ruled for almost 700 years. Their place was eventually taken by the Visigoths as the Western Roman Empire crumbled in the 5th century AD. The Moors,

who followed, flourished first in Córdoba, then in Seville, and, towards the end of their almost 800-year rule, in the Nasrid kingdom of Granada.

After the fall of Granada to the Christians in 1492, Spain entered an era of expansion and prosperity. The conquest of the New World made Seville one of the most affluent cities in Europe, but much of this wealth was squandered on wars by the Habsburg kings.

By the 18th century, Spain had fallen into economic decline; in the 19th and early 20th centuries poverty led to political conflict and, ultimately, to the Civil War.

The years after the Civil War saw continuing poverty, though mass tourism in the 1960s and '70s did much to ease this. With Franco's death and Spain's entry into the EU, the Spanish began to enjoy increasing prosperity and democratic freedoms. Andalusia still lagged behind, however. The Expo '92 was part of government policy to foster its economic growth.

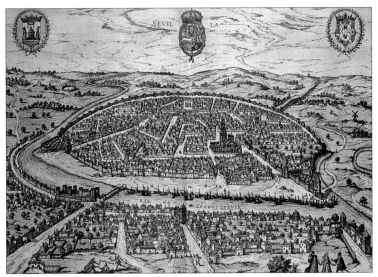

The 16th-century port of Seville, where ships brought wealth from the Americas to the Holy Roman Empire

◁ **18th-century lithograph of the Puerta de la Justicia in the Alhambra (see pp194–5)**

Early Andalusia

Neanderthal skull

Neanderthals inhabited Gibraltar around 50,000 BC. *Homo sapiens* arrived 25,000 years later and Neolithic tribespeople from Africa settled in Spain from about 7000 BC. By the time the Phoenicians arrived to trade in precious metals, they were met by a sophisticated Iberian culture. They later established trading links with the semi-mythical Iberian kingdom of Tartessus. The Greeks, already settled in northeastern Spain, started to colonize the south from about 600 BC. Meanwhile, Celts from the north had mixed with Iberians. This culture, influenced by the Greeks, created beautiful works of art. The Carthaginians arrived in about 500 BC and, according to legend, destroyed Tartessus.

AREAS OF INFLUENCE

▨ Greek

☐ Phoenician

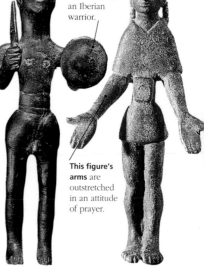

The short sword and shield denote an Iberian warrior.

This figure's arms are outstretched in an attitude of prayer.

Burial Sight at Los Millares
Los Millares (see p201) was the site of an early metal-working civilization in about 2300 BC. Up to 100 corpses were buried on a single site; the huge burial chambers were covered with earth to make a gently sloping mound.

IBERIAN BRONZE FIGURES
These bronze figurines from the 5th–4th centuries BC are votive offerings to the gods. They were discovered in a burial ground near Despeñaperros in the province of Jaén. The Romans regarded the Iberians who crafted them as exceptionally noble.

Cave Paintings
From approximately 25,000 BC, people painted caves in Andalusia. They portrayed fish, land animals, people, weapons and other subjects with a skilful naturalism.

TIMELINE

1,000,000 BC	50,000 BC	10,000 BC	8000 BC	6000 BC	4000 BC

1,000,000–750,000 BC Stones worked by hominids at Puerto de Santa María, Cádiz

Stone tool

50,000 BC Neanderthals inhabit Gibraltar

25,000–18,000 BC *Homo sapiens* make cave paintings and rock engravings

7000 BC Neolithic colonists arrive, perhaps from North Africa. Farming begins on Iberian Peninsula

4000 BC Burials at Cueva de los Murciélagos in Granada leave Neolithic remains; esparto sandals, religious offerings and other items

4500 BC Farmers begin to grow crops and breed cattle

Neolithic ochre pot

Goddess Astarte
The Phoenicians founded Cádiz in about 1100 BC. They brought their own goddess, Astarte, who became popular across Andalusia as the region absorbed eastern influences.

The headdress shows this is a votaress, devoted to her god.

The hand of this priestess is raised in benediction.

WHERE TO SEE EARLY ANDALUSIA

Cave paintings can be seen in the Cueva de la Pileta near Ronda la Vieja (p175) and in the Cuevas de Nerja (p180). At Antequera (p179) there are Bronze Age dolmens dating from 2500 BC; at Los Millares (p201) there are burial chambers. The replicas of the famous Tartessian Carambolo Treasure are in the Museo Arqueológico in Seville (p97) and Iberian stone carvings from Porcuna are exhibited in Jaén (p149).

Greek Urn
The ancient Greeks imported many artifacts from home; their style of decoration had a strong influence on Iberian art.

The Toro de Porcuna (500–450 BC) *was found at Porcuna near Jaén with other sculptures.*

Dama de Baza
This female figure, dating from around 500–400 BC, may represent an Iberian goddess. It is one of several such figures found in southern Spain.

Carambolo Treasure
Phoenician in style, this treasure is from Tartessus. Although many artifacts have been uncovered, the site of this kingdom has yet to be found.

2300 BC Beginning of the Bronze Age; dolmen-style burials take place at Los Millares *(see p201)*	**800–700 BC** Kingdom of Tartessus at its height, influenced by the Phoenicians	*Tartessian buckle*		**241 BC** First Punic War between Carthage and Rome

2000 BC	**1000 BC**	**800 BC**	**600 BC**	**400 BC**
1100 BC Foundation of Cádiz by the Phoenicians	**800 BC** Celts from northern Europe move southwards	**600 BC** Greek colonists settle on the coasts of Andalusia	**500 BC** Carthage colonizes southern Spain *Greek helmet*	**219 BC** Carthaginians take Sagunto, eastern Spain

Romans and Visigoths

The Romans came to Spain during a war against Carthage in 206 BC. Attracted by the wealth of the peninsula, they stayed for 700 years; in 200 years they conquered Spain and split it into provinces. Baetica, with Corduba (Córdoba) as its capital, corresponded roughly to what is now Andalusia. Cities were built, while feudal lords created **Visigothic capital** vast estates, exporting olive oil and wheat to Rome. Baetica became one of the wealthiest of Rome's provinces with a rich, Ibero-Roman culture. The Visigoths who followed continued to assert Roman values until the Moors arrived in AD 711.

ROMAN TERRITORY AD 100

▨ Roman Baetica

☐ Other Roman provinces

Hadrian
Emperors Hadrian and Trajan were born in Baetica. A great many politicians, writers and philosophers from the province also moved to Rome, some enjoying great fortune.

Private villas   Paved streets   Temple

Roman Mosaics in Andalusia
Private houses, temples and public buildings all had mosaic floors. Many themes, from the gods to hunting, were represented.

ITÁLICA RECONSTRUCTED
Scipio Africanus founded Itálica *(see p132)* in 206 BC after his defeat of the Carthaginians. The city reached its height in the 2nd and 3rd centuries AD and was the birthplace of the emperors Hadrian and Trajan. Unlike Córdoba, it was not built over in post-Roman times and today Itálica is a superbly preserved example of a Roman city.

TIMELINE

206 BC Scipio Africanus gains victory against the Carthaginians at Alcalá del Río; Itálica is founded

55 BC Birth of Seneca the Elder in Córdoba

AD 27 Andalusia is named Baetica

Suicide of Seneca

65 Suicide of Seneca the Younger after plotting against Nero

117 Hadrian is crowned Emperor

200 BC	100 BC	AD 1	100	200

200 BC Romans conquer southern Spain and reach Cádiz

61 BC Julius Caesar is governor of Hispania Ulterior (Spain)

Julius Caesar

98–117 Trajan, from Itálica, is emperor. Spanish senators enjoy influence in Rome

69–79 Emperor Vespasian grants Roman status to all towns in Hispania

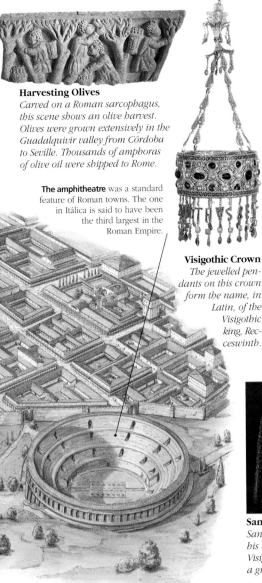

Harvesting Olives
Carved on a Roman sarcophagus, this scene shows an olive harvest. Olives were grown extensively in the Guadalquivir valley from Córdoba to Seville. Thousands of amphoras of olive oil were shipped to Rome.

The amphitheatre was a standard feature of Roman towns. The one in Itálica is said to have been the third largest in the Roman Empire.

Visigothic Crown
The jewelled pendants on this crown form the name, in Latin, of the Visigothic king, Recceswinth.

WHERE TO SEE ROMAN AND VISIGOTHIC ANDALUSIA

Extensive Roman remains can be seen at the sights of Itálica *(see p132)*, Carmona *(p132)* and Ronda la Vieja *(p175)*; in Málaga there is a partially excavated Roman amphitheatre, and Roman columns can be seen at the Alameda de Hércules in Seville *(p88)*. The Museo Arqueológico in Seville *(p97)*, Córdoba *(p143)* and Cádiz *(p164)* all have Roman artifacts on display. Visigothic pillars and capitals can be viewed in the Mezquita in Córdoba *(pp144–5)*.

The Roman ruins *at Itálica (see p132) are situated 9 km (5.5 miles) north of Seville.*

San Isidoro and San Leandro
San Isidoro (560–635) of Seville, like his brother, San Leandro, converted Visigoths to Christianity; he also wrote a great scholastic work, Etymologies.

415 Visigoths arrive in Spain from northern Europe		**446** Tarraconensis in north still Roman; Rome attempts to win back rest of Spain	*Illuminated cover of Etymologies by San Isidoro*	
			632 Death of Prophet Muhammad	
300	**400**	**500**	**600**	
409 Vandals sack Tarraconensis (Tarragona)	**476** Visigoths control whole of Spain	**589** Third Council of Toledo in central Spain. Visigothic King Reccared converted from Arianism to Catholicism		**635** Death of San Isidoro of Seville

Theodosius

The Moorish Conquest

10th-century ivory cask

Called in to resolve a quarrel among the Visigoths, the Moors first arrived in 710. They returned in 711 to conquer Spain; within 10 years, the north alone remained under Christian control. The Moors named their newly conquered territories Al Andalus and in 929 they established an independent caliphate. Córdoba, its capital, was the greatest city in Europe, a centre for art, science and literature. In the 11th century the caliphate collapsed into 30 feuding *taifas* (party states). Almoravids, tribesmen from North Africa, invaded the region in 1086, and in the 12th century Almohads from Morocco ousted the Almoravids and designated Seville their capital.

MOORISH DOMAIN AD 800

☐ *Al Andalus*

Abd al Rahman III receives the Byzantine envoy.

Apocalypse
An 11th-century account of an 8th-century text, Commentaries on the Apocalypse *by Beato de Liébana, this illustration shows Christians going to war.*

Bronze Stag
This 10th-century caliphal-style bronze is from Medina Azahara.

THE COURT OF ABD AL RAHMAN III
Abd al Rahman III began his palace of Medina Azahara *(see p138)* in 936. This 19th-century painting by Dionisio Baixeres shows a Byzantine envoy presenting the caliph with the works of the Greek scientist Dioscorides. The Moors of Córdoba possessed much knowledge of the ancient world, which was later transmitted to Europe. The Medina was sacked by Berber mercenaries in 1010.

TIMELINE

Visigothic king and Moorish chief

756 Abd al Rahman I reaches Spain and asserts himself as ruler, declaring an independent emirate based around Córdoba

936 Construction of Medina Azahara begins *(see pp138–9)*

929 Abd al Rahman III proclaims caliphate in Córdoba

700	800	900

711 Invasion under Tariq ben Ziyad

710 First Moorish intervention in Spain

785 Construction of the Mezquita *(see pp144–5)* begins at Córdoba

822–52 Rule of Abd al Rahman II

Coin from the reign of Abd al Rahman III

912–61 Rule of Abd al Rahman III

961–76 Al Hakam II builds great library at Medina Azahara; expands Mezquita

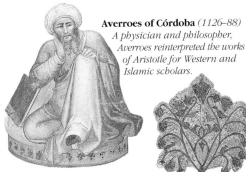

Averroes of Córdoba *(1126–88)*
A physician and philosopher, Averroes reinterpreted the works of Aristotle for Western and Islamic scholars.

Horseshoe arches were a major feature here, as in the Mezquita (*see pp144–5*) at Córdoba.

Mozarabic Bible
Moorish society integrated Jews and Mozarabs (Christians living an Islamic lifestyle). Illustrations like this one, from a 10th-century Bible, are in a Moorish decorative style.

Clerics prepare the manuscript to be given to Abd al Rahman III.

WHERE TO SEE MOORISH ANDALUSIA

The Mezquita in Córdoba (*see pp144–5*) and the ruins of the palace at Medina Azahara (*p138*) are the most complete remnants of Spain's Moorish caliphate. Artifacts found at Medina Azahara can be seen in the Museo Arqueológico in Córdoba (*see p143*). The Alcazaba at Almería (*see p200*) dates from the 10th century, when this city was still part of the caliphate, while the Alcazaba at Málaga (*see p181*) was built during the ensuing Taifa period. The Torre del Oro (*see p69*) and La Giralda (*see p78*) in Seville are both Almohad structures.

The Alcazaba *in Almería* (p200), *dating from the 10th century, overlooks the old town.*

Cufic Script
Islamic artists, forbidden to use representations of the human figure, made ample use of calligraphy for decoration.

Irrigation in Al Andalus
The water wheel was vital to irrigation, which the Moors used to grow newly imported crops such as rice and oranges.

Al Mansur

1012 *Taifas* emerge as splinter Moorish states

1031 Caliphate ends

1086 Almoravids invade

1120 Almoravid power starts to wane

1126 Birth of Averroes, Arab philosopher

1147 Almohads arrive in Seville; build Giralda and Torre del Oro

1000	1100	1200

976–1002 Al Mansur, military dictator, comes to power

1085 Fall of Toledo in north to Christians decisively loosens Moorish control over central Spain

1010 Medina Azahara sacked by Berbers

1135 Maimónides, Jewish philosopher, born in Córdoba

1175–1200 Height of Almohad power. Previously lost territory won back from Christians

Maimónides

The Reconquest

The war between Moors and Christians, which started in northern Spain, arrived in Andalusia with a landmark Christian victory at Las Navas de Tolosa in 1212; Seville and Córdoba fell soon afterwards. By the late 13th century only the Nasrid kingdom of Granada remained under Moorish control. Meanwhile, Christian monarchs such as Alfonso X and Pedro I employed Mudéjar

Christian horseman

(see p24) craftsmen to build churches and palaces in the reconquered territories – Mudéjar literally means "those permitted to stay". Granada eventually fell in 1492 to Fernando and Isabel of Aragón and Castilla, otherwise known as the Catholic Monarchs.

MOORISH DOMAIN IN 1350

 Nasrid kingdom

The Catholic Monarchs enter Granada; Fernando and Isabel were awarded this title for their services to Christendom.

Boabdil

Cantigas of Alfonso X
Alfonso X, who won back much of Andalusia from the Moors, was an enlightened Christian monarch. His illuminated Cantigas *are a vivid account of life in Reconquest Spain.*

Almohad Banner
This richly woven tapestry is widely believed to be the banner captured from the Moors by the Christians at the battle of Las Navas de Tolosa.

THE FALL OF GRANADA

This relief by Felipe de Vigarney (1480–c.1542), in Granada's Capilla Real *(see p190)*, shows Boabdil, the last Moorish ruler, surrendering the city in 1492. Trying to establish a Christian realm, the Catholic Monarchs converted the Moors by force and expelled the Jews. The same year, Columbus got funds for his voyage to America *(see p127)*.

TIMELINE

1226 Fernando III takes Baeza

1236 Fernando III conquers Córdoba

1252–84 Alfonso X reconquers much of Andalusia. Toledo Translators' School in the north continues to translate important works of Moorish literature

Pedro I of Castilla

1333 Moors add tower to the 8th-century Keep *(see p172)* on Gibraltar

1220   **1260**   **1300**   **1340**

1212 Almohad *(see p46)* power broken by Christian victory at Las Navas de Tolosa

1248 Fernando III takes Seville

1238 Nasrid dynasty established in Granada. Alhambra *(see p194)* begins

1350–69 Reign of Pedro I of Castilla, who rebuilds Seville Alcázar in Mudéjar style. His lack of Spanish patriotism provokes civil war against Henry II of Trastámara

Alfonso X

Chivalry
The Moors lived by chivalric codes – this jousting scene is in the Sala de los Reyes in the Alhambra (see p194).

Nasrid warriors

Crown
This Mudéjar-style crown, bearing the coats of arms of Castilla and León, is made of silver, ivory and coral.

Astrolabe
As this 15th-century navigation tool shows, the Moors had great technical expertise.

Boabdil's Demise
Legend has it that Boabdil wept as he left Granada. He moved to Laujar de Andarax (see p197) until 1493, then later to Africa.

WHERE TO SEE RECONQUEST ANDALUSIA

Many of the Reconquest buildings in Andalusia are Mudéjar in style *(see p24).* The most notable are the Palacio Pedro I in the Real Alcázar *(p83)* and parts of the Casa de Pilatos *(p77),* both in Seville. Christian churches built in Andalusia during the 13th, 14th and 15th centuries are also either completely Mudéjar in style or have Mudéjar features such as a minaret-like bell tower or portal; as, for example, the Iglesia de San Marcos *(p90)* in Seville. During this period the Nasrids of Granada built the most outstanding example of Moorish architecture in Spain, the Alhambra and Generalife *(pp194–6).* Seville Cathedral *(pp78–9)* was constructed in the 15th century as a high Gothic assertion of the Catholic faith.

The Palacio Pedro I (see p83) in Seville is considered to be the most complete example of Mudéjar architecture in Spain.

1369 Henry II of Trastámara personally kills Pedro I; lays seeds of monolithic Castilian regime

La Pinta, *one of Columbus's ships*

1492 Fall of Granada to the Catholic Monarchs

1380   **1420**   **1460**

Forced baptism of the Moors

1469 Marriage of Fernando of Aragón to Isabel of Castilla

1474 Isabel proclaimed queen in Segovia

1479 Fernando becomes king of Aragón; Castilla and Aragón united

1492 Columbus sails to America

Seville's Golden Age

Mexican Indian

The 16th century saw the rise of a monolithic Spanish state, led by the Catholic Monarchs. Heretics were persecuted and the remaining Moors treated so unjustly that they often rebelled. In 1503 Seville was granted a monopoly on trade with the New World and Spain entrusted with "converting" the Indians by the pope. In 1516 the Habsburg Carlos I came to the throne, later to be elected Holy Roman Emperor; Spain became the most powerful nation in Europe. Constant war, however, consumed the wealth that its main port, Seville, generated. By the 1680s the Guadalquivir had silted up, trade had passed to Cádiz and Seville declined.

SPANISH EMPIRE IN 1700

  Spanish territories

La Giralda *(see p78)*, once an Almohad minaret, is now the belfry of Seville's cathedral.

Carlos I *(1516–56)*
Carlos I of Spain was made Holy Roman Emperor Carlos V in 1521. His election enabled the Holy Roman Empire to gain access to the immense wealth that Spain, Seville in particular, generated at this time.

Map of Central America
Within 30 years of Columbus's first voyage, the distant lands and seas of Central America had become familiar territory to Spanish navigators.

SEVILLE IN THE 16TH CENTURY
This painting by Alonso Sánchez Coello (1531–88) shows Seville at its height. With the return of treasure fleets from the New World, astonishing wealth poured into the city and it became one of the richest ports in Europe. The population grew, religious buildings proliferated and artistic life found new vigour. Despite the prosperity of the city, poverty, crime and sickness were endemic.

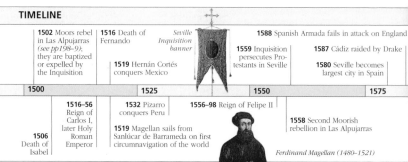

TIMELINE

1502 Moors rebel in Las Alpujarras *(see pp198–9)*; they are baptized or expelled by the Inquisition

1506 Death of Isabel

1516–56 Reign of Carlos I, later Holy Roman Emperor

1516 Death of Fernando

1519 Hernán Cortés conquers Mexico

1532 Pizarro conquers Peru

1519 Magellan sails from Sanlúcar de Barrameda on first circumnavigation of the world

Seville Inquisition banner

1556–98 Reign of Felipe II

1559 Inquisition persecutes Protestants in Seville

1558 Second Moorish rebellion in Las Alpujarras

1588 Spanish Armada fails in attack on England

1587 Cádiz raided by Drake

1580 Seville becomes largest city in Spain

Ferdinand Magellan (1480–1521)

| 1500 | 1525 | 1550 | 1575 |

Inquisition
Fears of heresy laid the ground for the Spanish Inquisition to be set up in the 15th century. In the 16th century autos-da-fé (trials of faith) were held in Seville in the Plaza de San Francisco (see p74).

Unloading and loading took place virtually in the heart of the city.

Velázquez
Born in Seville in 1599, Diego Velázquez painted his earliest works in the city, but later became a court painter in Madrid. This crucifix is a detail of a painting he made at the behest of Felipe IV.

Ships from other parts of Europe brought goods to the city; this merchandise would be traded later in the New World.

The Last Moors
The last Moors were expelled in 1609; this destroyed southern Spain's agriculture, which had taken over 700 years to develop.

WHERE TO SEE THE GOLDEN AGE IN ANDALUSIA

The Isabelline style (*see p24*), lasting testament to nationalistic fervour of the early 16th century, can be seen in the Capilla Real (*p190*) in Granada and the Palacio de Jabalquinto in Baeza (*pp152–3*). Baeza and Úbeda (*pp154–5*) both prospered during the Renaissance in Spain and contain some of the best architecture of this period in Andalusia. The Plateresque (*p25*) façade of the Ayuntamiento (*pp74–5*) in Seville is a good example of the style, and the Palacio Carlos V (*p191*) in Granada is the best example of Classical Renaissance architecture in Spain. The Archivo de Indias (*pp80–81*) was built according to the principles of Herreran style (*p25*). The Hospital de la Caridad (*p69*) is a fine 17th-century Baroque building.

The Capilla Real (see p190) *in Granada was built to house the bodies of the Catholic Monarchs, Fernando and Isabel.*

1598–1621 Reign of Felipe III

1608 Cervantes, active in Madrid and Seville, publishes *Don Quixote*

1609 Expulsion of Moors by Felipe III

Original edition of Don Quixote

1649 Plague in Seville kills one in three

1600	1625	1650	1675

1599 Velázquez born in Seville

1596 Sack of Cádiz by the English fleet

1617 Murillo born in Seville

1630 Madrid becomes Spain's largest city. Zurbarán moves to Seville

1665–1700 Carlos II, last of the Spanish Habsburgs

Young beggar by Murillo (1617–82)

Bourbon Kings

The 13-year War of the Spanish Succession saw Bourbons on the throne in place of the Habsburgs and, under the Treaty of Utrecht, the loss of Gibraltar to the British *(see pp172–3)*. Later, ties with France dragged Spain into the Napoleonic Wars: following the Battle of Trafalgar, the Spanish king Carlos IV abdicated and Napoleon Bonaparte placed his brother Joseph on the Spanish throne. The Peninsular War ensued and, with British help, the French were driven out of Spain. After the Bourbon restoration, Spain, weakened by further strife, began to lose her colonies. Andalusia became one of Spain's poorest regions.

Joseph Bonaparte

SPAIN IN EUROPE (1812)

▨	*Napoleonic dependencies*
☐	*Napoleonic rule*

Romantic Andalusia
Andalusia's Moorish legacy helped to establish it as a land of beauty and myth, making it popular with travellers of the Romantic era.

The Constitution is proclaimed to the people of Cádiz.

Carlos III
A Bourbon monarch of the Enlightenment and an innovator in matters of society and science, Carlos III tried to establish colonies of farm workers in the sparsely populated Sierra Morena.

THE 1812 CONSTITUTION

During the Peninsular War, Spain's Parliament met in Cádiz, and in 1812 produced an advanced liberal constitution. However, after the Bourbon restoration in 1814, Fernando VII banned all liberal activity. Ironically, during the First Carlist War, Fernando's daughter, Isabel II, contesting her right to the throne against her uncle Don Carlos, turned to the liberals for support.

TIMELINE

1701 Felipe V of Bourbon begins his reign

1717 American trade moves to Cádiz

1726 Spain tries to retake Gibraltar

1779–83 Great Siege of Gibraltar

1700	1725	1750	1775

1701–13 War of the Spanish Succession

1724 Felipe V abdicates but is reinstated

1713 Treaty of Utrecht; Gibraltar ceded to Britain

1746–59 Reign of Fernando VI

1759–88 Carlos III

1771 Royal Tobacco Factory in Seville is completed

1788–1808 Carlos IV

Battle of Bailén
In 1808, at Bailén, a Spanish army comprising local militias beat an experienced French army, taking 22,000 prisoners.

WHERE TO SEE BOURBON ANDALUSIA

Eighteenth-century Baroque architecture can be seen all over Andalusia. The prime examples in Seville are the former Royal Tobacco Factory, now the city's Universidad *(see pp96–7)*, and the Plaza de Toros de la Maestranza *(p68)*. Osuna *(p133)*, Écija *(p133)* and Priego de Córdoba *(p150)* all have fine examples of the style. The lower levels of Cádiz Cathedral *(p164)* are the most complete example of a Baroque church found in Spain. The Puente Isabel II *(p103)* is a fine example of 19th-century *arquitectura de hierro* (iron architecture).

Battle of Trafalgar
In 1805, the Spanish, allied at the time to Napoleon, lost their fleet to the British admiral, Nelson.

Support for the constitution came from a wide section of society, including women.

The Puente Isabel II *is an example of the architecture of Andalusia's "industrial" age.*

Washington Irving
In Tales of the Alhambra *(1832) the American diplomat Washington Irving perpetuated a highly romanticized view of Andalusia.*

Seville's Tobacco Factory
Carmen *(1845), by Prosper Mérimée (see p96), was inspired by the women – over 3,000 of them – who worked in the tobacco factory.*

Isabel II

1808 Joseph Bonaparte made king of Spain. Battle of Bailén	**1812** Liberal constitution drawn up in Cádiz		**1870–73** Reign of King Amadeo	**1873–4** First Republic
	1814–33 (Bourbon restoration) Reign of Fernando VII		**1868** Isabel II loses her throne in "glorious" revolution	
1800	**1825**	**1850**		**1875**
1805 Battle of Trafalgar	**1814** South American colonies begin struggle for independence	**1843** Isabel II accedes to throne	**1846–9** Second Carlist War	**1872–6** Third Carlist War
	1808–14 Peninsular War	**1833** First Carlist War	**1874** Second Bourbon restoration: Alfonso XII made king	

Alfonso XII

The Seeds of Civil War

Andalusia continued to decline, remaining so deeply feudal that by the early 20th century social protest was rife. The 1920s brought dictator General Primo de Rivera and relative, but short-lived, social order. In 1931, a Republican government, initially comprising liberals and moderate socialists, came to power. A rigid social order made real reforms slow to arrive, however, and 1931–36 saw growing conflict between extreme left and right wing (including the Falange) elements. Finally, in 1936, the Nationalist General Franco, leading a Moroccan garrison, invaded Spain, declaring war on the Republic.

General Franco

ANDALUSIA IN 1936

- Nationalist territory
- Republican territory

Women fought alongside men against the Nationalist army.

Moorish Revival
By the late 19th century, regionalism, andalucismo, *led to a revival of Moorish-style architecture. An example is Seville's Estación de Córdoba.*

Picasso
Pablo Picasso, shown in this self-portrait, was born in Málaga in 1881. His most famous work, Guernica, *depicts the tragic effects of the Civil War.*

THE REPUBLICAN ARMY
In Andalusia, Franco attacked the Republican army at the very start of the war. Cádiz and Seville fell to Nationalists, but other Andalusian towns held out longer. Franco seized Málaga in 1937, executing thousands of Republicans.

TIMELINE

1876 Composer Manuel de Falla born in Cádiz	**1882–1912** Growing militancy of farm workers	*Spanish soldiers, Cuban War*	
	1885–1902 Regency of María Cristina	**1895–8** Cuban War	

1880   **1890**   **1900**

1881 Pablo Picasso born	**1893** Guitarist Andrés Segovia born near Jaén	**1898** Cuba gains independence with US aid; Cádiz and Málaga begin to decline	**1902–31** Reign of Alfonso XIII
	1885 Anarchist group *Mano Negra* active in Andalusia		

Casas Viejas
In 1933, peasants were massacred after an uprising by anarchists at Casas Viejas in the province of Cádiz. The incident further served to undermine the Republican government.

WHERE TO SEE EARLY 20TH-CENTURY ARCHITECTURE IN ANDALUSIA

This period is characterized by architectural revivals. The regionalist style can be seen at the Plaza de España (*see p98*), the Museo Arqueológico (*p99*), and the Museo de Artes y Costumbres Populares (*p99*), all in the Parque María Luisa. The Teatro Lope Vega (*p97*) is in a Neo-Baroque style.

The Pabellón Real (see p99) *in the Parque María Luisa is a pastiche of the late Gothic, Isabelline (see p24) style.*

1929 Exposition
This trade fair was intended to boost Andalusia's economy. Unfortunately, it coincided with the Wall Street Crash.

Arms were supplied to the Republican army by the then Soviet Union.

Federico García Lorca
This poster is for Lorca's play, Yerma. *The outspoken poet and playwright was murdered by local Falangists in his home town, Granada, in 1936.*

General Queipo de Llano
Queipo de Llano broadcast radio propaganda to Seville as part of the Nationalists' strategy to take the city.

Republican poster

1923–30 Dictatorship of General Primo de Rivera

1933 Massacre at Casas Viejas

1929 Ibero-American Exposition, Seville

1936 Civil War starts

1910 **1920** **1930**

1917–20 Bolshevik Triennium; communists lead protests in Andalusia

José Antonio Primo de Rivera

1931–39 Second Republic

1933 Falange founded by José Antonio Primo de Rivera; later supports Franco

1936 Franco becomes head of state

1939 Civil War ends

Modern Andalusia

Andalusian flag

By 1945 Spain remained the only Nationalist state in Europe. She was denied aid until 1953, when Franco allowed US bases to be built on Spanish soil. The 1960s and '70s saw economic growth, Andalusia in particular benefiting from tourism. When Franco died in 1975 and Juan Carlos I came to the throne, Spain was more than ready for democracy; the regions clamoured for devolution from Franco's centralized government. In 1982 the Sevillian Felipe González came to power and, in the same year, Andalusia became an autonomous region.

AUTONOMOUS REGIONS

Present-day Andalusia

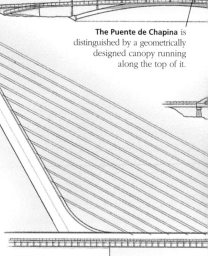

The Puente de Chapina is distinguished by a geometrically designed canopy running along the top of it.

Feria
Despite the repressive regime that Franco estab-lished, the spirit of the Andalusian people remained evident in events such as the feria in Seville.

The Hungry Years
After the Civil War, Spain was isolated from Europe and after World War II received no aid; amid widespread poverty and ration-ing, many Andalusians left to work abroad.

NEW BRIDGES

Despite its autonomy, Andalusia still lagged behind much of the rest of Spain eco-nomically. Funds were provided by central government to build the new infrastructure needed to support Expo '92. Five bridges, all of the most innovative, modern design, were built over the Guadalquivir river.

TIMELINE

1940 Franco refuses to allow Hitler to attack Gibraltar from Spanish territory

1953 Spain is granted economic aid in return for allowing US bases on Spanish soil

1966 Palomares incident: two US aircraft collide and four nuclear bombs fall to earth, one in the sea, but do not explode. The Duchess of Medina Sidonia, "the red duchess", leads protest march on Madrid

1976 Adolfo Suárez appointed prime minister and forms centre-right government

1940	1950	1960	1970

1940–53 The Hungry Years

Franco meets American President Eisenhower (1953)

1962 Development of Costa del Sol begins

1969 Spain closes its border with Gibraltar

1975 Franco dies. Third Bourbon restoration; Juan Carlos I accedes to the throne

Franco's Funeral *(1975)*
Franco's death was mourned as much as it was welcomed; most people, though, saw the need for democratic change.

Package Holidays
New building for mass tourism transformed Andalusia's coast.

WHERE TO SEE MODERN ANDALUSIA

The most striking buildings of modern Andalusia were built in the early part of the 1990s. Expo '92 left Seville with five new bridges over the Guadalquivir river, while at La Cartuja *(see p104)* Expo's core pavilions still stand, soon to be the site of new attractions. The new Teatro de la Maestranza *(pp68–9)*, in El Arenal, was also built during this period.

The Omnimax cinema (see p104) *on the former Expo '92 site was originally built as part of the Pavilion of Discoveries.*

The Puente del Alamillo (Harp) has a single upward arm supporting its weight.

The Puente de la Barqueta, a unique suspension bridge supported by a single overhead beam, spans 168 m (551 ft).

Expo '92
Hosted by Seville, Expo '92 placed Andalusia at the centre of a world stage. In 1996, however, Spain was still recovering the cost.

Felipe González
In 1982, the year after an attempted coup by the Civil Guard colonel Antonio Tejero, Felipe González, leader of the socialist PSOE, claimed a huge electoral victory.

1982 Felipe González elected prime minister; Andalusia becomes an autonomous region

1985 Spain-Gibraltar border opens

1996 In the general election González loses to a coalition led by Aznar

2004 The Spanish Socialist Workers' Party wins the general elections, a result that defies most predictions

2006 Seville FC are the UEFA Cup champions

1990	2000	2010	2020

1981 Colonel Tejero attempts coup and holds Spanish Parliament hostage; Juan Carlos intervenes

Colonel Tejero

2002 Spain converts to the euro

2006 In March, the Basque terrorist organization ETA announces a permanent ceasefire

2009 Andalusia's first subway system opens in Seville

2007 Madrid to Málaga high-speed AVE train line opens

SEVILLE AREA
BY AREA

Seville at a Glance

The capital of Andalusia is a compact and relaxing city with a rich cultural heritage. Conveniently, many of its principal sights can be found within or very near the city centre, which is set on the east bank of the Río Guadalquivir. Most visitors head straight for the cathedral and La Giralda, Real Alcázar and Museo de Bellas Artes. Among other highly popular monuments are the exquisite Renaissance palace of Casa de Pilatos and Seville's bullring, the Plaza de Toros de la Maestranza. There are, however, many other churches, monuments and neighbourhoods to discover in the four central areas described in this section, and more, further afield, across the river.

Baroque doorway, Parlamento de Andalucía *(see p89)*

EL ARENAL
Pages 62–9

The splendid ceiling of Museo de Bellas Artes *(see pp66–7)*

Plaza de Toros de la Maestranza seen from the river *(see p68)*

The Moorish Torre del Oro, built to defend Seville *(see p69)*

0 metres 400

0 yards 400

Patio of Real Fábrica de Tabacos, today the Universidad *(see p96)*

◁ La Giralda by night over the rooftops of El Arenal

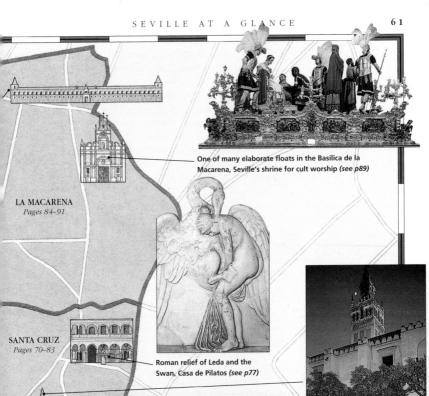

One of many elaborate floats in the Basílica de la Macarena, Seville's shrine for cult worship *(see p89)*

LA MACARENA
Pages 84–91

SANTA CRUZ
Pages 70–83

Roman relief of Leda and the Swan, Casa de Pilatos *(see p77)*

La Giralda rising above the massive Gothic cathedral *(see pp78–9)*

Sumptuous Mudéjar arches and decor in Salón de Embajadores, Real Alcázar *(see pp82–3)*

PARQUE MARIA LUISA
Pages 92–9

Plaza de España in the green oasis of Parque María Luisa *(see pp98–9)*

EL ARENAL

Bounded by the Río Guadalquivir and guarded by the mighty, 13th-century Torre del Oro, El Arenal used to be a district of munitions stores and shipyards.

Torre del Oro shown on 20th-century tiles

Today this quarter is dominated by the dazzling white bullring, Plaza de Toros de la Maestranza, where the Sevillians have been staging *corridas* for more than two centuries. The many classic bars and wine cellars in neighbouring streets get extra busy during the summer bullfighting season.

Once central to the city's life, the influence of the Guadalquivir declined as it silted up during the 17th century. By then El Arenal had become a notorious underworld haunt clinging to the city walls. After being converted into a canal in the early 20th century, the river was restored to its former navigable glory just in time for Expo '92. The east riverfront was transformed into a tree-lined, shady promenade with excellent views of Triana and La Cartuja across the river *(see pp104–5)*. Boat trips and sightseeing tours depart from the Torre del Oro. Close by is the smart, new Teatro de la Maestranza, where opera, classical music and dance take place before well-informed audiences.

The Hospital de la Caridad testifies to the city's continuing love affair with the Baroque. Its church is filled with famous paintings by Murillo, and the story of the Seville School is told with pride in the immaculately restored Museo de Bellas Artes further north. The city's stunning collection of great works by Zurbarán, Murillo and Valdés Leal is reason enough to visit Seville.

SIGHTS AT A GLANCE

Historic Buildings
Hospital de la Caridad ❺
Plaza de Toros
de la Maestranza ❸
Torre del Oro ❻

Museums
Museo de Bellas Artes
pp66–7 ❶

Churches
Iglesia de la Magdalena ❷

Theatres
Teatro de la Maestranza ❹

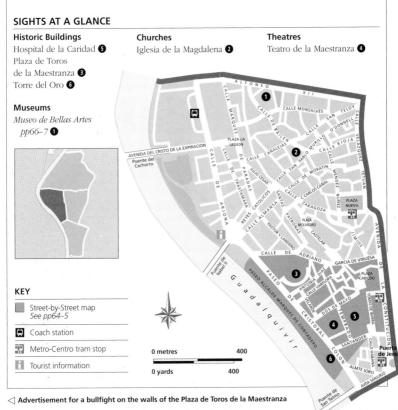

KEY

- Street-by-Street map
  See pp64–5
- 🚌 Coach station
- 🚊 Metro-Centro tram stop
- ℹ Tourist information

0 metres 400
0 yards 400

◁ **Advertisement for a bullfight on the walls of the Plaza de Toros de la Maestranza**

Street-by-Street: El Arenal

Statue of Carmen

Once home to the port of Seville, El Arenal also housed the artillery headquarters and ammunition works. Now its atmosphere is set by Seville's bullring, the majestic Plaza de Toros de la Maestranza, which is located here. During the bullfighting season *(see pp26–7)* bars and restaurants are packed, but for the rest of the year the backstreets remain quiet. The riverfront is dominated by one of Seville's best-known monuments, the Moorish Torre del Oro, while the long, tree-lined promenade beside Paseo de Cristóbal Colón is the perfect setting for a romantic walk along the Guadalquivir.

★ Plaza de Toros de la Maestranza
Seville's 18th-century bullring, one of Spain's oldest, has a Baroque façade in white and ochre ❸

Carmen *(see p96),* sculpted in bronze, stands opposite the bullring.

CALLE DE ADRIANO

CALLE ANTONIA DIAZ

PASEO DE CRISTOBAL COLON

Paseo Alcalde Marqués de Contadero

Teatro de la Maestranza
This showpiece theatre and opera house opened in 1991. Home of the Orquesta Sinfónica de Sevilla, it also features international opera and dance companies ❹

STAR SIGHTS

- ★ Plaza de Toros de la Maestranza
- ★ Torre del Oro
- ★ Hospital de la Caridad

The Guadalquivir
The river used to cause catastrophic inundations. After floods in 1947, a barrage was constructed. Today, peaceful boat trips start from the Torre del Oro.

El Buzo

This is one of many traditional tapas bars situated on or just off Calle Arfe. Nearby lies Mesón Sevilla Jabugo I, where jamón ibérico (see p225) *is served.*

El Postigo is an arts and crafts market.

↑ To Seville Cathedral

On Plaza de Cabildo, a well-hidden square, convent-made sweets are sold in El Torno.

★ Hospital de la Caridad
The Baroque church of this hospital for the elderly is lined with paintings by Bartolomé Esteban Murillo and Juan de Valdés Leal ❺

→ To Real Alcázar

Maestranza de Artillería

★ Torre del Oro
Built in the 13th century in order to protect the port, this crenellated Moorish tower now houses a small maritime museum ❻

| 0 metres | | 75 |
| 0 yards | | 75 |

KEY

- - - Suggested route

Museo de Bellas Artes ❶

The former Convento de la Merced Calzada has been restored to create one of the finest art museums in Spain. The convent, which was completed in 1612 by Juan de Oviedo, is built around three patios, which today are adorned with flowers, trees and *azulejos (see p76).* The museum's impressive collection of Spanish art and sculpture extends from the medieval to the modern, focusing on the work of Seville School artists such as Bartolomé Esteban Murillo, Juan de Valdés Leal and Francisco de Zurbarán.

Baroque cherubs in Sala 5

♿ 🚻 for disabled

La Inmaculada
This boisterous In-maculada (1672), by Valdés Leal (1622–90) is in Sala 8, a gallery devoted to the artist's forceful religious paintings.

First floor

★ San Hugo en el Refectorio *(1655)*
One of several works by Zurbarán for the monastery at La Cartuja (see p105), this scene depicts the Carthusian Order of monks first renouncing the eating of meat.

The Claustro de los Bojes is enclosed by Tuscan-style arches.

STAR EXHIBITS

- ★ La Virgen de la Servilleta
- ★ Domed Ceiling
- ★ Claustro Mayor
- ★ San Jerónimo Penitente by Pietro Torrigiano
- ★ San Hugo en el Refectorio by Zurbarán

★ San Jerónimo Penitente *(1528)*
Sculpted by the Florentine Torrigiano, this master-piece in terracotta brought the vitality of the Italian Renaissance to Seville.

★ La Virgen de la Servilleta
This Virgin and Child (1665–8), painted on a napkin (servilleta), is one of Murillo's most popular works.

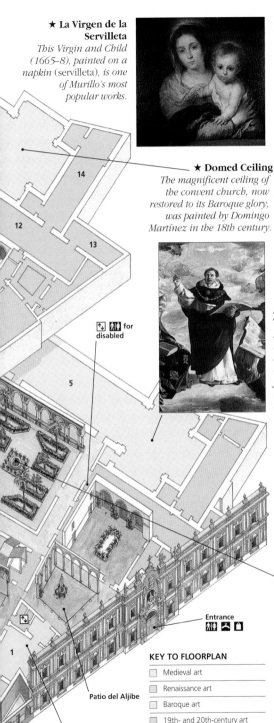

VISITORS' CHECKLIST

Pl del Museo 9. **Map** 5 B2. *Tel*
(95) 478 64 82. 🚌 B2, C3, C4.
⬤ 9am–8:30pm Tue–Sat, 9am–
2:30pm Sun. ♿ www.juntade-
andalucia.es/cultura

★ Domed Ceiling
The magnificent ceiling of the convent church, now restored to its Baroque glory, was painted by Domingo Martínez in the 18th century.

⬆ 🚻 for disabled

Apoteosis de Santo Tomás de Aquino
Zurbarán accomplished this work in 1631, at the age of 33. His sharp characterization of the figures and vivid use of colour bring it to life, as can be seen on this detail.

★ Claustro Mayor
The main cloister of the monastery was remodelled by architect Leonardo de Figueroa in 1724.

GALLERY GUIDE
Signs provide a self-guided chronological tour through the museum's 14 galleries, starting by the Claustro del Aljibe. Works downstairs progress from the 14th century through to Baroque; those upstairs from the Baroque to the early 20th century.

Entrance
🚻 🎫 📷

Patio del Aljibe

Ground floor

KEY TO FLOORPLAN
- ▢ Medieval art
- ▢ Renaissance art
- ▢ Baroque art
- ▢ 19th- and 20th-century art
- ▨ Non-exhibition space

For hotels and restaurants in this region see pp212–14 and pp228–30

Museo de Bellas Artes ❶

See pp66–7.

Madonna and Child in the Baroque Iglesia de la Magdalena

Iglesia de la Magdalena ❷

Calle San Pablo 10. **Map** 3 B1 (5 B2).
🚇 Plaza Nueva. **Tel** 95 422 96 03.
🕐 7:30–11am, 6:30–9pm Mon–
Sat; 7:30am–1:30pm, 6:30–9pm Sun.

This immense Baroque church
by Leonardo de Figueroa,
completed in 1709, is gradually
being restored to its former
glory. In its southwest corner
is the Capilla de la Quinta
Angustia, a Mudéjar chapel
with three cupolas. This chapel
survived from an earlier church
where the great Spanish painter
Bartolomé Murillo *(see pp66– 7)*
was baptized in 1618. The
font which was used for his
baptism today stands in the
baptistry of the present building. The sheer west front is
surmounted by a belfry painted
in vivid colours.

Among the religious works
in the church are a painting
by Francisco de Zurbarán, *St
Dominic in Soria*, housed in
the Capilla Sacramental (to the
right of the south door), and
frescoes by Lucas Valdés above
the sanctuary depicting *The
Allegory of the Triumph of Faith.*
On the wall of the north tran-
sept is a cautionary fresco
which depicts a medieval auto-
da-fé (trial of faith).

Plaza de Toros de la Maestranza ❸

Paseo de Colón 12. **Map** 3 B2 (5 B4).
🚇 Prado de San Sebastián. 🚇
Archivo de Indias. 🚌 C3, C4.
Tel 95 421 03 15. 🕐 9am–7pm
daily (to 8pm May–Oct); 9:30am–
3pm on bullfight days. 🎭 🖊

Seville's famous bullring is
arguably the finest in the whole
of Spain and is a perfect venue
for a first experience of the *corrida*, or bullfight *(see pp26– 7).*
Although the art of the matador
(bullfighter) is now declining in
popularity, the sunlit stage,
with its whitewashed walls,
blood red fences and merciless
circle of sand, remains crucial
to the city's psyche. Even if you
dislike the idea of bullfighting,
this arcaded arena, dating from
1761 to 1881, is an aesthetic
marvel and well worth a visit.

The bullring accommodates
as many as 12,500 spectators.
Guided tours start from the
main entrance on Paseo de
Colón. On the west side is the
Puerta del Príncipe (Prince's
Gate), through which the very
best of the matadors are carried
triumphant on the shoulders
of admirers from the crowd.

Passing the *enfermería*
(emergency hospital), visitors
reach a museum which details
the history of the bullfight in
Seville. Among its collection of
costumes, portraits and posters
are scenes showing early contests held in the Plaza de San
Francisco and a purple cape
painted by Pablo Picasso. The
tour continues to the chapel
where matadors pray for
success, and then on to the

stables where the horses of
the *picadores* (lance-carrying
horsemen) are kept.

The bullfighting season
starts on Easter Sunday and
continues intermittently until
October. Most *corridas* are
held on Sunday evenings.
Tickets can be bought from
the *taquilla* (booking office)
at the bullring itself.

**Entrance with 19th-century iron-
work, Teatro de la Maestranza**

Teatro de la Maestranza ❹

Paseo de Colón 22. **Map** 3 B2 (5 C5).
🚇 Prado de San Sebastián. 🚇 Puerta
Jerez. 🚌 C3, C4. **Tel** 95 422 65 73
(information). 🕐 for performances.
🎭 🖊 **www**.teatromaestranza.com

Close to the Plaza de Toros,
and with echoes of its circular
bulk, is Seville's 1,800-seat
opera house and theatre. It
opened in 1991 and many
international opera companies

Arcaded arena of the Plaza de Toros de la Maestranza, begun in 1761

Finis Gloriae Mundi by Juan de Valdés Leal in the Hospital de la Caridad

perform here *(see p245)*. Like many of the edifices built in the run-up to Expo '92 *(see pp56–7)*, it was designed in a rather austere style by architects Luis Marín de Terán and Aurelio del Pozo. Ironwork remnants of the 19th-century ammunition works that first occupied the site decorate the river façade. Tickets are sold from the box office in the adjacent Jardín de la Caridad.

Hospital de la Caridad **5**

Calle Temprado 3. **Map** 3 B2 (5 C5).
Prado de San Sebastian. Puerto Jerez. C3, C4. **Tel** 95 422 32 32.
9am–1:30pm, 3:30–6:30pm Mon–Sat, 9am–1pm Sun & public hols.

Founded in 1674, this charity hospital is still used today as a sanctuary for the elderly and the infirm. In the gardens opposite the entrance stands a statue of its benefactor, Miguel de Mañara. The complex was designed by Pedro Sánchez Falconete. The façade of the hospital church, with its whitewashed walls, terracotta stonework and framed *azulejos* *(see p76)* provides a glorious example of Sevillian Baroque.

Inside are two square patios adorned with plants, 18th-century Dutch *azulejos* and fountains with Italian statues depicting Charity and Mercy. At their northern end a passage to the right leads to another patio, where a 13th-century arch from the city's shipyards survives. A bust of Mañara stands amid rose bushes.

Inside the church there are many original canvases by some of the leading artists of the 17th century, despite the fact that some of its greatest artworks were looted by Marshal Soult at the time of the Napoleonic occupation of 1810 *(see p53)*. Immediately above the entrance is the ghoulish *Finis Gloriae Mundi* (The End of the World's Glories) by Juan de Valdés Leal, while opposite hangs his morbid *In Ictu Oculi* (In the Blink of an Eye). Many of the other works are by Murillo, including *St John of God Carrying a Sick Man*, portraits of the Child Jesus, *St John the Baptist as a Boy* and *St Isabel of Hungary Curing the Lepers*. Looking south from the hospital's

entrance you can see the octagonal Torre de Plata (Tower of Silver) rising above Calle Santander. Like the Torre del Oro nearby, it dates from Moorish times and was built as part of the city defences.

Torre del Oro **6**

Paseo de Colón s/n. **Map** 3 B2 (5 C5).
Plaza de Cuba. Puerta Jerez. C3, C4. **Tel** 95 422 24 19.
10am–2pm Tue–Fri, 11am–2pm Sat & Sun. Aug. (free Tue).

In Moorish times the Tower of Gold formed part of the walled defences, linking up with the Real Alcázar *(see pp82–3)* and the rest of the city. It was built as a defensive lookout in 1220, when Seville was under the rule of the Almohads *(see pp46–7)*, and had a companion tower on the opposite river bank. A mighty chain would be stretched between the two to prevent ships from sailing upriver. In 1760 the turret was added.

The gold in the tower's name may refer to gilded *azulejos* that once clad its walls, or to New World treasures unloaded here. The tower

The Torre del Oro, built by the Almohads

has been used as a chapel, a prison, a gun powder store and port offices. Now it is the Museo Marítimo, exhibiting maritime maps and antiques.

DON JUAN OF SEVILLE

Miguel de Mañara (1626–79), founder and subsequent benefactor of the Hospital de la Caridad, is frequently linked with Don Juan Tenorio. The amorous conquests of the legendary Sevillian seducer were first documented in 1630 in a play by Tirso de Molina. They have since inspired works by Mozart, Molière, Byron and Shaw. Mañara is thought to have led an equally dissolute life prior to his conversion to philanthropy – apparently this was prompted by a premonition of his own funeral which he experienced one drunken night.

The legendary Don Juan with two of his conquests

SANTA CRUZ

The Barrio de Santa Cruz, Seville's old Jewish quarter, is a warren of white alleys and patios that has long been the most picturesque corner of the city. Many of the best-known sights are grouped here: the cavernous Gothic cathedral with its landmark Giralda; the splendid Real Alcázar with the royal palaces and lush gardens of Pedro I and Carlos V; and the Archivo de Indias, whose documents tell of Spain's exploration and conquest of the New World. Spreading northeast from these great monuments is an enchanting maze of whitewashed streets. The

Ornate streetlamp, Plaza del Triunfo

artist Bartolomé Esteban Murillo lived here in the 17th century while his contemporary, Juan de Valdés Leal, decorated the Hospital de los Venerables with fine Baroque frescoes.

Further north, busy Calle de las Sierpes is one of Seville's favourite shopping streets. Its adjacent market squares, such as the charming Plaza del Salvador, provided backdrops for Cervantes' stories. Nearby, the ornate façades and interiors of the Ayuntamiento and the Casa de Pilatos, a gem of Andalusian architecture, testify to the great wealth and artistry that flowed into the city in the 16th century.

SIGHTS AT A GLANCE

Gardens
Jardines de Murillo ⑬

Streets and Plazas
Calle de las Sierpes ②
Plaza del Triunfo ⑨
Plaza Virgen de los Reyes ⑧

Churches
Seville Cathedral and
   La Giralda pp78–9 ⑦
Iglesia del Salvador ④

Historic Buildings
Real Alcázar pp82–3 ⑪
Archivo de Indias ⑩
Ayuntamiento ③

Casa de Pilatos ⑥
Hospital de los Venerables ⑫
Museo del Baile Flamenco ⑤
Palacio de Lebrija ①

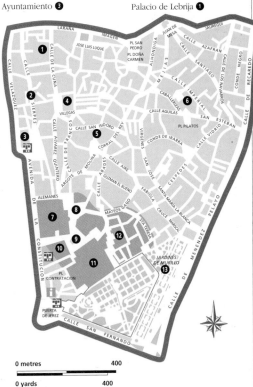

KEY

Street-by-Street map
See pp72–3

Metro-Centro tram stop

Tourist information

0 metres 400
0 yards 400

◁ **La Giralda seen from the gardens of the Real Alcázar**

Street-by-Street: Santa Cruz

Window grille, Santa Cruz

The maze of narrow streets to the east of Seville cathedral and the Real Alcázar represents Seville at its most romantic and compact. As well as the expected souvenir shops, tapas bars and strolling guitarists, there are plenty of picturesque alleys, hidden plazas and flower-decked patios to reward the casual wanderer. Once a Jewish ghetto, its restored buildings, with characteristic window grilles, are now a harmonious mix of up-market residences and tourist accommodation. Good bars and restaurants make the area well worth an evening visit.

Plaza Virgen de los Reyes
Horse carriages line this plaza which has an early 20th-century fountain by José Lafita **8**

Palacio Arzobispal, the 18th-century Archbishop's Palace, is still used by Seville's clergy.

★ Seville Cathedral and La Giralda
This huge Gothic cathedral and its Moorish bell tower are Seville's most popular sights **7**

Convento de la Encarnación
(See p80)

Archivo de Indias
Built in the 16th century as a merchants' exchange, the Archive of the Indies now houses documents relating to the Spanish colonization of the Americas **10**

Plaza del Triunfo
A Baroque column celebrates the city's survival of the great earthquake of 1755. Opposite is a moder statue of the Immacu late Conception **9**

Calle Mateos Gago
This street is filled with souvenir shops and tapas bars. Bar Giralda at No. 2, whose vaults are the remains of a Moorish bath, is particularly popular for its wide variety of tapas (see pp224–5).

LOCATOR MAP
See Street Finder, maps 5–6

Plaza Santa Cruz
is adorned by an ornate iron cross from 1692.

★ **Hospital de los Venerables**
This 17th-century home for elderly priests has a splendidly restored Baroque church ⑫

Callejón del Agua
This alley alongside the Alcázar walls offers enchanting glimpses into plant-filled patios. Washington Irving (see p53) stayed at No. 2.

| 0 metres | | 50 |
| 0 yards | | 50 |

★ **Real Alcázar**
Seville's Royal Palaces are a rewarding combination of exquisite Mudéjar (see p24) craftsmanship, regal grandeur and beautifully landscaped gardens ⑪

STAR SIGHTS

★ Seville Cathedral and La Giralda

★ Real Alcázar

★ Hospital de los Venerables

KEY

– – – Suggested route

Mosaic, from Itálica *(see p132)*, in the Palacio de Lebrija

Palacio de Lebrija ❶

Calle Cuna 8. **Map** 1 C5; 3 C1 (5 C2). *Tel* 95 422 78 02. ☐ 10am–1pm year round; also: mid-Jun–Sep: 5–7:30pm; Oct–mid-Jun: 4:30–7pm. ⬤ Sun. 📷 💳 www.palaciodelebrija.com

The home of the family of the Countess Lebrija, this mansion illustrates palatial life in Seville. The ground floor houses Roman and medieval exhibits. A guided tour of the first floor features a library and art, such as the Moorish inspired *azulejos (see p76)*.

The house itself dates from the 15th century and has some Mudéjar *(see p24)* features. Many of its Roman treasures were taken from the ruins at Itálica *(see p132)*, including the mosaic floor in the main patio. The *artesonado* ceiling above the staircase came from the palace of the Dukes of Arcos

in Marchena, near Seville. Ancient roman glass ware, coins and later examples of marble from Medina Azahara *(see p138)* are displayed in rooms off the main patio.

Calle de las Sierpes ❷

Map 3 C1 (5 C3).

The street of the snakes, running north from Plaza de San Francisco, is Seville's main pedestrianized shopping promenade. Long-established stores selling the Sevillian essentials – hats, fans and the traditional *mantillas* (lace headdresses) stand alongside clothes boutiques, souvenir shops, bargain basements and lottery kiosks. The best time to stroll along it is when the *sevillanos* themselves do – during the early evening *paseo*.

The parallel streets of Cuna and Tetuán on either side also offer some enjoyable window-shopping. Look out for the splendid 1924 tiled advert for Studebaker automobiles *(see p76)* at Calle Tetuán 9.

At the southern end of Calle de las Sierpes, on the wall of the Banco Central Hispano, a plaque marks the site of the Cárcel Real (Royal Prison), where the famous Spanish writer Miguel de Cervantes (1547–1616) *(see p51)* was incarcerated. Walking north from here, Calle Jovellanos to the left leads to the Capillita de San José. This small, rather atmospheric chapel, built in the 17th century, contrasts

sharply with its commercial surroundings. Further on, at the junction with Calle Pedro Caravaca, you can take a look back into the anachronistic, upholstered world of the Real Círculo de Labradores, a private men's club founded in 1856. Right at the end of the street, take the opportunity to peruse Seville's best-known *pastelería* (cake shop), La Campana.

Ayuntamiento ❸

Plaza Nueva 1. **Map** 3 C1 (5 C3). 🚆 Plaza Nueva. *Tel* 95 459 01 01. ☐ 5:30 & 6pm Tue–Thu. 💳

Plateresque doorway, part of the façade of Seville's Ayuntamiento

Seville's city hall stands between the historic Plaza de San Francisco and the modern expanse of Plaza Nueva.

In the 15th–18th centuries, Plaza de San Francisco was the venue for autos-da-fé, public trials of heretics held by the Inquisition *(see p51)* . Those found guilty would be taken to the Quemadero and burnt alive. (This site is now the Prado de San Sebastián, north of Parque María Luisa, *see pp98–9*.) These days, Plaza de San Francisco is the focus of activities in Semana Santa and Corpus Christi *(see pp34–5)*.

Plaza Nueva was once the site of the Convento de San Francisco. In its centre is an equestrian statue of Fernando III, who liberated Seville from the Moors and was eventually canonized in 1671 *(see p48)*.

The Ayuntamiento, begun in 1527, was finished in 1534. The east side, looking on to

Tables outside La Campana, Seville's most famous *pasteleria*

Plaza de San Francisco, is a fine example of the ornate Plateresque style *(see p25)* favoured by the architect Diego de Riaño. The west front is part of a Neo-Classical extension built in 1891. It virtually envelops the original building, but richly sculpted ceilings survive in the vestibule and in the lower Casa Consistorial (Council Meeting Room). This room contains Velázquez's *Imposition of the Chasuble on St Ildefonso*, one of many artworks in the building. The upper Casa Consistorial has a dazzling gold coffered ceiling and paintings by Zurbarán and Valdés Leal *(see pp66–7)*.

Baroque façade of the Iglesia del Salvador on the Plaza del Salvador

Iglesia del Salvador ❹

Pl del Salvador. **Map** 3 C1 (6 D3). *Tel* 95 421 16 79. ⬤ 3–7:30pm year round; also: Sep–Jun: 11:30am–6:30pm Mon–Sat; Jul & Aug: 10am–5:30pm Mon–Sat. 🗒

This church has been completely restored. Its cathedral-like proportions result in part from the desire of Seville's Christian conquerors to outdo the Moors' architectural splendours. A mosque first occupied the site; part of the Moorish patio survives beside Calle Córdoba, boxed in by arcades incorporating columns with Roman and Visigothic capitals.

By the 1670s the mosque, long since consecrated for Christian worship, had fallen into disrepair. Work started on a new Baroque structure, designed by Esteban García.

The church was completed in 1712 by Leonardo de Figueroa. Inside, the nave is by José Granados, architect of Granada cathedral *(see p190)*. In the Capilla Sacramental there is a fine statue, *Jesus of the Passion*, made in 1619 by Juan Martínez Montañés (1568–1649). In the northwest corner, a door leads to the ornate Capilla de los Desamparados and a Moorish patio. Over the exit on Calle Córdoba, the bell tower rests on part of the original minaret.

Adjacent to the church is the Plaza del Salvador, a meeting place for Seville's youngsters.

The bronze statue commemorates the sculptor Montañés. On the east side of the church, the Plaza Jesús de la Pasión is given over to shops catering to weddings – the Iglesia del Salvador is a favourite among *sevillanos* for getting married.

Museo del Baile Flamenco ❺

Calle Manuel Rojas Marcos 3. **Map** 3 C1 (6 D3). *Tel* 95 434 03 11. ⬤ 9am–7pm daily. 📷 🗒
www.museoflamenco.com

Although flamenco was supposedly born across the river, in Triana, the Barrio de Santa Cruz has become its de facto home in Seville. This museum of flamenco dance, occupying a restored 18th-century house on a small street between the Plaza del Alfalfa and the cathedral, is intended as an introduction of the art form to the visitor. As much as a space for exhibits in the traditional sense, it is a venue for live performances of flamenco and a school offering classes in flamenco music and dance.

THE SIGN OF SEVILLE

The curious abbreviation "NO8DO" is emblazoned everywhere from the venerable walls of the Ayuntamiento to the sides of the municipal buses. It is traditionally said to stand for "*No me ha dejado*" ("She has not deserted me"). These words were reputedly uttered by Alfonso the Wise, after the city remained loyal to him in the course of a dispute with his son Sancho during the Reconquest *(see pp48–9)*. The double-loop symbol in the middle represents a skein of wool, the Spanish word for which is *madeja*, thus *no (madeja) do*.

The traditional emblem of Seville, here in stone on the Ayuntamiento

The Art of Azulejos

Cool in summer, durable and colourful, glazed ceramic tiles have been a striking feature of Andalusian façades and interiors for centuries. The techniques for making them were first introduced by the Moors – the word *azulejo* derives from the Arabic *az-zulayj* or "little stone". Moorish *azulejos* are elaborate mosaics made of unicoloured stones.

16th-century *azulejos*, Salones de Carlos V *(p82)*

In Seville the craft flourished and evolved in the potteries of Triana *(see pp102–3)*. A later process, developed in 16th-century Italy, allowed tiles to be painted in new designs and colours. The onset of the Industrial Revolution enabled *azulejos* to be mass-produced in ceramics factories including, until 1980, the famous "Pickman y Cia" at the monastery of La Cartuja *(see p105)*.

MUDÉJAR-STYLE AZULEJOS

The Moors created fantastic mosaics of tiles in sophisticated geometric patterns as decoration for their palace walls. The colours used were blue, green, black, white and ochre.

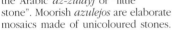

16th-century Mudéjar tiles, Casa de Pilatos

Interlacing motifs, Patio de las Doncellas

Mudéjar tiles in the Patio de las Doncellas, Real Alcázar

Sign for the Royal Tobacco Factory (now part of the Universidad, *see pp96–7*) made in painted glazed tiles in the 18th century

AZULEJOS FOR COMMERCIAL USE

As techniques for making and colouring *azulejos* improved, their use was extended from interior decor to decorative signs and shop façades. Even billboards were produced in multicoloured tiles. The eye-catching results can still be seen all over Andalusia.

Contemporary glazed ceramic beer tap

Azulejo billboard advertising the latest model of Studebaker Motor Cars (1924), situated on Calle Tetuán, off Calle de las Sierpes *(see p74)*

Genoan fountain and Gothic balustrades in the Mudéjar Patio Principal of the Casa de Pilatos

Casa de Pilatos ❻

Plaza de Pilatos 1. **Map** 4 D1 (6 E3).
Tel 95 422 52 98. ◯ 9am–6pm daily.
🖼 🗖 1st floor. ♿ ground floor.

In 1518 the first Marquess of Tarifa departed on a Grand Tour of Europe and the Holy Land. He returned two years later, enraptured by the architectural and decorative wonders of High Renaissance Italy. He spent the rest of his life creating a new aesthetic, which was very influential. His palace in Seville, called the House of Pilate because it was thought to resemble Pontius Pilate's home in Jerusalem, became a luxurious showcase for the new style.

Over the centuries, subsequent owners added their own embellishments. The Casa de Pilatos is now the residence of the Dukes of Medinaceli and is still one of the finest palaces in Seville.

Visitors enter it through a marble portal, commissioned by the Marquess in 1529 from Genoan craftsmen. Across the arcaded Apeadero (carriage yard) is the Patio Principal. This courtyard is essentially Mudéjar *(see p24)* in style with *azulejos* and intricate plasterwork. It is

Lantern in the entrance portal

surrounded by irregularly spaced arches capped with delicate Gothic balustrades. In its corners stand three Roman statues, Minerva, a dancing muse and Ceres, and a Greek fourth statue, a 5th century BC original of the goddess Athena. In its centre is a fountain imported from Genoa. To the right, through the Salón del Pretorio with its coffered ceiling and marquetry, is the Corredor de Zaquizamí. Among the antiquities in adjacent rooms are a bas-relief of *Leda and the Swan* and two Roman reliefs commemorating the Battle of Actium of BC 31. Further along, in the Jardín Chico there is a pool with a bronze of Bacchus.

Coming back to the Patio Principal, you turn right into the Salón de Descanso de los Jueces. Beyond this is a rib-vaulted chapel, which has a sculpture dating from the 1st century AD, *Christ and the Good Shepherd*. Left through the Gabinete de Pilatos, with its small central fountain, is the Jardín Grande. The Italian architect, Benvenuto Tortello, created the loggias in the 1560s.

Returning once more to the main patio, behind the statue

of Ceres, a tiled staircase leads to the apartments on the upper floor. It is roofed with a wonderful *media naranja* (half orange) cupola built in 1537. There are Mudéjar ceilings in some rooms, which are filled with family portraits, antiques and furniture. Plasterwork by Juan de Oviedo and frescoes by Francisco de Pacheco still survive in rooms which bear these artists' names.

West of the Casa de Pilatos, the Plaza de San Ildefonso is bounded by the Convento de San Leandro, famous for the *yemas* (sweets made from egg yolks) sold from a *torno* (drum). Opposite the convent is the Neo-Classical Iglesia de San Ildefonso, which has statues of San Hermenegildo and San Fernando by Pedro Roldán.

Escutcheons in the coffered ceiling of the Salón del Pretorio

For hotels and restaurants in this region see pp212–14 and pp228–30

Seville Cathedral and La Giralda ⓻

16th-century stained glass

Seville's cathedral occupies the site of a great mosque built by the Almohads *(see pp46–7)* in the late 12th century. La Giralda, its bell tower, and the Patio de los Naranjos are a legacy of this Moorish structure. Work on the Christian cathedral, the largest in Europe, began in 1401 and took just over a century to complete. As well as enjoying its Gothic immensity and the works of art in its chapels and Treasury, visitors can climb La Giralda for superb views over the city.

★ La Giralda
The bell tower is crowned by a bronze weathervane (giraldillo) depicting Faith, from which it takes its name. A replica has replaced the original vane.

Group entrance

★ Patio de los Naranjos
In Moorish times worshippers would wash hands and feet in the fountain under the orange trees before praying.

THE RISE OF LA GIRALDA

The minaret was finished in 1198. In the 14th century the original Muslim bronze spheres at its top were replaced by Christian symbols. In 1568 Hernán Ruiz added the Renaissance belfry, which blends perfectly with the Moorish base.

1198

1400

1557 (plan)

1568

Puerta del Perdón

Roman pillars brought from Itálica *(see p132)* surround the cathedral steps.

Retablo Mayor
*Santa María de la Sede,
the cathedral's patron
saint, sits at the high
altar below a waterfall
of gold. The 44 gilded
relief panels of the
retablo were carved
by Spanish and
Flemish sculptors
between 1482
and 1564.*

VISITORS' CHECKLIST

Avenida de la Constitucion s/n.
Map 3 C2 (5 C4). **Tel** 95 421 49
71. 🚇 *Prado de San Sebastian.*
⬜ **Cathedral & La Giralda**
*11am–5:30pm Mon–Sat; 2:30–
6:30pm Sun (9:30am–4:30pm
Jul–Aug).* 📷 🅾 ♿ ✝ *8:30am,
10am, noon, 5pm daily (also 9am,
8pm Sat, 11am, 1pm, 6pm Sun).*

**The Sacristía
Mayor** houses
many works of
art, including
paintings by
Murillo.

Main entrance

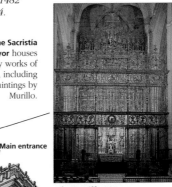

★ Capilla Mayor
*The overwhelming, golden
Retablo Mayor in the
main chapel is
enclosed by
monumental iron
grilles forged in
1518–32.*

**The Tomb of
Columbus** dates from
the 1890s. His coffin
is carried by bearers
representing the king-
doms of Castile, León,
Aragón and Navarra *(see p48).*

**Puerta
del Bautismo**

Iglesia del Sagrario, a
large 17th-century
chapel, is now used
as a parish church.

STAR FEATURES

★ La Giralda

★ Patio de los
Naranjos

★ Capilla Mayor

Puerta de la Asunción
*Though Gothic in style, this portal
was not completed until 1833. A
stone relief of the Assumption of the
Virgin decorates the tympanum.*

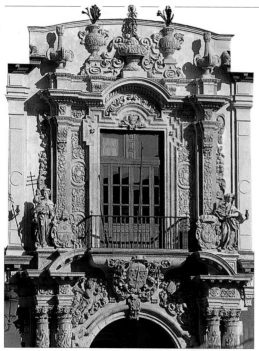

Upper part of the Baroque doorway of the Palacio Arzobispal

Plaza Virgen de los Reyes ❽

Map 3 C2 (6 D4). **Palacio Arzobispal** 🚫 *to the public.* **Convento de la Encarnación** 🚫 *to the public.*

The perfect place to pause for a while and admire the Giralda *(see pp78–9)*, this plaza presents an archetypal Sevillian tableau: horse-drawn carriages, orange trees, gypsy flower-sellers and religious buildings. At its centre is an early 20th-century monumental lamppost and fountain by José Lafita, with grotesque heads copied from Roman originals in the Casa de Pilatos *(see p77)*.

At the north of the square is the Palacio Arzobispal (Arch-bishop's Palace), begun in the 16th century, finished in the 18th, and commandeered by Marshal Soult during the Napoleonic occupation of 1810 *(see pp52–3)*. A fine Baroque palace, it has a jasper staircase and paintings by Zurbarán and Murillo. On the opposite side of

the square is the whitewashed Convento de la Encarnación, which was founded in 1591. The convent stands on grounds that have also been the site of a mosque and of a hospital.

The Plaza Virgen de los Reyes was once home to the Corral de los Olmos, a rogues' inn which features in the writings of Miguel de Cervantes *(see p51)* – on one of the convent walls a plaque bears an inscription testifying to this.

Plaza del Triunfo ❾

Map 3 C2 (6 D4).

Lying between the cathedral *(see pp78–9)* and the Real Alcázar *(see pp82–3)*, the Plaza del Triunfo was built to celebrate the triumph of the city over an earthquake in 1755. The quake devastated the city of Lisbon, over the border in Portugal, but caused comparatively little damage in Seville – a salva-tion attributed to the city's great devotion to the

Decorative Giralda relief on the Archivo de Indias

Virgin Mary. She is honoured by a Baroque column beside the Archivo de Indias. In the centre of the Plaza del Triunfo a monument commemorates Seville's belief in the Immacu-late Conception.

In Calle Santo Tomás, off the southeastern corner of the Plaza del Triunfo, lies a build-ing used by the Archivo de Indias. Formerly the Museo de Arts Contemporáneo – now in the Monasterio de Santa Mariá de las Cuevas *(see p105)* – the building is no longer open to the public. Dating from 1770 it was once a barn where tithes collected by the Church were stored. Parts of the Moorish city walls were uncovered during the renovation of the building.

Archivo de Indias ❿

Avda de la Constitución s/n. **Map** 3 C2 (6 D5). 🏛 *Archivo de Indias.* 🚇 *Prado de San Sebastian.* **Tel** 95 421 12 34. ⬜ *8am–3pm Mon–Fri. During special exhibitions: 9am–4pm Mon–Sat, 10am–2pm Sun.*

Façade of the Archivo de Indias by Juan de Herrera

The archive of the Indies punches home Seville's pre-eminent role in the colonization and exploitation of the New World. Built between 1584–98 to designs by Juan de Herrera, co-architect of El Escorial near Madrid, it was originally a *lonja* (exchange), where merchants traded. In 1785, Carlos III had all Spanish documents relating to the "Indies" collected under one roof, creating a fascinating archive. It contains letters from Columbus, Cortés, Cervantes, and George Washington, the first American president, and the extensive correspondence of Felipe II. The vast collection amounts to some 86 million handwritten pages and 8,000 maps and drawings. A programme of document digitization is ongoing.

Visitors to the Archivo de Indias climb marble stairs to library rooms where drawings and maps are exhibited in a reverential atmosphere. Displays change on a regular basis; one might include a watercolour map from the days when the city of Acapulco was little more than a castle, drawings recording a royal *corrida* (bullfight) held in Panama City in 1748 or designs and plans for a town hall in Guatemala.

Real Alcázar **⑪**

See pp82–3.

Hospital de los Venerables **⑫**

Plaza de los Venerables 8. **Map** 3 C2 (6 D4). Archivo de Indias. **Tel** *95 456 26 96.* 10am–1:30pm, 4–7:30pm daily. except Sun evening.

Located in the heart of the Barrio de Santa Cruz, the Hospital of the Venerables was founded as a home for elderly priests. It was begun in 1675 and completed around 20 years later by Leonardo de Figueroa. It was restored as a cultural centre by FOCUS (Fundación Fondo de Cultura de Sevilla).

It is built around a central, sunken patio. The upper floors, along with the infirmary and the cellar, are used as galleries for exhibitions. A separate guided tour visits the hospital church, a showcase of Baroque splendours, with frescoes by Juan de Valdés Leal and his son Lucas Valdés.

Other highlights include the sculptures of St Peter and St Ferdinand by Pedro Roldán, flanking the east door; and *The Apotheosis of St Ferdinand* by Lucas Valdés, top centre in the *retablo* of the main altar. Its frieze (inscribed in Greek) advises visitors to "Fear God and Honour the Priest".

In the sacristy, the ceiling has an effective *trompe l'oeil* depicting *The Triumph of the Cross* by Juan de Valdés Leal.

Jardines de Murillo **⑬**

Map 4 D2 (6 E5).

These formal gardens at the southern end of the Barrio de Santa Cruz once used to be orchards and vegetable plots in the grounds of the Real Alcázar. They were donated to the city in 1911. Their name commemorates Seville's best-known painter, Bartolomé Murillo (1617–82), who lived in nearby Calle Santa Teresa. A long promenade, Paseo de Catalina de Ribera, pays tribute to the founder of the Hospital de las Cinco Llagas, which is now the seat of the Parlamento de Andalucía *(see p89)*. Rising

Monument to Columbus in the Jardines de Murillo

above the garden's palm trees is a monument to Columbus, incorporating a bronze of the *Santa María*, the caravel that bore him to the New World in the year of 1492 *(see p127)*.

Fresco by Juan de Valdés Leal in the Hospital de los Venerables

Real Alcázar ⓫

Mudéjar stucco

In 1364 Pedro I *(see p48)* ordered the construction of a royal residence within the palaces built by the city's Almohad *(see pp46–7)* rulers. Within two years, craftsmen from Granada and Toledo had created a jewel box of Mudéjar patios and halls, the Palacio Pedro I, which now forms the heart of Seville's Real Alcázar. Later monarchs added their own distinguishing marks – Isabel I *(see p49)* despatched navigators to explore the New World from her Casa de la Contratación, while Carlos V *(see p50)* had grandiose, richly decorated apartments built.

Jardín de Troya

Gardens of the Alcázar
Laid out with terraces, fountains and pavilions, these gardens provide a delightful refuge from the heat and bustle of Seville.

★ **Salones de Carlos V**
Vast tapestries and lively 16th-century azulejos decorate the vaulted halls of the apartments and chapel of Carlos V.

Patio del Crucero lies above the old baths.

PLAN OF THE REAL ALCÁZAR

The complex includes the Palacio Pedro I and Spanish National Trust offices. The palace's upper floor is used by the Spanish royal family.

KEY

 Area illustrated above

Gardens

★ **Patio de las Doncellas**
The Patio of the Maidens boasts plasterwork by the top craftsmen of Granada.

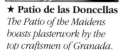

★ **Salón de Embajadores**
Built in 1427, the dazzling dome of the Ambassadors' Hall is made up of carved and gilded, interlaced wood.

VISITORS' CHECKLIST

Patio de Banderas. **Map** 3 C2 (6 D4). **Tel** 95 450 23 23. Archivo de Indias. Prado de San Sebastian. C3, C4. 9:30am–7pm Tue–Sat, 9:30am–5pm Sun (Oct–Mar: to 5pm Tue–Sat, 1:30pm Sun).

Horseshoe Arches
Azulejos and complex plasterwork decorate the Ambassadors' Hall, which has three symmetrically arranged, ornate archways, each with three horseshoe arches.

Casa de la Contratación

The Patio de la Montería was where the court met before hunting expeditions.

The façade of the Palacio Pedro I is a unique example of Mudéjar style.

Patio de las Muñecas
With its adjacent bedrooms and corridors, the Patio of the Dolls was the domestic heart of the palace. It derives its name from two tiny faces that decorate one of its arches.

Puerta del León (entrance)

STAR FEATURES

★ Patio de las Doncellas

★ Salón de Embajadores

★ Salones de Carlos V

Patio del Yeso
The Patio of Plaster, a garden with flower beds and a water channel, retains features of the earlier, 12th-century Almohad Alcázar.

LA MACARENA

The north of Seville, often overlooked by visitors, presents a characterful mix of decaying Baroque and Mudéjar churches, old-style neighbourhood tapas bars and washing-filled back streets. Its name is thought to derive from the Roman goddess, Macaria, the daughter of the hero Hercules. La Macarena is a traditional district and the power of church and family is still strong there.

The best way to enter this quarter is to walk north up Calle Feria to the Basílica de la Macarena, a cult-worship shrine to Seville's much-venerated Virgen de la Esperanza Macarena. Beside this

Roman column, Alameda de Hércules

modern church stands a restored entrance gate and remnants of defensive walls, which enclosed the city during the Moorish era.

Among many churches and convents in this quarter, the Monasterio de San Clemente and Iglesia de San Pedro retain the spirit of historic Seville, while the Convento de Santa Paula offers a rare opportunity to peep behind the walls of a closed religious community. The 13th-century Torre de Don Fadrique in Convento de Santa Clara is a notable sight to the west of the area. Further north is the former Hospital de las Cinco Llagas, now restored as the seat of Andalusia's Parliament.

SIGHTS AT A GLANCE

Churches and Convents
Basílica de la Macarena ❹
Convento de Santa Paula ❾
Iglesia de San Marcos ❽
Iglesia de San Pedro ❿
Iglesia de Santa Catalina ⓫
Monasterio de San Clemente ❶

Historic Buildings
Camera Obscura ❺
Parlamento de Andalucía ❻
Torre de Don Fadrique ❷

Monuments
Murallas ❼

Markets
Alameda de Hércules ❸

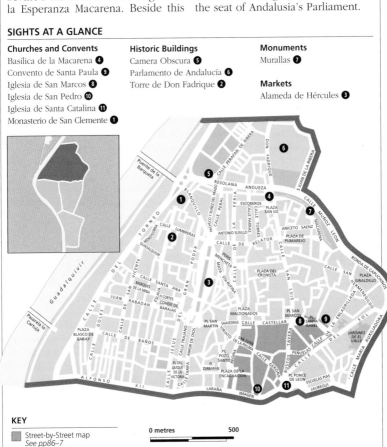

KEY

◼ Street-by-Street map
See pp86–7

0 metres   500
0 yards   500

◁ **Float of Virgen de la Esperanza Macarena during the Semana Santa processions**

Street-by-Street: La Macarena

A stroll in this area provides a glimpse of everyday life in a part of Seville that has so far escaped developing the rather tourist-oriented atmosphere of Santa Cruz. Calle de la Feria, the main street for shopping and browsing, is best visited in the morning when there is plenty of activity and its market stalls are filled with fresh fish and vegetables. Early evening, meanwhile, is a good time to discover the area's large number of fine churches, which are open for Mass at that time. It is also the time when local people visit the bars of the district for a drink and tapas.

Tiled image of Santa Paula

Palacio de las Dueñas
Boxed in by the surrounding houses, this 15th-century Mudéjar palace has an elegant patio. It is the private residence of the Dukes of Alba, whose tiled coat of arms can be seen above the palace entrance.

Iglesia San Juan de la Palma is a small Mudéjar church. Its brickwork belfry was added in 1788.

Calle de la Feria
On Thursday mornings, El Jueves, Seville's oldest market, takes place on this street full of shops.

★ **Iglesia de San Pedro**
The church where Velázquez was baptized is a mix of styles, from Mudéjar to these modern tiles on its front ⑩

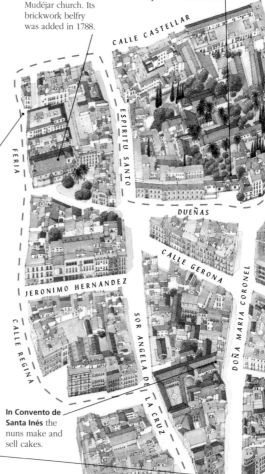

CALLE CASTELLAR

ESPIRITU SANTO

FERIA

DUEÑAS

CALLE GERONA

JERONIMO HERNANDEZ

DOÑA MARIA CORONEL

SOR ANGELA DE LA CRUZ

CALLE REGINA

In Convento de Santa Inés the nuns make and sell cakes.

KEY

— — — Suggested route

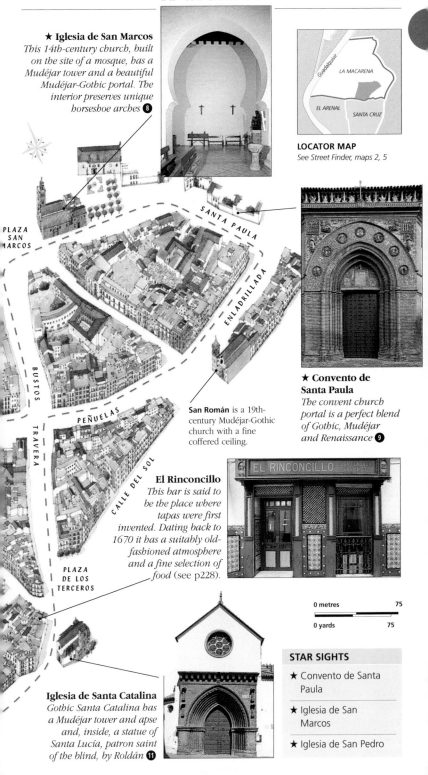

★ Iglesia de San Marcos

This 14th-century church, built on the site of a mosque, has a Mudéjar tower and a beautiful Mudéjar-Gothic portal. The interior preserves unique horseshoe arches **8**

LOCATOR MAP
See Street Finder, maps 2, 5

LA MACARENA

EL ARENAL   SANTA CRUZ

PLAZA SAN MARCOS

SANTA PAULA

ENLADRILLADA

BUSTOS

TRAVERA

PEÑUELAS

San Román is a 19th-century Mudéjar-Gothic church with a fine coffered ceiling.

★ Convento de Santa Paula

The convent church portal is a perfect blend of Gothic, Mudéjar and Renaissance **9**

El Rinconcillo

This bar is said to be the place where tapas were first invented. Dating back to 1670 it has a suitably old-fashioned atmosphere and a fine selection of food (see p228).

CALLE DEL SOL

PLAZA DE LOS TERCEROS

Iglesia de Santa Catalina

Gothic Santa Catalina has a Mudéjar tower and apse and, inside, a statue of Santa Lucía, patron saint of the blind, by Roldán **11**

0 metres   75
0 yards   75

STAR SIGHTS

★ Convento de Santa Paula

★ Iglesia de San Marcos

★ Iglesia de San Pedro

Monasterio de San Clemente ❶

Calle Reposo 9. **Map** 1 C3. 🚌 *C3, C4.* **Tel** *95 437 80 40.* **Church**
⬜ *for Mass only: 8am Mon–Sat, 10am Sun & public hols.*

Behind the ancient walls of the Monasterio de San Clemente is a tranquil cloister with palms and fruit trees, and an arcade with a side entrance to the monastery's church.

This atmospheric church can also be entered through an arch in Calle Reposo. Its features range from the 13th to 18th centuries, and include a fine Mudéjar *artesonado* ceiling, *azulejos (see p76)* dating from 1588, a Baroque main *retablo* by Felipe de Rivas and early 18th-century frescoes by Lucas Valdés.

Torre de Don Fadrique ❷

Convento de Santa Clara, Calle Santa Clara 40. **Map** 1 C4. **Tel** *66 055 52 84.* 🔲 *currently for refurbishment.*

One of the best-preserved historical surprises in Seville, this 13th-century tower stands like a chess-piece castle in the

Torre de Don Fadrique in the patio of Convento de Santa Clara

Marble columns at the southern end of Alameda de Hércules

Convento de Santa Clara. This is entered from Calle Santa Clara, passing through an arch to a sleepy patio with orange trees and a fountain. To the left is a second courtyard, where the tower is hidden away. The Gothic entrance to the courtyard was built during the 16th century as part of Seville's first university and transplanted here in the 19th century.

Constructed in 1252, the tower formed part of the defences for the palace of the Infante Don Fadrique. On the façade Romanesque windows sit below Gothic ones. More than 80 steps lead to the upper floor, from which there are impressive views across the city towards La Giralda and Puente de la Barqueta.

The convent of Santa Clara was founded in 1260, though the present buildings date from the 15th century. The Mannerist entrance portico is by Juan de Oviedo. Inside, the nave has a Mudéjar coffered ceiling and an outstanding main *retablo* sculpted by Juan Martínez Montañés in 1623.

Gargoyle on the Torre de Don Fadrique

Alameda de Hércules ❸

Map 2 D4.

This tree-lined boulevard was originally laid out in 1574. The former marshy area was thus turned into a fashionable promenade for use by *sevillanos* of the Golden Age *(see pp50–51)*.

Since the relocation of the Sunday morning flea market to Charco de la Pava *(see p104)*, efforts have been made to improve the Alameda, long seen as one of Seville's seedier areas.

At the southern end of the boulevard stand two marble columns. They were brought here from a Roman temple dedicated to Hercules in what is now Calle Mármoles (Marbles Street), where three other columns remain. Time-worn statues of Hercules and Julius Caesar cap the Alameda's columns.

The area boasts an eclectic mix of bars, restaurants, cafes and Moroccan-style tea houses.

Basílica de la Macarena ❹

Calle Bécquer 1. **Map** 2 D3. 🚌 *C1, C2, C3, C4.* **Tel** *95 437 01 95.* 🕐 *9am–2pm, 5–9pm daily.* **Treasury** 🕐 *9:30am–1pm, 5–8pm daily.* ◐ *Easter hols.* 📷

The Basílica de la Macarena was built in 1949 in the Neo-Baroque style by Gómez Millán as a new home for the much-loved Virgen de la Esperanza Macarena. It butts on to the 13th-century Iglesia de San Gil, where the Virgin was housed until a fire in 1936.

The image of the Virgin stands above the main altar amid waterfalls of gold and silver. It has been attributed to Luisa Roldán (1656–1703). The wall-paintings by Rafael Rodríguez Hernández have themes focusing on the Virgin.

In the museum housed in the Treasury there are magnificent processional garments as well as gowns made from *trajes de luces* (suits of lights), donated by famous and no doubt grateful bullfighters. The floats used in Semana Santa *(see p38)*, among them La Macarena's elaborate silver platform, can also be admired.

Float of the Virgen de la Macarena in Semana Santa processions

Camera Obscura ❺

C/ Resolana s/n. 🕐 *10am–2:30pm, 5–8:30pm.* **Tel** *902 10 10 81.*

The Camera Obscura at the Tower of Perdigones, located in Seville's old quarter, has fantastic views of the 1992 World Expo fairground, Cartuja Island and the Guadalquivir River. It projects real time images, with movement, by using mirrors and magnifying glasses over a periscope.

VIRGEN DE LA MACARENA

Devotions to the Virgen de la Macarena reach their peak during Semana Santa *(see p38)*, when her statue is borne through the streets on a canopied float decorated with swathes of white flowers, candles and ornate silverwork. Accompanied by hooded penitents and cries of *¡guapa!* (beautiful!) from her followers, the virgin travels along a route from the Basílica de la Macarena to the cathedral *(see pp78–9)* in the early hours of Good Friday.

Renaissance façade and Baroque portal of Parlamento de Andalucía

Parlamento de Andalucía ❻

C/ Parlamento de Andalucia s/n. **Map** 2 E3. 🕐 *By written application or call the protocol office.* **Tel** *954 59 22 88.* ♿ 📷 **www.**parlamentodeandalucia.es

The Parliament of Andalusia has its seat in an impressive Renaissance building, the Hospital de las Cinco Llagas (five wounds). The hospital, founded in 1500 by Catalina de Ribera, was originally sited near Casa de Pilatos. In 1540 work began on what was to become Europe's largest hospital. Designed by a succession of architects, its south front has a Baroque central portal by Asensio de Maeda.

The hospital was completed in 1613, and admitted patients until the 1960s. In 1992 it was restored for the Parliament.

At the heart of the complex, the Mannerist church, built by Hernán Ruiz the Younger in 1560, has today been turned into a debating chamber.

Virgen de la Macarena – the main reredos in Basílica de la Macarena

Murallas ❼

Map 2 E3.

A section of the defensive walls that once enclosed Seville survives along calles Andueza and Muñoz León. It runs from the rebuilt Puerta de la Macarena at the Basílica de la Macarena (*see p89*) to the Puerta de Córdoba some 400 m (1,300 ft) further east.

Dating from the 12th century, it was constructed as a curtain wall with a patrol path in the middle. The original walls had over 100 towers; the Torre Blanca is one of seven that can be seen here. At the eastern end stands the 17th-century Iglesia de San Hermenegildo, named after the Visigothic king who was allegedly martyred on the site. On the southern corner of this church remains of Moorish arches can be seen.

Iglesia de San Marcos ❽

Plaza de San Marcos. **Map** 2 E5 (6E1). **Tel** 95 450 26 16.
◯ 7:30–8:30pm Mon–Sat.

This 14th-century church retains several Mudéjar features, notably its Giralda-like tower (based on the minaret of an earlier mosque) and the decoration on the Gothic portal on Plaza de San Marcos. The restoration of the interior, gutted by fire in 1936, has highlighted unique horseshoe arches in the nave. A statue of St Mark with book and quill pen, attributed to Juan de Mesa, is in the far left corner. In the plaza at the back of the

The Gothic-Mudéjar portal of the 14th-century Iglesia de San Marcos

church is the Convento de Santa Isabel, founded in 1490. It became a women's prison in the 19th century. The church dates from 1609. Its Baroque portal, facing onto Plaza de Santa Isabel, has a bas-relief of *The Visitation* sculpted by Andrés de Ocampo.

Convento de Santa Paula ❾

C/ Santa Paula 11. **Map** 2 E5 (6 F1). **Tel** 95 453 63 30. ◯ 10am–1pm Tue–Sun. 🎫 📷

Seville has many enclosed religious complexes, but few are accessible. This is one of them, a convent set up in 1475 and still home to 40 nuns. The public is welcome to enter through two different doors in the Calle Santa Paula. Bang on the brown one, marked No. 11, to have a look at the convent museum. Steps lead to two galleries crammed with

religious paintings and artifacts. The windows of the second look onto the nuns' cloister, which echoes with laughter in the afternoon recreation hour. The nuns make a phenomenal range of marmalades and jams, which visitors may purchase in a room near the exit.

Ring the bell by a brick doorway nearby to visit the convent church, reached by crossing a meditative garden. Its portal vividly combines Gothic arches, Mudéjar brick-work, Renaissance medallions, and ceramics by the Italian artist, Nicola Pisano. Inside, the nave has an elaborate wooden roof carved in 1623. Among its statues are St John the Evangelist and St John the Baptist, carved by Juan Martínez Montañés.

St John the Baptist by Montañés in the Convento de Santa Paula

---

SEVILLIAN BELL TOWERS

Bell towers rise above the rooftops of Seville like bookmarks flagging the passing centuries. The influence of La Giralda (*see p78*) is seen in the Moorish arches and tracery adorning the 14th-century tower of San Marcos, and the Mudéjar brickwork which forms the base for San Pedro's belfry. The churches of Santa Paula and La Magdalena reflect the ornate confidence of the Baroque period, while the towers of San Ildefonso illustrate the Neo-Classical tastes of the 19th century.

San Marcos

San Pedro

Santa Paula

Intricate pattern on a chapel door in the Iglesia de San Pedro

Iglesia de San Pedro ⑩

Plaza San Pedro. **Map** 2 D5 (6 E2). **Tel** 95 422 91 24. ☐ 8:30–11:30am, 7–8:30pm Mon–Sat; 9:30am–1:30pm, 7–8:30pm Sun. ♿

The church where the painter Diego Velázquez was baptized in 1599 presents a typically Sevillian mix of architectural styles. Mudéjar elements survive in the lobed brickwork of its tower, which is surmounted by a Baroque belfry. The principal portal, facing Plaza de San Pedro, is another Baroque adornments added by Diego de Quesada in 1613. A statue of St Peter looks disdainfully down at the heathen traffic below.

The poorly lit interior has a Mudéjar wooden ceiling and west door. The vault of one of its chapels is decorated with exquisite geometric patterns formed of interlacing bricks. Behind the church, in Calle Doña María Coronel, cakes and biscuits are sold from a revolving drum in the wall of the Convento de Santa Inés. An arcaded patio fronts its restored church, with frescoes by Francisco de Herrera and a nun's choir separated from the public by a screen. The preserved body of Doña María Coronel, the convent's 14th-century founder, is honoured in the choir every 2 December.

Iglesia de Santa Catalina ⑪

Plaza Ponce de Léon. **Map** 2 D5 (6 E2). **Tel** 95 421 74 41. ◐ for restoration until 2011.

Built on the former site of a mosque, this 14th-century church has a Mudéjar tower modelled on La Giralda (see p78) (best viewed from Plaza Ponce de Léon) which has been spared the customary Baroque hat. On the west side, by Calle Alhóndiga, the Gothic portal is originally from the Iglesia de Santa Lucía, which was knocked down in 1930. Within its entrance is a horseshoe arch. At the far left end of the nave, the Capilla Sacramental is by Leonardo de Figueroa. On the right, the Capilla de la Exaltación has a decorative ceiling, circa 1400, and a figure of Christ by Pedro Roldán.

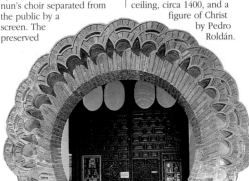

Detail of horseshoe arch in the Iglesia de Santa Catalina

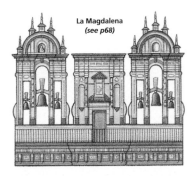

La Magdalena (see p68)

San Ildefonso (see p77)

PARQUE MARIA LUISA

The area south of the city centre is dominated by the extensive, leafy Parque María Luisa, Seville's principal green area. A great part of it originally formed the grounds of the Baroque Palacio de San Telmo, dating from 1682. Today the park is devoted to recreation; with its fountains, flower gardens and mature trees it provides a welcome place to relax during the long, hot summer months. Just north of the park lies Prado de San Sebastián, the former site of the *quemadero*, the platform where many victims of the Inquisition *(see p51)* were burnt do death. The last execution took place here in 1781.

Many of the historic buildings situated within the park were erected for the Ibero-American Exposition of 1929. This international jamboree sought to reinstate Spain and Andalusia on the world map. Exhibitions from Spain, Portugal and Latin America were displayed in attractive, purpose-built pavilions that are today used as museums, embassies, military headquarters and also cultural and educational institutions. The grand five-star Hotel Alfonso XIII and the crescent-shaped Plaza de España are the most striking legacies from this surge of Andalusian pride. Nearby is the Royal Tobacco Factory, forever associated with the fictional gypsy heroine, Carmen, who toiled in its sultry halls. Today it is part of the Universidad, Seville's university.

Ceramic urn in the Parque María Luisa

SIGHTS AT A GLANCE

Museums
Museo Arqueológico ❼
Museo de Artes y Costumbres Populares ❻

Theatres
Teatro Lope de Vega ❹

Gardens
Parque María Luisa pp98–9 ❺

Historic Buildings
Hotel Alfonso XIII ❶
Palacio de San Telmo ❷
Universidad ❸

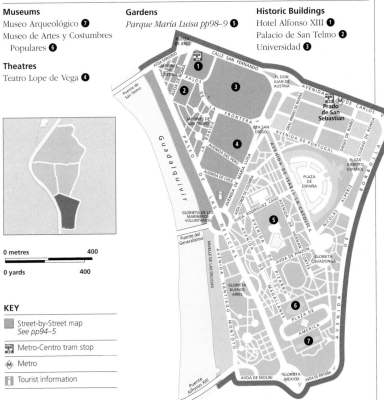

0 metres 400
0 yards 400

KEY

▮ Street-by-Street map
See pp94–5

▥ Metro-Centro tram stop

Ⓜ Metro

ℹ Tourist information

◁ **Horse-drawn carriage on Calle San Fernando**

Street-by-Street: Around the Universidad

Statue of El Cid by Anna Huntington

South of the Puerta de Jerez, a cluster of stately buildings stands between the river and Parque María Luisa. The oldest ones owe their existence to the Guadalquivir itself – the 17th-century Palacio de San Telmo was built as a training school for mariners, while the arrival of tobacco from the New World prompted the construction of the monumental Royal Tobacco Factory, today the Universidad de Sevilla. The 1929 Ibero-American Exposition added pavilions in various national and historic styles and also the opulent Hotel Alfonso XIII, creating an area of proud and pleasing architecture that will entertain visitors as they walk towards the Parque María Luisa.

To Triana

Paseo de las Delicias
This riverside walk flanks the Jardines de San Telmo. Its name means the "walk of delights".

Pabellón de Chile
is now the Escuela de Artes Aplicadas (School of Applied Arts).

Pabellón de Perú
Modelled on the Archbishop's Palace in Lima, this pavilion has a vividly carved façade. It is typical of the nationalistic designs used for the Exposition buildings.

Pabellón de Uruguay

PASEO DE LAS DELICIAS

LA RABIDA

GUADALQUIVIR

AVENIDA DE MARIA LUISA

Costurero de la Reina
Today it serves as the municipal tourist office, but the "Queen's sewing box" used to be a garden lodge.

Monument to El Cano, who completed the first world circumnavigation in 1522 after Magellan was killed on route.

| 0 metres | 75 |
| 0 yards | 75 |

KEY

– – – Suggested route

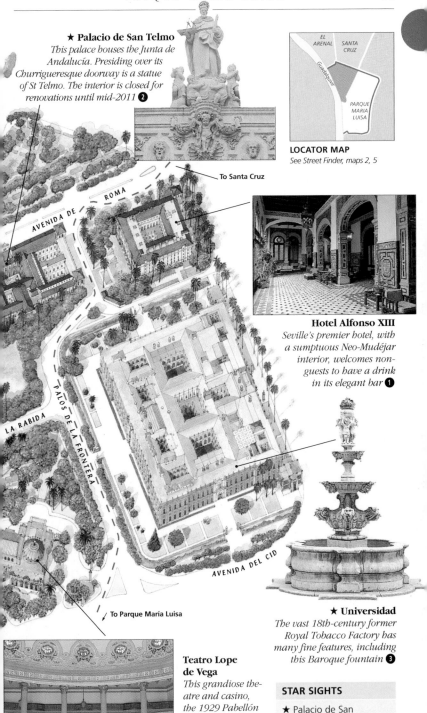

★ Palacio de San Telmo
This palace houses the Junta de Andalucía. Presiding over its Churrigueresque doorway is a statue of St Telmo. The interior is closed for renovations until mid-2011 **②**

To Santa Cruz

LOCATOR MAP
See Street Finder, maps 2, 5

Hotel Alfonso XIII
Seville's premier hotel, with a sumptuous Neo-Mudéjar interior, welcomes non-guests to have a drink in its elegant bar **①**

To Parque María Luisa

★ Universidad
The vast 18th-century former Royal Tobacco Factory has many fine features, including this Baroque fountain **③**

Teatro Lope de Vega
This grandiose theatre and casino, the 1929 Pabellón de Sevilla, is now a major venue for staging the arts and exhibitions **④**

STAR SIGHTS

★ Palacio de San Telmo

★ Universidad

Hotel Alfonso XIII ❶

Calle San Fernando 2. **Map** 3 C3
(6 D5). 🚇 *Puerta Jerez.* 🚌 *Prado de San Sebastian.* **Tel** *95 491 70 00.* ♿ *except toilets.* **www**.alfonsoxiii.com

At the southeast corner of Puerta de Jerez is Seville's best-known luxury hotel, named after King Alfonso XIII *(see p54)*, who reigned from 1902 until 1931, when Spain became a republic. It was built between 1916–28 for visitors to the 1929 Ibero-American Exposition *(see p55)*. The building is in Regionalista style, decorated with *azulejos (see p76)*, wrought iron and ornate brickwork. Its centrepiece is a grand patio with a fountain and orange trees. Non-residents are welcome to visit one of the hotel's bars or restaurants.

Central patio with fountain in the elegant Hotel Alfonso XIII

Churrigueresque adornments of the portal of Palacio de San Telmo

Palacio de San Telmo ❷

Avenida de Roma s/n. **Map** 3 C3.
🚇 *Puerta Jerez.* 🚌 *Plaza de Cuba.* **Tel** *95 503 55 05.* 🚫 *for renovations until mid-2011.* 🚫 ♿ 📷
www.juntadeandalucia.es

This imposing palace was built in 1682 to serve as a marine university, training navigators and high-ranking officers. It is named after St Telmo, patron saint of navigators. In 1849 the palace became the residence of the Dukes of Montpensier – until 1893 its vast grounds included what is now the

Parque María Luisa *(pp98–9)*. The palace became a seminary in 1901, and today it is the presidential headquarters of the regional government.

The palace's star feature is the exuberant Churrigueresque portal overlooking Avenida de Roma by Antonio Matías de Figueroa, completed in 1734. Surrounding the Ionic columns are allegorical figures of the Arts and Sciences. St Telmo can be seen holding a ship and charts, flanked by the sword-bearing St Ferdinand and St Hermenegildo with a cross. The north façade, which is on Avenida de Palos de la Frontera, is crowned by a row of Sevillian celebrities. These sculptures were added in 1895 by Susillo. Among them are representations of several notable artists such as Murillo, Velázquez and Montañés.

Façade detail of the Universidad

Universidad ❸

Calle San Fernando 4. **Map** 3 C3.
🚇 *Puerta Jerez.* 🚌 *Prado de San Sebastian.* **Tel** *95 455 10 00.* 🕐 *8am–8:30pm Mon–Fri.* ⬤ *public hols.* **www**.us.es

The former Real Fábrica de Tabacos (Royal Tobacco Factory) is now part of Seville University. It was a popular attraction for 19th-century travellers in search of Romantic Spain. Three-quarters of Europe's cigars were then manufactured here, rolled on the thighs of over 3,000 *cigarreras* (female cigar-makers), who were said "to be more impertinent than chaste", as the writer Richard Ford observed in his 1845 *Handbook for Spain*. The factory complex is the largest building in Spain after El Escorial in

CARMEN

The hot blooded *cigarreras* working in Seville's Royal Tobacco Factory inspired the French author, Prosper Mérimée, to create his famous gypsy heroine, *Carmen*. The short story he wrote in 1845 tells the tragic tale of a sensual and wild woman who turns her affections from a soldier to a bullfighter and is then murdered by her spurned lover. Bizet based his famous opera of 1875 on this impassioned drama, which established Carmen as an incarnation of Spanish romance.

Carmen and Don José

Madrid and was built between 1728–71. The moat and watch-towers show the importance given to protecting the king's lucrative tobacco monopoly. To the right of the main entrance is the former prison where workers caught smuggling tobacco were kept. To the left is the chapel, now used by university students.

The discovery of tobacco in the New World is celebrated in the principal portal, which has busts of Columbus (see p127) and Cortés. This part of the factory was once used as residential quarters – to either side of the vestibule lie small patios with plants and ironwork. Ahead, the Clock Patio and Fountain Patio lead to the former working areas. The tobacco leaves were first dried on the roof, then shredded by donkey-powered mills below. Production now takes place in a modern factory situated on the other side of the river, by the Puente del Generalísimo.

Baroque fountain in one of the patios in the Universidad

Teatro Lope de Vega ❹

Avenida María Luisa s/n. **Map** 3 C3.
🚉 & Ⓜ Prado de San Sebastian.
Tel 95 459 08 67 (ticket office).
◯ for performances. ♿
www.teatrolopedevega.org.

Lope de Vega (1562–1635), often called "the Spanish Shakespeare", wrote more than 1,500 plays. This Neo-Baroque theatre which honours him was opened in 1929 as a casino and theatre for the Ibero-American Exposition (see

Dome of the Neo-Baroque Teatro Lope de Vega, opened in 1929

p55). Its colonnaded and domed buildings are still used to stage performances and exhibitions (see pp244–5). Visitors to the Café del Casino can relax and enjoy a coffee amid its faded opulence.

Parque María Luisa ❺

See pp98–9.

Museo de Artes y Costumbres Populares ❻

Pabellón Mudéjar, Parque María Luisa. **Map** 4 D5. **Tel** 95 4712 391.
◯ 9am–8:30pm Tue–Sat, 9am–2:30pm Sun & public hols. 🚫 ♿

Housed in the Mudéjar Pavilion of the 1929 Ibero-American Exposition (see p55), this museum is devoted to the popular arts and traditions of Andalusia. Exhibits in the basement include a series of

workshop scenes detailing crafts such as leatherwork, ceramics and cooperage. There is also an informative account of the history of the azulejo. Upstairs is a display of 19th-century costumes, furniture, musical instruments and rural machinery. Romantic images of flamenco, bullfighting, and the Semana Santa and Feria de Abril (see p38) are a compendium of the Sevillian cliché.

Museo Arqueológico ❼

Plaza de América, Parque María Luisa.
Map 4 D5. **Tel** 95 478 64 74. ◯
9am–8:30pm Tue–Sat, 9am–2:30pm
Sun & public hols. 🚫 ♿

The Renaissance pavilion of the 1929 Ibero-American Exposition is now Andalusia's museum of archaeology. The basement houses Paleolithic to early-Roman exhibits, such as copies of the remarkable Tartessian Carambolo treasures (see p43). This hoard of 6th-century BC gold jewellery was discovered near Seville in 1958.

Upstairs, the main galleries are devoted to the Roman era, with statues and fragments rescued from Itálica (see p132). Highlights include a 3rd-century BC mosaic from Écija (see p133) and sculptures of local-born emperors Trajan and Hadrian. The rooms continue to Moorish Spain via Palaeo-Christian sarcophagi, Visigothic relics and artifacts discovered at Medina Azahara (see p138).

Museo de Artes y Costumbres Populares, the former Mudéjar Pavilion

Parque María Luisa ⑤

This vast park takes its name from Princess María Luisa de Orleans, who donated part of the grounds from the Palacio de San Telmo *(see p96)* to the city in 1893. The area was landscaped by Jean-Claude

Statue of María Luisa (1929) Forestier, director of the Bois de Boulogne in Paris, who created a leafy setting for the pastiche pavilions of the 1929 Ibero-American Exposition *(see p55)*. The most dazzling souvenirs from this extravaganza are the Plaza de España and Plaza de América, both the work of Anibal González, which set the park's theatrical mood. Sprinkling fountains, flowers and cool, tree-shaded avenues all go to make this park a refreshing retreat from the heat and dust of the city.

★ **Plaza de España**
Tiled benches line this semicircular plaza, centrepiece of the 1929 Exposition.

Glorieta de la Infanta has a bronze statue honouring the park's benefactress, the Princess María Luisa de Orleans.

Starting point for horse and carriage rides

Glorieta de Bécquer
Allegorical figures, depicting the phases of love, add charm to this tribute to Gustavo Adolfo Bécquer (1836–70), the Romantic Sevillian poet. It was sculpted by Lorenzo Coullaut Valera in 1911.

Isleta de los Patos
In the centre of the park is a lake graced by ducks and swans. A gazebo situated on an island provides a peaceful resting place.

Fuente de los Leones
Ceramic lions guard this octagonal fountain, which is surrounded by myrtle hedges. Its design was inspired by the fountain in the Patio de los Leones at the Alhambra (see p195).

★ Museo de Artes y Costumbres Populares
The pavilions of Plaza de América evoke the triumph of the Mudéjar, Gothic and Renaissance styles. The Pabellón Mudéjar houses a museum of Andalusian folk arts ❻

Pabellón Real

The Monte Gurugú is a mini-mountain with a tumbling waterfall.

★ Museo Arqueológico
The Neo-Renaissance Pabellón de las Bellas Artes today houses a regional archaeological museum. Many finds from nearby Roman Itálica (see p132) are among the exhibits ❼

Ceramics
Brightly painted Sevillian ceramics from Triana decorate the park in the form of floral urns, tiled benches and playful frogs and ducks placed around the fountains.

STAR FEATURES

★ Plaza de España

★ Museo Arqueológico

★ Museo de Artes y Costumbres Populares

ACROSS THE RIVER

On the west bank of the Guadalquivir, old Seville meets the new. Since Roman times, pottery has been made in Triana, an area named after the emperor Trajan. It has traditionally been a working-class district, famous for the bullfighters and flamenco artists that came from its predominantly gypsy community. With cobbled streets and shops selling ceramics, it still has an authentic, lived-in feel. Iglesia de Santa Ana is a fine Mudéjar-Gothic church. From the riverside restaurants and bars along Calle Betis there are views of Seville's towers and belfries.

Tile from Triana, a manufacturing centre for *azulejos* and ceramics

In the 15th century, a Carthusian monastery was built in what was then a quiet area north of Triana – hence the name that the district acquired: Isla de la Cartuja. Later Columbus resided here, planning his future exploits. Mainly due to this connection, La Cartuja was the site for Expo '92 *(see pp104–5)*. The monastery buildings were restored and several pavilions of strikingly modern design built. The majority of the pavilions now house offices; a branch of the University of Seville is also here. The Expo site has been redeveloped to include the Isla Mágica theme park *(see p104)*.

SIGHTS AT A GLANCE

Theme Parks
Cartuja '93 ❷
Charco de la Pava
 Flea Market ❸
Isla Mágica ❶

Traditional Areas
Triana pp102–3 ❺

Churches and Monasteries
Iglesia de Nuestra Señora
 de la O ❻
Iglesia de Santa Ana ❼
Monasterio de Santa María de
 las Cuevas ❹

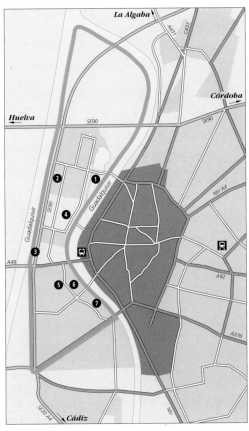

0 kilometres 1

0 miles 1

KEY

	Seville city centre
	Built-up area
	Greater Seville
🚉	Railway station
🚌	Coach terminus
▬	Motorway
▬	Major road
═	Minor road

◁ Pabellón de Andalucía, built for the Expo '92 on Isla de la Cartuja

Triana ●

Named after the Roman emperor Trajan, this quarter has, since early times, been famous for its potteries. Plenty of workshops still produce and sell tiles and ceramics. Once Seville's gypsy quarter, this *barrio* also has a reputation for producing great bullfighters, sailors and flamenco artists. It remains a traditional working-class district, with compact, flower-filled streets and a tangibly independent atmosphere. Visitors to Triana can buy tiles and wander through its narrow streets during the day, and enjoy the lively bars and romantic views across the Río Guadalquivir at night.

Statue, Plaza del Altozano

To Nuestra Señora de la O *(see p105)*

Callejón de l Inquisición

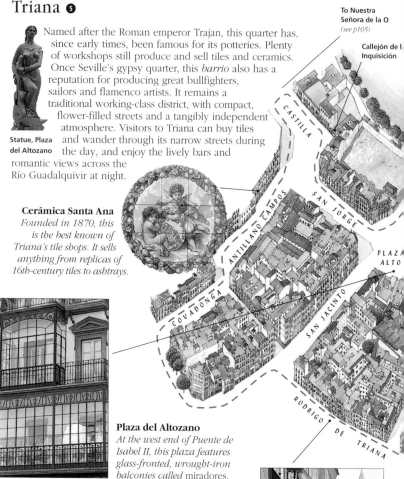

Cerámica Santa Ana
Founded in 1870, this is the best known of Triana's tile shops. It sells anything from replicas of 16th-century tiles to ashtrays.

Plaza del Altozano
At the west end of Puente de Isabel II, this plaza features glass-fronted, wrought-iron balconies called miradores.

Santa Justa and Santa Rufina as represented by Murillo (c.1665)

SANTA JUSTA AND SANTA RUFINA

Two Christians working in the Triana potteries in the 3rd century have become Seville's patron saints. The city's Roman rulers are said to have thrown the young women to the lions after they refused to join a procession venerating Venus. This martyrdom has inspired many works by Sevillian artists, including Murillo and Zurbarán *(see pp66–7)*. The saints are often shown with the Giralda, which, apparently, they protected from an earthquake in 1755.

Calle Rodrigo de Triana
This street in white and ochre is named after the Andalusian sailor who first caught sight of the New World on Columbus's epic voyage of 1492 (see p51).

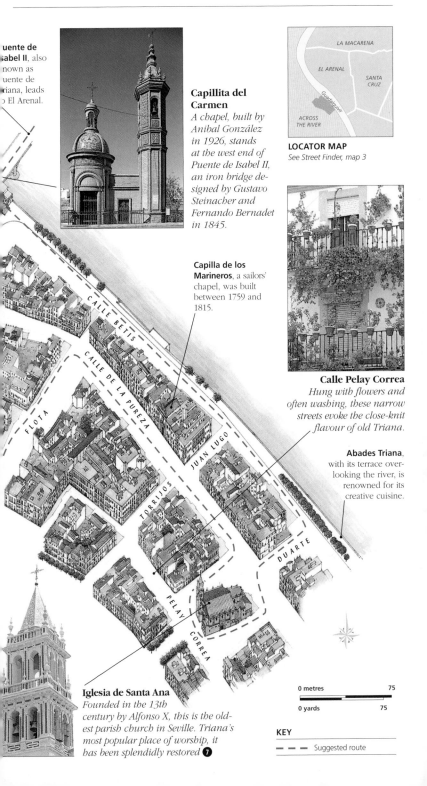

Puente de Isabel II, also known as Puente de Triana, leads to El Arenal.

Capillita del Carmen
A chapel, built by Aníbal González in 1926, stands at the west end of Puente de Isabel II, an iron bridge designed by Gustavo Steinacher and Fernando Bernadet in 1845.

LOCATOR MAP
See Street Finder, map 3

LA MACARENA
EL ARENAL
SANTA CRUZ
Guadalquivir
ACROSS THE RIVER

Capilla de los Marineros, a sailors' chapel, was built between 1759 and 1815.

Calle Pelay Correa
Hung with flowers and often washing, these narrow streets evoke the close-knit flavour of old Triana.

Abades Triana, with its terrace overlooking the river, is renowned for its creative cuisine.

CALLE BETIS
CALLE DE LA PUREZA
FLOTA
JUAN LUGO
TORRIJOS
DUARTE
PELAY CORREA

Iglesia de Santa Ana
Founded in the 13th century by Alfonso X, this is the oldest parish church in Seville. Triana's most popular place of worship, it has been splendidly restored **7**

| 0 metres | 75 |
| 0 yards | 75 |

KEY
– – – Suggested route

A thrill ride at the Isla Mágica theme park

Isla Mágica ❶

Pabellón de España, Isla de la Cartuja.
Map 1 B3. *Tel* 902 16 17 16. ☐
varies, see website for opening hours (which change throughout the year) as well as package deals (hotel and park entry). ☑ www.islamagica.es

Opened in 1997, the Isla Mágica theme park occupies part of the Isla de la Cartuja site redeveloped for Expo '92 *(see pp56–7),* including the Pabellón de España and the the dramatically leaning Pabellón de Andalucía.

The park recreates the exploits of the explorers who set out from Seville in the 16th century on voyages of discovery to the New World. The first of the eight zones which visitors experience is Seville, Port of the Indies, followed by among others Quetzal, the Fury of the Gods, the Gateway to the Americas, Amazonia, the Pirate's Lair and El Dorado. The Jaguar is the most thrill-

ing ride, a rollercoaster hurtling at 85 km/h (53 mph) along its looping course, but head also for The Anaconda, a flume ride, and The Orinoco Rapids on which small boats are buffeted in swirling water. The Fountain of Youth is designed for children, with carousels and fighting pirates.

Shows in the park include street performances and dance shows as well as IMAX cinema screenings. The shows provide the historical background and incorporate special effects and audience participation. New shows are added every season with some shows running throughout the season and others featuring for just a few weeks. Check the Isla Magica website for up-to-date information.

Cartuja '93 ❷

Paseo del Oeste (renamed Calle Leonardo da Vinci). **Map** 1 A3.

This science and technology park occupies the western side of the Expo '92 site. Visitors can walk along Calle Leonardo da Vinci and the service roads for close-up views of some of Expo '92's most spectacular pavilions. These buildings, however, now part of the Andalusian World Trade Centre, belong to public and private companies and are closed to visitors, although there are plans to develop the area. Groups of buildings south and east of the Parque Alamillo

The Pabellón de Andalucía, built on Isla de la Cartuja for Expo '92

are part of Seville University, which has links with Cartuja '93. To its south lie the gardens surrounding the ancient Monasterio de Santa María de las Cuevas *(see p105).*

Charco de la Pava Flea Market ❸

☐ *Sat & Sun am.*

Situated beyond the Olympic Stadium, along the River Guadalquivir, is the Charco de La Pava flea market. The market occupies a large open space on the far side of the Cartuja and is held on Sunday mornings. It is a popular spot among locals and tourists who come here for a leisurely browse through the bric-a-brac. Stretched out along the ground are all manner of goods for sale, from rusty farming tools to brass ornaments, paintings and old photographs. The market was, for many years, held at Alameda de Hércules *(see p88)* in the La Macarena area to the north of the city.

Despite its proximity to the city centre, Charco de la Pava, and the area immediately surrounding it, has little in the way of cafés and restaurants, so stock up with a hearty breakfast before heading out in search of a bargain.

Passenger boat at the Isla Mágica theme park

For hotels and restaurants in this region see pp212–14 and pp228–30

Main entrance of the Carthusian Monasterio de Santa María de las Cuevas, founded in 1400

Monasterio de Santa María de las Cuevas ❹

Calle Americo Vespucio 2, Isla de la Cartuja. **Map** 1 A4. **Tel** 95 503 70 70. **Monastery &Centro Andaluz de Arte Contemporaneo** ◻ Oct–Mar: 10am–8pm (last adm 7:30pm) Tue–Fri, 11am–8pm Sat, 10am–3pm Sun; Apr–Sep: 10am–9pm (last adm 8:30pm) Tue–Fri, 11am–9pm Sat, 10am–3pm Sun. ◻ (free Tue). ♿ ◻ www.caac.es

This huge complex, built by the Carthusian monks in the 15th century, is closely tied to Seville's history. Columbus stayed and worked here, and even lay buried in the crypt of the church, Capilla Santa Ana, from 1507 to 1542. The Carthusians lived here until 1836 and commissioned some of the finest works of the Seville School, including masterpieces by Zurbarán and Montañés, now housed in the Museo de Bellas Artes (see pp66–7).

In 1841 Charles Pickman, a British industrialist, built a ceramics factory on the site. After decades of successful business, production ceased in 1980 and the monastery was restored as a central exhibit for Expo '92. Also of interest are the Capilla de Afuera by the main gate, and the Casa Prioral, which has an exhibition of the restoration. There is a Mudéjar cloister of marble and brick. The chapter house has tombstones of rich patrons of the monastery.

The Centro Andaluz de Arte Contemporáneo features contemporary art exhibitions, as part of the Museo de Arte Contemporaneo. The centre's permanent collection is mostly by 20th century Andalusian artists while its temporary exhibitions include paintings, photographs, installations and performance art by international artists. Past exhibitions have featured everything from sculpture to internet art.

Triana ❺

See pp102–3.

The colourful belfry of Nuestra Señora de la O in Triana

Iglesia de Nuestra Señora de la O ❻

C/ Castilla. **Map** 3 A1. **Tel** 95 433 75 39. ◻ daily.

The Church of Our Lady of O, built in the late 17th century, has a brightly painted belfry decorated with azulejos made locally. Inside, Baroque sculptures include a Virgin and Child with silver haloes, attributed to Duque Cornejo, in the far chapel to the left as you enter. On the other side of the high altar is a fine group by Pedro Roldán depicting St Anne, St Joachim and Mary, the Virgin; a Jesus of Nazareth bearing his cross in the main chapel on the far wall is also by the same sculptor.

The church is in Calle de Castilla, whose name comes from the notorious castle in Triana where the Inquisition had its headquarters from the 16th century. The Callejón de la Inquisición, a nearby alley, leads down to the river.

Iglesia de Santa Ana ❼

C/ de la Pureza 84. **Map** 3 B2. **Tel** 95 427 08 85. ◻ 9am-3pm, 7–9pm daily.

One of the first churches built in Seville after the Reconquest (see pp48–9), Santa Ana was founded in 1276 but was much remodelled over the centuries. Today it is a focal point for the residents and cofradias (the religious brotherhoods) of Triana.

The vaulting of the nave is similar to Burgos cathedral's vaulting, suggesting that the same architect worked on the two churches. The west end of the nave has a 16th-century retablo, richly carved by Alejo Fernández. The sacramental chapel in the north wall has a Plateresque entrance.

In the baptistery is the Pila de los Gitanos, or Gypsy Font, which is believed to pass on the gift of flamenco song to the children of the faithful.

A 90-Minute Walk in Seville

This walk begins in one of the city's most elegant parks and explores one of its oldest *barrios* (neighbourhoods): the medieval Jewish quarter of Santa Cruz. The tiny alleys and squares of Santa Cruz conceal a museum to one of the city's great painters, Murillo, as well as a host of churches and many crafts galleries and restaurants. The walk then takes you through Seville's grandest square before heading for the Guadalquivir River, a historic bridge and the Triana area, famous for its ceramics district and home of Seville's flamenco culture.

Cross, Plaza Santa Cruz

A sun-drenched alley in the neighbourhood of Santa Cruz

Plaza Santa Cruz to the Rio Guadalquivir

This small square, with its birdcage and garden, sits close to both the Jardines de Murillo ①, where there is a monument to Columbus, and the walls of the Real Alcazar. Take Calle Santa Teresa past the museum and birthplace of painter Bartolomé Esteban Murillo (1618–82) ②; the pieces held here are minor compared to those kept in the

Patio of a house in the Santa Cruz quarter

KEY

- ••• Walk route
- Ⓜ Metro station
- 🚌 Bus stop
- 🚊 Metro-Centro tram stop

Museo des Bellas Artes *(see pp66–8)*. Opposite is the 16th-century Convento San José del Carmen, also known as Convento de las Teresas, an order of the Carmelites. Turning right near the top of Calle de Mateos Gagos, you pass the 17th-century Iglesia de Santa Cruz ③ with its triple carillon. Turn left into Calle Guzman El Bueno ("Guzman the Good"), named after the defender of Tarifa during the Moorish invasion. Guzman features some classic town mansions built around spacious interior patios. Cross into the Argote de Molina and walk behind the Palacio Arcobispal ④ down to the gates of the cathedral courtyard, the chief remaining Moorish section of this building; worshippers would wash here before entering the mosque.

Take a sharp right into Calle Hernan Colon, where odd little shops selling collectables jostle with souvenir stores. Colon leads into Plaza de San Francisco and the Ayuntamiento ⑤ (town hall), begun in 1527 by architect Diego de Riaño. It is one of the best examples of Renaissance architecture in Spain. Cross the square to Calle de Sierpes, one of Seville's oldest shopping streets. Sierpes is the place to buy fans, mantilla shawls and hats, not least at Maquedano (No. 40) ⑥ which always has an impressive window display. Where Sierpes meets tiny Plaza La Campana, turn

The Giralda tower seen from Plaza de San Francisco

Azulejos of Santa Ana church in Triana

left on Calle Martin Villa to Plaza del Duque de la Victoria and its statue of Velazquez. Turn right into Calle San Eloy; at its end is the Iglesia de la Magdalena ⑦, a church built in 1709 on the remains of an earlier Arabic mosque. Its interior features works by Zurburan and Valdés, and its exquisite representation of the Virgen del Amparo (protection) is a star of the Easter Semana Santa processions. It is claimed she intervened on behalf of petitioners during the after-shocks of the 1755 earth-quake and in the 19th century the church served as a refuge for homeless children. Circle to the front of the church and right into Calle San Pablo, which becomes Reyes Catolicos, leading straight to Puente de Isabel II ⑧. Built in 1852 on the found-ations of a long-lost 12th-century Arab bridge, it's also known as Puente de Triana.

Puente de Isabel II to Puente de San Telmo
The bridge enters the *barrio* of Triana, forever associated with flamenco, bullfighting and

Sidewalk café in the Triana district, close to the Guadalquivir River

ceramics (*azulejos*). For workshops and shops, bear right into Calles San Jorge and then left into Antillano ⑨ and Alfareria. This runs into Calle Rodrigo de Triana. Turn left into Calles Victoria and right into Pelay Correa to reach Seville's oldest church, the 13th-century Iglesia Santa Ana ⑩. Its interior features major works by 16th-century sculptors such as Jurate and Ocampo. Behind the church, take a right on Triana's bar-lined riverfront, Calle del Betis ⑪, with views across to the Plaza de Toros, the Torre del Oro and, to the left, sculptor Eduardo Chillida's modernist peace monument, *La Tolerancia* (Tolerance). Betis runs to the 1931 Puente de San Telmo, which leads to the Jardines de Cristina ⑫, a major bus hub, and to Calle San Fernando ⑬, which passes the Universidad and continues to the Jardines de Murillo.

Puente de Isabel II, stretching over the Guadalquivir River ⑧

Street Finder Index

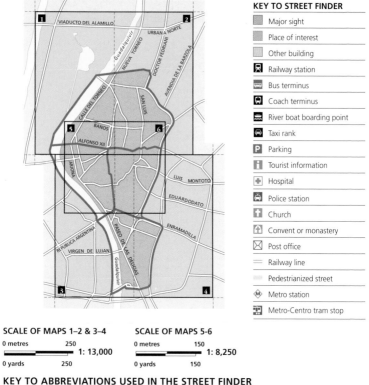

KEY TO STREET FINDER

- Major sight
- Place of interest
- Other building
- Railway station
- Bus terminus
- Coach terminus
- River boat boarding point
- Taxi rank
- Parking
- Tourist information
- Hospital
- Police station
- Church
- Convent or monastery
- Post office
- Railway line
- Pedestrianized street
- Metro station
- Metro-Centro tram stop

SCALE OF MAPS 1–2 & 3–4

0 metres 250
1: 13,000
0 yards 250

SCALE OF MAPS 5–6

0 metres 150
1: 8,250
0 yards 150

KEY TO ABBREVIATIONS USED IN THE STREET FINDER

Avda	Avenida	**d**	de, del, de la,	**Pl**	Plaza	**Sra**	Señora
C	Calle		de las, de los	**Po**	Paseo	**Sta**	Santa

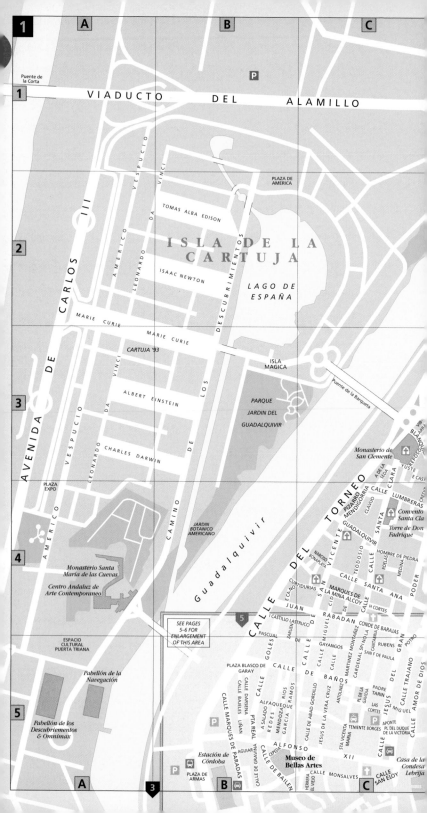

1

A **B** **C**

1

Puente de la Corta

V I A D U C T O D E L A L A M I L L O

P

PLAZA DE AMERICA

TOMAS ALBA EDISON

2

I S L A D E L A
C A R T U J A

LAGO DE
ESPAÑA

ISAAC NEWTON

MARIE CURIE

MARIE CURIE

CARTUJA '93

ISLA
MAGICA

3

ALBERT EINSTEIN

PARQUE
JARDIN DEL
GUADALQUIVIR

Puente de la Barqueta

CHARLES DARWIN

Monasterio de
San Clemente

PLAZA
EXPO

JARDIN
BOTANICO
AMERICANO

Convento
Santa Cla

Torre de Don
Fadrique

4

Monasterio Santa
María de las Cuevas

Centro Andaluz de
Arte Contemporaneo

CALLE SANTA ANA

MARQUES DE
LA MINA ALCOY

CONDE DE BARAJAS

CASTILLO LASTRUCCI

ESPACIO
CULTURAL
PUERTA TRIANA

SEE PAGES
5-6 FOR
ENLARGEMENT
OF THIS AREA

5

Pabellón de la
Navegación

GAYANGOS

RUBENS

PLAZA BLASCO DE
GARAY

PADRE
TARIN

5

Pabellón de los
Descubriementos
& Omnimax

P

TENIENTE BORGES

APONTE
PL. DEL DUQUE
DE LA VICTORIA

P

Estación de
Córdoba

Museo de
Bellas Artes

Casa de la
Condesa
Lebrija

ALFONSO

XII

P

PLAZA
DE ARMAS

CALLE SAN ELOY

A **B** **C**

3

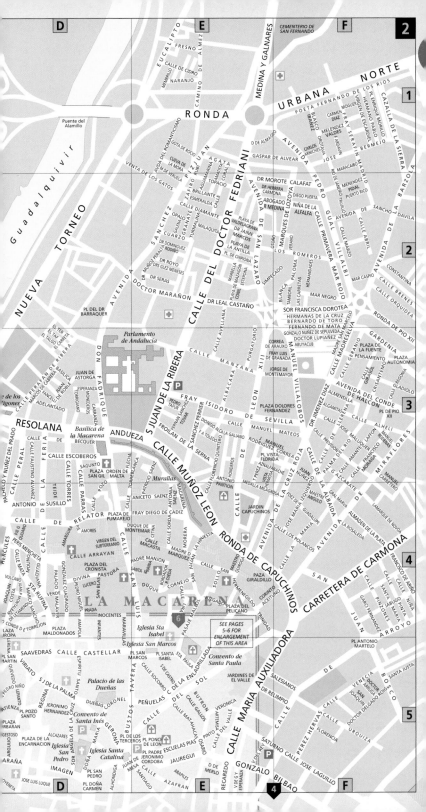

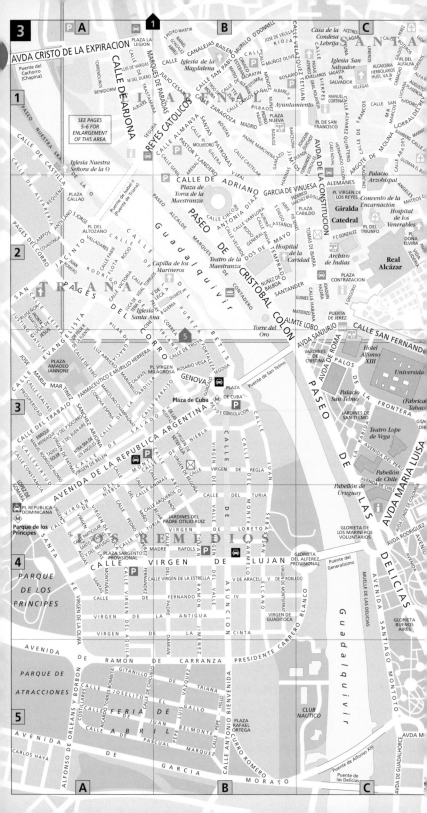

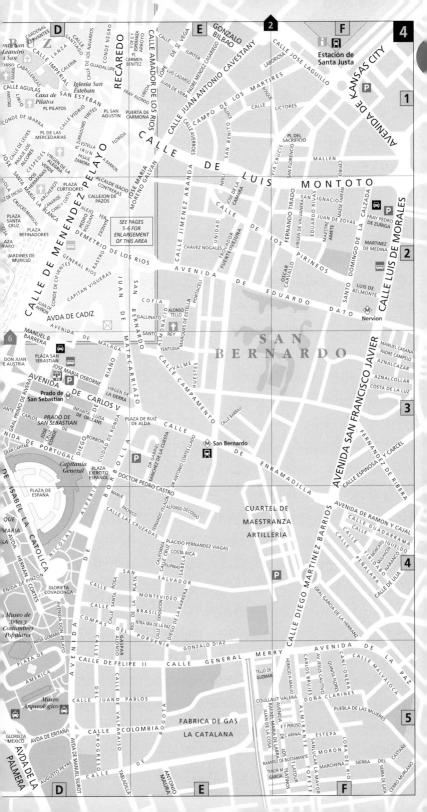

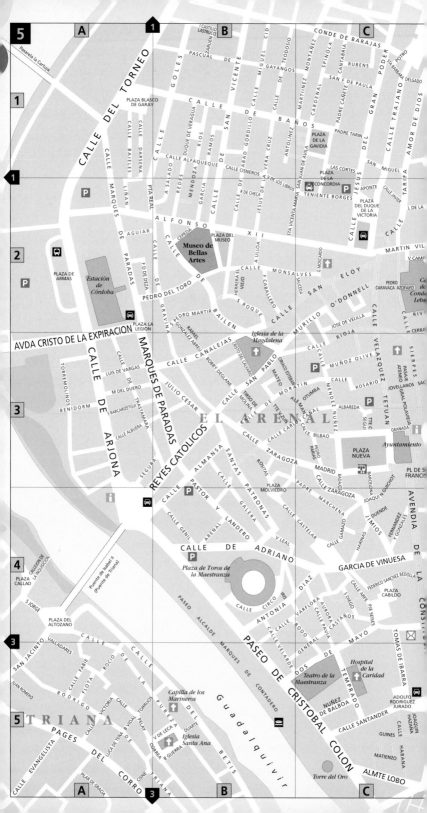

ANDALUSIA
AREA BY AREA

Andalusia at a Glance

Andalusia is a region of contrasts where snow-capped mountains rise above deserts and Mediterranean beaches, and Moorish palaces can be found standing next to Christian cathedrals. Its eight provinces, which in this guide are divided into four areas, offer busy towns such as Granada and Córdoba with their astonishing architectural treasures, in addition to sleepy villages, endless olive groves and nature reserves of great beauty.

Roof of the Mihrab in the Mezquita, Córdoba's top sight *(see pp144–5)*

The amphitheatre in the Roman city of Itálica *(see p44 and p132)*, just outside Seville

HUELVA AND SEVILLA
Pages 122–33

CADIZ AND MALAGA
Pages 158–83

Golden chalice from the rich treasury of Cádiz cathedral *(see p164)*

Arcos de la Frontera, one of the pretty *pueblos blancos* (white towns, *see pp174–5*) so typical of Andalusia

The Puente Nuevo, leading to Ronda's old town *(see pp176–7)*

◁ **Dawn at Montefrío in Granada province**

Baroque west front of the elegant
cathedral in Jaén *(see p148)*

The imposing Moorish castle of Baños de la Encina
(see p151) in the province of Jaén

CORDOBA
AND JAEN
Pages 134–5

GRANADA AND
ALMERIA
Pages 184–203

Magical Alhambra overlooking the Albaicín, Granada *(see pp190–96)*

0 kilometres   50

0 miles   25

Cabo de Gata, a nature reserve
with excellent beaches *(see p202)*

HUELVA AND SEVILLA

ndalusia's western extremities and the plains surrounding Seville are rarely explored by travellers in southern Spain. There are isolated beaches along Huelva province's Atlantic coast and good walking country in the northern sierras. The Parque Nacional de Doñana on the Guadalquivir delta is Europe's largest nature reserve; inland, orange groves straddle the river's valley.

As Roman legions under Scipio Africanus crossed southern Spain on their westward trek in the 3rd century BC, they founded a formidable metropolis, Itálica. Its ruins remain north of Seville.

Later, the Moors held the region as part of the Emirate of al Andalus. They peppered it with their whitewashed, fortified towns, of which Carmona, in Sevilla province, is a fine example.

After the Christian Reconquest *(see pp48–9)*, Moorish traditions persisted through Mudéjar architecture *(see pp24–5)*, blending with Baroque and Renaissance in cities such as Osuna, which flourished in the 16th century.

Huelva province is inextricably bound up with another chapter in the history of world conquest – in 1492 Columbus set out on his epic voyage from Palos de la Frontera, which at the time was an important port. He stayed nearby, at the Franciscan Monasterio de la Rábida, built earlier that century. Running along Huelva's northern border is a ridge of mountains, of which the forested Sierra de Aracena forms part. This ridge continues into Sevilla province as the Sierra Norte de Sevilla. Here, goats forage, birds of prey fly overhead and streams gush through chasms. The landscape erupts in a riot of wild flowers in spring, turning brown as the searing summer sets in.

The Parque Nacional de Doñana preserves the dunes and marshlands near the mouth of the Guadalquivir to the south. Here, teeming birdlife and wetland fauna thrive on the mudflats and shallow, saline waters.

Iglesia de Nuestra Señora del Rocío, El Rocío, where many pilgrims converge each Pentecost Sunday

◁ The famed *jamón ibérico* (cured ham) hanging in a bar in Jabugo, Sierra de Aracena

Exploring Huelva and Sevilla

Cosmopolitan Seville *(see pp58–117)* is the natural base from which to explore the far-flung corners of Huelva and Sevilla provinces, such as the little-visited and awesomely beautiful Sierra de Aracena and the rugged Sierra Norte. The Atlantic coast offers a virtually unbroken stretch of beaches and the Parque Nacional de Doñana features a fascinating marsh landscape abundant in wildlife. Between the coast and the mountains are rolling agricultural plains, interrupted by vineyards in fertile El Condado. Among the region's historic towns are Écija and Osuna, with fine Baroque features, while the history of Columbus can be traced in the towns around Huelva.

The mines of Riotinto, Sierra de Aracena

Cumbres Mayores · Arroyomolinos de León · Mérida

Sierra · Morena

Rosal de la Frontera · N433 · Aroche · N435 · Embalse de Aracena · Santa Olalla del Cala

Cortegana · Jabugo · Aracena

SIERRA DE ARACENA · Higuera de la Sierra

Santa Bárbara de Casa

Paymogo

Cabezas Rubias · N435 · El Ronq

Zalamea la Real · ❷ MINAS DE RÍOTINTO

Calañas · El Castillo de las Guardas

Tharsis · A478 · HUELVA

Alosno · Valverde del Camino · Aznalcóllar

Villanueva de los Castillejos · Embalse de Sancho

Sanlúcar de Guadiana

San Bartolomé de la Torre · A495 · Trigueros · N435 · EL CONDADO · ❶❶ · Sanlú la Ma

San Silvestre de Guzmán · Gibraleón · Niebla · Palma del Condado · A49

Villablanca · N431 · HUELVA · ❻ · San Juan del Puerto · Bollullos del Condado · Pilas

AYAMONTE ❸ · Cartaya · Lepe · MONASTERIO DE LA RÁBIDA ❼ ❽ PALOS DE LA FRONTERA · Almonte · A483 · Villafranc Guadal

❹ · PUNTA UMBRÍA ❺ · ❾ MOGUER

ISLA CRISTINA · ❿ MAZAGÓN · ❶❷ EL ROCÍO

Golfo de Cádiz · A494 · MATALASCAÑAS · ❶❹

❶❸ · NAC DE

KEY

══	Motorway
—	Major road
═	Minor road
—	Scenic route
—•—	Main railway
—	Minor railway
▬▬	International border
⚬⚬	Provincial border
△	Summit

Fishing boats at anchor in the harbour of Punta Umbría

For additional map symbols see back flap

GETTING AROUND

The busy A4 linking Córdoba with Seville slices
through the eastern half of the region, bypassing Écija
and Carmona, then streaks on down to Jerez de la
Frontera and Cádiz as the AP4. Another motorway, the
A92, brings traffic from Málaga and Granada. All join a
ring-road at Seville, with the A49 continuing to Huelva
and Portugal. All these cities are also connected by rail.
A complex and inexpensive bus network run by many
different companies links most towns. To explore the
more remote parts of the region, particularly mountain
roads, it is essential to have private transport.

A well-known *bodega* advertisement in
the rolling hills of the Sierra de Aracena

SIGHTS AT A GLANCE

0 kilometres   20

0 miles   10

A ham shop in Jabugo, Sierra de Aracena

Sierra de Aracena ❶

Huelva. **Road map** A2. �"El Repilado. 🚍 Aracena. 🛈 Plaza San Pedro s/n, Aracena (959 12 82 06). 🚍 Sat. **www**.sierradearacena.net

This wild mountain range in northern Huelva province is one of the most remote and least visited corners of Andalusia. Its slopes, covered with cork, oak, chestnut and wild olive, are cut by rushing streams and many extremely tortuous mountain roads.

The main town of the region, Aracena, squats at the foot of a ruined Moorish fortress on a hillside pitted with caverns. One of these, the **Gruta de las Maravillas**, can be entered to see its underground lake in a chamber hung with stalactites. Near the fortress, the **Iglesia del Castillo**, which was built in the 13th century by the Knights Templar, has a Mudéjar tower and foundations.

The village of **Jabugo** also nestles amid these mountains. It is famed across Spain for its tasty cured ham, *jamón ibérico*, or *pata negra (see p223)*.

🍴 Gruta de las Maravillas
Pozo de la Nieve. **Tel** 959 12 83 55. 🕐 10am–1:30pm, 3–6pm. 📷 🎫

Minas de Riotinto ❷

Huelva. **Road map** A2. 🚍 Riotinto. **Tel** 959 59 00 25. 🕐 10:30am–3pm, 4–7pm daily. 🔵 1 & 6 Jan, 25 Dec 📷 ♿ 🎫 **www**.parque mineroderiotinto.com

A fascinating detour off the N435 between Huelva city and the Sierra de Aracena leads to the opencast mines at Riotinto. These have been excavated since Phoenician times; the Greeks, Romans and Visigoths exploited their reserves of iron, copper, silver and mineral ores.

The lip of the crater overlooks walls of rock streaked with green and red fissures. Below, the trucks at work in the mines appear toy-sized. The **Museo Minero** in the village explains the history of the mines and of the Riotinto Company. At weekends and on public holidays there is a train tour in restored 1900 carriages.

🏛 Museo Minero
Plaza del Museo s/n. **Tel** 959 59 00 25. 🕐 daily. 📷 ♿ 🎫 🔲

Ayamonte ❸

Huelva. **Road map** A3. 🚶 18,000. 🚍 🛈 Avda Ramon y Cajal, s/n (959 47 09 88). 🚍 Sat morning.

Before the road bridge over the lower Guadiana river was completed in 1992, anyone crossing between southern Andalusia and the Algarve coast of Portugal had to pass through Ayamonte. The small, flat-bottomed car ferry across the jellyfish-infested mouth of the Guadiana river still operates and is an alternative for those making the journey between the two countries. Visitors can watch the ferry from the tower of Ayamonte's **Iglesia San Francisco**, which has a fine Mudéjar ceiling.

Isla Cristina ❹

Huelva. **Road map** A3. 🚶 18,000. 🚍 🛈 Calle San Francisco 12 (959 33 26 94). 🚍 Thu. **www**. islacristina.org

Once a distinct island, Isla Cristina is now surrounded by marshes. Situated near the mouth of the Guadiana river, it is an important fishing port, home to a fleet of tuna and sardine trawlers. With a fine sandy beach, it has, in recent years, also become a popular summer resort. There is an excellent choice of restaurants situated on the main seafront, which serve delicious, freshly landed fish and seafood.

Tuna and sardine trawlers moored for the night in the port of Isla Cristina

For hotels and restaurants in this region see pp214–15 and pp230–31

Frescoes depicting the life of Columbus at Monasterio de la Rábida

Punta Umbría ❺

Huelva. **Road map** A3. 🏘 14,000.
🚌 ℹ️ Ciudad de Huelva s/n (959
49 51 60). 🚢 Mon.

Punta Umbria is one of the main beach resorts in Huelva province. It sits at the end of a long promontory, with the Marismas del Odiel wetlands to one side and an outstanding sandy beach bordering the Gulf of Cádiz to the other. The Riotinto Company first developed the resort in the late 19th century for its British employees. These days, however, it is mainly Spanish holiday-makers who stay in the beachside villas.

A long bridge crosses the marshes, giving road access from Huelva. It is more fun to follow a trail blazed by Riotinto expatriates seeking the sun and take the ferry across the bird-rich wetlands.

Huelva ❻

Huelva. **Road map** A3. 🏘 130,000.
🚉 🚌 ℹ️ Avenida Alemania 12
(959 25 74 03). 🚢 Fri.

Founded as Onuba by the Phoenicians, the town had its grandest days as a Roman port. It prospered again in the early days of trade with the Americas, but Seville soon took over. Its decline culminated in 1755, when Huelva was almost wiped out by the great Lisbon earthquake. Today, industrial suburbs sprawl around the

Odiel quayside, from which the Riotinto Company once exported its products all over the commercial world.

That Columbus set sail from Palos de la Frontera, across the estuary, is Huelva's main claim to international renown. This fact is celebrated in the excellent **Museo Provincial**, which also has several exhibitions charting the history of the mines at Riotinto. Some archaeological finds from the very early days of mining are cleverly presented. To the east of the centre the Barrio Reina Victoria is a bizarre example of English suburbia in the very heart of Andalusia. It is a district of bungalows in mock-Tudor style, built by the Riotinto Company for its staff in the early 20th century.

Bronze jug, Museo Provincial, Huelva

South of the town, at Punta del Sebo, the Monumento a

Colón, a rather bleak statue of Columbus created by Gertrude Vanderbuilt Whitney in 1929, dominates the Odiel estuary.

🏛 **Museo Provincial**
Alameda Sundheim 13. **Tel** 959 65
04 24. 🕐 9am–8pm Tue–Sat,
9am– 3pm Sun & public hols. ♿

Monasterio de la Rábida ❼

Huelva. **Road map** A3. 🚍 from
Huelva. **Tel** 959 35 04 11. 🕐 10am–
1pm, 4–6:15pm Tue–Sun. 📷 🎬
www.monasteriodelarabida.com

In 1491, a dejected Genoese explorer found refuge in the Franciscan friary at La Rábida, across the Odiel estuary from Huelva. King Fernando and Queen Isabel had refused to back his plan to sail west to the East Indies. The prior, Juan Pérez, who as the confessor of the queen had great influence, eventually succeeded in getting this decision reversed. The following year, this sailor, by name Columbus, became the first European to reach the Americas since the Vikings.

La Rábida friary, which was built on Moorish ruins in the 15th century, is now a shrine to Columbus. Frescoes painted by Daniel Vásquez Díaz in 1930 glorify Columbus's life. The Sala de las Banderas contains a small casket of soil from every Latin American country. Worth seeing are the Mudéjar cloisters, the lush gardens and the beamed chapterhouse.

COLUMBUS IN ANDALUSIA

Cristóbal Colón – Christopher Columbus to the English-speaking world – was born in Genoa in Italy, trained as a navigator in Portugal and conceived the idea of reaching the Indies by sailing westwards. In 1492 he sailed from Palos de la Frontera and later the same year landed on Watling Island in the Bahamas, believing that he had fulfilled his ambition.

Columbus made three further voyages from bases in Andalusia, reaching mainland South America and other islands in what is now termed the West Indies in deference to his mistake. He died at Valladolid in 1506.

Columbus takes his leave before setting sail

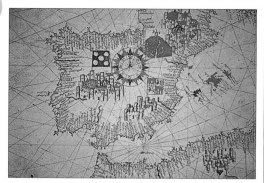

Historic map, Casa Museo de Martín Alonso Pinzón, Palos de la Frontera

Palos de la Frontera ❽

Huelva. **Road map** A3. 🏘 *12,000.*
🚋 ℹ️ *Parque Botánico José Celestino Mutis, Paraje de la Rábida (959 53 05 35).* 🚌 *Sat.*

Palos is an unprepossessing agricultural town on the eastern side of the Río Odiel's marshy delta. Yet it is a major attraction on the Columbus heritage trail.

On 3 August 1492, Columbus put out to sea from Palos in his caravel, the *Santa María*, with the *Pinta* and the *Niña*, whose captains were Martín and Vicente Pinzón, brothers from Palos. A statue of Martín Pinzón stands in the town's main square, and his former home has been turned into a small museum of exploration, named the **Casa Museo de Martín Alonso Pinzón**.

The Gothic-Mudéjar **Iglesia San Jorge**, dates from the 15th century. It has a fine portal, through which Columbus left after hearing Mass before his famous voyage. Afterwards, he boarded the *Santa María* at a pier which is now forlornly silted up.

These days, Palos's prosperity comes from the thousands of hectares of strawberry beds in the surrounding fields, which soak up the sun.

🏛 **Casa Museo de Martín Alonso Pinzón**
Calle Colón 24. **Tel** *959 35 01 99.*
◯ *Mon–Sat.*

Moguer ❾

Huelva. **Road map** A3. 🏘 *15,000.*
🚋 ℹ️ *Calle Castillo s/n (959 37 18 98).* 🚌 *Thu.* **www**.aytomoguer.es

A beautiful, whitewashed town, Moguer is a network of shaded courtyards and narrow streets lined with flower boxes. It is a delight to stroll around, exploring treasures such as the 16th-century hermitage of **Nuestra Señora de Montemayor** and the Neo-Classical **Ayuntamiento**. Moguer is also the birthplace of the poet and 1956 Nobel laureate, Juan Ramón Jiménez. The **Museo de Zenobia y Juan Ramón Jiménez**

charts the poet's life and work, and is located in his restored former home.

The walls of the 14th-century **Convento de Santa Clara** enclose some splendid, stone-carved Mudéjar cloisters. The nuns' dormitory, kitchen and refectory capture some of the atmosphere of their life inside the enclosure.

The **Monasterio de San Francisco** is worth seeing for its church, with a superb white tower and Baroque portals.

🏛 **Museo de Zenobia y Juan Ramón Jiménez**
Calle Juan Ramón Jiménez 10.
Tel *959 37 21 48.* ◯ *Tue–Sun.*
◯ *Sun pm & public hols.* 🏷 🎟

🔒 **Convento de Santa Clara**
Plaza de las Monjas. **Tel** *959 37 01 07.* ◯ *Tue–Sat.* ◯ *often closed on Sat for events; public hols.* 🏷

Mazagón's sandy beach on the Costa de la Luz

Mazagón ❿

Huelva. **Road map** A3. 🏘 *3,500.*
🚋 ℹ️ *Edificio Mancomunidad, Avda de los Conquistadores s/n (663 87 96 34).* 🚌 *Fri evening.*

One of the more remote beach resorts of the Costa de la Luz, Magazón shelters among pine woods 23 km (14 miles) southeast of Huelva. Virtually deserted in winter, it comes to life in summer when mainly Spanish holiday-makers arrive to fish, sail and enjoy the huge, and often windswept, beach. Visitors to the resort may still take pleasure in the solitude, however, while walking for miles along the endless Atlantic shoreline and among the sand dunes.

The 16th-century Nuestra Señora de Montemayor in Moguer

Moorish walls surrounding Niebla in El Condado

El Condado ⓫

Huelva. **Road map** B2. 🚌 🚗
Palma del Condado. 🛈 *Calle Campo
Castillo s/n, Niebla Huelva (959 36 22
70).* **www**.castillodeniebla.com

The rolling, fecund hills to
the east of Huelva produce
several of Andalusia's finest
wines. El Condado, defined
roughly by Niebla, Palma
del Condado, Bollullos del
Condado and Rociana del
Condado, is the heart of this
wine-growing district.

Niebla is of ancient origin. Its
bridge is Roman, but its solid
walls are Moorish, as is the
now ruined, 12th-century **Castillo de Niebla**, also known as
Castillo de los Guzmanes.

Around Niebla, vineyards
spread out over the landscape,
which is dotted with villages
close to the main *bodegas*.
These include Bollullos del
Condado, which has the
largest cooperative winery in
Andalusia and also the **Museo
del Vino**. Here you can learn
about wine-growing techniques
and also taste their wines
before making your purchase.

Bollullos and Palma del
Condado are good examples
of the popular young white
wines produced in the region.

Palma del Condado is best
visited in September when the
inhabitants celebrate the year's
vendimia (grape harvest).

🏰 **Castillo de Niebla**
C/ Campo Castillo s/n. **Tel** 959 36
22 70. ◯ 10am–2pm, 3–6pm
Mon–Sun.

🍷 **Museo del Vino**
Plaza Idelfonso Pinto s/n, Bollullos
Idel Condado. 🈲 *closed for
renovations.*

El Rocío ⓬

Huelva. **Road map** B3. 🚶 *2,500.*
🚌 🛈 *Centro Doñana, Avda de la
Canaliega s/n. 959 44 38 08.* 🛒 *Tue.*

Bordering the wetlands of the
Doñana region *(see pp130–31),*
the village of El Rocío is for
most of the year a tranquil,
rural backwater which attracts
few visitors.

At the Romería del Rocío
(see pp38–9) in May, however,
nearly a million people converge on the village. Many are
pilgrims who travel from all
over Spain by bus, car, horse,

or even on gaudily decorated
ox-carts or on foot. They come
to **Ermita de Nuestra Señora
del Rocío,** which has a statue
reputed to have been behind
miraculous apparitions since
1280. Pilgrims are joined by
revellers, who are enticed by
the promise of plentiful wine,
music and a great party.

Matalascañas ⓭

Huelva. **Road map** A3. 🚶 *1,200.*
🚌 🛈 *Avenida de las Adelfas s/n.
959 43 00 86.* 🛒 *Thu.*

Matalascañas is the largest
Andalusian beach resort
west of the Guadalquivir
river. Thousands holiday
here, lying in the sun, riding,
sailing or water-skiing by
day and dancing to the
latest disco beat at night. At
the Romería del Rocío, the
resort overflows with pilgrims
and revellers.

Matalascañas is totally self-
contained. To one side there
are dunes and forests stretching as far as Mazagón, to the
other the wild peace of the
Doñana *(see pp130–31).*

Iglesia de Nuestra Señora del Rocío in the village of El Rocío

Parque Nacional de Doñana ⑭

The National Park of Doñana is ranked among Europe's greatest wetlands. Together with its adjoining protected areas (Parque Natural de Doñana), the park covers over 50,000 hectares (185,000 acres) of marshes and sand dunes. The area used to be hunting grounds *(coto)* belonging to the Dukes of Medina Sidonia and was never suitable for human settlers. The wildlife flourished and, in 1969, the area became officially protected. In addition to a wealth of endemic species, thousands of migratory birds stay in winter when the marshes flood again, after months of drought.

Bird-spotting from boat on the Guadalquivir

Shrub Vegetation
Backing the sand dunes is a thick carpet of lavender, rock rose and other low shrubs.

Prickly Juniper
This species of juniper (Juniperus oxycedrus) *thrives in the wide dune belt, putting roots deep into the sand. The trees may get buried beneath the dunes.*

Palacio del Acebrón
El Rocío
La Rocina
H612
El Acebuche
Matalascañas
Palacio de Doñana
Laguna de Santa Olay

Coastal Dunes
Softly rounded, white dunes, up to 30 m (99 ft) high, fringe the park's coastal edge. The dunes, ribbed by prevailing winds off the Atlantic, shift constantly.

Monte de Doñana, the wooded area behind the sand dunes, provide shelter for lynx, deer and boar.

Official Tour
Numbers of visitors are controlled very strictly. On official day tours along rough tracks, the knowledgeable guides point out elusive animals while ensuring minimal environmental impact.

KEY

☐	Marshes
☐	Dunes
•••	Parque Nacional de Doñana
•••	Parque Natural de Doñana
▬	Road
☆	Viewpoint
ℹ	Visitors' centre
P	Parking
🚌	Coach station

Deer
Fallow deer (Dama dama) *and larger Red deer* (Cervus elaphus) *roam the park. Stags engage in fierce contests in late summer as they prepare for breeding.*

Wild cattle use the marshes as water holes.

José Antonio Valverde

Marisma de Iznalcázar

Marisma Gallega

Río Guadiamar

Río Guadalquivir

Sanlúcar de Barrameda

Fábrica de Hielo

0 kilometres   5

0 miles   5

VISITORS' CHECKLIST

Road map B3. **Marginal areas** ◯ daily. ◉ 1 Jan, 6 Jan, Pentecost, 25 Dec. ℹ️ **La Rocina**: **Tel** *959 43 95 69;* ℹ️ **Palacio del Ace-brón**: exhibition "Man and the Doñana". ◯ 10am–9pm. ℹ️ El **Acebuche**: reception, exhibition, café, shop. ◯ 8am–9pm. **Tel** *959 43 96 29.* **Self-guided footpaths:** La Rocina and Charco de la Boca; El Acebrón from Palacio del Acebrón; Laguna del Acebuche from Acebuche. **Inner park areas** ◯ summer: Mon–Sat; winter: Tue–Sun. Guided tour only. Jeeps leave El Acebuche 8:30am & 3pm. Booking compulsory. **Tel** *959 44 38 08.* 📷 ◯ phone first. **www**.reddeparques nacionales.mma.es

Imperial Eagle
The very rare Imperial eagle (Aquila adalberti) *preys on small mammals.*

Greater Flamingo
During the winter months, the salty lakes and marshes provide the beautiful, pink Greater flamingo (Phoenicopterus ruber) *with crustaceans, its main diet.*

THE LYNX'S LAST REFUGE
The lynx is one of Europe's rarest mammals. In Doñana about 40 individuals of Spanish lynx (Lynx pardinus) have found a refuge. They have yellow-brown fur with dark brown spots and pointed ears with black tufts. A research programme is under way to study this shy animal, which tends to stay hidden in scrub. It feeds mainly on rabbits and ducks, but sometimes also deer fawn.

The elusive lynx, only spotted with patience

Scenic view over the rooftops of Lebrija with their distinctive red tiles

Lebrija

Sevilla. **Road map** B3. 🏠 *24,000.*
🚌 🚉 🛈 *Casa de Cultura, Calle
Tetuán 15 (95 597 40 68).* 🛒 *Tue.*

The pretty, walled town of
Lebrija enjoys panoramic
views over the neighbouring
sherry-growing vineyards of
the Jerez region *(see p226).*

Narrow cobbled streets lead
to **Iglesia de Santa María de la
Oliva**. This is a 12th-century
Almohad mosque with many
original Islamic features, which
was consecrated as a church
by Alfonso X *(see p48).*

Itálica

Sevilla. **Road map** B2. 🚌 *from
Plaza de Armas, Seville.* **Tel** *95 562
22 66.* 🕙 *Apr–Sep: 8:30am–9pm
Tue–Sat, 9am–3pm Sun & public hols;
Oct–Mar: 9am–6:30pm Tue–Sat,
10am–4pm Sun.*

Scipio Africanus established
Itálica in 206 BC, as one of
the first cities founded by the
Romans in Hispania. Later, it
burgeoned, both as a military
headquarters and as a cultural
centre, supporting a population of several thousand.
Emperors
Trajan and
Hadrian
were both
born in Itálica.
The latter bestowed
imperial largesse on
the city during his reign
in the 2nd century AD,
adding marble temples
and other fine buildings.
Archaeologists have
speculated that the changing

**Roman mosaic
from Itálica**

course of the Guadalquivir
may have led to the demise
of Itálica. Certainly, the city
declined steadily after the fall
of the Roman Empire, unlike
Seville, which flourished.

At the heart of the site you
may explore the crumbling
remains of a vast amphitheatre,
which once seated 25,000.
Next to it is a display of finds
from the site, although many
of the treasures are displayed
in the Museo Arqueológico in
Seville *(see p97).* Visitors can
wander among the traces of
streets and villas. Little remains
of the city's temples or baths,
as most stone and marble was
plundered by builders over
the subsequent centuries.

The village of **Santiponce**
lies just outside the site. Here,
some better-preserved Roman
remains, including baths and a
theatre, have been unearthed.

Sierra Norte

Sevilla. **Road map** B2. 🚉 *Estación de
Cazalla y Constantina.* 🚌 *Constantina;
Cazalla.* 🛈 *Calle Paseo del Moro 2,
Cazalla de la Sierra (95 488 35 62).*

An austere mountain range
flanks the northern border of
Sevilla province. Known as
the Sierra Norte de Sevilla, it
is a part of the greater
Sierra Morena,
which forms a
natural frontier
between Anda-
lusia and the
plains of La Man-
cha and Extremadu-
ra. The region is
sparsely populated and, as it is
relatively cool in summer, it

can offer an escape from the
relentless heat of Seville. In
winter, you may meet the occasional huntsman carrying a
partridge or hare.

Cazalla de la Sierra, the
main town of the area, seems
surprisingly cosmopolitan and
is popular with young *sevillanos* at weekends. It has
made a unique contribution
to the world of drink, namely
Liquor de Guindas. This is a
concoction of cherry liqueur
and aniseed, whose taste is
acquired slowly, if at all.

Constantina, to the east, is
more peaceful and has superb
views across the countryside.
A romantic aura surrounds
the ruined castle, which is situated high above the town.

Grazing cow in the empty expanses
of the Sierra Norte de Sevilla

Carmona

Sevilla. **Road map** B2. 🏠 *25,000.*
🚌 🛈 *Alcázar de la Puerta de
Sevilla s/n (95 419 09 55).* 🛒 *Mon
& Thu.* **www**.turismo.carmona.org

Travelling east from Seville
on the NIV E5, Carmona is
the first major town you come
to. It rises above expansive
agricultural plains. Sprawling
suburbs spill out beyond the
Moorish city walls, which can
be entered through the old
Puerta de Sevilla. Inside,
there is a dense concentration
of mansions, Mudéjar churches,
squares and cobbled streets.

The grandeur of Plaza de San
Fernando is characterized by
the strict Renaissance façade
of the old **Ayuntamiento**. The
present town hall, located just
off the square, dates from the

Tomb of Servilia, Necrópolis Romana, Carmona

18th century; in its courtyard are some fine Roman mosaics. Close by lies **Iglesia de Santa María la Mayor**. Built in the 15th century over a mosque, whose patio still survives, this is the finest of the churches. Dominating the town, however, are the imposing ruins of the **Alcázar del Rey Pedro**, once a palace of Pedro I, also known as Pedro el Cruel (the Cruel) *(see p48)*. Parts of it now form a parador *(see p210)*.

Just outside Carmona is the **Necrópolis Romana**, the extensive remains of a Roman burial ground. A site museum displays some of the worldly goods buried with the bodies. These include statues, glass and jewellery, as well as urns.

🏛 **Ayuntamiento**
Calle Salvador 2. *Tel* 95 414 00 11.
🕐 8am–3pm Mon–Fri. 🌑 public hols.

🏛 **Necrópolis Romana**
Avenida Jorge Bonsor 9. *Tel* 95 414 08 11. 🕐 Tue–Sat. 🌑 public hols.

Écija ⓲

Sevilla. **Road map** C2. 🏠 40,000.
🚌 ℹ *Plaza de España 1, Ayuntamiento (95 590 29 33).*
🗓 Thu. **www**.turismoecija.com

Ecija is nicknamed "the frying pan of Andalusia" owing to its famously torrid climate. In the searing heat, the palm trees which stand on the Plaza de España provide some blissful shade. This is an ideal place to sit and observe daily life. It is also the focus of evening strolls and coffee-drinking.

Écija has 11 Baroque church steeples. Most are adorned with gleaming *azulejos (see p76)* and together they make an impressive sight. The most florid of these is the **Iglesia de Santa María** overlooking Plaza de España. **Iglesia de San Juan**, adorned with an exquisite bell tower, is a very close rival.

The **Palacio de Peñaflor** is also in Baroque style. Its pink marble doorway is topped by twisted columns, while a pretty wrought-iron balcony runs along the front façade.

🏛 **Palacio de Peñaflor**
C/Caballeros 32. *Tel* 95 483 02 73.
🕐 daily (courtyard only).

Osuna ⓴

Sevilla. **Road map** C3. 🏠 17,500. 🚌 🚍 ℹ C/Carrera 82, Antiguo Hospital (95 481 57 32). 🗓 Mon.

Osuna was once a key Roman garrison town before being eclipsed during the Moorish era. The Dukes of Osuna, who wielded immense power, restored the town to prominence in the 16th century. During the 1530s they founded the grand collegiate church, **Colegiata de Santa**

María. Inside is a Baroque *retablo*, and paintings by José de Ribera. The dukes were also the founders of the town's **Universidad**, a rather severe building with a beautiful patio.

Some fine mansions, among them the Baroque **Palacio del Marqués de la Gomera**, are also a testament to the former glory of this town.

Estepa ㉑

Sevilla. **Road map** C3. 🏠 12,000.
🚌 ℹ Carre Aguilar y cano s/n (95 591 20 66). 🗓 Mon, Wed & Fri. **www**.estepa.com

Legend has it that when the invading Roman army closed on Estepa in 207 BC, the townsfolk committed mass suicide rather than surrender.

These days, life in this small town in the far southeast of Sevilla province is far less dramatic. Its fame today derives from the production of its renowned biscuits – *mantecados* and *polvorones (see p213)*. Wander among the narrow streets of iron-grilled mansions, and sit on the main square to admire the beautiful black and white façade of the Baroque church, **Iglesia del Carmen**.

Iglesia del Carmen statuary

Wall painting on the ornate Baroque façade of Palacio de Peñaflor, Écija

CORDOBA AND JAEN

*C*órdoba, with its magnificent mosque and pretty Moorish patios, is northern Andalusia's star attraction. Córdoba province encompasses the Montilla and Moriles wine towns and also Baroque treasures such as Priego de Córdoba. Jaén's mountain passes are gateways to the province's beautiful Renaissance towns of Úbeda and Baeza, and to the great wildlife reserves of the mountain ranges.

Córdoba, on Andalusia's great river Guadalquivir, was a Roman provincial capital over 2,000 years ago, but its golden age came with the Moors. In the 10th century it was the western capital of the Islamic empire, rivalling Baghdad in wealth, power and sophistication. Today it is an atmospheric city, its ancient quarters and buildings reflecting a long and glorious history.

Córdoba's surrounding countryside is dotted with monuments to its Moorish past – like the Caliph's palace of Medina Azahara. To the south lies the Campiña, an undulating landscape covered in regiments of olives and vines, and green and gold expanses of sunflowers and corn. Here and there are whitewashed villages and hilltop castles with crumbling walls.

Running across the north of Córdoba and Jaén provinces is the Sierra Morena. Deer and boar shelter in the forest and scrub of this broad mountain range. The sierras dominate Jaén province. The great Río Guadalquivir springs to life as a sparkling trout stream in the Sierra de Cazorla, the craggy wilderness along its eastern border. Through the ages, mule trains, traders, highwaymen and armies have used the cleft in Sierra Morena, known as Desfiladero de Despeñaperros, to cross from La Mancha and Castilla to Andalusia.

Ancient castles perched on heights, once strategic outposts on the Muslim/ Christian frontier, now overlook the peaceful olive groves punctuated by historic towns preserving gems of post-Reconquest architecture.

The city of Jaén with its cathedral in the foreground, as viewed from Castillo de Santa Catalina

◁ Elaborate stonework and Islamic inscriptions on the mihrab of Córdoba's Mezquita

Exploring Córdoba and Jaén

This region of rolling fields and craggy heights is divided by the fertile Guadalquivir valley. On the northern banks of the river is Córdoba with its famous Mezquita. The wild, uninhabited Sierra Morena lies to the north, while southward is a prosperous farming area dotted with historic towns, such as Priego de Córdoba. Further east, amid the olive groves of Jaén, are the Renaissance jewels, Baeza and Úbeda. From these towns it is an easy excursion to the nature reserve of Cazorla, which offers dramatic scenery and a glimpse of deer and wild boar.

Main street of Cabra during siesta

Olive groves stretching across the countryside

SIGHTS AT A GLANCE

The town of Cazorla on the border of
the nature reserve

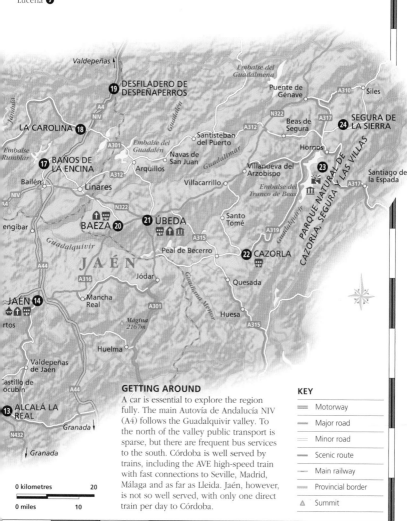

GETTING AROUND

A car is essential to explore the region
fully. The main Autovía de Andalucía NIV
(A4) follows the Guadalquivir valley. To
the north of the valley public transport is
sparse, but there are frequent bus services
to the south. Córdoba is well served by
trains, including the AVE high-speed train
with fast connections to Seville, Madrid,
Málaga and as far as Lleida. Jaén, however,
is not so well served, with only one direct
train per day to Córdoba.

KEY

▬▬	Motorway
▬	Major road
▭▭	Minor road
—	Scenic route
—	Main railway
▬	Provincial border
△	Summit

0 kilometres 20

0 miles 10

Palma del Río ❷

Córdoba. **Road map** C2.
19,500. 🏠 📷 **i** C/Santa Clara s/n
(957 64 43 70). 🚌 Tue.
www.palmadelrio.es

Remains of the walls built by
the Almohads in the 1100s are
a reminder of the frontier days
of this farming town. The
Romans established a settlement here, on the
main route from
Córdoba to Itálica
(see p132), almost
2,000 years ago.
The Baroque **Iglesia
de la Asunción**
dates from the
18th century. The
monastery of San
Francisco is now
a delightful hotel
(see p216), and
guests dine in
the 15th-century
refectory of the
Franciscan monks.
Palma is the home

**Bell tower,
La Asunción**

town of El Cordobés, one of
Spain's most famous matadors.
As a youth he would creep
out into the fields around the
town to practise with the
bulls. His biography, Or I'll
Dress You in Mourning, gives
a vivid view of Palma and of
the hardship that followed the
end of the Civil War.

Castillo de Almodóvar del Río ❸

Córdoba. **Road map** C2. **Tel** 957
63 40 55. ☐ May–mid-Sep: 11am–
2:30pm, 4–8pm (7pm mid-Sep–Apr).
🌐 **www**.castillodealmodovar.com

One of Andalusia's most
dramatic silhouettes breaks
the skyline as the traveller
approaches Almodóvar del Río.
The Moorish castle, with parts
dating back to the 8th century,
looks down on the white-
washed town and surrounding
fields of cotton and cereals.

**Detail of wood carving in the main
hall of Medina Azahara**

Medina Azahara ❹

Ctra Palma del Rio, km 5.5, Córdoba.
Road map C2. **Tel** 957 35 55 06. ☐
10am–6:30pm Tue–Sat (8:30pm
May–Sep), 10am–2pm Sun & public
hols. 🌐 (free for EU citizens).

To the northwest of Palma
del Río lie the remains of a
Moorish palace built in the
10th century for Caliph

Sierra Morena Tour ❶

The austere Sierra Morena runs across northern
Andalusia. This route through Córdoba province
takes in a region of oak- and pine-clad hills, where
hunters stalk deer and boar. It also includes the
open plain of Valle de los Pedroches, where storks
make their nests on church towers. The area, little
visited by tourists, is sparsely populated. Its individual character is more sober than the usual image
of Andalusia and it makes a delightful excursion
on a day out from Córdoba.

Hinojosa del Duque ④
"Catedral de la Sierra", the vast, 15th-
century pile of the Gothic-Renaissance
Iglesia San Juan Bautista, dominates th
town. It has a Churrigueresque
retablo.

RISING AT FUENTE OBEJUNA

On 23 April 1476, townsfolk
stormed the palace of the
hated lord, Don Fernando
Gómez de Guzmán. He
was hurled from a palace
window, then hacked to
pieces in the main plaza.
When questioned by a
judge who committed
the crime, the men
and women replied
as one, "Fuente Obe-
juna, señor!" Nobody was punished, at
least according to Lope de Vega's best-
known play, named after the village.

**Lope de Vega
(1562–1635)**

Peñarroya-Pueblonuevo ②
This was once an important
copper- and iron-
mining centre.

N432

Fuente Obejuna ③
The Plaza Lope de Vega
is often the venue for
Lope de Vega's famous
play. The parish church,
Nuestra Señora del
Castillo, was built in
the 15th century.

Bélmez ①
Remains of a 13th-century
castle crown a hill, from
which there are fine views.

Abd al Rahman III, who named it after his wife. More than 10,000 workers and 15,000 mules ferried building materials from as far as North Africa.

The palace is built on three levels and includes a mosque, the caliph's residence and fine gardens. Alabaster, ebony, jasper and marble decoration adorned its many halls and, it is said, shimmering pools of quicksilver added lustre.

Unfortunately, the glory was short-lived. The palace was sacked by Berber invaders in 1010. Then, over centuries, it was ransacked for its building materials. Now, the ruins give only glimpses of its former splendour – a Moorish main hall, for instance, with marble carvings and a fine wooden ceiling. The palace is being restored, but progress is slow.

Córdoba ❺

See pp140–46.

Montoro ❻

Córdoba. **Road map** D2. 🚶 9,600.
🚌 🛈 Plaza de España 8 (957 16 00 89). 🛒 Tue. **www**.montoro.es

Spread over five hills that span a bend in the River Guadalquivir, Montoro dates from the times of the Greeks and Phoenicians. Today the economy of this rather lethargic town depends on its olive groves. The solid bridge, which was designed by Enrique de Egas, was started in the time of the Catholic Monarchs

(see pp48–9) and took more than 50 years to finish. The townswomen sold their jewellery to raise funds for the bridge, hence its name: **Puente de las Donadas** (Bridge of the Donors).

Steep streets give the town charm. In Plaza de España are the **Ayuntamiento**, former seat of the ducal rulers, with a Plateresque façade, and the Gothic-Mudéjar **Iglesia de San Bartolomé**.

Leather bags and embossed saddlery are among several enduring crafts that are still produced in Montoro.

The 16th-century bridge spanning the Guadalquivir at Montoro

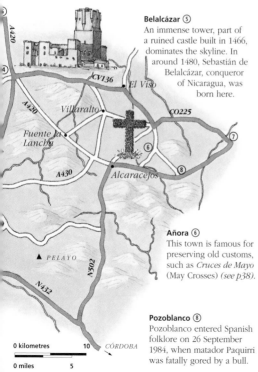

Belalcázar ⑤
An immense tower, part of a ruined castle built in 1466, dominates the skyline. In around 1480, Sebastián de Belalcázar, conqueror of Nicaragua, was born here.

Añora ⑥
This town is famous for preserving old customs, such as *Cruces de Mayo* (May Crosses) *(see p38)*.

Pozoblanco ⑧
Pozoblanco entered Spanish folklore on 26 September 1984, when matador Paquirri was fatally gored by a bull.

TIPS FOR DRIVERS

Length: 190 km (118 miles).
Stopping-off points: There are many shady places to stop along the way to have a picnic. Some of the villages along this route, such as Fuente Obejuna, have restaurants and bars.

Pedroche ⑦
A 56-m (184-ft) high granite church tower, with an alarming crack in it, rises above this village.

KEY

▨▨ Tour route

═ Other roads

▲ Mountain peak

Street-by-Street: Córdoba 🄕

The heart of Córdoba is the old
Jewish quarter near the Mezquita,
known as the Judería. A walk around
this area gives the visitor the sensa-
tion that little has changed since this
was one of the greatest cities in the
Western world. Narrow, cobbled
streets where cars cannot penetrate,
Statue of secluded niches, wrought iron
Maimónides gates, tiny workshops where
silversmiths create fine jewellery
– all appears very much as it was 1,000
years ago. Traffic roars along the riverfront,
past the replica of a Moorish water wheel
and the towering walls of the Great
Mosque. Most of the sights are in this
area, while modern city life takes
place some blocks north, around
the Plaza de las Tendillas.

Sinagoga
*Hebrew script covers the
interior walls of this
medieval synagogue, the
only one remaning in
Andalusia.*

Baños del Alcázar Califales
*These 10th century Arab
baths now house a museum
recreating the history and
uses of the baths.*

**Capilla de San
Bartolomé**, in
Mudéjar style,
contains elaborate
plasterwork.

★ Alcázar de los Reyes Cristianos
*Water terraces and fountains add to the
tranquil atmosphere of the gardens belonging to the palace-fortress of the Catholic
Monarchs, constructed in the 14th century.*

KEY

- - - Suggested route

To Barrio
de San
Basilio

STAR SIGHTS

★ Mezquita

★ Alcázar de los Reyes
Cristianos

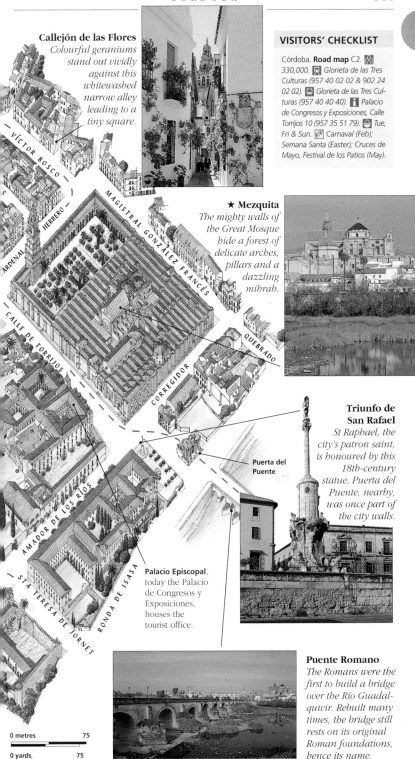

Callejón de las Flores
Colourful geraniums stand out vividly against this whitewashed narrow alley leading to a tiny square.

VISITORS' CHECKLIST

Córdoba. **Road map** C2.
330,000. Glorieta de las Tres Culturas (957 40 02 02 & 902 24 02 02). Glorieta de las Tres Culturas (957 40 40 40). Palacio de Congresos y Exposiciones, Calle Torrijos 10 (957 35 51 79). Tue, Fri & Sun. Carnaval (Feb); Semana Santa (Easter); Cruces de Mayo, Festival de los Patios (May).

★ Mezquita
The mighty walls of the Great Mosque hide a forest of delicate arches, pillars and a dazzling mihrab.

Triunfo de San Rafael
St Raphael, the city's patron saint, is honoured by this 18th-century statue. Puerta del Puente, nearby, was once part of the city walls.

Puerta del Puente

Palacio Episcopal, today the Palacio de Congresos y Exposiciones, houses the tourist office.

Puente Romano
The Romans were the first to build a bridge over the Río Guadalquivir. Rebuilt many times, the bridge still rests on its original Roman foundations, hence its name.

0 metres 75
0 yards 75

Exploring Córdoba

Córdoba's core is the old city around the Mezquita on the banks of the Guadalquivir. Its origins are probably Carthaginian; the name may be derived from Kartuba, Phoenician for "rich and precious city". Under the Romans it was a provincial capital and birthplace of philosopher Seneca. However, Córdoba's golden age was in the 10th century when Abd al Rahman III created an independent caliphate with Córdoba as its capital. Its influence spread to North Africa and the Balearic Islands. Córdoba was a centre of trade, industry and learning, where Jews and Christians lived alongside Muslims. Civil war *(see pp46–7)* ended the caliphate and the city was pillaged. It declined after falling to Fernando III in 1236, although a number of fine buildings have since been erected.

Sculpture by Mateo Inurria

Naranjas y Limones in Museo Julio Romero de Torres

⛪ Mezquita
See pp144–5.

♣ Alcázar de los Reyes Cristianos
C/Caballerizas Reales s/n. **Tel** *957 42 01 51.* 🕐 *8:30am–7:30pm Tue–Fri; 9:30am–4:30pm Sat; 9:30am–2:30pm Sun.* 🔴 *Mon.* 🖼

This palace-fortress was built in 1328 for Alfonso XI. Fernando II and Isabel stayed here during their campaign to conquer Granada from the Moors *(see p48)*. Later it was used by the Inquisition *(see p51)*, and then as a prison.

The gardens, with ponds and fountains, are open in the evenings in July and August. Behind the palace's walls are Roman mosaics.

✡ Sinagoga
Calle Judios 20. **Tel** *957 20 29 28.* 🕐 *10am–2pm, 3:30–5:30pm Tue–Sat; 10am–1:30pm Sun.*

Constructed around 1315, the small Mudéjar-style synagogue is one of three in Spain preserved from that era. The other two are both in Toledo, just south of Madrid. The women's gallery and decorative plaster-work, with Hebrew script, are of particular interest.

The synagogue lies in the Judería, the Jewish quarter, which has hardly changed since Moorish times. It is a labyrinth of narrow streets, with whitewashed houses and patios. In a plaza nearby is a statue of Maimónides, a 12th-century Jewish sage.

🏛 Baños del Alcázar Califales
Campo Santo de los Mártires. 🕐 *8:30am–7:30pm Tue–Fri; 9:30am–4:30pm Sat; 9:30am–2:30pm Sun & hols.* 🖼 *(free on Wed).*

Built in the Umayyad Palace under orders from Al-Hakam II in the 10th century, these Arab baths reflect the classical order of Roman baths: cold rooms, warm rooms and hot rooms. They are all vaulted and lit by star-shaped apertures and are remarkably well-preserved. A museum recreates the social and religious history and uses of the baths.

🏛 Museo Julio Romero de Torres
Plaza del Potro 1. **Tel** *957 49 19 09.* 🕐 *8:30am–7:30pm Tue–Fri, 9:30am–4:30pm Sat; 9am–2:30pm Sun & hols.* 🔴 *Mon.*

Julio Romero de Torres (1874– 1930), who was born in this house, captured the soul of Córdoba in his paintings. Many depict nudes in stilted poses; others are painfully mawkish, including the deathbed scene *Look How Lovely She Was* (1895). His unpredictable style varied from the macabre *Cante Hondo* (1930) to the humorous *Naranjas y Limones* (Oranges and Lemons) (1928).

🏛 Museo de Bellas Artes
Plaza del Potro 1. **Tel** *957 35 55 50.* 🕐 *2:30–8:30pm Tue, 9am–8:30pm Wed–Sat, 9am–2:30pm Sun.*

Located in a former charity hospital, this museum exhibits sculptures by local artist Mateo Inurria (1867–1924) as well as paintings by Murillo, Valdés Leal and Zurbarán of the Seville School *(see p66)*.

⛲ Plaza de la Corredera
Built in the 17th century in Castilian style, this handsome, arcaded square has been the scene of bullfights and other

Daily market in the arcaded Plaza de la Corredera

public events. The buildings are gradually being restored, but the cafés under the arches still retain an air of the past. A market is held here.

▦ Palacio de Viana
Plaza Don Gome 2. *Tel 957 49 67 41.*
⬭ 10am–7pm Tue–Sat; 10am–3pm
Sun. ⬤ Mon. 🖾

Tapestries, furniture, porcelain and paintings are displayed in this 17th-century mansion. Purchased by a savings

Central fountain in the garden of the 17th-century Palacio de Viana

bank in 1981, the former home of the Viana family is kept much as they left it. There are 14 beautiful patios and a delightful garden of citrus trees, date palms and rose bushes around a fountain.

🏛 Museo Arqueológico
Plaza Jerónimo Páez 7. *Tel 957 35 55 17.* ⬭ 2:30–8:30pm Tue, 9am–8:30pm Wed–Sat, 9am–2:30pm Sun & public hols. 🖾

Roman remains, including mosaics and pottery are on display in this Renaissance mansion. Other exhibits include Moorish items such as a 10th century bronze stag found at Medina Azahara *(see p138)*.

▦ Puente Romano
This arched bridge has Roman foundations, but was rebuilt by the Moors. Nearby, south of the Mezquita, stands the Puerta del Puente, designed by Hernán Ruiz in 1571.

Moorish bronze stag in the Museo Arqueológico

▦ Torre de la Calahorra
Tel 957 29 39 29. ⬭ daily. Oct–Apr: 10am–6pm; May–Sep: 10am–2pm, 4:30–8:30pm. 🖾

At the end of the Puente Romano, this defensive tower was built in the 1300s. It houses a museum about the life, culture and philosophy of 10th-century Córdoba.

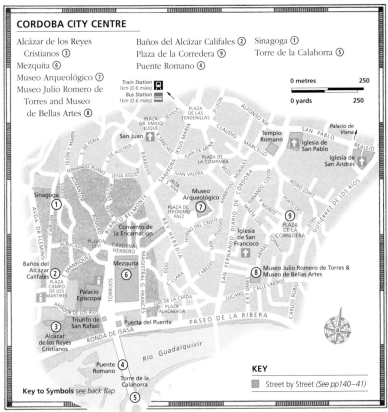

CORDOBA CITY CENTRE

Alcázar de los Reyes
  Cristianos ③
Mezquita ⑥
Museo Arqueológico ⑦
Museo Julio Romero de
  Torres and Museo
  de Bellas Artes ⑧

Baños del Alcázar Califales ②
Plaza de la Corredera ⑨
Puente Romano ④

Sinagoga ①
Torre de la Calahorra ⑤

Train Station
1km (0.6 miles) 🚆
Bus Station
1km (0.6 miles) 🚌

0 metres 250
0 yards 250

KEY
▨ Street by Street (See pp140–41)

Key to Symbols *see back flap*

Córdoba: the Mezquita

Córdoba's great mosque, dating back 12 centuries, embodied the power of Islam on the Iberian peninsula. Abd al Rahman I *(see p46)* built the original mosque between 785 and 787. The building evolved over the centuries, blending many architectural forms. In the 10th century al Hakam II *(see p46)* made some of the most lavish additions, including the elaborate *mihrab* (prayer niche) and the *maqsura* (caliph's enclosure). In the 16th century a cathedral was built in the heart of the reconsecrated mosque, part of which was destroyed.

Patio de los Naranjos
Orange trees grow in the courtyard where the faithful washed before prayer.

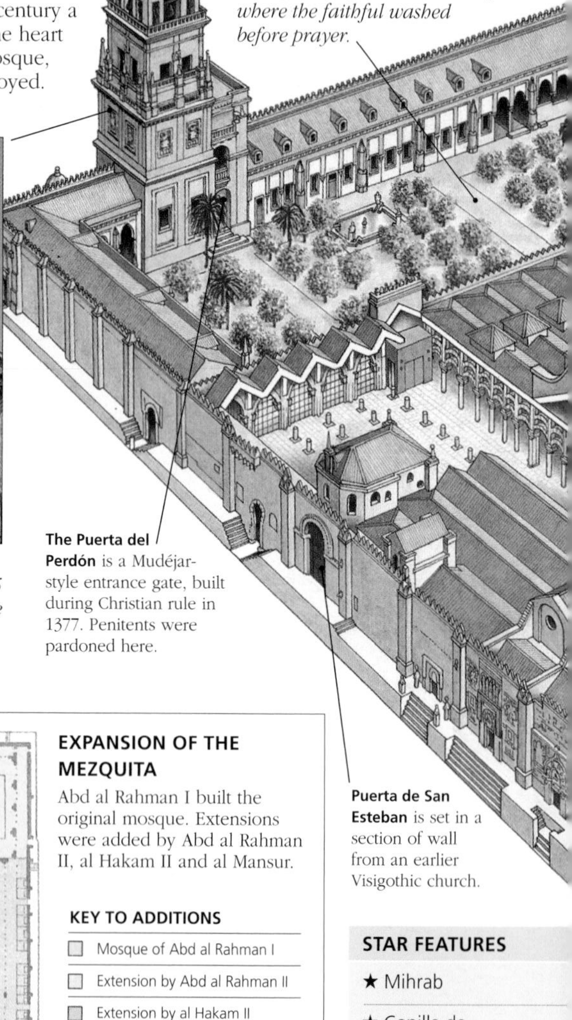

Torre del Alminar
This bell tower, 93 m (305 ft) high, is built on the site of the original minaret. Steep steps lead to the top for a fine view of the city.

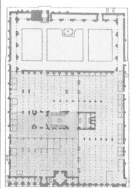

The Puerta del Perdón is a Mudéjar-style entrance gate, built during Christian rule in 1377. Penitents were pardoned here.

EXPANSION OF THE MEZQUITA

Abd al Rahman I built the original mosque. Extensions were added by Abd al Rahman II, al Hakam II and al Mansur.

KEY TO ADDITIONS

☐ Mosque of Abd al Rahman I
☐ Extension by Abd al Rahman II
☐ Extension by al Hakam II
☐ Extension by al Mansur
☐ Patio de los Naranjos

Puerta de San Esteban is set in a section of wall from an earlier Visigothic church.

STAR FEATURES

★ Mihrab

★ Capilla de Villaviciosa

★ Arches and Pillars

Cathedral
Part of the mosque was destroyed to accommodate the cathedral, started in 1523. Featuring an Italianate dome, it was chiefly designed by members of the Hernán Ruiz family.

The cathedral choir has Churrigueresque stalls, carved by Pedro Duque Cornejo in 1758.

Capilla Mayor

Capilla Real

★ Arches and Pillars
More than 850 columns of granite, jasper and marble support the roof, creating a dazzling visual effect. Many were taken from Roman and Visigothic buildings.

★ Mihrab
This prayer niche, richly ornamented, held a gilt copy of the Koran. The worn flagstones indicate where pilgrims circled it seven times on their knees.

★ Capilla de Villaviciosa
The first Christian chapel to be built in the mosque, in 1371, the Capilla de Villaviciosa has stunning multi-lobed arches.

The Patios of Córdoba

Since early times, family and social life in Andalusia have revolved around the courtyard or patio, which is at the heart of the classic Mediterranean house. The sleeping accommodation and living rooms were built round this space, which introduces air and light into the house. Brick arches, colourful tiles, ironwork, orange and lemon trees,

Regional pottery as patio decoration

and pots full of flowers add to the charm of these cool and tranquil retreats. Córdoba takes pride in all its patio gardens, be they palatial spaces in the grandest residences or tiny courtyards in humble homes, shared by many. There are traditional patios in the San Lorenzo and Judería quarters and in Barrio San Basilio, west of the Mezquita.

Whitewashed walls   **Tiled portrait of saint**   **Orange trees**

Festival de los Patios, *when scores of patios are thrown open to the public, takes place in early May* (see pp38–9). *The most beautifully decorated patio wins a prestigious prize.*

ANDALUSIAN PATIO

This scene, painted by García Rodríguez (1863–1925), evokes a style of patio that is still common in Andalusia. The patio walls are usually immaculately whitewashed, contrasting with the colourful display of geraniums and carnations in terracotta pots. Fragrant blooms of jasmine add to the atmosphere.

Moorish-style lamps, *which now have electric bulbs, light the patio in the late evening.*

Azulejos, *a reminder of the region's Moorish past, decorate many patios, adding to their colourful display.*

Cancelas *are attractively designed iron gates which screen the private patio from the street outside.*

A central fountain *or well traditionally provided water and remains a feature of many patios today.*

Montilla **7**

Córdoba. **Road map** C2. 🏠 *23,000.*
🚌 🚃 🛈 *Calle Capitan Alonso de
Vargas 3 (957 65 24 62).* 🛒 *Fri.*

Montilla is the centre of an
important wine-making region,
but one that finds it difficult
to emerge from the shadow
of a more famous rival. The
excellent white wine is made
in the same way as sherry *(see
pp30–31)* and tastes rather like
it but, unlike sherry, does not
need fortifying with alcohol.
Some *bodegas*, including
Alvear and **Pérez Barquero**, are
happy to welcome visitors.
  The Mudéjar **Convento de
Santa Clara** dates from 1512
and the **castle** from the 18th
century. The town library is in
the **Casa del Inca**, so named
because Garcilaso de la Vega,
who wrote about the Incas,
lived there in the 16th century.

**The historic crest of the Bodega
Pérez Barquero**

🍷 **Bodega Alvear**
Avenida María Auxiliadora 1. **Tel**
957 66 40 14. ⏰ *daily (call first to
arrange visit).* ● *Sun & public hols.*

🍷 **Bodega Pérez Barquero**
Avenida Andalucía 27. **Tel** *957 65 05
00.* ⏰ *phone ahead to make an
appointment.*

Aguilar **8**

Córdoba. **Road map** C2.
🏠 *13,500.* 🚌 🚃 🛈 *Cuesta
de Jesús 2, Edificio Antiguo Posito
(957 66 15 67).* 🛒 *Tue, Thu & Fri.*

Ceramics, wine and olive
oil are important products in
Aguilar, which was settled
in Roman times. There are
several seigneurial houses,
and the eight-sided **Plaza de
San José**. Built in 1810, it
houses the town hall. Nearby
is a Baroque clock tower.

Lucena **9**

Córdoba. **Road map** D2.
🏠 *40,000.* 🚌 🛈 *Castillo del
Moral s/n (957 51 32 82).* 🛒 *Wed.*
www.turlucena.com

Lucena prospers from furniture
making and from its brass and
copper manufactures, and
produces interesting ceramics.
Under the caliphs of Córdoba
(see p46) it was an important
trading and intellectual centre,
with a dynamic, independent,
Jewish community.
  Iglesia de Santiago, with a
Baroque turret, was built on the
site of a synagogue in 1503. The
Torre del Moral is the only
remaining part of a Moorish
castle. Granada's last sultan,
Boabdil, was captured in 1483,
and imprisoned here. Nearby,
the 15th-century **Iglesia de
San Mateo** has a flamboyant
Baroque sacristy and three
naves with delicate arches.
  On the first Sunday in May
Lucena stages an elaborate
ceremony which honours the
Virgen de Araceli.

Cabra **10**

Córdoba. **Road map** D2. 🏠 *21,000.*
🚌 🛈 *Calle Santa Rosalia 2 (957 52
01 10).* 🛒 *Mon.* **www**.cabra.net

Set amid fertile fields and
vast olive groves, Cabra was
an episcopal seat in the 3rd
century. On a rise stands the
former castle, which is now a

**Statue of Santo Domingo, Iglesia
Santo Domingo in Cabra**

school. There are also some
noble mansions and the
Iglesia Santo Domingo with
a Baroque façade.
  Just outside the town, the
Fuente del Río, source of the
Río Cabra, is a pleasantly leafy
spot in which to picnic.

Baena **11**

Córdoba. **Road map** D2. 🏠 *20,000.*
🚌 🛈 *Virrey del Pino 5 (957 67 17
57).* 🛒 *Thu.* **www**.baena.es

Baena's olive oil has been
famed since Roman times. At
the top of the whitewashed
town is **Iglesia Santa María
la Mayor**. On the Plaza de la
Constitución stands the handsome, modern town hall. The
Casa del Monte, an arcaded
mansion dating from the 18th
century, flanks it on one side.
  Easter week is spectacular,
when thousands of drummers
take to the streets *(see p34)*.

Decoration on façade of the 18th-century Casa del Monte, Baena

For hotels and restaurants in this region see pp215–16 and pp231–2

Jaén ⑭

The Moors knew Jaén as *geen*, meaning "way station of caravans". Their lofty fortress, later rebuilt as the Castillo de Santa Catalina, symbolizes Jaén's strategic importance on the route to Andalusia from the more austere Castile. For centuries this area was a battleground between Moors and Christians *(see pp48–9)*. The older, upper part of the city holds most interest. Around the cathedral and towards the Barrio San Juan are numerous seigneurial buildings, long winding streets and steep alleys. The city centre is filled with smart shops, and in the evenings the narrow streets near Plaza de la Constitución are filled with people enjoying the *tapeo* in the many bars.

Bamboo crucifix at Santa Clara

Mighty ramparts of Castillo de Santa Catalina

♟ Castillo de Santa Catalina

Carretera al Castillo. *Tel 953 12 07 33 (tourist centre), 953 23 00 00 (parador).* ⬜ *Tue–Sun.* ⬤ *public hols.*
Hannibal is believed to have erected a tower on this rocky pinnacle, high above the city. Later the Moors established a fortress, only to lose it to the crusading King Fernando III in 1246. A larger castle was then built with huge ramparts. This has been restored and a medieval-style *parador* (inn) built next door *(see pp210–11)*.

It is worthwhile taking the sinuous road up to the Torre del Homenaje and the castle chapel. Even more rewarding are the great views of the city, the mountains and the landscape, thick with olive trees.

♙ Catedral

Plaza de Santa Maria. ⬜ *daily.*
Andrés de Vandelvira, responsible for many of Ubeda's fine buildings *(see pp154–5)*, designed the cathedral in the 16th century. Later additions include two 17th-century towers that flank the west front. Inside are beautifully carved choir stalls and a museum with valuable works of art.

Every Friday, between 11:30am and 12:45pm, worshippers can view the Lienzo del Santo Rostro. St Veronica is said to have used this piece of cloth to wipe Christ's face, which left a permanent impression.

Statuary on the cathedral façade

♨ Baños Arabes

Palacio Villardompardo, Plaza Santa Luisa de Marillac. *Tel 953 24 80 68.* ⬜ *summer: 9am–8pm Tue–Fri, 9:30am–2:30pm Sat & Sun; winter: 9am–8:15pm Tue–Sat, 9am–3pm Sun.* ⬤ *Mon & public hols.*
These 11th-century baths are known as the baths of Ali, a Moorish chieftain. They were restored during the 1980s. The interior features horseshoe arches, ceilings decorated with tiny star-shaped windows, a hemispherical dome and two earthenware vats in which bathers once immersed themselves. The baths are entered through the Palacio Villardompardo, which also houses a museum of local arts and crafts.

OLIVE OIL

Olive oil is the life-blood of Jaén and its province. Since the Phoenicians, or possibly the Greeks, brought the olive tree to Spain it has flourished in Andalusia, particularly in Jaén, which today has an annual production of more than 200,000 tonnes of oil. Harvesting, mostly by hand, takes place from December onwards. Quality is controlled by a system known as *Denominación de Origen Controlada*. The best product, virgin olive oil, is made from the first cold-pressing, so that the full flavour, vitamins and nutrients of the oil are preserved.

Harvest time in one of the many olive groves in Andalusia

Horseshoe arches supporting the dome at the Baños Arabes

Shrine of Virgen de la Capilla in Iglesia San Ildefonso

🔒 Capilla de San Andrés

Tucked away in a narrow alley next to a college lies this Mudéjar chapel. It was founded in the 16th century, possibly on the site of a synagogue, by Gutiérrez González, who was treasurer to Pope Leo X and endowed with extensive privileges. A magnificent gilded iron screen by Maestro Bartolomé de Jaén is the highlight of the chapel.

🔒 Iglesia San Ildefonso

This mainly Gothic church has façades in three different styles. One is Gothic, with a mosaic of the Virgin descending on Jaén during a Moorish siege in 1430. A second is partly Plateresque *(see p25)* and the third, by Ventura Rodríguez in the late 18th century, is Neo-Classical. Inside, the high altar is by Pedro and José Roldán. There is also a chapel which enshrines the Virgen de la Capilla, Jaén's patron saint. The museum next door is devoted to the Virgin.

🔒 Real Monasterio de Santa Clara

Founded in the 13th century, just after the Reconquest of the city by Christian forces, this is one of the most ancient monasteries in Jaén. It has a lovely cloister, which dates from about 1581. The church has an *artesonado* ceiling and shelters a curious 16th-century bamboo image of Christ made in Ecuador. Sweet cakes are offered for sale by the nuns from the convent.

VISITORS' CHECKLIST

Jaén. **Road map** D2. 🚉
115,000. 🚉 *Paseo de la Estación
s/n (902 24 02 02).* 🚌 *Plaza Coca
de la Piñera s/n. 953 25 01 06.*
🛈 *Calle Maestra 18 (953 21 91
16).* 🛒 *Thu.* 🎭 *Semana Santa
(Easter); Festividad de Nuestra
Señora de la Capilla (11 Jun); Feria
de San Lucas (18 Oct); Romería
de Santa Catalina (25 Nov).*

🏛 Museo Provincial

Paseo de la Estación 27. **Tel** *953 31
33 39.* ◗ *2:30–8:30pm Tue, 9am–
8:30pm Wed–Sat, 9am–2:30pm Sun
& public hols.*

This building incorporates remains of the Iglesia de San Miguel and the façade of a 16th-century granary. A Palaeo-Christian sarcophagus, Roman mosaics and sculptures, and Greek and Roman ceramics are among the articles on display.

A short walk along Paseo de la Estación is the Plaza de las Batallas and a memorial to the defeats of Napoleon at Bailén *(see p53)* and of the Moors at Las Navas de Tolosa *(see p48).*

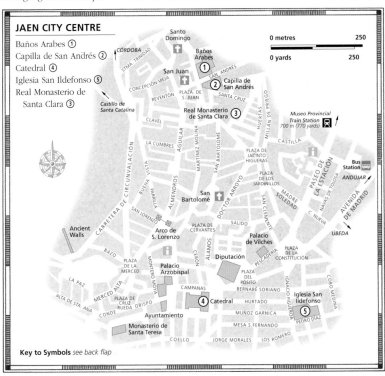

JAEN CITY CENTRE

Baños Arabes ①
Capilla de San Andrés ②
Catedral ④
Iglesia San Ildefonso ⑤
Real Monasterio de
Santa Clara ③

0 metres   250
0 yards   250

Key to Symbols *see back flap*

The Moorish Castillo de la Mota and the ruined church crowning the hill above Alcalá la Real

Priego de Córdoba ⑫

Córdoba. **Road map** D2.
🏠 *23,000.* 🚉 ℹ️ *Carrera de las Monjas 1 (957 70 06 25).* 🚌 *Sat.*
www.turismodepriego.com

Priego de Córdoba lies on a fertile plain at the foot of La Tiñosa, the highest mountain in Córdoba province. It is a pleasant small town with an unassuming air, well away from the main routes, and yet it claims to be the capital of Córdoba Baroque. The title is easy to accept in view of the dazzling work of local carvers, gilders and ironworkers.

The town's labyrinthine old quarter was the site of the original Arab settlement. But the 18th century, when silk manufacture prospered, was Priego's golden age. During this time elegant houses were built and money was lavished on fine Baroque architecture, particularly churches.

A restored Moorish fortress, standing on Roman foundations, introduces visitors to the fine medieval quarter which is called **Barrio de la Villa**. White-washed buildings line its narrow streets and flower-decked squares. Paseo Colombia leads to the Adarve, a long promenade with views of the surrounding countryside.

The nearby **Iglesia de la Asunción** is an outstanding structure. Originally Gothic in style, it was converted to a Baroque church by Jerónimo

Sánchez de Rueda in the 18th century. Its *pièce de résistance* is the sacristy chapel, created in 1784 by local artist Francisco Javier Pedrajas. Its sumptuous ornamentation in the form of sculpted figures and plaster scrolls and cornices can be overwhelming. The main altar is in Plateresque style *(see p25)*.

The **Iglesia de la Aurora** is another fine Baroque building. At midnight every Saturday the cloaked brotherhood, Nuestra Señora de la Aurora, parades the streets singing songs to the Virgin and collecting alms.

Silk merchants built many of the imposing mansions that follow the curve around the Calle del Río. Niceto Alcalá Zamora was born at No. 33 in 1877.

A brilliant orator, he became Spain's president in 1931, but was forced into exile during the Civil War. Today this building is the tourist office.

At the end of the street is the **Fuente del Rey**, or King's Fountain. This is a Baroque extravaganza, with three pools, 139 spouts gushing water, and includes Neptune among its exuberant statuary.

May is one of the liveliest months to visit Priego. Every Sunday a procession celebrates the town's deliverance from a plague which devastated the population centuries ago.

Alcalá la Real ⑬

Jaén. **Road map** D2. 🏠 *22,000.* 🚉
ℹ️ *Fortaleza de la Mota (639 64 77 96).* 🚌 *Tue.* **www**.alcalareal.com

Alcalá was a strategic point held by the military Order of Calatrava during Spain's Reconquest *(see pp48–9)*. On the hilltop of La Mota are the ruins of the Moorish **Fortaleza de la Mota**, built by the rulers of Granada in the 14th century, with later additions. Nearby are ruins of the town's main church. There are splendid views over the countryside and the historic town, with its air of past glories. The Renaissance **Palacio Abacial** and **Fuente de Carlos V** are the chief attractions to be found around the plaza in the centre of the town.

Fine statuary ornaments the 16th-century Fuente del Rey at Priego de Córdoba

Jaén ⑭

See pp148–9.

Andújar ⑮

Jaén. **Road map** D2. 🏛 *40,000.* 🚉
🚌 ℹ️ *Torre del Reloj Plaza de Santa Maria s/n. 953 50 49 59.* 🏪 *Tue.*

This strategically situated town was once the site of Iliturgi, an Iberian town which was destroyed by Scipio's army in the Punic Wars (*see p44*). A 15-arched bridge built by the Roman conquerors still spans the Guadalquivir river.

In the central plaza is the Gothic **Iglesia San Miguel**, with paintings by Alonso Cano. The **Iglesia Santa María la Mayor** features a Renaissance façade and a splendid Mudéjar tower. Inside is the painting *Christ in the Garden of Olives* (c.1605) by El Greco.

The town is also renowned for its potters, who still turn out ceramics in traditional style. Olive oil (*see p148*), which is produced in Andújar, figures strongly in the local cuisine.

Santuario Virgen de la Cabeza ⑯

Padres Trinitarios. **Road map** D2. *Tel 953 54 90 15.* 🕙 *10am–8pm daily.*
♿ www.santuariovirgencabeza.org

North of Andújar, amid the oak trees and bull ranches of the Sierra Morena, is the Santuario Virgen de la Cabeza. Within this grim stone temple

Replica of the statue of the Virgin Mary, Santuario de la Cabeza

Roman bridge spanning the Guadalquivir at Andújar

from the 13th century, is a much-venerated Virgin. According to tradition her image was sent to Spain by St Peter.

Much of the building and the original statue of the Virgin were destroyed in 1937 in the Civil War (*see pp54–5*). For nine months 230 civil guards held out against Republican forces. 20,000 men attacked the sanctuary before it burned down. Captain Santiago Cortés, the commander of the civil guard, died from his battle wounds.

On the last Sunday in April every year, many thousands make a pilgrimage to the sanctuary to pay homage to the Virgin (*see p39*).

Baños de la Encina ⑰

Jaén. **Road map** D2. 🚉 *from Linares & Jaén. Tel Callejón del Castillo 1. 953 61 32 29 (Ayuntamiento).* 🕙 *Wed–Sun.* www.bdelaencina.com

Caliph al-Hakam II (*see p46*) ordered the construction of this fortress in the foothills of the Sierra Morena in AD 967. Rising above the village, it is a daunting sight with its 15 towers and soaring ramparts. Its heights give views across pastures and olive groves.

During the spring fair there is a *romería* (*see p38*) to the town's shrine of the Virgen de la Encina. According to local tradition, the Virgin made a miraculous appearance on an *encina* (holm oak tree).

La Carolina ⑱

Jaén. **Road map** E1. 🏛 *15,500.*
🚌 ℹ️ *Carretera Madrid–Cádiz km 269. 953 68 08 82.* 🏪 *Tue & Fri.*

Founded in 1767, La Carolina was populated by settlers from Germany and Flanders.

This was an ill-fated plan to develop the area and to make it safer for travellers. The person in charge, Carlos III's minister, Pablo de Olavide, had a palace built on the main square. Just outside town is a monument to a battle at Las Navas de Tolosa in 1212. Alfonso VIII, king of Castile, was led

Façade of the palace of Pablo de Olavide

by a shepherd over the hills to Las Navas, where he crushed the Moors. His victory began the reconquest of Andalusia (*see pp48–9*).

Desfiladero de Despeñaperros ⑲

Jaén. **Road map** E1. ℹ️ *Visitors Centre, Auto via de Andalucia (A4) km 257 Santa Elena, Jaén. 953 66 43 07.*

This spectacular pass in the Sierra Morena is the main gateway to Andalusia. Armies, stage-coaches, mule-trains and brigands all used the pass, so hold-ups were common.

The four-lane Autovía de Andalucía and a railway line thread their way through the chasm, which offers views of rock formations – *Los Organos* (the organ pipes) and the *Salto del Fraile* (monk's leap).

Street-by-Street: Baeza ⑳

Coat of arms, Casa del Pópulo

Nestling amid olive groves, beautiful Baeza is a small town, unusually rich in Renaissance architecture. In 2003 it was named a UNESCO World Heritage site. Called Beatia by the Romans and later the capital of a Moorish fiefdom, Baeza is portrayed as a "royal nest of hawks" on its coat of arms. It was conquered by Fernando III in 1226 – the first town in Andalusia to be definitively won back from the Moors – and was then settled by Castilian knights. An era of medieval splendour followed, reaching a climax in the 16th century, when Andrés de Vandelvira's splendid buildings were erected. In the early 20th century, Antonio Machado, one of his generation's greatest poets, lived here for some years.

★ Palacio de Jabalquinto
An Isabelline (see p24) style façade, flanked by elaborate, rounded buttresses, fronts this splendid Gothic palace.

Antigua Universidad
From 1542 until 1825, this Renaissance and Baroque building was the site of one of Spain's first universities.

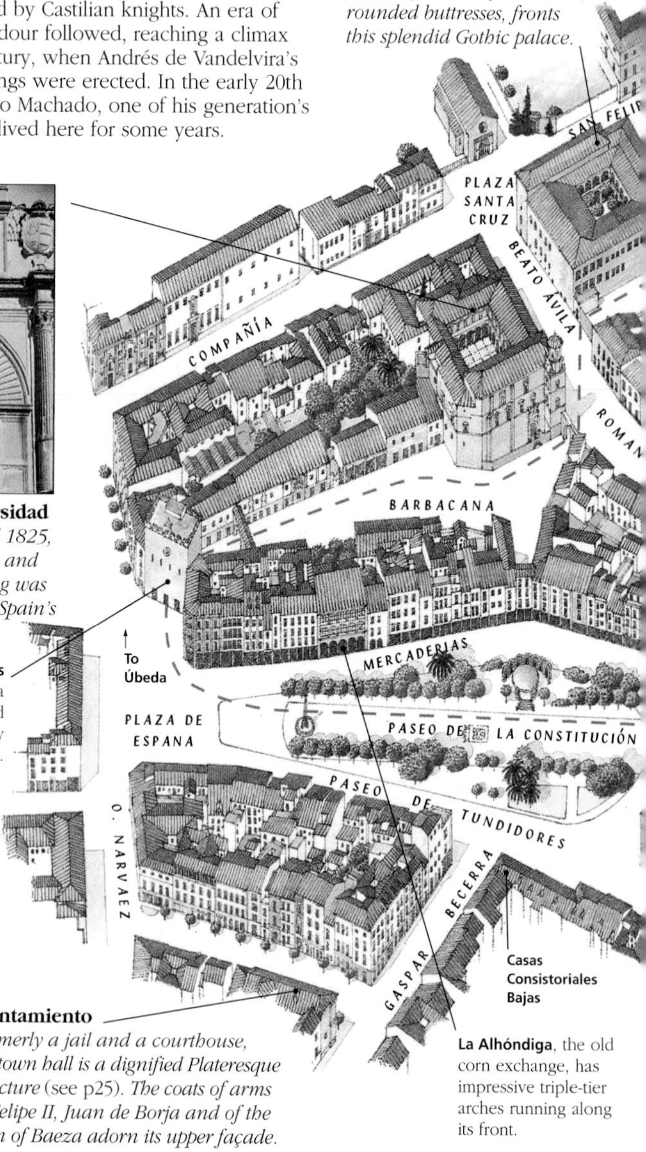

Torre de los Aliatares is a 1,000-year-old tower built by the Moors.

To Úbeda

PLAZA DE ESPANA

Ayuntamiento
Formerly a jail and a courthouse, the town hall is a dignified Plateresque structure (see p25). The coats of arms of Felipe II, Juan de Borja and of the town of Baeza adorn its upper façade.

Casas Consistoriales Bajas

La Alhóndiga, the old corn exchange, has impressive triple-tier arches running along its front.

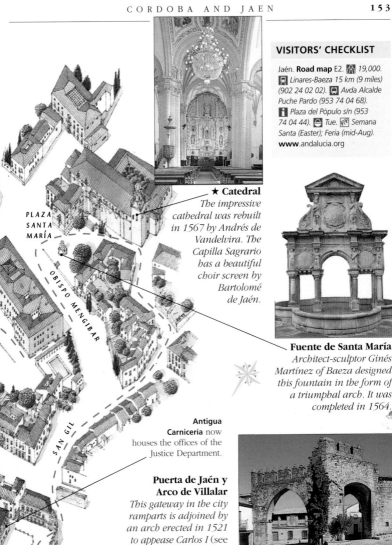

★ Catedral
The impressive cathedral was rebuilt in 1567 by Andrés de Vandelvira. The Capilla Sagrario has a beautiful choir screen by Bartolomé de Jaén.

PLAZA
SANTA
MARÍA

OBISPO MENGIBAR

SAN GIL

VISITORS' CHECKLIST

Jaén. **Road map** E2. 19,000. Linares-Baeza 15 km (9 miles) (902 24 02 02). Avda Alcalde Puche Pardo (953 74 04 68). Plaza del Pópulo s/n (953 74 04 44). Tue. Semana Santa (Easter); Feria (mid-Aug). www.andalucia.org

Fuente de Santa María
Architect-sculptor Ginés Martínez of Baeza designed this fountain in the form of a triumphal arch. It was completed in 1564.

Antigua Carnicería now houses the offices of the Justice Department.

Puerta de Jaén y Arco de Villalar
This gateway in the city ramparts is adjoined by an arch erected in 1521 to appease Carlos I (see p50) after a rebellion.

| 0 metres | 75 |
| 0 yards | 75 |

KEY

Tourist information

‒ ‒ ‒ Suggested route

↓
To
Jaén

★ Plaza del Pópulo
The Casa del Pópulo, a fine Plateresque palace, now the tourist office, overlooks this square. In its centre is the Fuente de los Leones, a fountain with an Ibero-Roman statue flanked by lions.

STAR SIGHTS

★ Palacio de Jabalquinto

★ Catedral

★ Plaza del Pópulo

Úbeda ㉑

Hospital de Santiago, detail

Perched on the crest of a ridge, Úbeda is a showcase of Renaissance magnificence. Thanks to the patronage of some of Spain's most influential men of the 16th century, such as Francisco de los Cobos, secretary of state, and his great nephew, Juan Vázquez de Molina, a number of noble buildings are dotted about the town. The Plaza de Vázquez de Molina is surrounded by elegant palaces and churches and is undoubtedly the jewel in the crown. The narrow streets of the old quarter contrast sharply with modern Úbeda, which expands north of the Plaza de Andalucía. In 2003 Úbeda became a UNESCO World Heritage Site.

Maestro Bartolomé's choir screen at Capilla del Salvador

🏛 Capilla del Salvador

Three architects, Andrés de Vandelvira (credited with refining the Renaissance style), Diego de Siloé and Esteban Jamete helped design this 16th-century landmark. It was built as the personal chapel of Francisco de los Cobos, whose tomb lies in the crypt.

Although the church was pillaged during the Civil War *(see pp54–5)*, it retains a number of treasures. These include a carving of Christ, which is all that remains of an altarpiece by Alonso de Berruguete, Maestro Bartolomé de Jaén's choir screen, and a sacristy by Vandelvira.

Behind the church are two other buildings dating from the 16th century – Cobos's palace, which is graced by a Renaissance façade, and the Hospital de los Honrados Viejos (Honoured Elders). At the end of Baja del Salvador is the Plaza de Santa Lucía. A promenade leads from this point along the Redonda de Miradores, following the line of the old walls and offering views of the countryside.

🏛 Palacio de las Cadenas

Pl de Vázquez de Molina. **Tel** 953 75 08 97. ⬜ 8am–3pm, 5–10pm Mon–Fri; 9am–1pm Sat & Sun.
www.ubedainteresa.com
Two stone lions guard Úbeda's town hall, which occupies this palace built for Vázquez de Molina by Vandelvira during the mid-16th century. The building gets its name from the iron chains *(cadenas)* once attached to the columns supporting the main doorway.

Crowning the corners of the Classical façade are carved stone lanterns. A museum of local pottery is in the basement. The building also houses the tourist information office.

🏛 Parador de Úbeda

Plaza de Vázquez de Molina s/n. **Tel** 953 75 03 45. **Patio** ⬜ to non-guests daily. See also p203.
Built in the 16th century but considerably altered in the 17th century, this was the residence of Fernando Ortega Salido, Dean of Málaga and chaplain of El Salvador. The austere palace has been turned into a hotel, which is also known as the Parador del Condestable Dávalos in honour of a warrior famed during the Reconquest *(see pp48–9)*. Its patio is an ideal place to have a drink.

🏛 Santa María de los Reales Alcázares

Built on the site of an original mosque, this church, mainly dating from the 13th century, is now undergoing restoration. Inside there is fine ironwork by Maestro Bartolomé. The Gothic cloister, with pointed arches and ribbed vaults, and a Romanesque doorway, are particularly noteworthy.

Near the church is the Cárcel del Obispo (Bishop's Jail), so called because nuns punished by the bishop were confined there. Today the building contains the town's courthouse.

Stone lions guarding the Palacio de las Cadenas

Statuary on the main entrance of Iglesia de San Pablo

🛈 Iglesia de San Pablo

The three doors of this church all date from different periods. The main entrance is in late Gothic style while the others are in transitional Romanesque and Isabelline. Inside is an apse which dates from the 13th century and a beautiful 16th-century chapel by Vandelvira. The church is surmounted by a Plateresque tower (1537).

Nearby on Plaza de Vázquez de Molina is a monument to the poet and mystic San Juan de la Cruz (1549–91).

🏛 Museo Arqueológico

Casa Mudéjar, C/Cervantes 6. **Tel** *953 77 94 32.* ☐ *2:30–8:30pm Tue, 9am–8:30pm Wed–Sat, 9am–2:30pm Sun.* ● *public hols.*

This archaeological museum exhibits artifacts from Neolithic times to the Moorish era. The display includes tombstones from the 1st century AD and Moorish and Mudéjar works in wood and plaster. It is located in the 15th-century Casa Mudéjar, among the many palaces and churches gracing the streets of the old quarter.

🏥 Hospital de Santiago

Calle Obispo Cobos s/n. **Tel** *953 75 08 42.* ☐ *11am–3pm, 6–10pm Sat & Sun year round; also: winter: 8am–2:30pm, 5–10pm Mon–Fri; summer: 8am–3pm, 4–10pm Mon–Fri.*

Created on the orders of the Bishop of Jaén around 1562, this colossal former hospital was designed by Vandelvira. The façade is flanked by square towers. Marble columns grace the patio with its central fountain. A broad staircase leads up to the gallery roofed by a frescoed ceiling.

Today the building houses the Palacio de Congresos y Exposiciones. At the entrance is an information office, and in a corner of the patio there is a stone-vaulted café.

Nearby, on Avenida de la Constitución, is Úbeda's bull-ring, open during the *fiesta*.

VISITORS' CHECKLIST

Jaén. **Road map** E2. 🚏 35,000. 🚉 to Linares-Baeza (953 62 00 62 & 902 24 02 02). 🚌 Calle San José 6 (953 75 51 88). 🛈 Palacio Marques de Contadero, Calle Baja del Marques 4 (953 75 55 21). 🗓 Fri. 🎭 Semana Santa (Easter). **www.**ubedainteresa.com

Distinctive steeple above the Hospital de Santiago

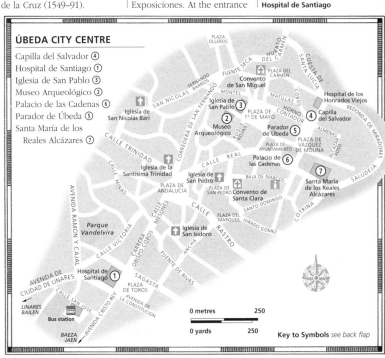

ÚBEDA CITY CENTRE

Capilla del Salvador ④
Hospital de Santiago ①
Iglesia de San Pablo ③
Museo Arqueológico ②
Palacio de las Cadenas ⑥
Parador de Úbeda ⑤
Santa María de los
    Reales Alcázares ⑦

0 metres   250
0 yards   250

Key to Symbols *see back flap*

Ruins of La Iruela, spectacularly situated above the road outside Cazorla

Cazorla ②

Jaén. **Road map** E2. 👥 8,500.
🚌 ℹ️ *Paseo del Santo Cristo 17
(953 71 01 02).* 🛒 *Mon & Sat.*

Cazorla was wealthy in ancient times when the Romans mined the surrounding mountains for silver. Today it is better known as the jumping-off point for those who wish to visit the Parque Natural de Cazorla, Segura y Las Villas.

Modern buildings have proliferated, but it is pleasant to stroll along the crooked streets between the Plaza de la Corredera and the charming Plaza Santa María. The ruined Iglesia de Santa María forms a picturesque backdrop to this popular meeting place. Above stands the **Castillo de la Yedra** which houses a folklore museum.

On the road leading to the park are the remains of **La Iruela**, a much-photographed fortress atop a rocky spur. On 14 May the locals pay

homage to a former resident of Cazorla, San Isicio, one of seven apostles who preached Christianity in Spain before the arrival of the Moors.

🏛 **Castillo de la Yedra**
Folklore Museum: **Tel** *953 71 16 38.*
⏰ *2:30–8:30pm Tue, 9am–8:30pm
Wed–Sat, 9am–2:30pm Sun & hols.*

Parque Natural de Cazorla, Segura y Las Villas ②

Jaén. **Road map** E2.
🚌 *Cazorla.* ℹ️ *Paseo del Santo
Cristo 17, Cazorla (953 72 01 02).*

First-time visitors are amazed by the spectacular scenery of this 214,336-ha (529,409-acre) nature reserve with its thick woodland, tumbling streams and abundant wildlife. Bristling mountains rise over 2,000 m (6,500 ft) above the source of the Guadalquivir River.

The river flows north through a delightful valley before reaching the Tranco de Beas dam, where it turns to run down towards the Atlantic.

Cars are allowed only on the main road. Many visitors explore on foot, but horses and bikes can be hired from the **Centro de Recepción e Interpretación de la Naturaleza**, in the reserve. It provides a lot of useful information. There are also opportunities for hunting and angling.

🏛 **Centro de Recepción
e Interpretación de la
Naturaleza**
Carretera del Tranco km 49, Torre del
Vinagre. **Tel** *953 71 30 40.* ⏰ *daily.*

Segura de la Sierra ②

Jaén. **Road map** E1. 👥 2,200.
🚌 ℹ️ *Ayuntamiento, Calle Regidor
Juan de Isla 1 (953 48 02 80).*

This tiny village at 1,200 m (4,000 ft) above sea level is dominated by its restored Moorish **castillo** (ask for keys in the village). From the ramparts there are splendid views of the harsh mountain ranges. Below is an unusual bullring, partly chipped out of rock. It sees most action at the *fiesta* in the first week of October.

Olive oil in the Segura de la Sierra area is one of four which bear Spain's prestigious *Denominación de Origen Controlada* label (see p148).

Moorish castillo at Segura de la Sierra, surrounded by olive groves

For hotels and restaurants in this region see pp215–16 and pp231–2

Wildlife in Cazorla, Segura and Las Villas

The nature reserve of Sierra de Cazorla, Segura and Las Villas protects a profusion of wildlife. Most is native to the region, but some species have been introduced or reintroduced for hunting. More than 100 species of birds live in

**Mouflon
(Ovis musimon)**

Cazorla, some very rare. It is the only habitat in Spain, apart from the Pyrenees, where the lammergeier can be seen. The extensive forests are home to a range of plant life, such as the indigenous *Viola cazorlensis (see p21)*, which grows among rocks.

The golden eagle (Aquila chrysaetus), *king of the air, preys on small mammals living in the reserve.*

Griffon vultures (Gyps fulvus) *circle high above the reserve, descending rapidly when they catch sight of their prey.*

The lammergeier (Gypaetus barbatus) *drops bones from a height on to rocks to smash them and eat the marrow.*

LANDSCAPE

The area's craggy limestone heights and riverside meadows are part of its attraction. Water trickles down the mountains, filling the lakes and brooks of the valley. This lush landscape provides ideal habitats for a diversity of wildlife.

Red deer (Cervus elaphus), *reintroduced to the area in 1952, are most commonly seen in the autumn months.*

The Spanish ibex (Capra pyrenaica) *is amazingly sure-footed on the rocky terrain. Today, the few that remain only emerge at dusk in order to feed.*

Otters (Lutra lutra) *live around lakes and streams and are active at dawn and dusk.*

Wild boar (Sus scrofa) *hide in woodland by day and forage at night for anything from acorns to roots, eggs of ground-nesting birds and small mammals.*

CADIZ AND MALAGA

Andalusia's southern provinces offer striking contrasts. Behind Málaga's suburbs are forested mountains with awesome natural wonders, such as the Garganta del Chorro. Behind the tourist resorts of the Costa del Sol is the Serranía de Ronda, habitat of elusive wildlife. Here, white Moorish towns command strategic hilltop locations. East of Gibraltar are the sherry towns of Cádiz province and the raw coastal strands of the Costa de la Luz.

In Málaga province the mountains fall steeply to the Mediterranean. The ancient port of Málaga town was a wintering place for English travellers in the 19th century; then in the 1960s, the narrow strip of coast to its east and west was claimed by the nascent tourist industry as the "Costa del Sol". A rash of high-rise development around the beaches of grey sand at its eastern end soon made the name "Torremolinos" synonymous with the excesses of cheap package holidays for the mass market. Meanwhile, at Marbella, further southwest, an exclusive playground for international film stars and Arab royalty was taking shape. Gibraltar, a geographical and a historical oddity, is a decisive full stop at the end of the Costa del Sol.

The mountains of North Africa loom across the Strait of Gibraltar, and the spirit of the Moors can be felt very clearly in Tarifa and Cádiz – author Laurie Lee's city "sparkling with African light".

Between these two towns is the Cádiz section of the Costa de la Luz ("Coast of Light") *(see p32)* which continues up north along the shores of Huelva province. Little developed, it is characterized by long stretches of windswept sand, popular with locals.

North of Cádiz is sherry country, with its hills and large vineyards. To taste sherry visit Jerez de la Frontera – a link in a chain of towns on the frontier of the Christian war to reconquer Andalusia from its Muslim rulers.

Ronda with its 18th-century bridge spanning the Guadalevín river

◁ **Beach life at Nerja, east of Málaga, one of the Costa del Sol's busy resorts**

Exploring Cádiz and Málaga

With a network of excellent roads across the region, the mountains of Málaga province's interior are easily accessible to holiday-makers who are staying on the Costa del Sol. Day trips can be made from either Marbella or Torremolinos to the glorious Montes de Málaga and Grazalema nature reserves or to the Serranía de Ronda, with lunch stops at classic *pueblos blancos*. In the heart of this characteristic Andalusian landscape lies the captivating town of Ronda, ensouled by clear, stark light and the lingering aura of Moorish times.

Further west, on the Atlantic coast beyond Tarifa where mass-market developers fear to tread, the same spirit lingers. The once great city of Cádiz and the small ports of El Puerto de Santa María, Chipiona and Sanlúcar de Barrameda all make excellent bases for exploring sherry country.

Outside dining at a restaurant close to the cathedral in Málaga

KEY

═══	Motorway
──	Major road
──	Minor road
──	Scenic route
──	Main railway
──	Minor railway
═══	International border
──	Provincial border
△	Summit

SIGHTS AT A GLANCE

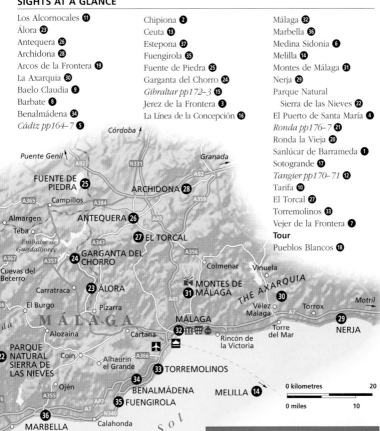

GETTING AROUND

Málaga's international airport *(see p264)* is the busiest airport in Andalusia. From here, the fast, new N340 dual carriageway traces the coastline as far as Algeciras, but bypasses Torremolinos, Fuengirola and Marbella. After Algeciras, the road narrows and continues to Cádiz. The highway A376 from San Pedro de Alcántara northwards to Ronda is a sensationally beautiful route. The A382 and A385 cut across the north from Jerez towards Antequera. The route then continues as a dual carriageway, known as the A92, to Granada. A railway running along the Costa del Sol links Málaga, Torremolinos and Fuengirola. Another heads north from Málaga, stopping at Álora, El Chorro and Fuente de Piedra. Although you will find it possible to explore remote corners of Cádiz and Málaga provinces using the complex bus network, it requires some patience.

The beach of Nerja, situated at the foot of Sierra de Almijara on the Costa del Sol

Entrance to the Barbadillo *bodega* in Sanlúcar de Barrameda

Sanlúcar de Barrameda ❶

Cádiz. **Road map** B3. 🏛 *62,000.*
🚌 🛈 *Calzada del Ejército s/n
(956 36 61 10).* 🛒 *Wed.*

A fishing port at the mouth of the Guadalquivir river, Sanlúcar is overlooked by the Moorish **Castillo de Santiago**. The Parque Nacional de Doñana (*see pp130–31*), over the river, can be reached by boat from the riverside quay. From here Columbus set off on his third trip to the Americas, in 1498, and in 1519 Ferdinand Magellan left the port intending to circumnavigate the globe.

However, Sanlúcar is now best known for its *manzanilla* (*see p30*), a light, dry sherry from, among other producers, **Bodegas Barbadillo**.

Tourists and wine enthusiasts alike can watch the sun set over the river, sip a *copita* (little glass) of *manzanilla* and enjoy the local shellfish, *langostinos*.

Sights in the town include the **Iglesia de Nuestra Señora de la O** (*see p24*), which has superb Mudéjar portals.

🍷 **Bodegas Barbadillo**
C/Luis de Eguilaz 11. **Tel** *956 38 55 00.* 📷 *11am Tue–Sat.* 🎫 🕭

Chipiona ❷

Cádiz. **Road map** B3. 🏛 *17,000.*
🚌 🛈 *Calle Del Castillo 5 (956 92 90 65).* 🛒 *Mon.* **www**.chipiona.org

A lively little resort town, Chipiona is approached through sherry vineyards. It has a great beach and a holiday atmosphere in the summer.

Days on the beach are followed by a *paseo* along the quay or the main street of the Moorish old town, where many cafés and ice-cream parlours (*heladerías*) stay open well past midnight. There are also street entertainers and horse-drawn carriages. The **Iglesia de Nuestra Señora de Regla**, the main church, has a natural spring feeding a fountain, and an adjoining cloister decorated with 17th-century *azulejos*.

Jerez de la Frontera ❸

Cádiz. **Road map** B3. 🏛 *186,000.*
🚆 🚌 🚌 🛈 *Alameda Cristina 7 (956 34 17 11).* 🛒 *Mon.*

Jerez, the capital of sherry production, is surrounded by chalky countryside blanketed with long rows of vines. British merchants have been involved for centuries in producing and shipping sherry, and have created Anglo-Andaluz dynasties like Sandeman and John Harvey – names which can be seen emblazoned over the *bodega* entrances. A tour of a *bodega*, through cellars piled high with *soleras* (*see p31*), will enable visitors to learn how to distinguish a *fino* from an *amontillado* and an *oloroso* sherry (*see p30*).

Jerez has a second claim to world fame, the **Real Escuela Andaluza de Arte Ecuestre** – the school of equestrian art. On selected days, in a display of exquisite dressage, the horses dance to music amid colourful pageantry. Visitors can arrange to watch horses being trained.

Nearby is **La Atalaya Theme Centre**, which includes two museums: the magical **Palacio del Tiempo**, home to the most impressive clocks in Europe, and **El Misterio de Jerez**, which pays tribute to the history of sherry in the area.

The old city walls flank the Barrio de Santiago. On Plaza de San Juan is the 18th-century **Palacio de Pemartín**, the home of the **Centro Andaluz de Flamenco**, which, through exhibitions and audiovisual shows, offers an insight to this music and dance tradition (*see pp28–9*). The 16th-century Gothic **Iglesia de San Mateo** is just one of several interesting churches nearby.

The partially restored, 11th-century **Alcázar** includes a well-preserved mosque, now a church. Just to the north of the Alcázar is the **Catedral del Salvador**, whose most interesting sight, *The Sleeping Girl* by Zurbarán, is in the sacristy.

🏛 **Real Escuela Andaluza de Arte Ecuestre**
Avenida Duque de Abrantes s/n.
Tel *956 31 96 35 (information, press 2 for English). Call to arrange visit.* 🎫 🕭 **www**.realescuela.org

🏰 **Alcázar**
Alameda Vieja s/n. **Tel** *956 14 99 55.*
🕐 *daily.* 🔴 *25 Dec, 1 & 6 Jan* 🎫 🕭

🏛 **La Atalaya Theme Centre**
Calle Cervantes 3. **Tel** *902 18 21 00.* 🕐 *Tue–Sun.* 🎫 🕭 🕭

🏛 **Palacio de Pemartín**
Centro Andaluz de Flamenco, Plaza de San Juan 1. **Tel** *956 81 41 32.*
🕐 *Mon–Fri.* 🔴 *public hols.*

Antique clock in Palacio del Tiempo, Jerez de la Frontera

El Puerto de Santa María ④

Cádiz. **Road map** B3. 🏠 *76,000.*
✈ 🚌 🚆 ⓘ *Calle Luna 22 (956 54 24 13).* 🗓 *Tue.* **www.elpuertosm.es**

Sheltered from the Atlantic wind and waves of the Bay of Cádiz, El Puerto de Santa María is a tranquil town which has burgeoned as one of the main ports for the exportation of sherry in Andalusia. A number of sherry companies, such as **Terry** and **Osborne**, have *bodegas* here, which can be visited for tours and tasting.

Among the town's sites are the 13th-century **Castillo San Marcos** and a **Plaza de Toros** – one of the largest and most famous bullrings in Spain. The town's main square, the Plaza Mayor, is presided over by the 13th-century, Gothic **Iglesia Mayor Prioral**, which is worth a look for its unusual choir.

Scattered around the town are several fine old *palacios*, or stately houses, adorned with the coats of arms of wealthy families who prospered in the port during colonial times.

The waterfront is lined with quite a few first-rate seafood restaurants, among them La Resaca (the Hangover), where, when it is dark, gypsies perform fiery flamenco.

⚓ **Castillo San Marcos**
Plaza Alfonso X, El Sabio. **Tel** 956 85 17 51. 🕐 Oct– May: Tue, Thu, Sat; Jun–Sep: Tue–Sun. 💳

🎪 **Plaza de Toros**
Plaza Elias Ahuja s/n. **Tel** 956 54 15 78. 🕐 Tue–Sun. ♿

🍷 **Bodegas Osborne**
Calle de los Moros. **Tel** 956 86 91 00. 🕐 Mon–Fri (phone to arrange). ● public hols. ♿ 💳

🍷 **Bodegas Terry**
Calle Toneleros s/n. **Tel** 956 85 77 00. 🕐 Mon–Fri (phone to arrange). ● public hols. ♿ 💳

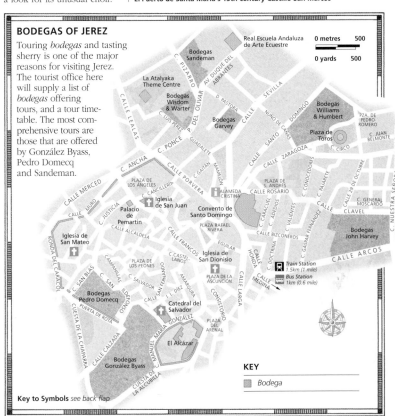

El Puerto de Santa María's 13th-century Castillo San Marcos

BODEGAS OF JEREZ

Touring *bodegas* and tasting sherry is one of the major reasons for visiting Jerez. The tourist office here will supply a list of *bodegas* offering tours, and a tour time-table. The most comprehensive tours are those that are offered by González Byass, Pedro Domecq and Sandeman.

Real Escuela Andaluza de Arte Ecuestre

Bodegas Sandeman
La Atalyaka Theme Centre
Bodegas Wisdom & Warter
Bodegas Garvey
Bodegas Williams & Humbert
Plaza de Toros
Bodegas John Harvey
Iglesia de San Juan
Palacio de Pemartin
Convento de Santo Domingo
Iglesia de San Mateo
Iglesia de San Dionisio
Bodegas Pedro Domecq
Catedral del Salvador
El Alcázar
Bodegas González Byass

🚆 Train Station 1.5km (1 mile)
🚌 Bus Station 1km (0.6 mile)

Key to Symbols see back flap

0 metres 500
0 yards 500

KEY
▢ Bodega

Cádiz 🄯

Egyptian mask, the Museo de Cádiz

Jutting out of the Bay of Cádiz, and almost entirely surrounded by water, Cádiz can lay claim to being Europe's oldest city. Legend names Hercules as its founder, although history credits the Phoenicians with establishing the town of Gadir in 1100 BC. Occupied by the Carthaginians, Romans and Moors in turn, the city also prospered after the Reconquest (see pp48–9) on wealth taken from the New World. In 1587 Sir Francis Drake raided the port in the first of many British attacks in the war for world trade. In 1812 Cádiz briefly became Spain's capital when the nation's first constitution was declared here (see p52).

Saint Bruno in Ecstasy by Zurbarán in the Museo de Cádiz

Exploring Cádiz

Writers have waxed lyrical over Cádiz for centuries: " … the most beautiful town I ever beheld … and full of the finest women in Spain," gushed Lord Byron in 1809. Modern Cádiz is a busy port, with a few ugly suburbs to get through before arriving at the historic centre. This is situated on a peninsula that juts sharply into the sea, and consists of haphazardly heaped, Moorish-style houses.

The joy of visiting Cádiz is to wander the harbour quayside, with its well-tended gardens and open squares, then plunging into the centre (see p166–7).

The old town is full of narrow, dilapidated alleys, where flowers sprout from rusting cans mounted on walls beside religious tile paintings. Markets pack into tiny squares, alive with the bartering of fish and vegetables, and street vendors selling pink boiled shrimps in newspaper.

The pride of Cádiz is Los Carnavales (see p39). Under the dictator Franco, Cádiz was the only city where the authorities failed to suppress the anarchy of carnival.

🄰 Catedral
🕐 10am–6:30pm Mon–Fri; 10am–4:30pm Sat; 1–6:30pm Sun.
Known as the Catedral Nueva (New Cathedral) because it was built over the site of an older one, this Baroque and Neo-Classical church is one of Spain's largest. Its dome of yellow tiles looks like gilt glinting in the sun. The carved

stalls inside came from a Carthusian monastery. In the crypt are the tombs of the composer Manuel de Falla (1876–1946) and writer José Maria Pemán (1897–1981), both natives of Cádiz. The cathedral's treasures are stored in a museum in Plaza Fray Félix and include jewel-studded monstrances of silver and gold and notable paintings.

CÁDIZ CATHEDRAL

🏛 Museo de Cádiz
Plaza de Mina s/n. *Tel* 956 20 33 68.
🕐 9:30am–8:30pm Tue–Sat, 9:30am–2:30pm Sun. 🔵 public hols. ♿
On the ground floor there are archaeological exhibits charting the history of Cádiz, including statues of Roman leaders, such as emperor Trajan, and Phoenician stone sarcophagi. Upstairs is one of Andalusia's largest art galleries, displaying

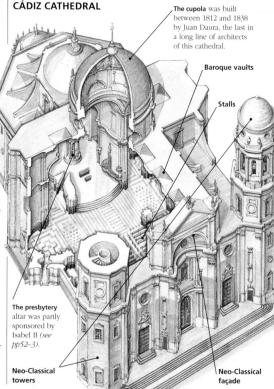

The cupola was built between 1812 and 1838 by Juan Daura, the last in a long line of architects of this cathedral.

Baroque vaults

Stalls

The presbytery altar was partly sponsored by Isabel II (see pp52–3).

Neo-Classical towers

Neo-Classical façade

works by Rubens, Murillo and Zurbarán, as well as paintings by recognized contemporary . Spanish artists. On the third floor is a collection of puppets made for village *fiestas* around Andalusia. There are also some more recent ones satirizing current political figures.

⛪ Oratorio de San Felipe Neri

Calle Santa Inés s/n. **Tel** 956 21 16 12. ⬜ 10am–1pm Mon–Sat.
On 19 March 1812 a major event took place in this 18th-century Baroque church: the proclamation of a liberal constitution for Spain (*see p52*). As Napoleon's troops besieged Cádiz during the Peninsular War (*see p50*), the members of the provisional parliament assembled in the church to draft a document that would inspire radicals throughout Europe. In its limitations of the power of the monarch and its provisions for citizens to enjoy unprecedented rights, the constitution was ahead of its time and ultimately doomed

Commemorative plaques on the Oratorio de San Felipe Neri

The Baroque Torre Tavira, the highest watchtower in Cádiz

to fail. No sooner had the French been driven out of Spain in 1814 than it was repealed by Fernando VII.

🏛 Torre Tavira

Calle Marqués del Real Tesoro 10. **Tel** 956 21 29 10. ⬜ daily. 🎫 🔲
In the mid-1700s, when much of Spain's trade with the Americas passed through the port of Cádiz, the city's merchants built themselves watchtowers from which to observe the coming and going of vessels – either for commercial interest in the cargoes or for their own amusement. More than 100 such towers remain as part of Cádiz's skyline, but only this one is open to the public.

Baroque in style, the tower rises above what was once the home of the Marqués de Ricaño (now a music academy); it stands in the

VISITORS' CHECKLIST

Cádiz. **Road map** B4.
🚉 150,000. 🚌 Plaza de Sevilla s/n (902 24 02 02). 🚌 Plaza de la Hispanidad s/n (902 19 92 08). 🛈 Plaza San Juan de Dios 11 (956 24 10 01). 🗓 Mon. 🎭 Los Carnavales (Feb), Semana Santa (Easter). **www**.cadizturismo.com

centre of the Old Town and is its highest point, reaching 45 m (150 ft) above sea level. Its penultimate floor contains the first camera obscura installed in Spain, but it is also worth visiting for the simple pleasure of the views over the rooftops and the sea from its four balconies.

Environs

At the northern lip of the Bay of Cádiz is Rota, a town best known for its Spanish-US naval base but which also claims to have the highest population of chameleons in Spain.

The southern limit of the bay is marked by the small island of Sancti Petri, believed by archaeologists to be the site of a Temple of Hercules built by the Phoenicians in the 12th century BC over the mythical burial site of the hero-turned-god.

Much of the bay lying between these two points forms the Bahía de Cádiz Nature Reserve; a shifting population of migratory wildfowl uses this area as a staging post between the Straits of Gibraltar and the Doñana National Park (*see pp130–31*).

EL VAPOR BOAT

Rather than drive up the isthmus into Cádiz, you can travel by ferry across the bay from El Puerto de Santa Maria (*see p163*). A fast catamaran provides a regular service, but a more charming way to make the trip is on board the wooden-hulled, double-decker *vaporcito* ("little steamer"), which takes 40 minutes to cross the bay. There are five sailings each way (six in summer). Take the first boat out and the last one back to fit in a full day's sightseeing. Tel: 629 46 80 14; www.vapordeelpuerto.com

El Vapor, a steamer crossing the Bay of Cádiz

A 90-Minute Walk Around Historic Cádiz

This walk begins at the Ayuntamiento (town hall) and takes in 3,000 years of Cádiz history, most of which is defined by the surrounding sea. The route starts on the eastern flank over the Bay of Cádiz. It heads into the heart of the city's warren of small alleys and squares before reaching the topiary gardens by the university. You are rarely out of sight of the sea, passing Cádiz's fish market, its most famous fish restaurant, its beach spa and the Atlantic seafront. The walk ends at the city's monumental cathedral, with its golden-coloured dome overlooking the ocean.

The Murallas de San Carlos, overlooking the Bay of Cádiz ⑤

A café-lined lane near the central Plaza San Juan de Dios

Plaza San Juan de Dios to Parque Genovés

The palm-lined Plaza San Juan offers many cafés and shops. The Neo-Classical Ayuntamiento ①, built in 1799, is chiefly the work of architect Torcuato Benjumeda. Head north from the square, taking Calle Nuevo ②, part of Cádiz's busy shopping district. Nuevo runs into Calle San Francisco up to Plaza de San Francisco ③, one of many tiny neighbourhood squares. Turn right into Isabel La Catolica, which becomes Calle Rafael de la Viesca and, via Doctor Zurita, enters the Plaza de España. The militaristic Monumento a las Cortes ④, erected in 1912, has special resonance for the people of Cádiz, and Spain itself. In 1812, Cádiz was home to a short-lived alternative parliament to Madrid, but this attempt to establish democratic rule was crushed by the monarchy. Across the plaza, turn left into Fernando El Catolico, which leads to the seafront Murallas (walls) de San Carlos ⑤, overlooking the Bay of Cádiz and the town of Puerto de Santa Maria opposite, an interesting destination in its own right. At the Murallas, follow Calle Honduras ⑥ left, hugging Cádiz's sea walls. You pass the Alameda Apodaca ⑦, one of numerous gardens boasting vast dragon trees, and the Baluarte (battlement) de la Candelaria ⑧, now a contemporary arts centre. Turn left again into Avenida Carlos III, passing the Universidad and the lovely Parque Genovés ⑨, with its avenue of symmetrical topiary trees, open-air theatre and café.

Taking a stroll in leafy Parque Genovés ⑨

TIPS FOR WALKERS

Starting point: *Plaza San Juan de Dios.*

Length: *4 km (3 miles)*

Getting there: *Plaza San Juan de Dios is next to the port and a few minutes' walk from rail and bus stations.*

Stopping-off points: *The family-owned Terraza on the Plaza de la Catedral s/n has outdoor seating with a fantastic view of the cathedral.*

Parador to Playa de la Caleta

At the end of the Parque is Cádiz's unattractive, modern parador hotel ⑩. From here, you can head into the heart of the Old Town. Turn left into Calle Benito Perez Galdos, passing Plaza de Falla and the gaudy, pink Gran Teatro Falla ⑪, both named after local composer Manuel de Falla, interred in the cathedral. The Neo-Mudéjar theatre was finished in 1919, after 30 years' construction, and is busiest during Cádiz's wild February Carnival *(see p39)*. Calle

View from one of the bell towers of the Catedral de Santa Cruz ⑱

KEY

••• Walk route

Alcala Sacramento, turn right into Plaza Topete and the city's bustling market, with stalls preparing delicious fresh seafood snacks. Cross the square to Calle Libertad and into Desamparados, then turn right into the leafy Plaza de la Cruz Verde ⑭, which, via Calle Maria Arteaga, joins Calle Rosa to reach the city's most famous beach, Playa de la Caleta, its 19th-century bathing station ⑮ (now government offices) and a nautical college. The beach overlooks the old harbour and two small forts, one of which, San Sebastián, was once the 1100 BC Phoenician settlement of Gadir and site of a temple to Kronos.

Caleta to Catedral

From Caleta, Calle de Nájera joins the Campo del Sur seafront, but it's worth turning left into Calle Venezuela into the fishermen's quarter and down to San Felix and the most famous fish restaurant in the region, El Faro (open: 1pm) ⑯. Both the restaurant and the tapas bar here live up to the local saying, "Don't leave Cádiz before eating at El Faro." Take Felix up to the seafront and turn left into Campo del Sur ⑰, where pastel-colour buildings stretch to the magnificent Catedral de Santa Cruz ⑱, begun in 1722 and finished only in 1838. Several architects contributed to its mix of Baroque, Rococo and Neo-Classical styles. The views from its bell towers repay the climb. Calle Pelota, opposite, leads back to Plaza San Juan.

Galdos changes name here to Calle Sacramento, the busiest of the shopping streets, and you pass the Oratorio de San Felipe Neri ⑫ and the unusual 18th-century Torre Tavira ⑬, named after its first keeper, Antonio Tavira. At 45 m (150 ft) above sea level, this lookout and camera obscura is the highest view-point in the city. At Calle

View of the cathedral from Torre Tavira ⑬

Carved *retablo*, Iglesia de Santa María la Coronada, Medina Sidonia

Medina Sidonia 6

Cádiz. **Road map** B4. 11,500.
Plaza Iglesia Mayor s/n (956 41 24 04). Mon.

As you drive along the N440, between Algeciras and Jerez, Medina Sidonia appears startlingly white atop a conical hill. The town was taken from the Moors in 1264 by Alfonso X, and during the 15th century the Guzmán family were established as the Dukes of Medina Sidonia to defend the territory between here and the Bay of Cádiz. After the Reconquest *(see pp48–9)*, the family grew rich from investments in the Americas, and Medina Sidonia became one of the most important ducal seats in Spain.

Many parts of the town's medieval walls still stand and cobbled alleys nestle beneath them.

The **Iglesia de Santa María la Coronada** is the town's most important building. Begun on the foundations of a castle in the 15th century, after the Reconquest, it is a fine example of Andalusian Gothic. Inside is a collection of religious works of art dating from the Renaissance, including paintings and a charming *retablo* with beautifully carved panels.

Vejer de la Frontera 7

Cádiz. **Road map** B4. 13,000.
In Ayuntamiento c/Marques de Tamarón 10 (956 45 17 36).
www.turismovejer.com

Attractively located on a hilltop above Barbate, Vejer de la Frontera was one of the first places occupied by the Muslim invaders in 711, shortly after they had defeated the Visigoths in battle close by (the exact site is not known).

The oldest part of town is enclosed by an irregular wall protected by three towers and entered by four gates. Within the walled area are the Arab castle and the parish church, the Iglesia Parroquial del Divino Salvador, which was built on the site of a mosque between the 14th and 16th centuries in a mixture of Gothic and Mudejar architecture.

Later buildings outside the walls include the Palacio del Marqués de Tamaron, a 17th- to 18th-century stately home.

The lighthouse on Cabo de Trafalgar, Costa de la Luz

Barbate 8

Cádiz. **Road map** B4. 22,000.
C/Vázquez de Mella 2 (956 43 39 62). **www**.barbate.es

The largest coastal settlement between Cádiz and Tarifa, Barbate stands at the mouth of the eponymous river, in an area of marshes and saltflats. There is not much of interest in the town itself, but two small tourist resorts attached to it are worth visiting.

A short way south down the coast is **Zahara de los Atunes**, which has grown up along one of the coast's best beaches. The epithet "of the tuna fish" is a reminder of an important industry in these waters. Barbate's culinary speciality is *mojama*, tuna that has been cured in the same way as *jamón serrano*. Inland from Zahara, around the main N340 coast road, are large swathes of wind turbines generating electricity for the national grid.

The fortified walls surrounding the Old Town of Vejer de la Frontera

WINDFARMS

North of Tarifa, the wind blows with such reliable force that it is used to drive wind turbines to generate electricity. Spain has the world's second-highest installed capacity of windpower after Germany, and the country aims to meet 20 per cent of its energy needs from renewable resources by 2020. Critics argue that windpower works only when the wind is strong enough and that the turbines are unsightly. Another objection, that the blades of the turbines are a hazard to birds, hasn't been substantiated by evidence.

The characteristic turbines of a windfarm north of Tarifa

The road north out of Barbate (past the fishing port) climbs over a headland fringed by cliffs and planted with dense pine woods to drop down to the small holiday resort of **Los Caños de Meca**, which grew up as a hippy hideaway in the 1970s and still has a carefree feel to it.

On a short sand spit nearby stands a light-house marking the **Cabo de Trafalgar** (Cape Trafalgar), which gave its name to the naval battle fought on 21 October 1805. Early in the morning of that day, Britain's Admiral Nelson decided to take on the combined fleet of Spanish and French ships that had left Cádiz two days earlier. The British were outnumbered and outgunned but defeated the enemy without the loss of a single ship. Nelson, however, was struck by a musket ball late in the battle and died soon after.

A statue of Trajan at Baelo Claudia

Baelo Claudia ●

Bolonia, Cádiz. **Road map** B4.
Tel 956 10 67 96. ☐ Jun–Sep: 9am–8pm Tue–Sat, 10am–2pm Sun; Oct, Mar–May: 9am–7pm Tue–Sat, 10am–2pm Sun; Nov–Feb: 9am–6pm Tue–Sat, 10am–2pm Sun. 🖼 (free to EU citizens). **www**.juntadeandalucia.es/cultura/museos

The Roman settlement of Baelo Claudia was established on the seashore in the 2nd

century BC and gradually grew in importance through trade with North Africa and its fish salting and pickling works.

Emperor Claudius (41–54 AD) elevated Baelo Claudia to the status of municipality, but its prestige was short-lived, since it was effectively destroyed by an earthquake in the 2nd century and finally abandoned in the 6th century. The ruins, which include a theatre, a necropolis and several erect columns, are in a picturesque spot next to a beautiful beach beside the small settlement of Bolonia.

Tarifa ⑩

Cádiz. **Road map** B4. 🏛 16,000. 🖼
🛈 Paseo de la Alameda s/n (956 68 09 93). 🖼 Tue. **www**.tarifaweb.com

Tarifa, Europe's windsurfing capital (see p32) takes its name from Tarif ben Maluk, an 8th-century Moorish commander.

The 10th-century **Castillo de Guzmán el Bueno** is the site of a legend. In 1292, Guzmán, who was defending Tarifa from the Moors, was told his hostage son would die if he did not surrender. Rather than give in, Guzmán threw down his dagger for the captors to use.

♠ Castillo de Guzmán el Bueno
Calle Guzmán el Bueno.
Tel 956 68 09 93. ☐ Tue–Sun. 🖼

Parque Natural de Los Alcornocales ⑪

Cádiz and Málaga. **Road map** B4.
🛈 Plaza San Jorge 1, Alcalá de los Gazules (956 41 33 07).
www.alcornocales.org

This nature reserve is named after the alcornocales, cork oak trees that are prevalent in many parts of it. They are easily identified because they have been stripped of their lower bark, leaving the vivid red heartwood showing.

Cork trees in the Parque Natural de Los Alcornocales

The far south of the natural park is crossed by deep valleys called canutos, in which rare vestiges of Europe's ancient fern-rich forests cling on.

Apart from its wildlife, the area has a few towns worth visiting, including Jimena de la Frontera, Castellar de la Frontera and Medina Sidonia (see p168), and several caves holding prehistoric paintings.

Tangier

Tangier is only 45 minutes by fast ferry from Tarifa, making it a perfect day trip. Despite its proximity, this ancient port, founded by the Berbers before 1000 BC, will be a sharp culture shock for those used to life in Europe. Tangier is vibrant with eastern colour, and the vast, labyrinthine Medina, the market quarter, pulsates with noise. From their workshops in back alleys, craftsmen make traditional goods for busy shops and stalls in the crowded streets. Yet behind wrought-iron railings the traveller will see tranquil courts decorated with mosaics, cool fountains and mosques.

Water seller, Grand Socco

View into the labyrinthine Medina from the Grand Socco

SIGHTS AT A GLANCE

American Legation ⑦
Dar El Makhzen ①
Grand Mosque ④
Grand Socco ⑥
Hôtel Continental ③
Kasbah ②
Rue es Siaghin ⑤

Key to Symbols *see back flap*

0 metres 100
0 yards 100

🏛 Dar El Makhzen

Place de la Kasbah. **Tel** 212 39 93 20 97. ◯ *Wed–Mon.* 🎞
Sultan Moulay Ismail, who unified Morocco in the 17th century, had this palace built within the Kasbah. The sultans lived here until 1912. It is now a museum of crafts such as ceramics, embroidery and ironwork. The exhibits are arranged round a central courtyard and in cool rooms with tiled ceilings. There are illuminated Korans in the Fez Room and a courtyard in the style of Andalusian Moorish gardens.

🏯 Kasbah

The Kasbah or citadel, where the sultans once held court, is at the Medina's highest point. It is separated from its alleys by sturdy walls and four massive stone gateways. From the battlements there are views over the Strait of Gibraltar.

The Kasbah encloses the Dar El Makhzen, the treasury house, the old prison and the law courts. Villas once owned by American and European celebrities, such as Paul Bowles, the author of *The Sheltering Sky,* are also within the Kasbah walls.

Façade of the Dar El Makhzen, the museum of Moroccan arts

☪ Grand Mosque

Green and white minarets rise above this massive edifice built in the 17th century by Sultan Moulay Ismail. An exquisitely carved gateway suggests more treasures within – non-Muslims, however, are forbidden from entering any mosque.

🏯 Grand Socco

Traders from the Rif mountains come to barter their goods at this busy main square at the heart of Tangier. The square's official name, Place du 9 Avril 1947, commemorates a visit by Sultan Muhammad V.

For hotels and restaurants in this region see pp216–18 and pp233–6

⚏ Rue es Siaghin

The Medina's 'Silversmith's Street' was Tangier's main thoroughfare in the 1930s and still offers a staggering array of merchandise; shop owners along the street will offer you mint tea in a bid to get you to buy.

Ceuta ⑬

Road map C4. 76,000. from Algeciras. Calle Edrissis, Baluarte de los Mallorquines (856 20 05 60). **www.ceuta.es**

The closest of Spain's two North African enclaves to Europe is worth visiting if you want to dip your toe into North Africa without leaving Spain (although you will need to show an identity card or passport on entering), or if are on your way to Morocco. Ceuta is only 12 miles from mainland Spain.

Ceuta is dominated by a hill called Monte Hacho, on which there is a fort occupied by the Spanish army. The city has Phoenician and Arab remains, churches dating from the 17th to the 19th centuries and several museums, including the **Museo de la Legion**, dedicated to the Spanish Foreign Legion.

Ceuta's shops offer the chance to indulge in some tax-free shopping. Both Ceuta and Melilla are surrounded by high fences, as they are European entry points for illegal immigrants from parts of Africa.

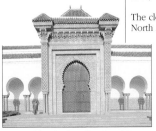

The carved façade of Tangier's Grand Mosque

⚏ American Legation

Rue du Portugal. **Tel** 212 39 93 53 17. Mon, Wed & Thu or by appt. This former palace was the United States' first diplomatic mission and remained the American Embassy until 1961. It is now an art museum and holds regular exhibitions.

⚏ Hôtel Continental

Rue Dar El Baroud. **Tel** 212 39 93 10 24. daily. Numerous intrigues have been played out in this hotel overlooking the port. Today it is a fine place to sit and drink tea.

European architectural influence in the North African enclave of Ceuta

🏛 Museo de la Legión

Paseo de Colon. **Tel** 699 97 61 51. 10am–1:30pm, 4–6pm Mon–Sat.

Melilla ⑭

Road map E5. 69,000. from Málaga or Almería. See p265 for travel info Palacio de Exposiciones y Congresos, Calle Fortuny 3 (952 67 54 44). **www.melillaturismo.com**

Spain's second North African enclave, settled by Spain in 1497, is located 150 km (90 miles) due south of Adra (in Almería), across the sea, on the Moroccan coast. It takes a little effort to get there, as Melilla is a six hour ferry ride from mainland Spain, but it is worth it as there is plenty to see, including the only Gothic architecture in Africa and Modernisme, the Catalan version of Art Nouveau architecture. Modern-day Melilla prides itself on being a place of peaceful co-existence between its main four component cultures: Christian, Muslim, Jewish and Hindu. All the principal sights are located in **Melilla La Vieja** (Old Melilla), a cluster of four fortified areas separated by moats or walls, built in the 14th century on a hammerhead promontory jutting out into the sea.

The 19th- and 20th-century parts of the city, however, are equally worth strolling around in, since they include an abundance of splendid Art Nouveau and Art Deco buildings. There are around 900 period edifices in Melilla. There's also a small beach.

THE INTERNATIONAL ERA

From 1932 until its incorporation into Morocco in 1956, Tangier was an international zone, tax free and under the control of a committee of 30 nations. This was an era that was characterized by financial fraud, espionage, large-scale smuggling, outrageous sexual licence and profligacy by wealthy tax exiles, such as heiress Barbara Hutton. Celebrities such as Henri Matisse, Jack Kerouac and Orson Welles added colour to the scene.

Orson Welles, once a familiar sight on the streets of Tangier

Gibraltar ⑮

Native Gibraltarians are descendents of British, Genoese Jews, Portuguese and Spanish who remained after the Great Siege *(see p52)*. Britain seized Gibraltar during the War of the Spanish Succession in 1704, and was granted it "in perpetuity" by the Treaty of Utrecht *(see p52)* nine years later. As the gateway to the Mediterranean, the Rock was essential to Britain in colonial times. Tensions over Gibraltar have eased in recent years, with more co-operation between Spain and Britain expected in the future. Each year, around 4 million people stream across the frontier at La Línea to visit this speck of England bolted on to Andalusia. Pubs, fish and chips, pounds sterling and bobbies on the beat all contrast with Spain.

Gibraltarian barbary ape

The Keep
The lower part of this Moorish castle, built in the 8th century, is still used to house Gibraltar's prison population.

Siege Tunnels
Soldiers' barracks and storerooms fill 50 km (31 miles) of tunnels.

Spanish border and customs

Cable Car
A cable car runs from the centre of the town to the Top of the Rock, Gibraltar's summit, which, at 450 m (1,475 ft) high, is often shrouded in mist.

The airport runway crosses over the main road from La Línea to Gibraltar.

173

St Michael's Cave
During World War II these caves served as a bomb-proof military hospital. These days classical concerts are performed here.

The Apes' Den is home to Gibraltar's tailless apes; legend has it that the British will keep the Rock only as long as the apes remain.

Europa Point, on the southernmost tip, looks across the Strait of Gibraltar to North Africa.

The 100-Ton Gun was put here in 1884; it took two hours to load and it could fire shells weighing 910 kg (2,000 lb).

Cable car station

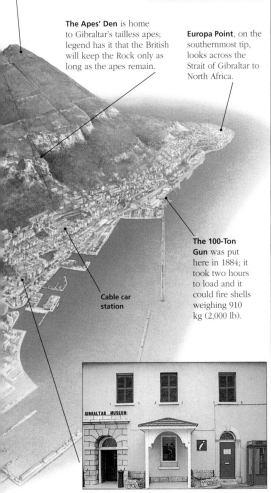

Gibraltar Museum
This museum, built on the foundations of Moorish baths, houses an exhibition of Gibraltar's history under British rule.

La Línea de la Concepción, with Gibraltar in the distance

La Línea de la Concepción 16

Cádiz. **Road map** C4. 60,000.
Avenida de 20 Abril s/n (956 76 99 50). Wed. **www**.lalinea.ws

La Línea is a town on the Spanish side of the border with Gibraltar. Its name, "The Line", refers to the old walls that once formed the frontier, but which were demolished during the Napoleonic wars to prevent the French using them for defence. Now it is a lively trading town, with several hotels patronized by people who want to avoid the higher prices of Gibraltar hotels.

The elegant marina at Sotogrande

Sotogrande 17

Cádiz. **Road map** C4. 2,000.
San Roque. C/San Felipe s/n
(956 69 40 05). Sun.

Just above Gibraltar, on the Costa del Sol, Sotogrande is an exclusive residential seaside town where wealthy Gibraltarians, who commute daily to the Rock, reside in exclusive villas. The marina is filled with expensive yachts and lined with excellent seafood restaurants.
Nearby there are several immaculately manicured golf courses *(see p32)*.

A Tour Around the Pueblos Blancos ⑱

Instead of settling on Andalusia's plains, where they would have fallen prey to bandits, some Andalusians chose to live in fortified hilltop towns and villages. The way of life in these *pueblos blancos* – so called because they are whitewashed in the Moorish tradition – has barely changed for centuries. Touring the *pueblos blancos*, which crown the mountains rising sharply from the coast, will show visitors a world full of references to the past. Yet today they are working agricultural towns, not just tourist sights.

Zahara de la Sierra ③ This fine *pueblo blanco*, a tightly huddled hillside village below a castle ruin, has been declared a national monument.

Ubrique ② This town, nestling at the foot of the Sierra de Ubrique, has become a flourishing producer of leather goods.

Grazalema ④ At the heart of the Parque Natural de la Sierra de Grazalema, this village has the highest rainfall in Spain. Lush vegetation fills the park.

Arcos de la Frontera ① This strategically positioned town has been fortified for centuries. From the commanding heights of this stronghold, there are views over the Guadalete valley.

Jimena de la Frontera ⑧ An expanse of cork and olive trees blankets the hills leading up to this village. A ruined Moorish castle, which is open to visitors, overlooks the surroundings where wild bulls graze peacefully.

SEVILLA

CADIZ, JEREZ

El Bosque

A372

Benamahoma

Embalse de Zah

CA5013

A3

④

③

A373

Benaocaz

A374

Embalse de los Hurones

Charco de los Hurones

CA5221

PARQUE NAT SIERRA DE GRAZALEM

SIERRA DE UBRIQUE

②

Cortes de la Frontera

A373

CA503

A375

Río Hozgarganta

PARQUE NATURAL DE LOS ALCORNOCALES- SIERRA DEL ALJIBE

Río Guadiaro

La Sauceda

CA3331

A369

Gaucín ⑦ From here there are unsurpassed vistas over the Mediterranean, the Atlantic, the great hump of Gibraltar and across the strait to the Rif mountains of North Africa.

⑧

0 kilometres | 10
0 miles | 5

Setenil ⑤
The streets of this white town are formed from the ledge of a gorge, carved from tufa rock by the river Trejo.

Ronda ⑥
With the Tajo gorge as an efficient moat, Ronda was one of the last towns recaptured from the Moors. It later became the cradle of modern bullfighting (see pp176–7).

KEY

▬▬ Tour route

═══ Other roads

TIPS FOR DRIVERS

Tour length: 205 km (135 miles).
Stopping-off points: Ronda has a wide range of hotels (see p218) and restaurants (see p235). Arcos de la Frontera has a parador (see p216), other hotels and some restaurants. Gaucín, Jimena de la Frontera and Zahara de la Sierra also have places to stay and eat. Grazalema has a resort for families and Setenil a couple of bars and a hotel. Ubrique has a hotel.

Arcos de la Frontera ⑲

Cádiz. **Road map** B3. 🏠 *30,000.*
🚌 ℹ *Plaza del Cabildo s/n (956 70 22 64).* 🛒 *Fri.*
www.ayuntamientoarcos.org

Arcos has been inhabited since prehistoric times. Its strategic position encouraged settlement, first as the Roman town of Arcobriga, and later as the stronghold of Medina Arkosh under the Caliphate of Córdoba (see p46). It was captured by Alfonso X's (see p48) Christian forces in 1264.

An archetypal white town, it has a labyrinthine Moorish quarter that twists up to its ruined castle. At its centre is the Plaza de España, one side of which gives views across sunbaked plains. Fronting the square are the superb **Parador de Arcos de la Frontera** (see p216) and the **Iglesia de Santa María de la Asunción**, a late Gothic-Mudéjar building worth seeing for its extravagant choir stalls and altarpiece. A small museum displays the church treasures. More striking is the massive, Gothic **Parroquia de San Pedro**. Its thick-set tower provides a view over the sheer drop down to the Guadalete river. Nearby is the **Palacio del Mayorazgo** with an ornate, Renaissance façade. The **Ayuntamiento** is also worth seeing, particularly to view its beautiful Mudéjar ceiling.

🏛 **Palacio del Mayorazgo**
Calle San Pedro 2.
Tel 956 70 30 13 (Casa de Cultura). 🕐 *daily.* ♿
🏛 **Ayuntamiento**
Plaza del Cabildo 1.
Tel 956 70 00 02.
🕐 *Mon–Fri.* 🔴 *public hols.*

Roman theatre set amid the ruins of Acinipo (Ronda la Vieja)

Ronda la Vieja ⑳

Málaga. **Road map** C3. 🚌 🚌
Ronda. Tel 952 21 36 40 & 630 42 99 49. ℹ *Plaza España 9 (952 87 12 72).* 🕐 *9am–3:30pm Wed–Sat, 10am–3pm Sun.* **Cuevas de la Pileta** *by guided tour (twice daily).*
www.turismoderonda.es

Ronda la Vieja is the modern name for the remains of the Roman city of Acinipo, 12 km (7 miles) northwest of Ronda (see pp176–7). An important town in the 1st century AD, it later declined, unlike the growing town of Ronda, which was called Arunda by the Romans.

The ruins are beautifully sited on a hillside where only a fraction of the town has been excavated. The town's most important sight is the theatre, but lines of stones also mark foundations of houses, and of the forum and other public buildings.

Along the C339, 22 km (12 miles) from Ronda la Vieja, are the Cuevas de la Pileta, the site of prehistoric cave paintings dating from about 25,000 BC (see p43).

The Gothic-Mudéjar Iglesia de Santa María de la Asunción

Street-by-Street: Ronda ⑳

Plate handpainted in Ronda

One of the most spectacularly located cities in Spain, Ronda sits on a massive rocky outcrop, straddling a precipitous limestone cleft. Because of its impregnable position this town was one of the last Moorish bastions, finally falling to the Christians in 1485. On the south side perches a classic Moorish *pueblo blanco* (see p174) of cobbled alleys, window grilles and dazzling whitewash – most historic sights are in this old town. Across the gorge in El Mercadillo, the newer town, is one of Spain's oldest bullrings.

★ Puente Nuevo
Building the "New Bridge" over the nearly 100 m (330 ft) deep Tajo gorge was a feat of civil engineering in the late 18th century.

Convento de Santo Domingo was the local headquarters of the Inquisition.

To El Mercadillo, Plaza de Toros and Parador de Ronda (see p218)

Casa del Rey Moro
From this 18th-century mansion, built on the foundations of a Moorish palace, 365 steps lead down to the river.

Mirador El Campillo

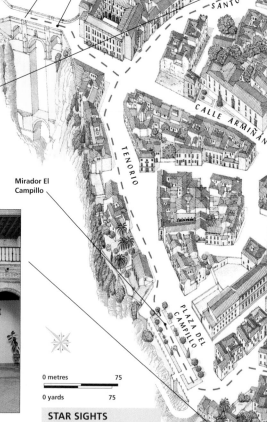

SANTO DOMINGO

CALLE ARMIÑÁN

TENORIO

PLAZA DEL CAMPILLO

0 metres 75
0 yards 75

★ Palacio Mondragón
Much of this palace was rebuilt after the Reconquest (see pp48–9), but its arcaded patio is adorned with original Moorish mosaics and plasterwork.

STAR SIGHTS

★ Palacio Mondragón

★ Puente Nuevo

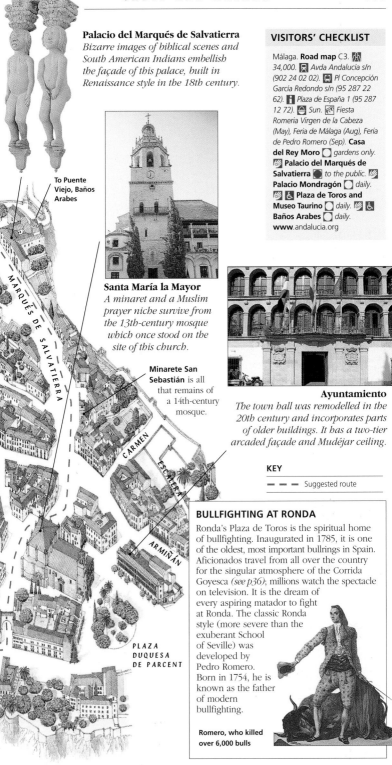

Palacio del Marqués de Salvatierra

Bizarre images of biblical scenes and South American Indians embellish the façade of this palace, built in Renaissance style in the 18th century.

To Puente Viejo, Baños Arabes

Santa María la Mayor

A minaret and a Muslim prayer niche survive from the 13th-century mosque which once stood on the site of this church.

Minarete San Sebastián is all that remains of a 14th-century mosque.

MARQUÉS DE SALVATIERRA

CARMEN

ESCALERA

ARMIÑÁN

PLAZA DUQUESA DE PARCENT

VISITORS' CHECKLIST

Málaga. **Road map** C3. 34,000. Avda Andalucía s/n (902 24 02 02). Pl Concepción García Redondo s/n (95 287 22 62). Plaza de España 1 (95 287 12 72). Sun. *Fiesta Romería Virgen de la Cabeza* (May), *Feria de Málaga* (Aug), *Feria de Pedro Romero* (Sep). **Casa del Rey Moro** gardens only. **Palacio del Marqués de Salvatierra** to the public. **Palacio Mondragón** daily. **Plaza de Toros and Museo Taurino** daily. **Baños Arabes** daily. www.andalucia.org

Ayuntamiento

The town hall was remodelled in the 20th century and incorporates parts of older buildings. It has a two-tier arcaded façade and Mudéjar ceiling.

KEY

– – – Suggested route

BULLFIGHTING AT RONDA

Ronda's Plaza de Toros is the spiritual home of bullfighting. Inaugurated in 1785, it is one of the oldest, most important bullrings in Spain. Aficionados travel from all over the country for the singular atmosphere of the Corrida Goyesca *(see p36)*; millions watch the spectacle on television. It is the dream of every aspiring matador to fight at Ronda. The classic Ronda style (more severe than the exuberant School of Seville) was developed by Pedro Romero. Born in 1754, he is known as the father of modern bullfighting.

Romero, who killed over 6,000 bulls

Parque Natural Sierra de las Nieves ㉒

Road map C3. Palacio de Mondragón, Plaza de Mondragón, Ronda (95 287 11 71).

One of Andalusia's least accessible areas, this UNESCO biosphere reserve southeast of Ronda extends between Parauta (to the east), Tolox (west), El Burgo (north) and Istán (south). Interestingly, it features both extreme highs and lows, reaching up to the peak of Torrecilla (1,919 m/6,295 ft) and down to one of the world's deepest potholes, GESM, which is 1,100 m (3,608 ft) deep. The sierra is popular for caving and rock climbing, and it also has some moderate to difficult signposted walking trails.

A short way south, near Ojén, is the beauty spot of Refugio de Juanar, which offers gentle walks through mixed woodland to a viewpoint overlooking the coast.

Olive groves between the villages of Álora and Antequera

Álora ㉓

Málaga. **Road map** C3. 13,000. Plaza Baja de la Despedía (95 249 55 77). Mon. **www**.alora.es

Situated in the Guadalhorce River valley, Álora is an important agricultural centre. It is a classic white town (*pueblo blanco, see pp174–5*),

perched on a hillside overlooking an expanse of wheat fields, citrus orchards and olive groves.

The town's cobbled streets radiate from the 18th-century **Iglesia de la Encarnación**. At the weekly market, stalls of farm produce and clothing fill nearby streets. On the higher of Álora's twin hills stands the **Castillo**, with a cemetery of niche tombs set in neat blocks.

🏰 **Castillo Árabe**
Calle Ancha. **Tel** 95 249 83 80 (tourist office). ☐ daily.

Garganta del Chorro ㉔

Málaga. **Road map** C3. El Chorro. Parque Ardales. Avenida Constitución s/n (95 249 55 77).

Up the fertile Guadalhorce valley, 12 km (7 miles) on from Álora, is one of the geographical wonders of Spain. The Garganta del Chorro is an immense gaping chasm 180 m (590 ft) high, slashing through a limestone mountain. In some places, where the Guadalhorce river hurtles through the gorge, waters foaming white, it is only 10 m (30 ft) wide. Below the gorge is a hydroelectric plant, which detracts slightly from the wildness and impressive beauty of the place.

The nearby village of **El Chorro** offers a wide range of outdoor activities.

Fuente de Piedra ㉕

Málaga. **Road map** C3. C/Castillo 1 (95 273 54 53).

The largest of several lakes in an expanse of wetlands north of Antequera, the Laguna de la Fuente de Piedra teems with bird life, including huge flocks of flamingos. In March, every year, up to 25,000 of them arrive to breed before migrating back to West Africa. Visitors should be aware that if there is drought

The Garganta del Chorro, rising high above the Guadalhorce river

in the region, there will be fewer birds breeding.

Apart from flamingos, you will also be able to admire cranes, herons, bee-eaters, snow-white egrets, as well as many species of ducks and geese. Their numbers have been on the increase since conservation and anti-hunting laws were introduced and the area declared a sanctuary. A road off the N334 leads to the lake side, from where visitors can watch the birds. Be advised that restraint is required: it is forbidden to join the waders in the lake. Information is available from a visitors' centre near the village of Fuente de Piedra.

Limestone formations in the Parque Natural del Torcal

The triumphal 16th-century Arco de los Gigantes, Antequera

Antequera ㉖

Málaga. **Road map** D3.
42,000. Plaza San Sebastián 7 (95 270 25 05).
www.aytoantequera.com

This busy market town has long been strategically important; first as Roman Anticaria, and later as a Moorish border fortress defending Granada.

The **Iglesia de Nuestra Señora del Carmen**, with its massive Baroque altarpiece, is not to be missed. To the west of here, at the opposite end of the town, is the 19th-century **Plaza de Toros**, with its museum of bullfighting.

High on a hill overlooking the town is the **Castillo Arabe**, a 13th-century Moorish castle. Visitors cannot go inside, but can walk round the castle walls – the approach is through the 16th-century **Arco de los Gigantes**. There are fine views from the **Torre del Papabellotas**, on the best-preserved part of the wall. In the town below, the 18th-century **Palacio de Nájera** is the setting for the Municipal Museum, whose star exhibit is a 2,000-year-old bronze statue of a Roman boy.

In the outskirts of town are three large prehistoric **dolmens** that may have been the burial chambers of tribal leaders. Two of them – Viera and Menga – stand together, the latter the oldest and most impressive of all, dated at between 4,000 and 4,500 years old. A short distance away is the Dolmen de Romeral, which has a long corridor leading to a vaulted central chamber.

Plaza de Toros
Crta de Sevilla. **Tel** 95 270 81 42.
Tue–Sun. **Museo Taurino**
Sat, Sun, public hols.

Palacio de Nájera
Coso Viejo. **Tel** 95 270 40 21.
until 2011. Dolmens 9am–6pm Tue–Sat; 9:30am–2:30pm Sun. Tue.

El Torcal ㉗

Málaga. **Road map** D3. Antequera. Antequera (95 270 25 05).

A huge exposed hump of limestone upland battered into bizarre formations by wind and rain, the **Parque Natural del Torcal** is very popular with hikers. Most follow a network of footpaths leading from a visitors' centre in the middle; short walks (up to two hours) are marked by yellow arrows; longer walks are marked in red. There are canyons, caves, mushroom-shaped rocks and other geological curiosities to see. The park also boasts fox and weasel populations, and colonies of eagles, hawks and vultures. It also protects rare plants and flowers, among them species of wild orchid.

Archidona ㉘

Málaga. **Road map** D3. 8,200. Plaza Ochavada 2 (95 271 64 79). Mon.

This small town is worth a stop to see its extraordinary **Plaza Ochavada**. This is an octagonal square built in the 18th century in a French style, but which also incorporates traditional Andalusian features.

From the **Ermita Virgen de Gracia** on a hillside above the town, there are commanding views over rolling countryside.

The 18th-century, octagonal Plaza Ochavada in Archidona

Nerja ㉙

Málaga. **Road map** D3.
🏠 18,000. 🚌 🚶 Calle Puerta
del Mar 2 (95 252 15 31). 🚢 Tue.
www.nerja.org

This fashionable resort at the eastern extremity of the Costa del Sol lies at the foot of the beautiful mountains of the Sierra de Almijara, and is perched on a cliff above a succession of sandy coves. The main area for tourist activity in the resort centres around the promenade, running along a rocky promontory known as **El Balcón de Europa** (the Balcony of Europe). Ranged along its length are cafés and restaurants with outdoor tables, and there are sweeping views up and down the coast. On the edges of town, holiday villas and apartments proliferate.

Due east of the town are the **Cuevas de Nerja**, a series of

The town of Nerja overlooking the sea from El Balcón de Europa

vast caverns of considerable archaeological interest, which were discovered in 1959. Wall paintings (see p42) found in them are believed to be about 20,000 years old. Unfortunately they are closed to public view, but a few of the many cathedral-sized chambers are open to the public. One of

these has been turned into an impressive underground auditorium large enough to hold audiences of several hundred. Concerts are held there in the summer.

⌂ Cuevas de Nerja
Carretera de las Cuevas de Nerja.
Tel 95 252 95 20. ☐ daily. 📷

Málaga ㉜

Málaga. **Road map** D3.
🏠 650,000. ✈ 🚌 🚆 🚶 Pasaje
de Chinitas 4 (95 130 89 11). 🚢
Sun. **www**.malagaturismo.com

A thriving port, Málaga is Andalusia's second largest city. Initial impressions tend to be of ugly suburbs, high-rise blocks and lines of rusting cranes, but this belies a city that is rich with history, and is filled with monuments and the vibrancy of Andalusia.

Malaca, the Phoenician (see pp42–3) city, was an important trading port on the Iberian peninsula. After Rome's victory against Carthage in 206 BC (see p44), it became a major port for Roman trade with Byzantium. Málaga's heyday came in the years after 711, when it fell to the Moors and became their main port serving Granada. It was recaptured by the Christians in 1487 after a bloody siege. The Moors who stayed behind were expelled (see pp50–51) after a rebellion.

Following a long decline, the city flourished once again

during the 19th century, when Málaga wine became one of Europe's most popular drinks. Unfortunately, phylloxera, the vine disease that ravaged the vineyards of Europe, reached Málaga, putting paid to the prosperity of its vineyards. This, however, was when tourists – the British especially – began to winter here.

The old town at the heart of Málaga radiates from the **catedral**. It was begun in 1528 by Diego de Siloé, but it is a bizarre mix of styles. Its construction was interrupted by an earth-

Façade detail, Málaga Cathedral

quake in 1680. The half-built second tower, abandoned in 1765 when funds ran out, is the reason for the cathedral's nickname: La Manquita (the one-armed one).

Málaga's former Museo de Bellas Artes has been adapted to house a **Museo de Picasso**, displaying works by the native artist (see p54). The **Casa Natal de Picasso**, where

Amphitheatre

Puerta
Principal

Entrance

Puerta de
las Columnas

Plaza de Armas

The Axarquia **⑳**

Málaga. **Road map** D3. **ℹ** *Avda de la Constitución, Cómpeta (952 55 36 85).* **www**.competa.es

The hills behind Torre del Mar and Nerja make up the pretty upland region of the Axarquia, whose main town, **Vélez-Málaga**, has a few old streets and the remains of a castle to explore.

A better base for excursions is the attractive sweet wine-producing town of **Cómpeta**, 20 km (12 miles) from the coast by winding mountain roads. From here, there is an interesting "Mudejar route" down the hill and up the valley to **Archez** and **Salares**, villages whose church towers are undisguised brick minarets dating from the 15th and 13th centuries respectively.

Two other villages worth visiting are **Frigiliana**, close to the coast and easily accessible from Nerja; and **Comares** (north east of Vélez-Málaga), perched on top of an impressive outcrop of rock from which there are superb views.

Narrow street in the Barrio de San Sebastián, Vélez Málaga

Montes de Málaga **㉑**

Málaga. **Road map** D3. **🚌** *to Colmenar.* **ℹ** *Lagar de Torrijos, on C345 at km 544,3 (95 104 51 00).*

To the north and east of Málaga are the beautiful hills of Montes de Málaga. A wide area is undergoing reforestation and forms the **Parque Natural de Montes de Málaga**. Wildlife thrives in the strongly scented undergrowth of lavender and wild herbs. Occasionally, there are glimpses of wild cats, stone martens, wild boars, eagles and other birds of prey.

Walkers can follow marked trails. A farmhouse has been restored and converted into an ethnological museum. Along the C345 road between Málaga and the park, there are sensational views down to the sea.

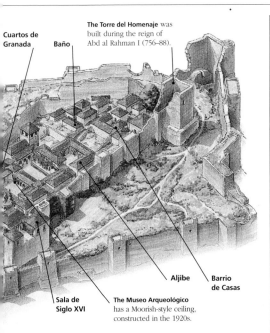

Cuartos de Granada

Baño

The Torre del Homenaje was built during the reign of Abd al Rahman I (756–88).

Sala de Siglo XVI

The Museo Arqueológico has a Moorish-style ceiling, constructed in the 1920s.

Aljibe

Barrio de Casas

Malaga's Alcazaba

Málaga's vast Alcazaba was built between the 8th and 11th centuries on the site of a Roman town. The two are curiously juxtaposed, with the Roman amphitheatre, discovered in 1951 and only partially excavated, just outside the entrance. The remains of Moorish walls can be seen, but the real attraction is the Museo Arqueológico, housing collections of Phoenician, Roman and Moorish artifacts, including fine ceramics.

the painter spent his early years, is now the headquarters of the Picasso Foundation.

On the hill directly behind the Alcazaba are the ruins of the **Castillo de Gibralfaro**, a 14th-century Moorish castle. Connected to the fortress by a pair of parallel ramparts, it can be reached through some beautiful gardens. There are views over the old town, the port and the Málaga bullring, immediately below. The road to the Parador de Málaga also leads to the top of this hill; there are commanding views over the city from both.

East of Málaga on the road to Vélez Málaga is the unspoilt family beach of Rincón de la Victoria *(see p33).*

🏛 **Museo de Picasso**
Calle San Agustín 8. **Tel** *95 260 27 31.* ⏲ *10am–8pm Tue–Sun.* 🏷

🏛 **Casa Natal de Picasso**
Plaza de la Merced 15. **Tel** *95 206 02 15.* ⏲ *9:30am–8pm Mon–Sun, 10am–2pm public hols.*

⛪ **Castillo de Gibralfaro**
⏲ *9am–6pm Tue–Sun.* 🏷

⛪ **Alcazaba**
Calle Alcazabilla s/n. **Tel** *95 221 60 05.* ⏲ *9:30am–7pm Tue–Sun.*

🏛 **Museo Arqueológico**
Calle Alcazabilla. **Tel** *95 221 60 05.* ⏲ *9:30am–7pm Tue–Sun.* 🏷

Torremolinos, the brash capital of the Costa del Sol's tourist industry

Torremolinos 33

Málaga. **Road map** D4. 50,000.
Plaza Blas Infante 1
(952 37 95 12). Thu.
www.ayto-torremolinos.org

Torremolinos grew from a village in the 1950s to one of the busiest resorts on the Costa del Sol, where British and, to a lesser extent, German holiday-makers enjoyed their cheap package holidays. It also developed its red-light district and a raffish nightlife to provide "recreation" for sailors of the US navy in port at Málaga.
   The town was cleaned up as part of a scheme that has seen huge sums spent on new squares, a promenade, green spaces and enlarging the beach with millions of tonnes of fine golden sand.
   Although Torremolinos still has scores of English bars run by expatriates, the atmosphere is now decidedly less brash, especially at

Carihuela beach, towards the adjoining resort of Benalmádena. Bajondillo beach is nearer the busy town centre.

Benalmádena 34

Málaga. **Road map** D4. *Tel 95 256 96 62.* 10:30am–2pm, 4–7:30pm Tue–Sun. **www**.stupabenalmadena.org

The Costa del Sol may be a surprising place to find the largest Buddhist monument in Europe, but this elegant stupa lends a welcome air of serenity to the sprawl of apartments around it.
   Inaugurated in 2003, the stupa was built by the local Buddhist community led by Lopon Tsechu Rinpoche, in co-operation with Benalmádena council. The unmistakeable golden spire reaches 33 m (108 ft) above the terrace on which the stupa stands and has diverse sacred objects sealed inside it.

Fuengirola 35

Málaga. **Road map** C4. 53,000.
Avda Jesús Santos Rein 6 (95 246 74 57). Tue, Sat & Sun.
www.fuengirola.org

The town of Fuengirola is another package-holiday resort, although some of the wilder elements of its mostly British clientele have moved on to newer pastures. Nowadays Fuengirola attracts mainly families.
   During the mild winter months, retired people from

Boxes of fresh fish, Fuengirola

the UK come to stroll along the promenade, go to English bars and waltz the afternoons away at hotel tea dances.

Marbella 36

Málaga. **Road map** C4.
120,000. *Glorieta de la Fontanilla s/n, Paseo Marítimo (95 277 14 42).* Mon & Sat (Puerto Banús). **www**.marbella.es

Marbella is one of Europe's most exclusive holiday resorts. Royalty, film stars and other

Yachts and motorboats in the exclusive marina of Marbella – the summer home of the international jet set

For hotels and restaurants in this region see pp216–18 and pp233–6

LIFE IN THE SUN

The idealized image of the Costa del Sol before tourism is of idyllic fishing villages where life was always at an easy pace. It is true to say that local economies have turned away from fishing and agriculture, and that the natural beauty of this coast has been marred by development. Any measured view, however, should consider the situation described by Laurie Lee, the writer who in 1936 wrote of "... salt-fish villages, thin-ribbed, sea-hating, cursing their place in the sun". Today, few Andalusians curse their new-found prosperity.

19th-century lithograph of the harbour at Málaga

members of the jet set spend their summers here, in smart villas or at one of Marbella's luxury hotels. In winter, the major attraction is the golf *(see pp32–3)*.

As well as modern developments, Marbella boasts a well-preserved, charming Old Town. A number of streets lead from the main road, Avenida Ramón y Cajal, to Plaza de los Naranjos, the main square, planted with orange trees (hence its name).

The remains of the town's Arab walls loom over adjacent Calle Carmen, which leads to the 17th-century **Iglesia de Nuestra Señora de la Encarnación**. Nearby is the **Museo del Grabado Contemporaneo** (Museum of Contemporary Engravings), which contains works by Miró and Picasso.

On the other side of Avenida Ramón y Cajal is the **Paseo de la Alameda**, a park with benches decorated with colourful ceramics. From here, the road to the seafront, Avenida del Mar, is lined with statues made from designs by Salvador Dalí.

Heading west, Avenida Ramón y Cajal becomes the N340. The first stretch is known as the "Golden Mile" because of its real-estate value. At the other end of the Golden Mile is Puerto Banús, the most exclusive marina in Spain.

Beyond Puerto Banús is **San Pedro de Alcántara**, really a separate town but officially part of Marbella. It is quiet, with a sleepy atmosphere, especially in the Plaza de la Iglesia, the town square. Most

of the smart holiday developments are located on the town's fringes, set amid a number of golf courses.

🏛 **Museo del Grabado Contemporáneo**
C/Hospital Bazan s/n. **Tel** 952 76 57 41. ⬜ *Tue–Sat.* ⬤ *public hols.* 📷

Estepona 🟠

Málaga. **Road map** C4. 👥 *46,000.* 🚉 ℹ *Avda San Lorenzo 1 (95 280 09 13).* ⬤ *Wed & Sun.* **www**.infoestepona.com

This fishing village, situated midway between Marbella and Gibraltar, has been altered, but not totally overwhelmed, by tourist developments. It is not particularly attractive at first sight, with big hotels and

Relaxing in sleepy San Pedro de Alcántara

The leafy Plaza de las Flores hidden in Estepona's backstreets

apartment blocks fronting the town's busy main tourist area. Behind, however, there are endearing pockets of all that is quintessentially Spanish – orange trees lining the streets, and the lovely **Plaza Arce** and **Plaza de las Flores**, peaceful squares where old men sit reading newspapers while around them children kick footballs about. There are also a few good, relatively inexpensive fish restaurants and tapas bars. The beach is pleasant enough and evenings in the town tend to be quiet, which makes the resort popular for families with young children.

Not far away from Estepona, however, is a popular nudist beach called the Costa Natura *(see pp32–3)*.

GRANADA AND ALMERIA

Eastern Andalusia is dominated by the Sierra Nevada, Iberia's highest range and one of Spain's premier winter sports venues. At its foot is Granada, once a Moorish kingdom, with a royal palace, the Alhambra, straight out of One Thousand and One Nights. *Ruined fortresses, relics of a warring past, dominate the towns of Granada province. In Almería's arid interior, film directors have put to use atmospheric landscapes reminiscent of Arabia or the Wild West.*

At the point where the mountains of the Sierra Nevada meet the plain, 670 m (2,200 ft) above sea level, nestles the ancient city of Granada, founded by the Iberians. For 250 years it was the capital of a Moorish kingdom whose borders enclosed both Almería and Málaga provinces. On a ridge overlooking the city rises the royal citadel of the Alhambra, a complex of spacious palaces and water gardens.

The mountainous terrain of Granada province is starkly impressive. Amid the ravines, crags and terraced fields of Las Alpujarras on the southern flank of the Sierra Nevada, the villages seem to cling to the sheer slopes.

Along the coastal strip of Granada province, avocados and custard apples flourish in the subtropical climate. Hotels, villas and holiday apartment blocks are also much in evidence here.

East of Granada, the landscape becomes more arid. Around the town of Guadix, founded in Phoenician and Roman times, thousands of people live in cave-houses. A statue of an Iberian goddess from pre-Roman times was found at Baza, and at Los Millares, near Almería, there are traces of a 4,000-year-old settlement.

Almería, a flourishing port in the Moorish era, has been revitalized by a new form of agriculture. Plastic greenhouses now cover hectares of its surrounding province, producing fruit and vegetables all year round.

Along the sparsely populated coast of Cabo de Gata, little-visited villages and bays doze in year-round sunshine.

The Renaissance castle of La Calahorra at the foot of the Sierra Nevada

◁ Patio de los Leones, Alhambra, Granada; a fountain resting on the backs of 12 lions

Exploring Granada and Almería

Granada and the Alhambra are the obvious highlights of this region, but are only a part of its appeal. Improved roads make it easy to reach most places within a few hours, and from Granada it is possible to explore the Sierra Nevada, plunge into the clear waters of the Costa Tropical, or wander through beautiful, spectacularly situated old towns, such as Montefrío and Alhama de Granada. From Almería it is a short hop to the Arizona-like country around Tabernas, where spaghetti westerns were made, or to the secluded beaches of the Parque Natural de Cabo de Gata. Each town and whitewashed village that lies in between has its own charm.

The Alhambra, with the snow-covered Sierra Nevada mountain range in the background

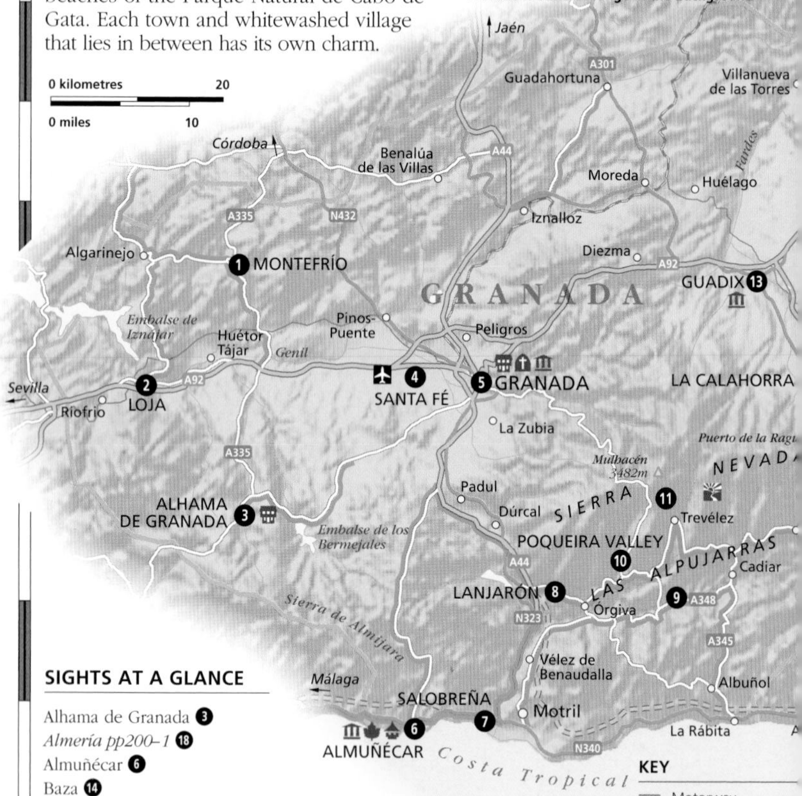

0 kilometres   20

0 miles   10

SIGHTS AT A GLANCE

Alhama de Granada **3**
Almería pp200–1 **18**
Almuñécar **6**
Baza **14**
Granada pp190–96 **5**
Guadix **13**
La Calahorra **12**
Lanjarón **8**
Loja **2**
Mojácar **23**
Montefrío **1**
Níjar **21**
Parque Natural de
  Cabo de Gata **19**
Poqueira Valley **10**

Roquetas de Mar **17**
Salobreña **7**
San José **20**
Santa Fé **4**
Sierra Nevada **11**
Sorbas **22**
Tabernas **16**
Vélez Blanco **15**

Tour
Las Alpujarras **9**

KEY

═══	Motorway
═ ═	Under construction
───	Major road
═══	Minor road
───	Scenic route
┄┄	Main railway
────	Minor railway
─ ─	Provincial border
△	Summit

Sierra de Segura

Sagra
2382m

Puebla de
Don Fadrique

A330

A317

Huéscar

Castillejar   Galera   Maria

**VÉLEZ
BLANCO**
15

Vélez Rubio

A92N

Embalse
de Negratin

Benamaurel   Cúllar   Chirivel

Zújar   Oria   Santa María
de Nieva

14 BAZA   Albox

Caniles   A334   Purchena Macael

Almanzora

Serón

Sierra
de Baza

ALMERÍA

Tetica de Bacares
2088m

Sierra de los Filabres

Lorca

A327

Pulpí

Huércal-Overa

N340   Cuevas del
A7   Almanzora

Vera

Garrucha

Fiñana   Uleila del Campo   **23** MOJÁCAR

Abla   Gérgal   A349

N340a   **22**
SORBAS

Sierra
Cabrera

aujar de
ndarax   Canjáyar   **16** TABERNAS

A92   Sierra Alhamilla

A348   Gádor   NÍJAR **21**   Carboneras

Sierra de
Gádor   Benahadux

*Punta de los
Muertos*

rja   Dalías   PARQUE NATURAL
DE CABO DE GATA

ALMERÍA 18   Rodalquilar

Punta de la Polacra

19

A7   El Cabo
de Gata   **20** SAN JOSÉ

El Ejido   N340

17
ROQUETAS
DE MER

Costa de Almería

Cabo de Gata

Avenida de Andalucía, the
main street in Lanjarón

Spaghetti-western-style landscape near Tabernas

GETTING AROUND

The A92 runs west to Guadix and
then turns south to Almería. The A92N
continues west from Guadix towards
Lorca. The N340 follows the coast via
Almería and the Costa Tropical. The
N323 links the coast with Granada and
the A348 connects the villages of the
Alpujarras.

There are three trains a day between
Granada and Almería, but no coastal rail
service. Frequent buses run from both
cities to towns on main routes.

Whitewashed houses on the edge of the gorge at Alhama de Granada, surrounded by olive groves

Montefrío ❶

Granada. **Road map** D3. 🏠 *7,000.*
🚌 🛈 *Plaza de España 1 (958 33
60 04).* 🖪 *Mon.*

Montefrío is the archetypal
Andalusian town, which,
approached by road from the
south, offers wonderful views
of tiled rooftops and whitewashed houses running up to
a steep crag. The village is
surmounted by remains of
Moorish fortifications and
the 16th-century Gothic
Iglesia de la Villa, which
is attributed to Diego
de Siloé. Located in
the centre of town
stands the **Iglesia de
la Encarnación**, in
Neo-Classical design;
the architect Ventura
Rodríguez (1717–85)
is credited with its
design. Montefrío
is also famed for
the high quality of
its pork products.

**Belfry of Templo de San
Gabriel at Loja**

Loja ❷

Granada. **Road map** D3. 🏠 *21,000.*
🚉 🚌 🛈 *Calle Licenciado Moreno, 1
(958 32 39 49).* 🖪 *Mon.* **www.
aytoloja.org**

A ruined Moorish fort rises
above the crooked streets of
the old town of Loja, which
was built at a strategic point on
the Río Genil. The Renaissance
Templo de San Gabriel (1566)
has a striking façade,
designed by Diego de Siloé.
Known as "the city of water",
Loja also has some beautiful

fountains. East of the town,
the fast-flowing Río Genil cuts
through **Los Infiernos** gorge.
Sample local trout in **Riofrío,**
to the west.

Alhama de Granada ❸

Granada. **Road map** D3. 🏠 *6,000.*
🚌 🛈 *Carrera de Francisco de
Toledo (958 36 06 86).* 🖪 *Fri.*
www.turismodealhama.org

Alhama is a charming
little town balanced
above a gorge. It
was known as Al
hamma (hot
springs) to the
Arabs. Their baths
can still be seen
in **Hotel Balneario**
on the edge of the
town. Alhama's fall
to the Christians
in 1482 led to the
final humiliation
of the Nasrid king-
dom at Granada in
1492 *(see p48).*
The 16th-century **Iglesia de
Carmen** has a number of
very fine paintings on its
dome, which had to
be restored after
damage incurred
during the Spanish
Civil War *(see pp54–5).*
Narrow, immaculately whitewashed streets lead to the
Iglesia de la Encarnación,
which was founded by the
Catholic Monarchs *(see
pp48–9)* in the 16th
century. Some of the
vestments worn by the
present-day priests are

said to have been embroidered
by Queen Isabel herself. The
church also has a Renaissance
bell tower designed by Diego
de Siloé. Nearby is the 16th-
century **Hospital de la Reina**,
now a library housing a fine
artesonado ceiling.

🏨 **Hotel Balneario**
Calle Balneario. *Tel 958 35 00 11.*
🕐 *Mar–Nov.*

🏨 **Hospital de la Reina**
Calle Vendederas s/n. *Tel 958 36
06 43.* 🕐 *11am–1:30pm, 4–8pm
Tue–Fri, 10am–1pm Sat.*

Santa Fé ❹

Granada. **Road map** D3. 🏠 *12,500.*
🚌 🛈 *Arco de Sevilla, Calle Isabel la
Católica, 7 (958 51 31 10).* 🖪 *Thu.*
www.lavegadegranada.es

The army of the Catholic
Monarchs camped here as it lay
siege to Granada *(see p48).* The
camp burned down, it is said,
after a maid placed a candle
too close to a curtain in Isabel's
tent. Fernando ordered a
model town to be built. Its
name, "holy faith", was
chosen by the devout
Isabel. In 1492 the
Moors made a
formal surrender at
Santa Fé and here,
in the same year, the
two monarchs backed
Columbus's voyage of
exploration *(see p127).* An
earthquake destroyed
some of the town in
1806. A Moor's severed
head, carved in stone,
decorates the spire of
the parish church.

**Spire-tip of the
church, Santa Fé**

Granada ❺

See pp190–96.

Almuñécar ❻

Granada. **Road map** D3. 👥 *22,000.*
🚌 🛈 *Avenida Europa s/n (958 63
11 25).* 🗓 *Fri.* **www**.almunecar.info

Almuñécar lies on southern
Spain's most spectacular coast,
the **Costa Tropical** *(see p32),*
where mountains rise to over
2,000 m (6,560 ft) from the
shores of the Mediterranean
Sea. The Phoenicians founded
the first settlement, called
Sexi, at Almuñécar, and the
Romans built an aqueduct
here. When the English writer
Laurie Lee made his long trek
across Spain in 1936, he
described Almuñécar as "a
tumbling little village fronted
by a strip of grey sand which
some hoped would be an attraction for tourists". On returning in the 1950s, he found a
village still coming to terms
with the Spanish Civil War *(see
pp54–5),* which he recounts in
his novel *A Rose for Winter.*

Almuñécar is now a holiday
resort. Above the old town is
the **Castillo de San Miguel**. In
its shadow are botanic
gardens, the **Parque Ornitológico** and a Roman fish-
salting factory. Phoenician

Castillo de San Miguel, overlooking the village of Almuñécar

artifacts are on display in the
**Museo Arqueológico Cueva
de Siete Palacios**.

♜ **Castillo de San Miguel**
◯ *Tue–Sun.* 📷

🦅 **Parque Ornitológico**
Plaza de Abderraman s/n. **Tel** *609
41 28 69.* ◯ *daily.* 📷

🏛 **Museo Arqueológico
Cueva de Siete Palacios**
Casco Antiguo. ◯ *Tue–Sun.* 📷

Salobreña ❼

Granada. **Road map** E3.
👥 *10,500.* 🚌 🛈 *Plaza de Goya
s/n (958 61 03 14).* 🗓 *Tue & Fri.*

From across the coastal plain,
Salobreña looks like a white
liner sailing above a sea of
waving sugar cane. Narrow

streets wend their way up a
hill first fortified by the Phoenicians. The hill later became
the site of the restored **Castillo
Arabe**, which gives fine views
of the peaks of the Sierra
Nevada *(see p197).* Modern
developments, bars and
restaurants line part of this
resort's lengthy beach.

♜ **Castillo Arabe**
Falda del Castillo, Calle Andrés
Segovia. **Tel** *958 61 03 14.*
◯ *Tue–Sun.* 📷 🎫

Lanjarón ❽

Granada. **Road map** E3.
👥 *24,000.* 🚌 🛈 *Avda de la
Alpujarra s/n (958 77 04 62).* 🗓 *Tue
& Fri.* **www**.lanjaron.es

Scores of snow-fed springs
bubble from the slopes below
the Sierra Nevada, and
Lanjarón, on the threshold of
Las Alpujarras *(see pp198–9),*
has a long history as a spa.
From June to October visitors
flock to the town to take the
waters and, under medical
supervision, enjoy various
water treatments for arthritis,
obesity, nervous tension and
other ailments. Lanjarón bottled
water is sold all over Spain.

The town occupies a lovely
site, but it can seem melan-
cholic. The exception to this
is during the early hours of
the festival of San Juan *(see
p35)* when a water battle
takes place. Anybody who
dares venture into the streets
gets liberally doused.

♨ **Balneario**
Balneario de Lanjarón. **Tel** *958 77
01 37.* ◯ *daily.* ⬤ *mid-Dec–mid
Feb.* 📷 ♿

The village of Salobreña viewed across fields of sugar cane

Granada ➎

Relief at the Museo Arqueológico

The guitarist Andres Segovia (1893–1987) described Granada as a "place of dreams, where the Lord put the seed of music in my soul". It was ruled by the Nasrid dynasty *(see pp48–9)* from 1238 until 1492 when it fell to the Catholic Monarchs. Before the Moors were expelled, artisans, merchants, scholars and scientists all contributed to the city's reputation as a centre for culture. Under Christian rule the city became a focus for the Renaissance. After a period of decline in the 19th century, Granada has become the subject of renewed interest and efforts are being made to restore parts of it to their past glory.

Entrance to the Moorish mihrab in the Palacio de la Madraza

🏛 Alhambra and Generalife
See pp194–6.

Façade of Granada cathedral

🏛 Catedral
C/Gran Via 5. **Tel** 958 22 29 59.
On the orders of the Catholic Monarchs, work on the cathedral began in 1523 to Enrique de Egas's Gothic-style plans. It continued under the Renaissance maestro Diego de Siloé, who also designed the façade. Corinthian pillars support his circular Capilla Mayor. Under its dome, windows of 16th-century glass depict Juan del Campo's *The Passion*. The west front was designed by local Baroque artist Alonso Cano. His grave and many of his works are housed in the cathedral. By the entrance arch are wooden statues of the Catholic Monarchs carved by Pedro de Mena in 1677.

🏛 Capilla Real
C/Oficios 3. **Tel** 958 22 92 39.
The Royal Chapel was built for the Catholic Monarchs between 1505 and 1507 by Enrique de Egas. A magnificent *reja* (grille)

by Maestro Bartolomé de Jaén encloses the mausoleums and high altar. The *retablo* by the sculptor Felipe de Vigarney has reliefs depicting the fall of Granada *(see pp48–9)*. Carrara marble figures of Fernando and Isabel repose next to those of their daughter Juana la Loca (the Mad) and her husband Felipe el Hermoso (the Handsome), both by the sculptor Bartolomé Ordóñez.

Steps lead down to the crypt where the corpses are stored in lead coffins. In the sacristy there are more statues of the two monarchs and many art treasures, including paintings by Van der Weyden and Botticelli. Glass cases house Isabel's crown and Fernando's sword.

🏛 Palacio de la Madraza
Calle Oficios 14. **Tel** 958 24 34 84.
⏰ Mon–Fri. 🔊
Originally an Arab university, this building later became the city hall. The façade dates from the 18th century. Inside is a Moorish hall with a finely decorated mihrab. Today the Palacio is part of the University of Granada.

🏛 Corral del Carbón
Calle Mariana Pineda s/n. **Tel** 958 22 59 90. ⏰ 10:30am–1pm, 5–8pm Mon–Fri; 10:30am–1pm Sat. 🔊
This galleried courtyard is a unique relic of the Moorish era. Originally it was a storehouse and inn for merchants. In Christian times it was a venue for theatrical performances. These days it houses local craft vendors and a cultural centre.

🏛 Casa de los Tiros
Calle Pavaneras 19. **Tel** 958 57 54 66. ⏰ 2:30–8:30pm Tue; 9am–8:30pm Wed–Sat; 9am–2:30pm Sun & public hols.
This fortress-like palace was built in Renaissance style in the 16th century. It was once the property of a family who were awarded the Generalife after the fall of Granada *(see pp48–9)*; among their possessions was a sword belonging to Boabdil *(see p49)*. The sword is represented on the façade. The building owes its name to the muskets in its battlements, *tiros* being the Spanish word for shot.

Reja by Maestro Bartolomé de Jaén enclosing the altar of the Capilla Real

🔭 Mirador de San Nicolás

From this square visitors can enjoy splendid sunset views. Tiled rooftops drop away to the Darro river, on the far side of which stands the Alhambra; the Sierra Nevada provides a suitably dramatic backdrop.

🔭 El Bañuelo

Carrera del Darro 31. *Tel 958 22 97 38.* 10am–2pm Tue–Sat. public hols. These brick-vaulted Arab baths, located near the Darro river, were built in the 11th century. Roman, Visigothic and Arab capitals were all incorporated into the baths' columns.

🏛 Museo Arqueológico

Carrera del Darro 43. *Tel 958 22 56 40.* 2:30–8:30pm Tue, 9am–8:30pm Wed–Sat, 9am–2:30pm Sun. The Renaissance Casa de Castril, with a Plateresque portal, houses this museum of Iberian, Phoenician and Roman antiquities, found in the province of Granada.

Cupola in the sanctuary of the Monasterio de la Cartuja

🏛 Palacio Carlos V

Alhambra. *Tel 958 02 79 00.* 9am–2pm Tue–Sat. public hols. This palace in the Alhambra houses the Museo Hispano-Musulmán and the Museo de Bellas Artes. The highlight of the quite thrilling Muslim art collection is a most exquisite 15th-century vase from the Alhambra, which has amazing blue and gold designs.

🏛 Monasterio de la Cartuja

Tel 958 16 19 32. daily A Christian warrior, El Gran Capitán, donated the land on which this monastery was built in 1516, in thanks for surviving a skirmish with the Moors. A cupola by Antonio Palomino tops the sanctuary. The Churrigueresque sacristy *(see p25)* is by mason Luis de Arévalo and sculptor Luis Cabello.

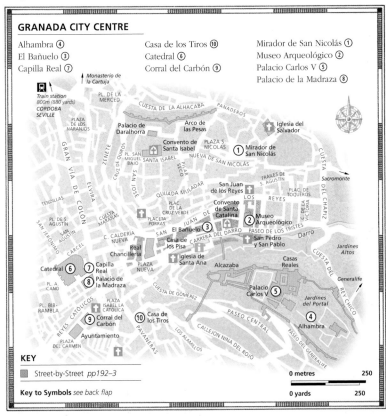

GRANADA CITY CENTRE

Monasterio de la Cartuja

Train station 800m (880 yards) CORDOBA SEVILLE

PL. DE LA MERCED
CUESTA DE LA ALHACABA
PANADEROS
PLAZA DE LOS NARANJOS
Palacio de Daralhorra
Arco de las Pesas
Iglesia del Salvador
Convento de Santa Isabel
PL. SAN MIGUEL BAJO
SANTA ISABEL
PLAZA S. NICOLÁS
NUEVA DE SAN NICOLÁS
① Mirador de San Nicolás
GRAN VÍA DE COLÓN
ZENETE
CRUZ QUIROS
SAN JOSÉ
PILAR SECO
Sacromonte
QUIJADA MULADAR
San Juan de los Reyes
FRAILES DE S. AGUSTÍN
LOS REYES
PLAC. DE TOQUEROS
TENDILLAS
ELVIRA
CUESTA MARAÑAS
PLAC. DE LA CRUZ VERDE
PLACETA PORRAS
Convento de Santa Catalina
JUAN DE
② Museo Arqueológico
PASEO DE LOS TRISTES
Darro
PL. DE S. AGUSTÍN
SAN AGUSTÍN
C. CALDERÍA NUEVA
③ El Bañuelo
SAN JUAN
CARRERA DEL DARRO
San Pedro y San Pablo
Jardines Altos
SAN JERÓNIMO
CÁRCEL
Real Chancillería
Casa de los Pisa
Iglesia de Santa Ana
Casas Reales
CUESTA ALTOS
Catedral ⑥
⑦ Capilla Real
PL. A. CANO
PLAZA NUEVA
Alcazaba
Generalife
⑧ Palacio de la Madraza
CUESTA DE GOMÉREZ
Palacio Carlos V ⑤
Jardines del Portal
REY CHICO
PL. BIB-RAMBLA
REYES CATÓLICOS
PLAZA ISABEL LA CATÓLICA
⑨ Corral del Carbón
⑩ Casa de los Tiros
PASEO CENTRAL
④ Alhambra
PLAZA DEL CARMEN
Ayuntamiento
PAVANERAS
CALLEJÓN NINA DEL ROJO
LOS ALAMILLOS
PASEO DEL GENERALIFE

KEY

Street-by-Street pp192–3

Key to Symbols see back flap

0 metres 250
0 yards 250

Street-by-Street: the Albaicín

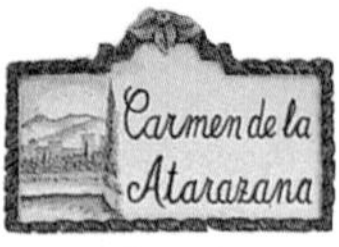

Ornate plaque for house in the Albaicín

This corner of the city, clinging to the hillside opposite the Alhambra, is where one feels closest to the city's Moorish ancestry. A fortress was first built here in the 13th century and there were once over 30 mosques, some of which can still be traced. Along narrow, cobbled alleys stand *cármenes*, villas with Moorish decoration and gardens, secluded from the world by their high walls. In the evening, when the scent of jasmine lingers in the air, take a walk up to the Mirador de San Nicolás. From here the view over a maze of rooftops and the Alhambra glowing in the sunset is magic.

Albaicín Street
Steep and sinuous, the Albaicín streets form a virtual labyrinth. Many street names start with Cuesta, *meaning slope.*

Real Chancillería
Commissioned by the Catholic Monarchs, the Royal Chancery dates from 1530. Its patio is attributed to de Siloé.

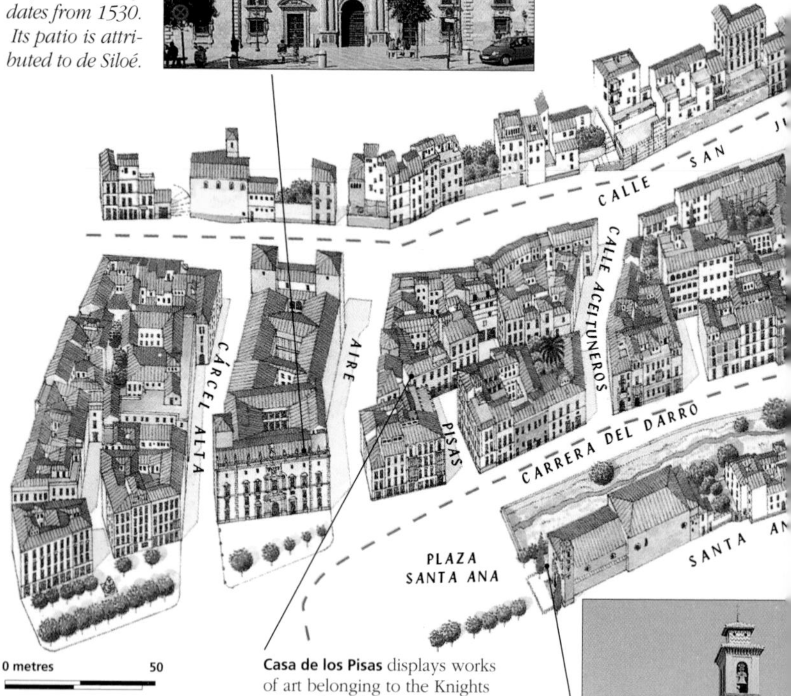

Casa de los Pisas displays works of art belonging to the Knights Hospitallers, founded by Juan de Dios in the 16th century.

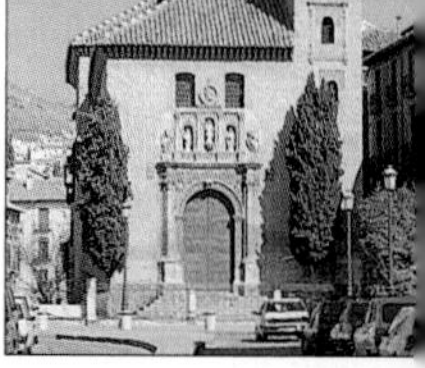

0 metres 50
0 yards 50

STAR SIGHTS

- ★ El Bañuelo
- ★ Museo Arqueológico
- ★ Iglesia de Santa Ana

★ Iglesia de Santa Ana
At the end of the Plaza Nueva stands this 16th-century brick church in Mudéjar style. It has an elegant Plateresque portal and, inside, a coffered ceiling.

Carrera del Darro
The road along the Río Darro leads past fine façades and crumbling bridges. At the top end, a café-terrace offers views of the Alhambra.

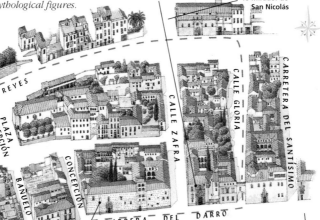

★ **Museo Arqueológico**
The ornate façade of this museum has Plateresque carvings, including reliefs of mythological figures.

VISITORS' CHECKLIST

Granada. **Road map** D3. 250,000. 12 km (7 miles) SE of city. Avenida de Andalucia s/n (902 24 02 02). Carretera de Jaen s/n (958 18 54 80). Santa Ana 4 (958 57 52 02); C/ Virgen Blanca 9 (902 40 50 45). Sat & Sun. Día de la Cruz (3 May), Corpus Christi (May/Jun). www.granadatur.com

KEY

– – – Suggested route

To Mirador de San Nicolás

To Sacromonte

Convento de Santa Catalina de Zafra was founded in 1521.

★ **El Bañuelo**
Star-shaped openings in the vaults let light into these well-preserved Moorish baths, which were built in the 11th century.

SACROMONTE

Granada's gypsies formerly lived in the caves honey-combing this hillside. Travellers such as Washington Irving *(see p53)* would go there to enjoy spontaneous outbursts of flamenco. Today, virtually all the gypsies have moved away, but touristy flamenco shows of variable quality are still performed here in the evenings *(see p244)*. A Benedictine monastery, the Abadía del Sacromonte, sits at the very top of the hill. Inside, the ashes of San Cecilio, Granada's patron saint, are stored.

Gypsies dancing flamenco, 19th century

Granada: Alhambra

A magical use of space, light, water and decoration characterizes this most sensual piece of architecture. It was built under Ismail I, Yusuf I and Muhammad V, caliphs when the Nasrid dynasty *(see p48)* ruled Granada. Seeking to belie an image of waning power, they constructed their idea of paradise on Earth. Modest materials were used (tiles, plaster and timber), but they were superbly worked. Although the Alhambra suffered from decay and pillage, including an attempt by Napoleon's troops to blow it up, it has undergone extensive restoration and its delicate craftsmanship still dazzles the eye.

Sala de la Barca

★ Salón de Embajadores
The ceiling of this sumptuous throne room, built between 1334 and 1354, represents the seven heavens of the Muslim cosmos.

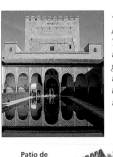

★ Patio de Arrayanes
This pool, set amid myrtle hedges and graceful arcades, reflects light into the surrounding halls.

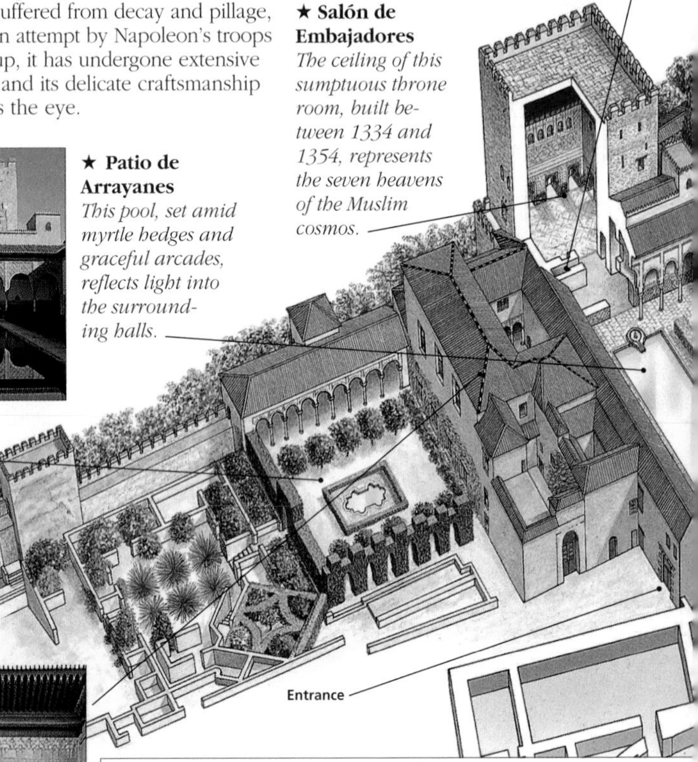

Patio de Machuca

Entrance

Patio del Mexuar
This council chamber, completed in 1365, was where the reigning sultan listened to the petitions of his subjects and held meetings with his ministers.

PLAN OF THE ALHAMBRA

To the Generalife

Ticket office

Parking

The Alhambra complex includes the Casas Reales, the 13th-century Alcazaba, the Palacio Carlos V *(see p50)* and the Generalife *(see p196)*, located just off the map.

KEY

- Casas Reales (shown above)
- Palacio Carlos V
- Alcazaba
- Portal and Medina
- Other buildings

Palacio del Partal

A tower and its pavilion, with a five-arched portico, are all that remain of the Palacio del Partal, the Alhambra's oldest palace.

VISITORS' CHECKLIST

Granada. *Tel* 902 44 12 21. Book by phone (from Spain: 902 22 44 60; from abroad: 0034 915 37 91 78) or online. 🚌 2. ⏰ 8:30am–8pm daily (6pm in winter). **Night visits:** summer: 10–11:30pm Tue–Sat; winter: 8–9:30pm Fri & Sat. ♿ ✎ 🚻 www.alhambra tickets.com. *Booking in advance & arriving early is recommended.*

Washington Irving's apartments

Baños Reales

Jardin de Lindaraja

The Sala de las Dos Hermanas, with its honeycomb dome, is regarded as the ultimate example of Spanish Islamic architecture.

Sala de los Reyes

This great banqueting hall was used to hold extravagant parties and feasts. Beautiful ceiling paintings on leather, from the 14th century, depict tales of hunting and chivalry.

Puerta de la Rawda

★ Sala de los Abencerrajes

This hall takes its name from a noble family, who were rivals of Boabdil (see pp48–9). According to legend, he had them massacred while they attended a banquet here. The pattern of the stalactited ceiling was inspired by Pythagoras' theorem.

The Palacio Carlos V *(see p50)*, a fine Renaissance building, was added to the Alhambra in 1526.

★ Patio de los Leones

Built by Muhammad V, this patio is lined with arcades supported by 124 slender marble columns. At its centre a fountain rests on 12 marble lions.

STAR FEATURES

★ Salón de Embajadores

★ Patio de Arrayanes

★ Patio de los Leones

★ Sala de los Abencerrajes

Granada: Generalife

Located north of the Alhambra, the Generalife was the country estate of the Nasrid kings. Here, they could escape the intrigues of the palace and enjoy tranquillity high above the city, a little closer to heaven. The name Generalife, or Yannat al Arif, has various interpretations, perhaps the most pleasing being "the garden of lofty paradise". The gardens, begun in the 13th century, have been modified over the years. They originally contained orchards and pastures for animals. The Generalife provides a magical setting for Granada's yearly International Music and Dance Festival *(see p35)*.

Patio de la Acequia
This enclosed oriental garden is built round a long central pool. Rows of water jets make graceful arches above it.

Jardines Altos (Upper Gardens)

Sala Regia

The Escalera del Agua is a staircase with water flowing gently down.

The Patio de los Cipreses, otherwise known as the Patio de la Sultana, was the secret meeting place for Soraya, wife of the Sultan Abu l Hasan, and her lover, the chief of the Abencerrajes.

Entrance

Patio del Generalife
Leading up from the Alhambra to the Generalife are the Jardines Bajos (lower gardens). Above them, just before the main compound, is the Patio del Generalife.

The Patio de Polo was the courtyard where palace visitors, arriving on horseback, would leave their horses.

The majestic peaks of the Sierra Nevada towering, in places, over 3,000 m (9,800 ft) above sea level

Las Alpujarras ❾

See pp198–9.

Poqueira Valley ❿

Barranco de Poqueira, Granada. **Road map** E3. ℹ *Plaza de la Libertad 7, Pampaneira (95 876 31 27).*

Many visitors to the Alpujarras get no further than this deep, steep-sided valley above Orgiva, and it is certainly the best place to head for on a short visit. It contains three pretty, well-kept villages climbing the slope. In ascending order, they are: **Pampaneira**, **Bubion** and **Capileira**. All are perfect examples of the singular architectural style of the Alpujarras, which has its closest relation in the Atlas Mountains of Morocco. The whitewashed houses of each village huddle together seemingly randomly ("a confused agglomeration of boxes" as the writer Gerald Brenan described them), with flat grey gravel roofs sprouting a variety of eccentrically tall chimneys. The streets between the houses are rarely straight, often stepped and tapering, and they sometimes disappear into short tunnels.

The countryside between the villages makes excellent walking or horse-riding country. The slopes are still divided by dry-stone walls into terraced fields that are fed by an ingenious irrigation system that distributes the melt water from the mountains above. Dilapidated mills and old threshing floors are other signs of a vanishing way of life.

Sierra Nevada ⓫

Granada. **Road map** E3. 🚌 *from Granada.* ℹ *Parque Nacional Sierra Nevada Centro de Visitantes "El Dornajo", Carretera de Sierra Nevada Km 23, Güéjar Sierra (95 834 06 25).* **www**.reddeparquesnacionales.mma.es /parques/sierra/index.htm

Fourteen peaks, more than 3,000 m (9,800 ft) high, crown the heights of the Sierra Nevada. The snow lingers until July and begins falling again in late autumn. Europe's highest road (closed to traffic) runs past a ski resort at 2,100 m (6,890 ft), and skirts the two highest peaks, **Pico Veleta** at 3,398 m (11,145 ft) and **Mulhacén** at 3,482 m (11,420 ft). Its altitude and closeness to the Mediterranean account for the range of fauna and flora native to this mountain range. It is a habitat for golden eagles, rare butterflies and over 60 species of flowers unique to the area.

The Sierra Nevada was declared a national park in 1999 and access restricted. The park authorities run guided minibus excursions to the higher slopes from its check-points on the two sides of the Sierra Nevada: Hoya de la Mora (above the ski station on the Granada side) and Hoya del Portillo (above Capileira in the Alpujarras). The Sierra Nevada observatory is located on the northern slopes at 2800m.

La Calahorra ⓬

Granada. **Road map** E3. 🚌 *Guadix.* ℹ *Town Hall, Plaza Ayuntamiento 1 (95 867 71 32).* 🕐 *10am–1pm, 4–6pm Wed.*

Grim, immensely thick walls encircle this castle, perched on a hillock above the village. Rodrigo de Mendoza, son of Cardinal Mendoza, ordered La Calahorra to be built for his bride between 1509 and 1512, using architects and craftsmen from Italy. Inside is a Renaissance courtyard with a staircase and Carrara marble pillars.

The castle of La Calahorra above the village of the same name

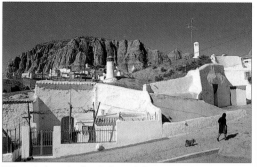

Whitewashed cave dwellings in the troglodyte quarter of Guadix

Guadix ⑬

Granada. **Road map** E3. 🏛 *20,100*.
🚌 🚏 🛈 *Avenida Mariana Pineda
s/n (958 66 26 65)*. 🚃 *Sat*.
www.guadixymarquesado.org

The troglodyte quarter, with
2,000 inhabited caves, is the
town's most remarkable sight.
The cave dwellers say they
prefer living in caves because
the temperature remains
constant all year. The **Museo Al
Fareria** and **Cueva-Museo de
Costumbres Populares** show
how they live underground.

Around 2,000 years ago
Guadix had iron, copper and
silver mines. The town thrived
under the Moors and after the
Reconquest (see pp48–9), but
declined in the 18th century.

Relics of San Torcuato, who
established the first Christian
bishopric in Spain, are kept
in the Cathedral museum. The
Catedral, begun in 1594 by
Diego de Siloé, was finished
between 1701 and 1796 by
Gaspar Cayón and Vicente de
Acero. Near the 9th-century
Alcazaba, the town's Mudéjar
Iglesia de Santiago has a fine
coffered ceiling. **Palacio de
Peñaflor**, dating from the 16th
century, is now fully restored.

🏛 **Museo Al Fareria**
C/San Miguel 59. ◯ *daily*. 🚫

🏛 **Cueva-Museo de
Costumbres Populares**
Ermita Nueva s/n. ◯ *daily*. 🚫

Baza ⑭

Granada. **Road map** E2. 🏛 *20,000*.
🚌 🛈 *Plaza Mayor s/n (958 86 13
25)*. 🚃 *Wed*.

Impressive evidence of ancient
cultures based around Baza
came to light in 1971, when a
large, seated, female figure was

Trevélez ④
Trevélez, in the shadow of Mulhacén,
is built in typical Alpujarran style and
is famous for its cured hams.

A Tour of Las Alpujarras ⑨

Las Alpujarras lie on the southern slopes of the
Sierra Nevada. The villages in this area cling
to valley sides clothed with oak and walnut trees.
Their flat-roofed houses are distinctive and seen
nowhere else in Andalusia. Local food is rustic.
A speciality is *plato alpujarreño*: pork fillet, ham,
sausage and blood sausage, accompanied by a
pinkish wine from the Contraviesa mountains.
Local crafts include handwoven rugs (see p242)
and curtains with Moorish-influenced designs.

Orgiva ①
This is the largest town of the
region, with a Baroque church
in the main street and a lively
Thursday market.

Poqueira Valley ②
Three villages typical
of Las Alpujarras in this
river valley are Capileira,
Bubión and Pampaneira
(see p197).

Fuente Agria ③
People come here from far
and wide to drink the iron-rich,
naturally carbonated waters.

▲ MULHACÉN
3,479 m
11,410 ft

S I E R R

GR421

Juviles

Pórtugos

Pitres

Guadalfeo

A348

GR413

LANJARÓN
GRANADA

A348

S I E R R A D E L A

found in a necropolis. She is the Dama de Baza (see p43), believed to represent an Iberian goddess, and estimated to be 2,400 years old. Subsequently, she was removed to the Museo Arqueológico in Madrid but a replica can be still seen in the **Museo Arqueológico** in Baza. The Renaissance **Colegiata de Santa María**, nearby, has a Plateresque entrance and a fine 18th-century tower.

During the first few days of September a riotous fiesta takes place (see p36). An emissary, El Cascamorras, is despatched from the neighbouring town of Guadix to try to bring back a coveted image of the Virgin from Baza's **Convento de la Merced**. He is covered in oil and chased back to Guadix by youths, also covered in oil. There, he is taunted again for returning empty-handed.

🏛 **Museo Arqueológico**
Plaza Mayor s/n. **Tel** 958 86 19 47.
🕐 10am–2pm, 4–6:30pm daily.

Vélez Blanco ⑮

Almeria. **Road map** F2. 🏔 2,200. 🚌 Vélez Rubio. ℹ️ Centro de Visitantes Almacén del Trigo, Avenida Marqués de los Vélez s/n (950 41 53 54). 🛒 Wed.

Dominating this pleasant little village is the mighty **Castillo de Vélez Blanco**. It was built from 1506 to 1513 by the first Marquis de Los Vélez, and its interior richly

The village of Vélez Blanco, over-looked by a 16th-century castle

adorned by Italian craftsmen. Unfortunately for the visitor its Renaissance splendour has since been ripped out and shipped to the Metropolitan Museum of New York. There is, however, a reconstruction of one of the original patios.

A blend of Gothic, Renaissance and Mudéjar styles (see pp24–5) can be seen in the **Iglesia de Santiago**, located in the village's main street.

Just outside Vélez Blanco is the **Cueva de los Letreros**, which contains paintings from around 4000 BC. One image depicts a horned man holding sickles; another the Indalo, a figure believed to be a deity with magical powers, still used as a symbol of Almería.

⚓ **Castillo de Vélez Blanco**
Tel 607 41 50 55.
🕐 Wed–Sun.

Ⴖ **Cueva de los Letreros**
Camino de la Cueva de los Letreros.
Tel 617 88 28 08.
🕐 noon–4pm daily. 🈂

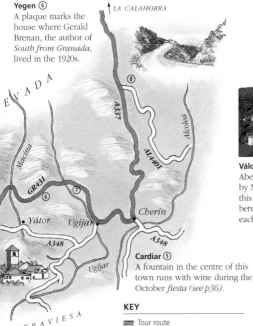

Yegen ⑥
A plaque marks the house where Gerald Brenan, the author of South from Granada, lived in the 1920s.

Cardiar ⑤
A fountain in the centre of this town runs with wine during the October fiesta (see p36).

KEY

🟫	Tour route
═	Other roads
▲	Mountain peak

0 kilometres 10
0 miles 5

Puerto de la Ragua ⑧
This pass, which leads across the mountains to Guadix, is nearly 2,000 m (6,560 ft) high and often snowbound in winter.

Válor ⑦
Aben Humeya, leader of a rebellion by Moriscos (see p50), was born in this village. A commemorative battle between Moors and Christians is staged each year in mid-September (see p36).

TIPS FOR DRIVERS

Tour length: 85 km (56 miles).
Stopping-off points: Orgiva and Trevélez have bars, rest-aurants and hotels (see p219). Bubión has hotels and one good restaurant (see p237). Capileira has bars and restaurants. Orgiva is the last petrol stop before Cadiar.

Almería ⑱

Taking a break in the Plaza Vieja

A colossal fortress bears witness to Almería's golden age, when it was an important port for the Caliphate of Córdoba. Known as al Mariyat (the Mirror of the Sea), the city was a centre for trade and textile industries, with silk, cotton and brocade among its chief exports. After the city fell to the Catholic Monarchs *(see pp48–9)* in 1489, it went into decline for the next 300 years. During the 19th and early 20th centuries, mining and a new port revived the city's fortunes, but this period ended abruptly with the start of the Civil War *(see pp54–5)*. Today a North African air still pervades the city, with its flat-roofed houses, desert-like environs and palm trees. North African faces are common as ferries link the city with Morocco.

Detail of the Renaissance portal of Almería cathedral

The 10th-century Alcazaba overlooking the old town of Almería

♣ Alcazaba
C/Almanzor s/n. **Tel** 950 17 55 00.
◯ *Tue–Sun.* ◼ *1 Jan, 25 Dec.*
Fine views over the city are offered by this 1,000-year old Moorish fortress. It has been restored and within its walls are pleasant gardens and a Mudéjar chapel. It was the largest fortress built by the Moors and covered an area of more than 25,000 sq m (269,000 sq ft). The walls extend for 430 m (1,410 ft). Abd al Rahman III started construction in AD 955, but there were considerable additions later. The fort withstood two major sieges but fell to the Catholic Monarchs *(see pp48–9)* in 1489. Their coat of arms can be seen on the Torre del Homenaje, which was built during the monarchs' reign.
In the past, a bell in the Alcazaba was rung to advise the farmers in the surrounding countryside when irrigation was allowed. Bells were also rung to warn the citizens of Almería when pirates had been sighted off the coast.

It is inadvisable for visitors to wander around the Alcazaba district alone or after dark.

⛪ Catedral
From North Africa, Berber pirates would often raid Almería. Consequently, the cathedral looks more like a fortress than a place of worship, with four towers, thick walls and small windows. A mosque once stood on the site. It was later converted to a Christian temple, but destroyed by an earthquake in 1522. Work began on the present building in 1524 under the direction of Diego de Siloé. Juan de Orea designed the Renaissance façade. He also created the beautifully carved walnut choir stalls. The naves and high altar are Gothic.

⛪ Templo San Juan
Traces of Almería's most important mosque can still be seen here – one wall of the present church is Moorish. Inside is a 12th-century mihrab, a prayer niche with cupola. The church, built over the mosque, was damaged in the Spanish Civil War and abandoned until 1979. It has since been restored.

▦ Plaza Vieja
Also known as the Plaza de la Constitución, this is a 17th-century arcaded square. On one side of the square is the Ayuntamiento, a flamboyant building with a cream and pink façade dating from 1899.

The pedestrianized 17th-century Plaza Vieja, surrounded by elegant arcades

Puerta de Purchena

Located at the heart of the city, the Puerta de Purchena was once one of the main gateways in the city walls. From it run a number of shopping streets, including the wide Paseo de Almería. A tree-lined thoroughfare, this is the focus of city life, with its cafés, Teatro Cervantes and nearby food market.

Centro Rescate de la Fauna Sahariana

C/General Segura 1. **Tel** 950 28 10 45. ◯ call ahead for an appointment.
At the rear of the Alcazaba, this rescue centre shelters endangered species from the Sahara, in particular different kinds of gazelle. Having flourished in Almería's arid climate, some animals have been shipped to restock African nature reserves.

Museo de Almería

Carretera de Ronda 91. **Tel** 950 17 55 10. ◯ 2:30–8:30pm Tue; 9am–8:30pm Wed–Sat; 9am–2:30pm Sun. ◲ (free for EU citizens).

Brightly coloured entrance to a gypsy cave in La Chanca district

Almería's two main prehistoric civilizations, Los Millares and El Algar, are explained in this archaeological museum that has 900 exhibits chosen from a collection of 80,000 pieces.

Saharan gazelle

Environs
One of the most important examples of a Copper Age settlement in Europe, **Los Millares**, lies 17 km (10.5 miles) north of Almería.

As many as 2,000 people occupied the site from around 2700 to 1800 BC (see pp42–3). Discovered in 1891, remains of houses, defensive ramparts and a necropolis that contains more than 100 tombs have since been uncovered.

The community here lived from agriculture but also had the capability to forge tools, arms and adornments from copper, which was mined in the nearby of Sierra de Gador.

Los Millares

Santa Fé de Mondújar. **Tel** 677 90 34 04. ◯ 10am–2pm Wed–Sun.
www.losmillares.info

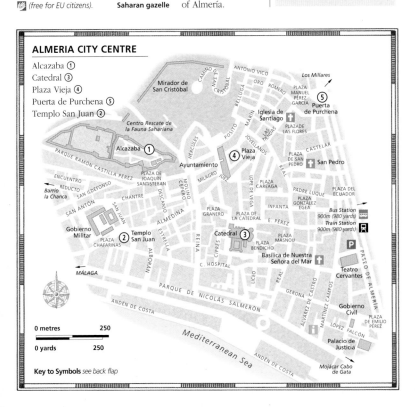

ALMERIA CITY CENTRE

Alcazaba ①
Catedral ③
Plaza Vieja ④
Puerta de Purchena ⑤
Templo San Juan ②

0 metres 250
0 yards 250

Key to Symbols see back flap

Still from *For a Few Dollars More* by Sergio Leone

SPAGHETTI WESTERNS

Two Wild West towns lie off the N340 highway west of Tabernas. Here, visitors can reenact classic film scenes or watch stunt men performing bank hold-ups and saloon brawls. The Poblados del Oeste were built during the 1960s and early 1970s when low costs and eternal sunshine made Almería the ideal location for spaghetti westerns. Sergio Leone, director of *The Good, the Bad and the Ugly*, built a ranch here and film-sets sprang up in the desert. Local gypsies played Indians and Mexicans. The deserts and Arizona-style badlands are still used occasionally for television commercials and series, and by film directors such as Steven Spielberg.

Tabernas ⑯

Almería. **Road map** F3. 🏘 3,000.
🚌 ℹ️ *on main road (950 52 50 30).* 🛒 Wed.

A Moorish hilltop fortress presides over the town of Tabernas and the surrounding dusty, cactus-dotted scenery of eroded hills and dried-out riverbeds. The harsh, rugged scenery has figured in many so-called spaghetti westerns.

Not far from Tabernas is a solar energy research centre, where hundreds of heliostats follow the course of southern Andalusia's powerful sun.

Roquetas de Mar ⑰

Almería. **Road map** F3. 🏘 34,000.
ℹ️ *Avenida Mediterraneo 2 (950 33 32 03).*

Much of Almería's southern coastal plain is given over to massive plastic greenhouses in which vegetables and flowers are raised for export. Interrupting the greenhouses is the resort of Roquetas de Mar, which has a 17th-century castle and a squat lighthouse, both used for exhibitions. Roquetas also has an aquarium with tropical and Mediterranean species of fish.

🐠 **Aquarium**
Avda Reino de España.
Tel 950 16 00 36. 🔲 *daily.*
🌐 **www.aquariumroquetas.com**

Almería ⑱

See pp200–1.

Parque Natural de Cabo de Gata ⑲

Almería. **Road map** F3. 🚌 *to San José.* ℹ️ *Centro de Visitantes de las Amoladeras, Carretera Cabo de Gata km 6 (950 16 04 35).*
Park 🔲 *10am–3pm daily.*

Towering cliffs of volcanic rock, sand dunes, salt flats, secluded coves and a few fishing settlements can be found in the 29,000-ha (71,700-acre) Parque Natural de Cabo de Gata. The end of the cape, near the Arrecife de las Sirenas (Sirens' Reef), is marked by a lighthouse. The park includes a stretch of sea-bed about 2 km (1.2 miles) wide, which allows protection of the marine flora and fauna; the clear waters attract divers and snorkellers.

The area of dunes and salt-pans between the cape and the Playa de San Miguel is a habitat for thorny jujube trees. Thousands of migrating birds stop here en route to and from Africa. Among the 170 or so bird species recorded in the park there are flamingoes, avocets, Dupont's larks and griffon vultures. Attempts are also being made to reintroduce the monk seal, which died out in the 1970s. At the northern end of the park, where there is a cormorants' fishing area, is Punta de los Muertos, ("dead man's point"); this takes its name from the bodies of shipwrecked sailors that are said to have washed ashore there.

San José ⑳

Almería. **Road map** F3. 🏘 1,000.
🚌 ℹ️ *Calle Correos s/n (950 38 02 99).* 🛒 *Sun (Easter & summer).*

Located on a fine, sandy bay, San José is a small but fast-growing sea resort within the Parque Natural de Cabo de Gata. Rising behind it is the arid **Sierra de Cabo de Gata**, a range of bleak grandeur.

Lighthouse overlooking the cliffs of the Parque Natural de Cabo de Gata

The harbour at the traditional fishing village of La Isleta

Nearby are fine beaches, including Playa de los Genoveses (see p33). Along the coast are **Rodalquilar**, a town once important for gold-mining, and **La Isleta**, a fishing hamlet.

Níjar ㉑

Almería. **Road map** F3. 🏘 3,000.
🚌 🛈 Plaza García Blanes, Bajo (950 36 01 23). 🛒 Wed. **www.**nijar.es

Set amid a lush oasis of citrus-trees on the edge of the Sierra Alhamilla, Níjar's fame stems from the colourful pottery and the *jarapas*, handwoven rugs and blankets, that are made here. The town's historic quarter is typical of Andalusia, with narrow, streets and wrought-iron balconies.

The **Iglesia de Nuestra Señora de la Anunciación,** dating from the 16th century, has a coffered Mudéjar ceiling, delicately inlaid. The barren plain between Níjar and the sea has begun to blossom thanks to irrigation.

In Spanish minds, the name of Níjar is closely associated with a poignant and violent incident that occurred here in the 1920s, and which later became the subject of a play by Federico García Lorca.

Sorbas ㉒

Almería. **Road map** F3. 🏘 3,000.
🚌 🛈 Centro de Visitantes los Yesares, Calle Terraplen, 9 (950 36 44 76). 🛒 Thu.

Balanced on the edge of a deep chasm, Sorbas overlooks the Río de Aguas, which flows far below. There are two buildings in this village worth a look: the 16th-century **Iglesia de Santa María** and a 17th-century mansion said to have once been a summer retreat for the Duke of Alba.

Another point of interest for visitors is the traditional, rustic earthenware turned out and sold by Sorbas' local potters.

Located near to Sorbas is the peculiar **Yesos de Sorbas** nature reserve. This is an unusual region of karst, where water action has carved out hundreds of subterranean galleries and chambers in the limestone and gypsum strata. Speleologists are allowed to explore the caves, but only if they are granted permission by Andalusia's environmental department. On the surface, the green, fertile valley of the Río de Aguas cuts through dry, eroded hills. Local wildlife in this area includes tortoises and peregrine falcons.

Mojácar ㉓

Almería. **Road map** F3. 🏘 7,000.
🚌 🛈 Calle Glorieta, 1 (950 61 50 25). 🛒 Wed & Sun.

From a distance, the village of Mojácar shimmers like the mirage of a Moorish citadel, its white houses cascading over a lofty ridge near to the sea. The village was taken by the Christians in 1488 and the Moors were later expelled. In the years after the Spanish Civil War (see pp54–5) the village fell into ruin, as much of its population emigrated. In the 1960s Mojácar was discovered by tourists, giving rise to a new era of prosperity. The old gateway in the walls is still here, but otherwise the village has been completely rebuilt.

Pensión façade in the picturesque, recently rebuilt village of Mojácar

BLOOD WEDDING AT NIJAR

Bodas de Sangre (Blood Wedding), a play by Federico García Lorca (see p55), is based on a tragic event that occurred in 1928 near the town of Níjar. A woman called Paquita la Coja agreed, under pressure from her sister, to marry a suitor, Casimiro. A few hours before the ceremony, however, she fled with her cousin. Casimiro felt humiliated and Paquita's sister, who had hoped to benefit from the dowry, was furious. The cousin was found shot dead and Paquita half-strangled. Paquita's sister and her husband, Casimiro's brother, were found guilty of the crime. Shamed by this horrific scenario, Paquita hid from the world until her death in 1987. Lorca never visited Níjar, but based his play on newspaper reports.

The dramatist Federico García Lorca (1899–1936)

TRAVELLERS'
NEEDS

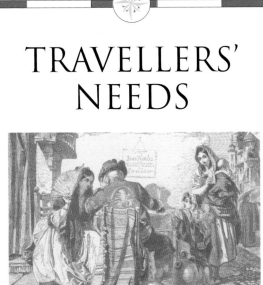

WHERE TO STAY

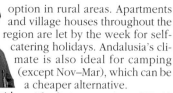

Doorman, Hotel
Alfonso XIII

Some of the most charming places to stay in Spain are in Andalusia. They range from restored castles to family guesthouses, and from one of the most luxurious hotels in Europe to an organic farm deep in the countryside. For budget travel there are pensions and youth hostels, and for hikers there are mountain refuges. A night or two in a B&B is an increasingly popular option in rural areas. Apartments and village houses throughout the region are let by the week for self-catering holidays. Andalusia's climate is also ideal for camping (except Nov–Mar), which can be a cheaper alternative.

The listings on pages 212–19 describe some of the region's best hotels in every style and all price ranges, from basic to luxurious.

The Hospedería de San Francisco in Palma del Río (see p216)

WHERE TO LOOK

In Seville, the most appealing places to stay are mainly in the centre of town, especially around the Santa Cruz district (see pp70–83), where there is a broad range of hotels. As in most cities, the cheapest hotels tend to be small family-run pensions in the backstreets.

Parking is always a problem in the town centre, so if you drive, you may have to book into a hotel with secure private parking, or look around the city's outer suburbs. You can ask your hotel to direct you to attended car parks in the city. A reasonable alternative is to stay in a town close to Seville, such as Carmona (see pp132–3).

Granada has two main hotel districts: around the Alhambra (see pp194–5), which is quiet, and around the centre, which is livelier, noisier and usually cheaper. Central hotels make the best base for going out on the town at night.

In Córdoba the Judería (see pp140–41) is the most convenient place to stay if you plan to get around on foot. If you drive, you may prefer a hotel on the outskirts of the city.

Hotels in Andalusia's coastal resorts are mainly the modern chains that cater for package holiday-makers, although there are also many small, family-owned seaside hotels favoured by the Spanish and visitors alike. If you want somewhere more relaxing, there are good small hotels a short way inland; the countryside here is dotted with them. Look out for them in the white towns between Arcos de la Frontera (see p175) and Ronda (see pp176–7), and around Cazorla (see p156).

Two small private chains have a growing network of hotels in western Andalusia: the luxury Fuerte group and the budget Tugasa chain.

HOTEL GRADING AND FACILITIES

Hotels in Andalusia are awarded categories and stars by the regional tourist authorities. Hotels (H is the abbreviation) are awarded between one and five stars and pensions (P) between either one and two stars. The star-rating system assesses the quantity of facilities a hotel has (such as whether there is a lift or air-conditioning) rather than the quality of service to expect. Most hotels have restaurants that can be

The hillside terrace of the Alhambra Palace hotel (see p218), with views across Granada

◁ **Bar on Calle Gerona, Seville**

used by non-residents. Hotel-Residencias (HR), however, do not have dining rooms, although they may serve breakfast.

PARADORS

Paradors are government-run hotels which fall into the three- to five-star classi-fications. The best ones occupy historic monuments, such as castles, monasteries, palaces and old hunting lodges, but a number of them have been purpose-built in attractive settings. Though a parador will not always be the best hotel in town, they can be counted on to deliver a predictable level of comfort: regional dishes will always be on the menu and rooms are generally comfortable and often spacious. The bedroom furniture varies little from parador to parador.

If you are travelling around the paradors during high season, or intending to stay in smaller paradors, it is wise to book ahead through agents for the paradors *(see p209)*.

PRICES

Hotels are obliged by law to display their range of prices behind reception and in every room. As a rule, the more stars a hotel has, the more you pay. Rates for a double room start from 30 euros per night in a cheap one-star pension and can go as high as 250 euros in a five-star hotel.

Prices vary according to the room, and the region and season. The rural hotels are generally cheaper than the city ones. All the prices quoted on pages 212–19 are based on the rates for mid-season or high season. High season is usually July and August, but it can also run from April to October. City hotels charge inflated rates during major *fiestas*, such as Semana Santa *(see p38)* in Seville. Easter is a popular travel period for the Spanish themselves, and it is usually

Swimming pool in a courtyard of the Hotel Alfaros, Córdoba *(see p215)*

included in the high-season price range, so be sure to enquire about availability and prices in advance.

Note that most hotels will quote prices per room and meal prices per person without *IVA* (VAT).

Five-star hotel restaurant logo

BOOKING AND CHECKING IN

You do not need to book ahead if you are travelling off-season in rural Andalusia, unless you want to stay in a particular hotel. On the other hand, it is essential to reserve rooms by phone, through a travel agent or on the Internet if you travel in high season. You will also need to book if you want a specific room, with a good view, with a double bed (twin beds are the norm), or away from a noisy road. Hotels in many coastal resorts close in the winter, so check that any hotels you want to stay in are open.

Some hotels will request a deposit of 20–25 per cent for booking during peak times, or for a long stay. This can be arranged by credit card and phone, even in smaller hotels. Others will hold your booking until an agreed arrival time. Try to make

cancellations at least a week in advance, or you may lose all or some of your deposit. A reserved room will be held only until 6pm unless you can inform the hotel that you are going to arrive late.

When you book in you will be asked for your passport or identity card, to comply with police regulations. It will be returned to you when your details have been copied.

You are expected to check out of your room by noon or to pay for another night. Most hotels are happy to keep your luggage for you until later that day.

The impressive entrance of a hotel housed in a former Sevillian mansion

Mosaic tiling in the courtyard of a hostel

PAYING

These days most hotels, except the most basic of bed and breakfasts, accept credit cards. In some large hotels you may be asked to sign a blank credit card pay slip on arrival. Under Spanish law it is fraudulent to ask you to do this, and you are advised to refuse to sign.

No hotel in Andalusia will take cheques, even when backed by a guarantee card or drawn on a Spanish bank.

In Spain it is customary to tip the porter and the chambermaid in a hotel by €1–2. The usual tip to leave in hotel restaurants is 5–10 per cent of the bill, although some restaurants will have already included a service charge.

SELF-CATERING

Villas and holiday flats let by the week are plentiful along the Costa del Sol and the coasts of Granada and Almería. Most cities will also have holiday let accommodation in central, well-furnished apartments that are cheaper than a comparable hotel. The local tourism office can supply information about letting agencies.

Inland, an increasing number of village and farm houses are now also being let all over the region. In the UK, a number of private companies, among them **The Individual Traveller's Spain,** act as agents for owners of apartments and houses. Many agents belong to an organization called the **RAAR** (Red Andaluza de Alojamientos Rurales or Andalusian Rural Accommodation Network), through which it is possible to make direct bookings.

Prices charged for self-catering accommodation sometimes vary considerably: prices are determined by location, the season and type of property. A four-person villa with a pool costs as little as €240 for a week if it is inland and up to and over €950 per week if it is in a prime coastal location.

Another possibility is the *villa turística* (holiday village) which is half hotel, half holiday apartments. The guests can hire rooms with kitchens and use a restaurant.

BED AND BREAKFAST

Andalusia's 500 or more *casas rurales* offering bed and breakfast range from a stately *cortijo* (manor house) to a small organic farm. Do not expect usual hotel service or a long list of facilities. However, you may be met with a friendly

---

DIRECTORY

HOTELS

Asociación de Hoteles de Sevilla
Calle San Pablo 1, Casa A Bajo, 41001 Seville. **Tel** 95 422 15 38. www. hotelesdesevilla.com

Asociación de Hoteles Rurales de Andalucía (AHRA)
Avda Niceto Alcalá Zamora 12, 14800 Priego de Córdoba. **Tel** 95 754 08 01. www.ahra.es

Fuerte Hotels
www.fuerteshoteles.com

Tugasa Hotels
www.tugasa.com

PARADORS

Central de Reservas
Calle Requena 3, 28013 Madrid. **Tel** 90 254 79 79. www.parador.es

Keytel
402 Edgware Rd, London W2 1ED. **Tel** (020) 7616 0300. www.keytel.co.uk

SELF-CATERING & BED & BREAKFAST

The Individual Traveller's Spain
Tel (08700) 780 194. www.individualtravellers. com

RAAR
Sagunto 8-10-3, 04004 Almería. **Tel** 950 28 00 93. www.raar.es

YOUTH HOSTELS

Central de Reservas de Inturjoven
Calle Miño 24, 41011 Seville. **Map** 3 A4. **Tel** 90 251 00 00. **Fax** 95 503 58 40. www.inturjoven.com

MOUNTAIN REFUGES

Federación Andaluza de Montañismo
Calle Santa Paula 23, 2° Planta, 18001 Granada. **Tel** 95 829 13 40. (opening hours: summer: 9am–2pm Mon–Fri; rest of year: 8:30am–1:30pm, 4–8pm Mon–Thu; 9am–1:30pm Fri). www.fedamon.com

CAMPING

Club de Camping y Caravanning de Andalucía
Calle Francisco Carrión Mejías 13, 41003 Seville. **Tel** 95 422 77 66.

Federación Andaluza de Campings
Tel 958 22 35 17. www. campingsandalucia.es

Camping and Caravanning Club
Tel 0845 130 7631. www.campingand caravanningclub.co.uk

DISABLED

IHD
EURL, Boîte Postale 62, 83480 Puget-sur-Argens, France. **Tel** (0494) 81 61 51. **Fax** (0494) 81 61 43.

Viajes 2000
Paseo de la Castellana 228–30, 28046 Madrid. **Tel** 91 323 25 23. **Fax** 91 314 73 07. www.viajes2000.com

Some youth hostels can be charmingly rustic

welcome and be spoiled with good home cooking.

A stay at a bed and breakfast can be booked through **RAAR**, the owners' association, or directly. If you are booking from abroad you may be asked to send a 10 per cent deposit and to stay for at least two nights.

YOUTH HOSTELS AND MOUNTAIN REFUGES

To use Andalusia's extensive network of *albergues juveniles* (youth hostels) you have to buy an international YHA card from a hostel or show a card from your country. Bed and breakfast costs between €10 and €15 per person. You can book a bed or room in a hostel directly or through the central booking office of Inturjoven – **Central de Reservas de Inturjoven.**

If you backpack in remote mountain areas, you can stay in *refugios*, which are shelters with basic kitchens and dormitories. The *refugios* are marked on all good large-scale maps of the mountains and national parks. They are administered by the **Federación Andaluza de Montañismo.**

CAMP SITES

There are more than 110 camp sites scattered across the region of Andalusia, many of them along the coasts but there are also some outside the major cities and in the popular countryside areas. Most have electricity and running water;

some also have launderettes, restaurants, shops, play areas for children and pools.

It is a wise to take with you a camping *carnet* (card). It can be used to check in at sites, and it also gives you third-party insurance. *Carnets* are issued by the AA, the RAC, and by camping and caravanning clubs.

A map of all the region's camp sites, with descriptions of each facility, and links to their websites, is available from the **F.A.C. (Federación Andaluza de Campings)**.

DISABLED TRAVELLERS

Hotel managers will advise on wheelchair access and staff will always assist, but few hotels are equipped for the disabled. However, some of the youth hostels are. **RADAR** *(see*

Logo for a five-star hotel

p257), the Royal Association for Disability and Rehabilitation, publishes a useful booklet called *Holidays and Travel Abroad*, and **Accessible Tourism** *(see p257)* publishes a fact sheet on Spain.

In Spain, the Confederación Coordinadora Estatal de Minusválidos Fisicos de España, also known as **Servi-COCEMFE** *(see p257)*, and **Viajes 2000** have details of hotels with special facilities in Andalusia.

IHD (International Help for the Disabled) arranges accessible accommodation, nurses, transport and other help for visitors to the Costa del Sol.

FURTHER INFORMATION

Every year the **Dirección General de Turismo** in Andalusia publishes its *Guía de Hoteles, Pensiones, Apartamentos, Campings y Agencias de Viajes*. This gives the star-ratings and a resumé of facilities of all hotels, pensions, camp sites and youth hostels in the area.

Having chosen the type of accommodation you want and where you want to stay, it is wise to fax or phone directly to obtain the most up-to-date information on prices and facilities. In the hotel listings *(pp212–19)*, the hotels have been listed under high season rates. This means that prices for specific rooms on certain nights, or for an apartment or pension out of season, may turn out to be cheaper.

A pretty room in a bed-and-breakfast hotel

Andalusia's Best: Paradors

Parador is an old Spanish word for a lodging place for travellers of respectable rank. In the late 1920s a national network of state-run hotels called Paradors was established. Many of them are converted castles, palaces or monasteries, although some have been purpose-built in strategic tourist locations. The paradors are generally well sign-posted, making them easy to find. All offer a high degree of comfort and service and have restaurants in which regional cuisine is served.

Parador de Ronda
This parador sits on the edge of the Tajo gorge, opposite Ronda's old town. Some rooms have in-comparable views. (See p218.)

Parador de Carmona
Carmona's Moorish-style parador, in the palace of Pedro the Cruel, makes a relaxing base from which to ex-plore nearby Seville. (See p214.)

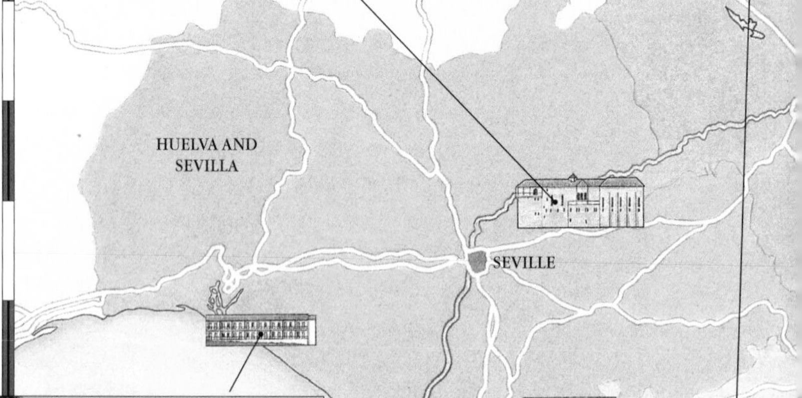

HUELVA AND
SEVILLA

SEVILLE

CADIZ AND
MALAGA

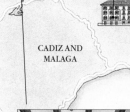

Parador de Mazagón
This purpose-built parador, in a peaceful and scenic spot near a long sandy beach, makes a convenient base for exploring the Coto Doñana. (See p215.)

Parador de Arcos de la Frontera
Situated in one of the archetypal pueblos blancos *(white towns) this parador has a wide terrace offering panora-mic views over the river Guadalete.* (See p216.)

| 0 metres | 500 |
| 0 yards | 500 |

Parador de Cazorla
A secluded mountain lodge, Cazorla's parador is set amid the dense forests of one of the principal nature reserves in Andalusia, close to the source of the Guadalquivir river. (See p215.)

Parador de Jaén
A re-created fortress, complete with small arched windows and vaulted chambers, this parador stands on top of a hill above the city. (See p216.)

Parador de Úbeda
This is one of many fine Renaissance buildings in Úbeda. It has a delightful patio fringed by slender columns. (See p216.)

CORDOBA
AND JAEN

GRANADA
AND ALMERIA

Parador de Granada
Advance booking is essential if you want to stay in this atmospheric 15th-century convent, built in the gardens of the Alhambra at the instruction of the Catholic Monarchs. (See p219.)

Parador de Mojácar
A modern white building, imitating the Cubist style of Mojácar's architecture, this parador stands by a beach and has a spacious sun terrace. (See p219.)

Choosing a Hotel

Hotels have been selected across a wide price range for facilities, good value, and location. All rooms have private bath, TV, air conditioning, and are wheelchair accessible unless otherwise indicated. Most have Internet access, and in some cases, fitness facilities may be offsite. The hotels are listed by area. For map references, *see pp112–17.*

PRICE CATEGORIES
The following prices are for a standard double room per night in the high season, with tax and service charge included.
€ Under €75
€€ €75–125
€€€ €125–175
€€€€ €175–225
€€€€€ Over €225

SEVILLE

EL ARENAL Hotel Montecarlo
€€€
Gravina 51, 41007 **Tel** *954 21 75 03* **Fax** *954 21 68 25* **Rooms** *51*   **Map** *1 B5 (5 B2)*

This beautiful 18th-century gentleman's house, with two courtyards decorated with wrought-iron gates and railings and some magnificent tiling, is located in the best part of the city, within easy reach of historical sites, the Guadalquivir and the commercial district. The restaurant staff are exceptionally friendly. **www.hotelmontecarlosevilla.com**

EL ARENAL Taberna del Alabardero
€€€
C/Zaragoza 20, 41001 **Tel** *954 50 27 21* **Fax** *954 56 36 66* **Rooms** *7*   **Map** *3 B1 (5 B3)*

The former home of Sevillian poet J Antonio Castevany, this little hotel is set in a mansion above one of the city's finest restaurants *(see p228)*. Each of the individually decorated bedrooms is furnished with beautiful antiques and stylish fabrics. The central courtyard is illuminated through a stained-glass roof. **www.tabernadelalabardero.com**

EL ARENAL Vincci la Rabida
€€€
C/Casterlar 24, 41001 **Tel** *954 50 12 80* **Fax** *954 21 66 00* **Rooms** *81*   . **Map** *3 B1 (5 C4)*

Located close to shops, restaurants and the bullring, this 18th-century palace has guestrooms that combine warm, earthy tones with dark furnishings and comfortable wrought-iron beds. Some rooms have views of the pretty central courtyard. **www.vinccihoteles.com**

EL ARENAL Hotel Melia Colon
€€€€
Canalejos 1, 41001 **Tel** *954 50 55 99* **Fax** *595 22 09 38* **Rooms** *217*   **Map** *3 B1 (5 B3)*

A renovated, luxury hotel in the old quarter. The Melia Colon is a tradition in the world of bullfighting, mainly thanks to its location – between the Giralda, the cathedral, the Torre del Oro and the bullring, surrounded by restaurants and bars. The ideal place to spot Spain's "beautiful people" during Semana Santa. **www.solmelia.com**

LA CAMPANA Hotel Cervantes
€€€€
C/Cervantes, 10, 41004 **Tel** *954 90 02 80* **Fax** *954 90 05 36* **Rooms** *72*   **Map** *6 D1*

This Best Western hotel is located in the lively area of La Campana, within reach of the main sights and a 20-minute walk from the Isla Magica theme park. Two great glass ceilings make this a bright and elegant establishment with a typical Sevillian interior courtyard. **www.hotel-cervantes.com**

LA CARTUJA Barcelo Renacimiento
€€€
Isla de la Cartuja, 41092 **Tel** *954 46 22 22* **Fax** *954 46 04 28* **Rooms** *295*   **Map** *1 C2*

An avant-garde, modern, top-quality hotel located on the isle of La Cartuja, a 20-minute walk from the historic quarter. The Barcelo Renacimiento is considered the best hotel in the city for congresses, conferences and other business functions. Wi-Fi and a convention centre add to the corporate appeal. **www.barcelorenacimiento.com**

LA MACARENA Hotel Tryp Macarena
€€
San Juan de Ribera, 2, 41009 **Tel** *954 37 58 00* **Fax** *954 38 18 03* **Rooms** *331*   **Map** *2 E3*

Although a little way from the historic centre of the city, the Tryp Macarena remains an attractive offering, thanks to its proximity to a bus stop. The rooftop pool is very welcome after a day spent sightseeing. It can be somewhat noisy at times, but its position close to the Guadalquivir River is good. **www.solmelia.com**

LA MACARENA Patio de la Cartuja
€€
C/Lumbreras 8 & 10, 41002 **Tel** *954 90 02 00* **Fax** *954 90 20 56* **Rooms** *56*   **Map** *1 C4*

A group of old mansions with large patios has been converted into this unusual hotel. Situated in the bohemian neighbourhood of La Macarena, the apartments are simple, but well equipped. The hotel is a short walk from the cathedral and Santa Cruz. It also has a car park, a rare commodity inSeville. **www.patiosdesevilla.com**

LA MACARENA Casa Romana Hotel Boutique
€€€
C/Trajano 15, 41003 **Tel** *954 91 51 70* **Fax** *954 37 31 91* **Rooms** *26*   **Map** *1 C5 (5 C1)*

Rooms at the Casa Romana are distributed around the picturesque central courtyard. Featuring all the comforts you would expect of a four-star hotel, the rooms are tastefully decorated in subdued elegance, while some have Jacuzzis. Website-offer specials including flamenco tickets with your hotel reservation. **www.hotelcasaromana.com**

Key to Symbols *see back cover flap*

LA MACARENA Casa Sacristía de Santa Ana

Almeda de Hercules 22, 41002 **Tel** *954 91 57 22* **Fax** *954 90 53 16* **Rooms** *25*   €€€   **Map** *1 C4*

An 18th century sacristy has been meticulously restored and is now a charming hotel with rooms opening onto a central courtyard. It's located right in Plaza Almeda de Hercules, with numerous bars and restaurants close by. There's also an excellent in-house restaurant and free Wi-Fi. **www.sacristiadesantaana.com**

LA MACARENA Alcoba del Rey de Sevilla

C/Bécquer 9, 41002 **Tel** *954 91 58 00* **Fax** *954 91 56 75* **Rooms** *15*   €€€€   **Map** *2 D3*

This is a stylish little hotel, full of small details that create a romantic atmosphere. Furnishings include lovely glasswork, *azulejos* (tiles), silk cushions and objets d'art – all of which are for sale. Each of the rooms is named after a personality from the Moorish period and elegantly decorated. **www.alcobadelrey.com**

MAESTRANZA Picasso

Calle San Gregorio 1, 41004 **Tel** *954 21 08 64* **Fax** *954 21 08 64* **Rooms** *15*   €   **Map** *3 C2 (6 D5)*

The Picasso is located in the very heart of Seville, on the route of the Semana Santa procession, which can be enjoyed from the balconies of the rooms. This prime position makes it a popular option during the Easter period, so be sure to book in advance. Close to all the main sights, and ten minutes from the Seville Fair. **www.grupo-piramide.com**

SANTA CRUZ Hosteria del Laurel

Plaza de los Venerables 5, 41004 **Tel** *954 22 02 95* **Fax** *954 21 04 50* **Rooms** *20*   €€   **Map** *4 D2 (6 E4)*

Located in a historic building in the heart of Santa Cruz is this hotel, whose bar and restaurant *(see p229)* attract a local clientele. Hosteria del Laurel is within easy reach of shops and historic sites such as the Real Alcazar, the cathedral and the bullring. This is a very pleasant area in which to go for a stroll. **www.hosteriadellaurel.com**

SANTA CRUZ La Casa del Maestro

C/Almudena 5, 41002 **Tel** *954 50 00 07* **Fax** *954 50 00 06* **Rooms** *11*   €€   **Map** *6 E2*

Once the home of the celebrated flamenco guitarist Niño Ricardo, this charming yellow-and-ochre townhouse is built around a patio bursting with plants and flowers. Rooms tend to be on the small side, but they are full of thoughtful touches, such as a jug of iced water and chocolates placed by the bed. **www.lacasadelmaestro.com**

SANTA CRUZ YH Giralda Hotel

C/Abades 30, 41004 **Tel** *954 22 83 24* **Fax** *954 22 70 19* **Rooms** *14*   €€   **Map** *3 D1 (6 D4)*

The YH-Giralda has a great location in the heart of the Barrio Santa Cruz. The building is a converted 18th-century palace, and it has been completely refurbished whilst still retaining its original character. All the rooms are sound-proofed and have en-suite baths, air-conditioning and heating. **www.yh-hoteles.com**

SANTA CRUZ Hotel Alminar

C/Álvarez Quintero 52, 41004 **Tel** *954 29 31 93* **Rooms** *12*   €€€   **Map** *3 C1 (6 D4)*

Located on a quiet street just metres from the cathedral, this small hotel provides elegant charm in an historic build-ing. Rooms have tasteful, neutral, modern decor, with Internet and mini-bars in each room. There's a central court-yard patio for relaxation and public parking nearby. **www.hotelalminar.com**

SANTA CRUZ Petit Palace Santa Cruz

C/Muñoz y Pavón 18, 41004 **Tel** *954 22 10 32* **Fax** *954 22 50 39* **Rooms** *46*   €€€   **Map** *6 E3*

Located in a typically Andalusian building, this boutique hotel features a modern, state-of-the-art interior design. Rooms are spacious and well equipped, offering – among other things – Wi-Fi access, flat-screen TVs and fluffy bathrobes. **www.hthoteles.com**

SANTA CRUZ EME fusionhotel

C/Alemanes 27, 41004 **Tel** *954 56 00 00* **Fax** *954 56 10 00* **Rooms** *60*   €€€€   **Map** *3 C2 (6 D4)*

Perfectly situated directly in front of the Cathedral and the Giralda, this five star hotel has panoramic terraces, stunning views, a swimming pool and spa and four fine restaurants. For true luxury, book one of the "Estancias Collection" rooms, with 24-hour butler service, private terraces and swimming pools. **www.emehotel.com**

SANTA CRUZ Hotel Inglaterra

Plaza Nueva 7, 41001 **Tel** *954 22 49 70* **Fax** *954 56 13 36* **Rooms** *90*   €€€€   **Map** *3 B1 (5 C3)*

The present building was built in 1967, but the hotel dates from 1857, when it was the pride of Seville. Furnished with exquisite Seville tiles, antique furniture and paintings, the Inglaterra overlooks Plaza Nueva and city hall in the historic centre, and is just a two-minute walk from the cathedral and the Giralda. **www.hotelinglaterra.es**

SANTA CRUZ Alfonso XIII

C/San Fernando 2, 41004 **Tel** *954 91 70 00* **Fax** *954 91 70 99* **Rooms** *147*   €€€€€   **Map** *3 C3*

Seville's legendary hotel, built in the neo-Mudéjar style as a royal guesthouse, is still fit for kings. Elegance and formal service are assured, and bedrooms have opulent furnishings. Crystal chandeliers, marble columns and palm trees adorn the public spaces. There is also a posh cocktail bar. It is being renovated until 2011 but remains open. **www.alfonsoxiii.com**

SANTA CRUZ Casa Numero Siete

C/Virgenes 7, 41004 **Tel** *954 22 15 81* **Fax** *954 21 45 27* **Rooms** *6*   €€€€€   **Map** *3 D1 (6 E3)*

One of the loveliest and most romantic hotels in Seville, this elegant guesthouse occupies a mansion and features just a handful of rooms. The decor includes a range of antiques and family heirlooms. Casa Numero Siete also has an opulent sitting room with a bar. The breakfasts here are delicious. **www.casanumero7.com**

SANTA CRUZ Las Casas del Rey de Baeza

€€€€€

Plaza Jesus de la Redencion 2, 41003 **Tel** *954 56 14 96* **Fax** *954 56 14 41* **Rooms** *41* **Map** *4 D1 (6 E4)*

Located in a beautiful, unique setting, this hotel expertly fuses past and present. Bright, whitewashed walls blend with the ochres and reds of the courtyard, which is shaded by arched walkways. Indoors, cool stone flooring and natural tones lead to the rooms, where chic interiors pay tribute to modernity. **www.hospes.es**

TRIANA Abba Triana Hotel

€€

Plaza Chapina, 41010 **Tel** *954 26 80 00* **Rooms** *137* **Map** *3 A1 (5 A3)*

Enjoy spectacular views of the Guadalquivir River at this new hotel, featuring the latest technological advances and modern decor. Have a swim in the rooftop pool, or explore the surrounding area: the Abba Triana is within easy and enjoyable walking distance from all the city's attractions. **www.abbatrianahotel.com**

HUELVA AND SEVILLA

ALCALA DE GUADAIRA Hotel Oromana

€€

Av de Portugal, 41500 **Tel** *955 68 64 00* **Fax** *955 68 64 00* **Rooms** *31*

On the fringes of the historic town of Alcalá, just 15 km (9 miles) from Seville, this country hotel is located in a handsome mansion built in the 1920s. It is surrounded by huge gardens with an outdoor pool. Welcoming, helpful staff, and a good restaurant serving local specialities add to the appeal. **www.hoteloromana.com**

ARACENA Finca Buen Vino

€€€

Los Marines, 21293 **Tel** *959 12 40 34* **Fax** *959 50 10 29* **Rooms** *4*

A wonderful guesthouse located in an elegant villa on a hilltop surrounded by olive and citrus groves. The owners grow their own organic produce, which they use to prepare breakfasts, afternoon teas and cordon-bleu dinners (guests only). Stay in the villa, or rent a cottage in the grounds. **www.fincabuenvino.com**

ARACENA La Casa Noble

€€€€€

C/Campito 35, 21200 **Tel** *959 12 77 78* **Rooms** *6*

This unique Andalusian home dating from 1914 has been meticulously restored to ensure guests have every modern comfort while its historic charm is retained. Rooms have imported mattresses, luxurious linens, rain showers and Jacuzzis, and there are beautiful castle views. The staff prides itself on offering personal attention. **www.lacasanoble.net**

AYAMONTE Riu Atlantico

€€€

Punta del Moral, 21470 **Tel** *959 62 10 00* **Fax** *959 62 10 03* **Rooms** *359*

The beachside Riu Atlantico is located near the Portuguese border and very close to the famous Isla Canela golf course. An oasis providing tranquillity and first-rate service, it is surrounded by pools and a tropical landscape. Guests can enjoy a full-service spa, gymnasium and sauna. Room prices include breakfast and dinner. **www.riu.com**

CARMONA Casa de Carmona

€€€

Plaza de Lasso 1, 41410 **Tel** *954 19 10 00* **Fax** *954 19 01 89* **Rooms** *34*

This 16th-century palace decorated with a blend of contemporary and period styles has been converted into a hotel that has featured in numerous fashion magazines. The luxurious rooms and suites are filled with art and opulent furniture, and there is a superb restaurant. A good base for exploring Sevilla province. **www.casadecarmona.com**

CARMONA Parador de Carmona

€€€

C/Alcázar, 41410 **Tel** *954 14 10 10* **Fax** *954 14 17 12* **Rooms** *63*

This magnificent clifftop parador was built as a fortress by the Moors and later became the palace of the Christian king Pedro the Cruel. It is hung with tapestries and scattered with antiques, and the plush rooms have superb views of the countryside. There is a huge outdoor pool, and one of the best restaurants in the region. **www.parador.es**

CASTILLEJA DE LA CUESTA Hacienda de San Ignacio

€€€

C/Real 190, 41950 **Tel** *954 16 92 90* **Fax** *954 16 14 37* **Rooms** *13*

Once a Jesuit monastery, then an Andalusian hacienda, this is now a relaxed estate set within whitewashed walls. Huge palms tower above the graceful central patio, and the fine restaurant is located in the former olive mill. The rooms are functional, with few comforts, but the public areas are stunning. **www.haciendasanignacio.com**

CAZALLA DE LA SIERRA Las Navezuelas

€

Ctra Cazella-Ed Pedroso, 41370 **Tel** *954 88 47 64* **Fax** *954 88 45 94* **Rooms** *10*

The spacious rooms in this family-run farmhouse are furnished with handmade fabrics. Staying here gives visitors a rare opportunity to experience living in an authentic Andalusian *cortijo* (farmstead). The rooms look out over vast orchards of olive trees and cork oaks, and home-cooked meals are served in the restaurant. **www.lasnavezuelas.com**

CAZALLA DE LA SIERRA Hospederia La Cartuja

€€

Ctra Cazella-Constantina km 2.5, 41370 **Tel** *954 88 45 16* **Fax** *954 88 47 07* **Rooms** *14*

This old monastery has been converted into a charming refuge for artists by its crusading owner. Painters, sculptors and musicians sometimes offer their art in exchange for their stay, and there is a gallery exhibiting works by resident artists, all of which can be purchased. Choose from rooms, suites or a cottage. **www.cartujadecazalla.com**

MAZAGON Parador de Mazagón   🍴 ♨ 🗐   €€€

*Ctra San Juan de Puerto-Matalascañas km 30, 21130 **Tel** 959 53 63 00 **Fax** 959 53 62 28 **Rooms** 63*

This modern parador on the Huelva coast is situated between a sandy beach and a pine forest, offering superb views of the surrounding area. This hotel is a good base for visiting the Parque Nacional de Doñana, but it also offers many on-site activities, including a swimming pool and a relaxing Jacuzzi. **www.parador.es**

El ROCIO Hotel Toruño   🍴 🗐   €€

*Plaza Acebuchal 22, 21750 **Tel** 959 44 23 23 **Fax** 959 44 23 38 **Rooms** 30 ·*

A charming whitewashed villa a short distance from the hermitage containing the image of the virgin of El Rocío. The Toruño is set on the fringes of the Parque Nacional de Doñana, one of Europe's most important wetlands and wildlife reserves, and is popular with bird-watchers. Prices double during the El Rocío pilgrimage. **www.toruno.es**

CORDOBA AND JAEN

BAEZA Hotel Fuentenueva   🍴 ♨ 🗐   €€

*Calle del Carmen 15, 23440 **Tel** 953 74 31 00 **Fax** 953 74 32 00 **Rooms** 13*

Relocated in a 19th-century house converted from a former women's prison, this hotel offers all modern conveniences, as well as a few special touches. These include a library, cafeteria, conference hall, a Japanese garden and Wi-Fi. Rooms boast hydromassage baths and sleek, modern decor. There are also 6 self-catering apartments. **www.fuentenueva.com**

CAZORLA Molino de la Farraga   ♨   €€

*Camino de la Hoz, 23470 **Tel** 953 72 12 49 **Fax** 953 72 12 49 **Rooms** 8*

A renovated 200-year-old mill on the fringes of the lovely village of Cazorla, the Molino is perfect for anyone seeking tranquillity. Shrouded by abundant greenery, the whitewashed building is surrounded by rambling gardens, and the rooms are simple but very pretty. There is also an annexe for greater privacy. **www.molinolafarraga.com**

CAZORLA Parador de Cazorla   📶 🍴 ♨   €€€

*Sierra de Cazorla, 23470 **Tel** 953 72 70 75 **Fax** 953 72 70 77 **Rooms** 34*

The forests and mountains of the Sierra de Cazorla, a major Andalusian nature reserve, are the superb setting for this modern parador, designed with the rural setting in mind. Nestling into the side of the hill, the hotel offers fine views from the well-equipped bedrooms. The restaurant serves local game in season. **www.parador.es**

CORDOBA Maestre   📶 🍴 🗐   €

*C/Romero Barros 4-6, 17003 **Tel** 957 47 24 10 **Fax** 957 47 53 95 **Rooms** 26*

Near the Mezquita, in the centre of Córdoba, this is a simple hotel with basic amenities. It is set around a series of pretty Andalusian patios with colourful tiles, fountains and trailing plants, and is perfectly placed for sightseeing. The Maestre offers both rooms and self-catering apartments. Private underground parking. **www.hotelmaestre.com**

CORDOBA Casa de los Azulejos   🍴 🗐   €€

*C/Fernando Colón 5, 14002 **Tel** 957 47 00 00 **Fax** 957 47 54 96 **Rooms** 8*

The "House of the Tiles" is an enchanting 17th-century mansion set around a patio with exquisite local tiles, pretty wrought-iron fixtures and greenery. The rooms are cool and modern, with extras such as Internet connection. A terrific restaurant offers a fusion of Andalusian and South American cuisine. **www.casadelosazulejos.com**

CORDOBA Eurostar Ciudad de Córdoba   📶 🍴 🗐   €€€

*Avenida de Cadiz, 14003 **Tel** 957 10 36 00 **Fax** 957 10 36 01 **Rooms** 90*

A hotel with a warm interior design in the historic and cultural heart of the city, a ten-minute taxi ride to the shopping and financial district. The hotels are renowned as an excellent business centre, but it also holds regular exhibitions of painting, photography and other visual arts. **www.eurostarsciudaddecordoba.com**

CORDOBA Hospes Palacio de Baílio   📶 🍴 ♨ 🎴 🗐   €€€

*Ramirez de las Casas Deza 10-12, 14012 **Tel** 957 49 89 93 **Fax** 957 49 89 94 **Rooms** 53*

This hotel is a restored complex of a palace built between the 16th and 17th centuries, granaries, coach houses and stables, surrounded by beautiful gardens and courtyards with jasmine, lemon and orange trees. The interior is a lovely fusion of old and modern styles; rustic stone walls mix with modern furnishings. **www.hospes.es**

CORDOBA Hotel Eurostar Las Adelfas   📶 🍴 ♨ 🎴 🗐   €€€

*Avenida de la Arruzafa, 14012 **Tel** 957 27 74 20 **Fax** 957 27 27 94 **Rooms** 101*

One of the quietest residences in the city thanks to its setting in the exclusive area of El Brillante, just ten minutes from the city centre. The hotel is noted for its cuisine, and its garden terrace is a favourite eating place. It has a large swimming pool surrounded by a lawn terrace with plenty of loungers. **www.eurostarslasadelfas.com**

CORDOBA Hotel Hesperia   📶 🍴 ♨ 🎴 🗐   €€€

*Avenida Fray Albino, 1, 14009 **Tel** 957 42 10 42 **Fax** 957 29 99 97 **Rooms** 104*

Situated on the Guadalquivir River, with wonderful views over the town, the Hesperia has a spectacular pool in the centre of a traditional Andalusian courtyard. La Azotea café-bar on the rooftop terrace is a very special place in the middle of this city. The rooms are modern in design, with free Wi-Fi. **www.hesperia-cordoba.com**

CORDOBA Maciá Alfaros   🖼 🍽 🛏 📋   €€€€
C/Alfaros 18, 14001 **Tel** *957 49 19 20* **Fax** *957 49 22 10* **Rooms** *144*

In a busy street, but soundproofed against traffic noise, the Alfaros is a sleek contemporary hotel built around three courtyards in neo-Mudéjar style. One of the marble courtyards contains an elegant swimming pool. Geared towards business travellers, the hotel offers facilities such as Wi-Fi. Rooms are comfortable. **www.maciahoteles.com**

JAÉN Hotel Husa Europa   🖼 🍽 📋   €€
Plaza de Belen 1, 23001 **Tel** *953 22 27 04* **Fax** *953 22 26 92* **Rooms** *38*

Strategically located on the Andalusian Renaissance Trail (Jaen-Baeza-Ubeda), this peaceful hotel is in the centre of the city's main restaurant and tapas area. Refurbished in 1999, it is ideal for both business and leisure travellers. The sports centre nearby has a large heated pool. Breakfast is continental only. **www.husa.es**

JAEN Parador de Jaen   🖼 🍽 🛏 🏃 🍽 📋   €€€
Castillo de Santa Catalina, CP, 23009 **Tel** *953 23 00 00* **Fax** *953 23 09 30* **Rooms** *71*

In an elevated position on the Santa Catalina Hill, this parador offers stunning vistas across the city of Jaen. The interior is in true Arabic style, with crossed stone arches in the public rooms. All the bedrooms have panoramic views. Regional specialties in the restaurant include cold garlic soup and partridge terrine. **www.parador.es**

PALMA DEL RIO Hospedería de San Francisco   🍽 🛏 📋   €€
Av de Pio XII 35, 14700 **Tel** *957 71 01 83* **Fax** *957 71 02 36* **Rooms** *35*

Built in the 15th century as a Franciscan monastery, this hotel houses some bedrooms in former monks' cells, furnished with hand-painted basins and bedcovers woven by nuns. The kitchen uses organic produce from the hotel's own gardens, and meals are served in the atmospheric old refectory. **www.casasypalacios.com**

UBEDA El Postigo Zenit   🖼 🍽 🛏 🏃 📋   €€
C/Postigo 5, 23400 **Tel** *953 75 00 00* **Fax** *953 75 53 09* **Rooms** *26*

This is a modern hotel; the decor includes warm colours accented with stone, and the hotel has all creature comforts to ensure a comfortable stay. Enjoy a drink in the social room, which has a fireplace, or soak up the sun by the lovely swimming pool. There's free Wi-Fi throughout the hotel. **www.zenithoteles.com**

UBEDA Parador de Úbeda   🍽 📋   €€€
Plaza Vàzquez de Molina 1, 23400 **Tel** *953 75 03 45* **Fax** *953 75 12 59* **Rooms** *36*

Presiding over Úbeda's central square, this parador is located in a former 16th-century aristocratic palace. Blue and white tiles adorn the façade, and the house surrounds a Renaissance two-storey patio. The spacious, high-ceilinged rooms are decorated with traditional furniture, and the restaurant serves regional cuisine. **www.parador.es**

ZUHEROS Zuhayra   🍽 📋   €
C/Mirador 10, 14870 **Tel** *957 69 46 93* **Fax** *957 69 47 02* **Rooms** *18*

The principal charm of this simple rural hotel is its location, in a white town on the edge of a range of high hills. The building is modern but imitates the style of the noble mansion it replaced. It is a perfect base for hiking in the Sierra Subbética, and the hotel rents mountain bikes. The restaurant serves local specialities. **www.zercahoteles.com**

CADIZ AND MALAGA

ARCOS DE LA FRONTERA Casa Grande   🍽 📋   €€
C/Maldonado 10, 11630 **Tel** *956 70 39 30* **Fax** *956 71 70 95* **Rooms** *7*

A charming family-run hotel set in a whitewashed 18th-century mansion that still bears the escutcheon of its original owner. Each of the originally decorated rooms is full of character. The hotel is warm, intimate and full of personal touches, such as home-made marmalade for breakfast. Great views from the roof terrace. **www.lacasagrande.net**

ARCOS DE LA FRONTERA Parador de Arcos de la Frontera   🖼 🍽 📋   €€€
Plaza del Cabildo, 11630 **Tel** *956 70 05 00* **Fax** *956 70 11 16* **Rooms** *24*

Formerly a magistrate's house, this mansion perched on a cliff above the Old City is now a smart parador. A huge terrace offers great views of the ancient spires and rooftops below, and the rooms are set around a series of beautifully tiled patios with wells and fountains. Rooms are plush and comfortable, some with Jacuzzis. **www.parador.es**

CADIZ Pension Centro-Sol   📋   €€
Manzanares, 7, 11010 **Tel** *956 28 31 03* **Fax** *956 28 31 03* **Rooms** *19*

A charming, friendly little pension in a picturesque part of the city. The neo-classical building has a striking tiled entrance, situated in one of Cadiz's charming alleyways. It is near both bus and train stations, and only 15 minutes away from the beach at Santa Maria del Mar. **www.hostalcentrosolcadiz.com**

CADIZ Hotel Playa Victoria   🖼 🍽 🛏 🏃 📋   €€€
Glorieta Ingenerio La Cierva, 4, 11010 **Tel** *956 20 51 00* **Fax** *956 26 33 00* **Rooms** *188*

On the seafront, the eco-friendly Playa Victoria prides itself on its recycling policy. It is built in an intriguing combination of local oyster stone and blue glass, with traditional marble and wood inside. Designer furnishings feature prominently in the public rooms, and there is a spectacular sculpture hanging from the ceiling. **www.palafoxhoteles.com**

CANOS DE MECA La Breña   ⊞ ≅ ▤   €€

Av Trafalgar 4, 11160 (Cádiz) **Tel** *956 43 73 68* **Fax** *956 43 73 68* **Rooms** *7*

The beaches of the Costa de la Luz are some of the most beautiful and unspoilt in Spain. This charming beachside hotel is painted crisp blue and white, and the rooms and suites are simple and spacious. Most offer fine sea views. La Breña has an excellent restaurant with a modern Andalusian menu. Closed Nov–Jan. **www.hotelbrena.com**

CASTELLAR DE LA FRONTERA Casa Convento La Almoraima   ⊞ ≅ ⍓ ▤   €€

Finca La Almoraima, 11350 **Tel** *956 69 30 50* **Fax** *956 69 32 14* **Rooms** *20*

Surrounded by a protected forest of Mediterranean cork trees, this stunning mansion and former convent has been turned into a tranquil hotel. The cloisters are now a flower-filled patio, and the public areas are decorated with antiques. The rooms are simple, and the hotel can arrange tours of the region. **www.la-almoraima.com**

CORTES DE LA FRONTERA Casa Rural Ahora   ⊞ ▤   €

C/Lepanto 40, Bda El Colmenar, 29013 **Tel** *&* **Fax** *952 15 30 46* **Rooms** *9*

A rural retreat with an ecological restaurant and various therapies on offer, Ahora is situated in a picturesque valley with a bubbling brook running through it. The beach is only one hour away. Alternatively, spend your time indulging in Turkish baths, massages and clay treatments. The perfect spot for relaxation and rejuvenation. **www.ahoraya.es**

GIBRALTAR The Rock   ▨ ⊞ ≅ ⍓ ▤   €€€€

3 Europa Road, Gibraltar **Tel** *956 77 30 00* **Fax** *956 77 35 13* **Rooms** *104*

Built in 1932 by the Marquess of Bute, Gibraltar's first five-star hotel still trades on its old-fashioned colonial style and service. Perched on the cliff side, high above the town and harbour, it offers all imaginable amenities, from a hair and beauty centre to a casino. Popular with both business and leisure travellers. **www.rockhotelgibraltar.com**

GRAZALEMA Hotel Fuerte Grazalema   ▨ ⊞ ≅ ⍖ ▤   €€

Baldio de los Alamillos Carretera A-372, 11610 **Tel** *956 13 30 00* **Fax** *956 13 30 01* **Rooms** *77*

In the heart of the Grazalema Nature Reserve, close to the white village of Grazalema and a short drive to Ronda, the Fuerte Grazalema is perfect for nature lovers. The hotel offers bike and horse rental, as well as organized trekking trips and activities for children. Regional cuisine is a speciality. There is also an Internet room. **www.fuertehoteles.com**

MALAGA Sallés Hotel Málaga Centro   ▨ ⊞ ≅ ⍓ ▤   €€

C/Marmoles 6, 29007 **Tel** *952 07 02 16* **Fax** *952 28 33 60* **Rooms** *148*

This refurbished four star hotel in the heart of Málaga offers smartly decorated rooms with spacious bathrooms, a free non-alcoholic mini-bar, and a rooftop swimming pool for cooling off and admiring the views. The rooms are decorated in two different ways; either warm and classic or modern and functional. **www.salleshotel.com**

MARBELLA El Fuerte   ▨ ⊞ ≅ ⍓ ▤   €€€€

Av El Fuerte, 29602 **Tel** *952 92 00 00* **Fax** *952 82 44 11* **Rooms** *263*

The El Fuerte was the first purpose-built hotel in Marbella and is still one of the best. It is unmissable – a big pink building surrounded by tropical gardens. Some rooms have mountain views, but the best look out to sea. Next to the beachfront, the hotel has a heated pool, an outdoor pool and a health and beauty centre. **www.fuertehoteles.com**

MARBELLA Marbella Club Hotel   ▨ ⊞ ≅ ⍓ ▤   €€€€€

Blvr Principe von Hohenlohe, 29600 **Tel** *952 82 22 11* **Fax** *952 82 98 84* **Rooms** *137*

Built for a prince in the 1950s, this is now an ultra-luxurious beachside complex with two pools (one indoors) and extensive subtropical gardens. Located in the Golden Mile (between Marbella and Puerto Banus), it includes a world-class golf course and a spa. The rooms, suites and villas feature private heated pools. **www.marbellaclub.com**

MIJAS Club Puerta del Sol   ▨ ⊞ ≅ ⍖ ⍓ ▤   €€

Ctra Fuengirola-Mijas km 4, 29650 **Tel** *952 48 64 00* **Fax** *952 48 54 62* **Rooms** *130*

A whitewashed modern hotel complex in the foothills of the Sierra de Mijas offering spacious rooms. There are impressive views of Fuengirola and the coast. Facilities include tennis courts, a gym, indoor and outdoor pools and a host of other sport amenities. It is child-friendly, and the beaches are nearby. **www.hotelclubpuertadelsol.com**

NERJA Hostal Miguel   €

C/Almirante Ferrádiz 31, 29780 **Tel** *&* **Fax** *952 52 15 23* **Rooms** *9*

This friendly, eclectic hostel with Moroccan touches first opened in the 1960s. The rooms are decorated in a subdued style, and all have ceiling fans, mini-fridges and airy balconies. Breakfast can be taken on the rooftop terrace, and the lounge has a selection of books and magazines. **www.hostalmiguel.com**

OJEN La Posada del Ángel   ⊞ ⍖ ▤   €€

C/Mesones 21, 29610 **Tel** *952 88 18 08* **Rooms** *17*

La Posada del Ángel offers 17 carefully decorated rooms, each with its own individual flavour, but all rich in Andalusian charm. The hotel is located 15 minutes from Marbella, in the whitewashed town of Ojén, in the Sierra de las Nieves. Special activities are available, including painting holidays. **www.laposadadelangel.com**

EL PUERTO DE SANTA MARÍA Monasterio de San Miguel   ▨ ⊞ ≅ ⍓ ▤   €€

C/Virgen de los Milagros 27, 11500 **Tel** *956 54 04 40* **Fax** *956 54 05 25* **Rooms** *150*

Located in an 18th-century Baroque monastery, this hotel is well placed for visits to Cádiz, the bodegas of Jerez and the tapas bars and nightlife of Puerto de Santa Maria. The rooms don't quite match up to the opulent public areas, but there are extensive gardens and excellent facilities. The hotel arranges free transport to the beach. **www.jale.com**

RINCON DE LA VICTORIA Molino de Santillán 🄿 🚻 ♒ 🐾 🗐   €€

Ctra de Macharaviaya km 3, 29730 **Tel** *952 40 09 49* **Fax** *952 40 09 50* **Rooms** *22*

Perched on a wooden hilltop, this is a charming hotel set in a traditional Andalusian finca. Rooms are painted in warm colours, and all offer memorable views. The hotel offers a wide range of outdoor activities and is close to the beaches. Home-grown organic produce is served in the restaurant. Closed Jan 7–31. **www.molinodesantillan.es**

RONDA Parador de Ronda 🄿 🚻 ♒ 🐾 🗐   €€€

Plaza España, 29400 **Tel** *952 87 75 00* **Fax** *952 87 81 88* **Rooms** *78*

Edging up to Ronda's famous cliff, yet close to the town centre, this modern, purpose-built parador has stunning views over the gorge, especially from the top-floor suites. The bedrooms are full of light and stylishly decorated. The parador is surrounded by huge gardens, with an outdoor pool right on the cliff edge. **www.parador.es**

SANLUCAR DE BARRAMEDA Los Helechos 🄿 🚻 🗐   €

Plaza Madre de Dios 9, 11540 **Tel** *956 36 13 49* **Fax** *956 36 96 50* **Rooms** *54*

Decorated with tiles and potted plants, Los Helechos is a delightful, relaxing seaside hotel. Rooms are light, spacious and prettily, if simply, decorated, and they are set around a plant-filled courtyard. The friendly staff are very informative and can arrange visits to the nearby Parque Nacional de Doñana. **www.hotelloshelechos.com**

TARIFA Hurricane 🚻 ♒ 🐾 🗐   €€€

Ctra N340 km 78, 11380 **Tel** *956 68 49 19* **Fax** *956 68 03 29* **Rooms** *33*

Tarifa is a mecca for windsurfers, and the Hurricane is a temple to the sport. It is an imaginative, open-plan building set in subtropical gardens that lead out to the beach. Rooms are decorated in true Andalusian style. It is one of the least crowded corners of the Spanish coast, with fine views across the sea to Africa. **www.hotelhurricane.com**

TOLOX Cerro de Hijar 🚻 ♒   €€

Cerro de Hijar, 29019 **Tel** *952 11 21 11* **Fax** *952 11 97 45* **Rooms** *18*

This hotel offers stunning views of the surrounding natural beauty and the pretty white village of Tolox. The estate is Andalusian in style, with a central patio and spacious rooms. All kinds of outdoor pursuits can be arranged, including horse riding and excursions. The award-winning restaurant serves local specialities and own-made wines. **www.cerrodehijar.com**

TORREMOLINOS Hotel Miami 🚻 ♒   €

C/Aladino 14, 29019 **Tel** *952 38 52 55* **Fax** *952 37 85 08* **Rooms** *26*

The Miami offers welcome respite from the Costa del Sol's modernity. It has whitewashed walls, tiles, wrought-iron fixtures, balconies and potted plants. Rooms are simple, and vary in terms of size and amenities, but they are all comfortable, and the staff are friendly and helpful. The pool is an added bonus. **www.residencia-miami.com**

VEJER DE LA FRONTERA Casa Cinco 🚻 🗐   €€

C/Sancho IV El Bravo 5, 11150 **Tel** *956 45 50 29* **Fax** *956 45 11 25* **Rooms** *4*

This beautiful little hostel on the town's hilltop aims to stimulate all five senses. All the rooms are decorated individually, with a mixture of contemporary and traditional furnishings from around the world. Thoughtful details such as CD players add to its charm. Bookings are for a minimum of two nights. **www.hotelcasacinco.com**

GRANADA AND ALMERIA

ALMERIA AM Husa Catedral 🄿 🚻 🏃 🗐   €€

Plaza Catedral 8, 04002 **Tel** *950 27 81 78* **Fax** *950 27 81 17* **Rooms** *110*

This charming four star hotel, located in a former manor house dating from 1850, has a great location in the Cathedral Plaza. Rooms are elegantly decorated in neutral tones. There is free Wi-Fi throughout the hotel, a solarium and rooftop terrace with commanding views. Breakfast is included. **www.husa.es**

GRANADA Pensión Landázuri 🚻   €

Cuesta de Gomérez 24, 18009 **Tel** *958 22 14 06* **Rooms** *15*

Perhaps the nicest budget option in Granada, this tiled pension has two terraces offering great city views. All the rooms are simple, but surprisingly spacious, and those on the top floor (book in advance) enjoy great views of the Alhambra. Not all rooms have en-suite bathrooms; those that don't are extremely cheap. **www.pensionlandazuri.com**

GRANADA Posada del Toro 🄿 🚻 🏃 🗐   €€

C/Elvira 25, 18010 **Tel** *958 22 73 33* **Fax** *958 21 62 18* **Rooms** *15*

Rustic charm combines with modern comforts at this welcoming hotel within an 1862 building which has been comprehensively renovated. Close to the Albaicín, Plaza Nueva (where you can catch a bus to the Alhambra) and the cathedral, Pilar del Toro offers Internet connection in every room. **www.posadadeltoro.com**

GRANADA Room Mate Migueletes 🄿 🏃 🗐   €€€

C/Benalúa 11, 18010 **Tel** *958 21 07 00* **Fax** *958 21 07 02* **Rooms** *25*

This small, exclusive hotel is fantastically located in the Albaicín, just steps aways from Plaza Nueva. Among the 25 rooms available, there are also two suites: one with Jacuzzi and fabulous views of the Alhambra; the other located in a tower with views of both the Old Town and the Alhambra. Charming and romantic. **www.casamigueletes.com**

GRANADA Parador de Granada ⬚ 🏤 🗐 €€€€€

C/Real de la Alhambra, 18009 **Tel** *958 22 14 40* **Fax** *958 22 22 64* **Rooms** *36*

This elegant parador in the jasmine-scented gadens of the Alhambra was once a convent, and the cloister has been transformed into an oasis filled with flowers and trees. From the elegant bedrooms, you can hear the fountains of the Generalife and enjoy blissful views of the city and the ancient palace. Book well in advance. **www.parador.es**

LOJA La Bobadilla ⬚ 🏤 ≋ 🏃 🗐 €€€€€

Finca La Bobadilla, 18300 **Tel** *958 32 18 61* **Fax** *958 32 18 10* **Rooms** *62*

Looking rather like a labyrinthine Andalusian village surrounded by its own estate, this is one of the most luxurious hotels in Europe. Each of the rooms and suites is different, but all are fitted with every imaginable amenity. There is a lake-sized pool, and guests can take part in a wide range of sports and activities. **www.barcelolabobadilla.com**

MECINA BOMBARÓN Casas Rurales Benarum 🏤 ≋ 🏃 €

C/Casas Blancas 1, 18450 **Tel** *958 85 11 49* **Rooms** *12*

Nestled in a quiet town in Las Alpujarras, this hotel provides luxurious comfort in a relaxing environment. Each cabin is equipped with kitchen, living room with fireplace, washing machine, barbecue area and a bathroom with hydro-massage shower. Outdoor activities available include archery, hiking and hot-air ballooning. **www.benarum.com**

MOJACAR Parador de Mojácar ⬚ 🏤 ≋ 🗐 €€€

Playa de Mojácar, 04638 **Tel** *950 47 82 50* **Fax** *950 47 81 83* **Rooms** *98*

The architecture of this purpose-built parador on the sunny coast of Almería echoes that of the dazzling white-cube houses in nearby Mojácar. It has excellent facilities for all manners of water sports. The light, airy bedrooms have terraces with wonderful sea views, and the restaurant offers local specialities. **www.parador.es**

MONACHIL La Almunia del Valle 🏤 ≋ 🗐 €€€

Camino de la Umbria, 18193 **Tel** *& Fax 958 30 80 10* **Rooms** *10*

High in the Sierra Nevada mountains, this is a stylish rural retreat surrounded by extensive gardens. In winter, it is just 20 minutes by car from the ski slopes, and the hotel offers all-inclusive packages. In summer, guests can lounge by the pool, enjoy the mountain views or take a stroll through the shady gardens. **www.laalmuniadelvalle.com**

MOTRIL Casa de los Bates ≋ 🗐 €€€

Ctra Nacional 340 km 329.5, 18600 **Tel** *958 34 94 95* **Fax** *958 83 41 31* **Rooms** *4*

A country villa set in its own gardens, with stunning views of the sea, the mountains and the castle of Salobreña, the Casa de los Bates is a chic retreat with an aristocratic ambience – antiques, family portraits and a grand piano. The rooms are furnished in pastel tones, and for breakfast you can enjoy fresh tropical juice. **www.casadelosbates.com**

NIGUELAS Alquería de Los Lentos 🏤 ≋ 🏃 🗐 €€

Camino de los Molinos, 18657 **Tel** *958 77 78 50* **Fax** *958 77 78 48* **Rooms** *16*

The Alquería provides a sumptuous retreat, convenient for those who wish to travel to the Alpujarras, the Sierra Nevada and Granada. All rooms are suites, and they are all well appointed and pleasantly decorated. Romantics can check out the "Corral de la Luna" (Stable of the Moon), which offers intimacy and warmth. **www.alquerialoslentos.com**

ORGIVA Taray 🏤 ≋ 🗐 €€

Ctra A-348 km 18 (Tablate-Abuñol), 18400 **Tel** *958 78 45 25* **Fax** *958 78 45 31* **Rooms** *15*

A whitewashed rural hotel set in lovely gardens, with olive groves and orange trees. The bedrooms are large enough to be small apartments, but the Taray has even larger suites. A good base for pursuing outdoor activities such as horse riding, the hotel is also equipped for disabled visitors, with specially adapted rooms. **www.hoteltaray.com**

PECHINA Balneario de Sierra Alhamilla ⬚ 🏤 🗐 €€

Pechina, 4359 **Tel** *950 31 74 13* **Fax** *950 31 75 51* **Rooms** *19*

This spa hotel in the Sierra de Alhamilla has been restored to its 18th-century glory. The thermal waters have long been known for their healing properties – the Romans and then the Arabs built spas on this spot. Treatments include soaking in an outdoor thermal pool with underwater jets, mud packs and massages.

ROQUETAS DE MAR Hotel Playaluna ⬚ 🏤 ≋ 🏃 🗐 €€€€

Urb. Playa Serena, Roquetas de Mar, 04740 **Tel** *950 18 48 00* **Fax** *950 18 48 14* **Rooms** *496*

Facing Serena Beach, this hotel also has a great pool for which towels are provided (free). Catering for children with three clubs for differing ages, it is ideal for families. It has an Internet room and a very good health and beauty centre limited to the over-16s. All-inclusive deals are available, plus there are great offers online. **www.hotelesplaya.com**

SAN JOSE Cortijo El Sotillo 🏤 ≋ 🗐 €€€

Ctra San José, 04118 **Tel** *950 61 11 00* **Fax** *950 61 11 05* **Rooms** *20*

An elegant 18th-century farmhouse set in the beautiful natural parks of Cabo de Gata and Nijar, El Sotillo is the perfect place for a walking holiday, with hikes into the volcanic hills. The beaches of this stunning stretch of coastline are just a short drive away. The restaurant uses produce from the estate. **www.cortijoelsotillo.com**

TURRE El Nacimiento ≋ €

Cortijo El Nacimiento, 4639 **Tel** *950 39 06 73* **Rooms** *5*

This remote old farmhouse is set in unspoilt countryside. Bed and breakfast and home-cooked vegetarian dinners (on request) using organic produce from their farm. Rooms are cosy and pretty, and there are fabulous views from the terrace. Best of all is the natural swimming pool in the grounds. Closed mid-Jan–mid-Feb. **www.page.to/elnacimiento**

RESTAURANTS, CAFES AND BARS

One of the joys of eating out in this region is the sheer sociability of the Andalusians. Family and friends, often with children in tow, start early with tapas, and usually continue eating until after midnight. The food has a regional bias – the best

Sign advertising house specialities

restaurants have grown from taverns and tapas bars serving fresh, home-cooked food. The restaurants listed on pages 228–37 have been selected for food and conviviality. A guide to tapas and a glossary is on pages 224–5, and pages 226–7 show what to eat and drink.

The dining room of El Churrasco restaurant, Córdoba (see p232)

ANDALUSIAN CUISINE

The food of Andalusia falls into two categories: coastal and inland. Five of the region's eight provinces have stretches of coastline and a sixth, Seville, has a tidal river and several seaports (Cádiz, Sanlúcar, Barbate and Zahara among them) nearby. The cooking of the coastal regions is distinguished by a huge variety of fish and shellfish. The most famous of the many fish dishes of Andalusia is *pesca'ito frito* (fried fish). Fish is integral to the Spanish diet, while meat is an expensive once- or twice-a-week dish – although ham and cheaper

meats, such as knuckle ribs and chops, often appear on tapas menus.

Inland, rich stews with hams and sausages, and game, pork, lamb and chicken dishes are served. Vegetables and salads are excellent, as is Andalusia's signature dish, gazpacho, a soup made from vine-ripened tomatoes and peppers.

Andalusia is the world's largest producer of olive oil, whose flavour is basic to the region's cooking.

MEAL HOURS

In Spain, breakfast, or *desayuno*, is eaten twice. The first is a light meal, often toasted bread with butter and jam and *café con leche* (milky coffee). A more substantial breakfast follows between 10 and 11am, perhaps in a café: a *bocadillo* or *mollete* (a sandwich or roll) with ham, sausage or cheese; a thick slice of *tortilla de patatas* (potato omelette); or a *suizo*

Standing up, enjoying a tapa

or *torta de aceite* (sweet rolls). *Churros* (fried dough strips) are sold mainly from stalls in autumn and winter.

By 1pm, some people will have stopped in a bar for a beer or wine with tapas. By 2 or 2:30pm offices and business close for *al-muerzo* (lunch), the main meal of the day, eaten between 2 and 3pm, followed by a *siesta* hour. By 5:30 or 6pm cafés, *salones de té* (tea rooms) and *pastelerías* (pastry shops) fill up for *la merienda* (tea): pastries, cakes and sandwiches with coffee, tea or juice.

By 8:30pm tapas bars are becoming busy. *La cena* (supper) is eaten from about 9pm, although some places begin service earlier for tourists. In summer people eat as late as midnight, although many country restaurants close around 11pm.

Spaniards tend to lunch out on weekdays and dine out at weekends. Sunday lunch is usually a family affair.

HOW TO DRESS

While a jacket and tie are rarely required, Spanish people dress smartly, especially in city restaurants. In the beach resorts, dress is casual, although shorts are frowned on at night.

READING THE MENU

The Spanish for menu is *la carta*. The Spanish *menú* means a fixed-price menu of the day. The day's specialities

Bar in Calle Gerona, behind the Iglesia de Santa Catalina (see p91), Seville

are often chalked on a board or clipped to the menu. Some finer restaurants offer a *menú de degustación*, which allows you to sample six or seven of the chef's special dishes.

La carta will start with *sopas* (soups), *ensaladas* (salads), *entremeses* (hors d'oeuvres), *huevos y tortillas* (eggs and omelettes) and *verduras y legumbres* (vegetable dishes). Some of the vegetable, salad and egg dishes may be suitable for vegetarians, while others may contain a few pieces of ham, so ask first.

Main courses are *pescados y mariscos* (fish and shellfish) and *carnes y aves* (meat and poultry). Paella and other rice dishes often come as the first course. Follow rice with meat, or start with *serrano* ham or salad and follow with paella. It is quite normal to order just one or two courses from any part of the menu.

Desserts and puddings are grouped as *postres*, but fresh fruit is the preferred choice for desserts in Andalusia.

CHILDREN

Children are generally very welcome, but there are seldom special facilities for them. *Ventas*, or country restaurants, are the exception; they often have play areas.

Stylish dining room of the exclusive Egaña Oriza, Seville *(see p230)*

SMOKING

Fine restaurants will have a selection of *puros* (cigars) which are offered with coffee and brandy. No-smoking areas are now more common with the introduction of anti-smoking laws in the European Union, but small establishments may still be smoky.

WHEELCHAIR ACCESS

Since restaurants are rarely designed for wheelchairs, you (or hotel staff) should call to book and to discuss access to restaurant and toilets. Spanish law now requires all new-build public buildings to have wheelchair access, so newer restaurants will offer easier disabled access and facilities such as adapted restrooms and wheelchair space in dining areas.

WINE CHOICES

Dry *fino* wines are perfect with shellfish, *serrano* ham, olives, soups and first courses. Wines to accompany meals are usually from Ribera del Duero, Rioja, Navarra or Penedés. A tapas bar might serve Valdepeñas or La Mancha wines. *Oloroso* wines are often drunk as a digestif. *(See also What to Drink pp226–7 and The Land of Sherry pp30–31.)*

WHAT IT COSTS

The cheapest places to eat are usually tapas bars and smaller, family-run establishments *(bar-restaurantes)*. A *menú del día* is offered in the majority of restaurants. It is usually three courses and priced well below choices from *la carta*.

Ordering from *la carta* in a restaurant can push your final bill way above average, especially if you choose pricey items like *ibérico* ham and fresh seafood. If you find "bargain prices" for swordfish, hake, sole and other fish, then it is probably frozen. Expect shellfish such as lobster and large prawns, and fish such as sea bass and bream, to be priced by weight. The bill *(la cuenta)*, includes service charges and sometimes a small cover charge. Prices on the menus do not include six per cent *IVA* (VAT), which, as a rule, is added when the bill is totalled. Tipping is just that, a discretionary gratuity. The Spanish rarely tip more than five per cent, often just rounding up the bill.

Credit cards are accepted in restaurants everywhere, but do not expect to pay by credit card in a tapas bar or café.

Relaxed ambience at the Manolo Bar in the Parque María Luisa *(see pp98–9)*, Seville

The Flavours of Andalusia

Andalusia is vast, bordered on one side by the Mediterranean and on the other by the Atlantic. Inland are lofty mountains and undulating hills, endless olive groves and bright fields of sunflowers. The cuisine is as varied as the terrain, with a huge array of seafood, superb meat and game, and a harvest of sun-ripened fruit and vegetables. The *tapeo* (tapas-bar-hopping) is a regional institution and, around Granada, these little morsels are still served free with drinks. Along the coast, especially the Costa del Sol, the influx of foreigners has brought glamorous international restaurants but, inland, traditional recipes are still the norm at old-fashioned inns.

Olives and olive oil

Diners choosing from a selection at a tapas bar

TAPAS

The *tapeo*, or tapas crawl, is an intrinsic part of daily life in Andalusia. Each bar is usually known for a particular speciality: one might be well known for its home-made *croquetas* (potato croquettes, usually filled with ham or cod), while another will serve exceptional hams, and yet another might make the best *albóndigas* (meatballs) in the neighbourhood. Tapas are often accompanied by a glass of chilled, dry *fino* sherry, or perhaps a cold draught beer *(una caña)*. Tapas were once free, but that tradition has largely died out.

SEAFOOD

It's not surprising, given its extensive coastline, that southern Spain offers every imaginable variety of seafood, including cod, hake, prawns, crayfish, clams, razor clams, octopus, cuttlefish, sole and tuna. Almost every seaside resort will offer *pescaíto frito*, originally a Malaga dish, made with whatever fish is freshest that day. In Cádiz, they are served appealingly in a paper cone, and in nearby Sanlúcar you must not miss the sweet and juicy *langostinos* (king prawns).

Jamón iberico belota   Morcilla with onion   Morcilla with rice   Salchichón iberico belota

Chorizo rosario picante

Lomo embuchado

Selection of delicious Spanish *embutidos* (cured meats)

REGIONAL DISHES AND SPECIALITIES

Andalusia embodies many of the images most closely associated with Spain – the heady rhythms of flamenco, striking white villages and bull-fighting. And tapas – in Andalusia, you can easily make a meal of these delectable treats, and every bar has an excellent range. Don't miss the mouthwatering hams from Jabugo and Trevélez which are famed throughout Spain, or the platters of freshly fried fish liberally doused with lemon juice. An ice-cold sherry (the word comes from Jérez, where most sherry is produced) is deliciously refreshing in the searing summer heat and is the most popular tipple at southern fiestas. While pork, particularly *jamon* (cured ham) remains the most appreciated local meat, duck, beef and lamb are also favourites, subtly flavoured with aromatic bay leaves.

Pomegranates

Gazpacho *This famous chilled soup is made with ripe tomatoes, breadcrumbs, garlic, vinegar, olive oil and red peppers.*

Andalusian vegetable seller displaying fresh local produce

used in Andaluz cuisine, and the typical southern breakfast is toasted country bread topped with thin slices of tomato and drizzled with olive oil – utterly delicious. The hot climate is perfect for fruit and vegetables, including luscious peaches, papayas, persimmons, and mangoes, as well as tomatoes, asparagus, aubergines (eggplants) and artichokes. The chilled tomato soup, *gazpacho*, is a classic, but *salmorejo*, which is thicker and topped with a sprinkling of chopped boiled eggs and ham, is even tastier.

MEAT AND GAME

Pork is king in Andalusia. The famous hams of Jabugo (in the southwest) and Trevélez (near Granada) are among the finest produced in Spain, and are made with

Prawns and sardines on display at the fishmarket

free-range, black-footed pigs fed on a diet of acorns. Beef is also popular; endless fields full of glossy black bulls (some raised for bull-fighting but most for meat) are a common sight, and one of the most popular local dishes is *rabo de toro* (bull's tail). All kinds of cured meats are made here, often to traditional recipes which have remained unchanged for centuries. In the wild inland Sierras, you'll find an abundance of game in season, along with the traditional country staples of lamb and rabbit.

FRUIT AND VEGETABLES

The undulating Andalusian fields and hillsides are densely covered with beautiful olive groves, and the best oils are graded as carefully as fine wines. Olive oil is liberally

ON THE MENU

Chocos con habas Cuttlefish is cooked with beans, white wine and plenty of bay leaves.

Pato a la Sevillana Succulent duck, cooked slowly with onion, leeks, carrots, bayleaf and a dash of sherry, this is a speciality of Seville.

Rabo de Toro An Andaluz classic, made with chunks of bull's tail, slowly braised with vegetables, bay leaf and a dash of sherry until tender.

Salmorejo Cordobés A creamy tomato dip thickened with breadcrumbs.

Torta de Camarones Delicious fritters filled with tiny, whole shrimp.

Tortilla del Sacromonte A speciality of Granada: omelette with brains, kidney or other offal, peppers and peas.

Huevos a la Flamenca *Eggs are baked in a terracotta dish with vegetables, ham and chorizo sausage.*

Pescaíto Frito *A seaside favourite, this is a platter of small fish tossed in batter and fried in olive oil.*

Tocino de Cielo *This is a creamy custard dessert with a caramel topping. Its name means "heavenly lard".*

Choosing Tapas

Tapas, sometimes called *pinchos,* are small snacks that originated in Andalusia in the 19th century to accompany sherry. Stemming from a bartender's practice of covering a glass with a saucer or *tapa* (cover) to keep out flies, the custom progressed to a chunk of cheese or bread being used, and then to a few olives being placed on a platter to accompany a drink. Once free of charge, tapas are usually paid for nowadays, and a selection makes a delicious light meal. Choose from a range of appetizing varieties, from cold meats to elaborately prepared hot dishes of meat, seafood or vegetables.

Mixed green olives

Patatas bravas *is a piquant dish of fried potatoes with a spicy red sauce.*

Albondigas *(meatballs) are a hearty tapa, often served with a spicy tomato sauce.*

Almendras fritas *are fried, salted almonds.*

Banderillas *are canapes skewered on toothpicks. The entire canape should be eaten at once.*

Calamares fritos *are squid rings and tentacles which have been dusted with flour before being deep fried in olive oil. They are usually served garnished with a piece of lemon.*

Jamón serrano *is salt-cured ham dried in mountain (serrano) air.*

ON THE TAPAS BAR

Alcachofas Artichokes, typically served pickled in vinegar

Almejas Clams

Berenjenas rebozadas Roasted aubergines (eggplants)

Boquerones al natural Fresh anchovies in garlic and olive oil. Often served fried as well.

Buñuelos de bacalao Salt cod fritters

Cacahuetes Peanuts

Calamares a la romana Fried squid rings

Callos Tripe

Caracoles Snails

Carne en salsa Meat in a thick sauce

Champiñones Button mushrooms fried and served in a light sauce with garlic and parsley

Chiporones a la plancha Grilled cuttlefish with a garlic and parsley sauce

Chopitos Cuttlefish fried in batter

Chorizo al vino Chorizo sausage cooked in red wine

Chorizo diablo Chorizo served flamed with brandy

Costillas Spare ribs

Criadillas Bulls' testicles

Croquetas Croquettes

Ensaladilla Rusa Russian salad, with vegetables and mayonnaise

Gambas pil pil Spicy, garlicky fried king prawns (shrimp)

Habas con jamón Tender broad beans fried with *jamón serrano*

Magro Pork in a paprika and tomato sauce

Manitas de cerdo Pig's trotters

Mejillones Mussels

TAPAS BARS

Even a small village will have at least one bar where the locals go to enjoy drinks, tapas and conversation with friends. On Sundays and holidays, favourite places are packed with whole families enjoying the fare. In larger towns it is customary to move from bar to bar, sampling the specialities of each. A tapa is a single serving, whereas a *ración* is two or three. Tapas are usually eaten standing or perching on a stool at the bar rather that sitting at a table, for which a surcharge is usually made.

Diners make their choice at a busy tapas bar

Chorizo, *a popular sausage flavoured with paprika and garlic, may be eaten cold or fried and served hot.*

Salpicón de mariscos *is a luxurious cold salad of assorted fresh seafood in a zesty vinaigrette.*

Gambas a la plancha *is a simple but flavourful dish of grilled prawns (shrimp).*

Tortilla española *is the ubiquitous Spanish omelette of onion and potato bound with egg.*

Queso manchego *is a sheep's-milk cheese from La Mancha.*

Pollo al ajillo *consists of small pieces of chicken (often wings) sautéd and then simmered with a garlic-flavoured sauce.*

Merluza a la romana Hake fried in a light batter

Migas Breadcrumbs, fried and flavoured with a variety of savoury ingredients

Montaditos Mini sandwiches made with a variety of fillings

Morcilla Black (blood) pudding

Muslitos del mar Crab-meat croquette, skewered onto a claw

Orejas de cerdo Pig's ear

Paella Rice dish made with meat, fish and/or vegetables

Pan de ajo Garlic bread

Patatas a lo pobre Potato chunks sauteéd with onions and red and green peppers

Patatas alioli Potato chunks in a garlic mayonnaise

Pescaítos fritos Fish given a light dusting of flour and fried

Pescaditos Small fried fish

Pimientos Fried green peppers

Pimientos rellenos Stuffed peppers

Pinchos morunos Moorish kebabs, usually of pork

Pulpo Baby octopus

Quesos Spanish cheeses

Rabo de toro Bull's tail

Revueltos Scrambled eggs with asparagus or mushrooms

Salmonetes Red mullet

Sardinas Sardines, fried or grilled

Sepia a la plancha Grilled cuttlefish

Sesos Brains, usually lamb or calf

Truita de patates Catalan name for *tortilla española*

Verdura a la plancha Grilled vegetables

What to Drink in Andalusia

Andalusia is the third-largest of Spain's wine regions and produces some of the world's best-known wines; particularly sherry *(see pp30–31)*. Wine is such a large part of the culture that festivals celebrating the *vendimia* (grape harvest) are held all over the region *(see p36)*. Bars and cafés are an institution in Andalusia, and much public life takes place over morning coffee. Start the day with coffee at the counter in a café, have sherry or beer at midday, wine with lunch, and finish lunch or dinner with coffee and a *copa* of brandy.

A jug of sangria

Autumn grape harvest or *vendimia* celebrated all over Andalusia

Fino from Jerez

Manzanilla from Sanlúcar

Fino from Montilla

WINE

Andalusia produces a few young white table wines, notably Castillo de San Diego, Marqués de la Sierra and wines from El Condado *(see p129)*. Most table wines – *tinto* (red), *blanco* (white) and *rosado* (rosé) – come from other parts of Spain. In more up-market establishments these tend to be Rioja, Ribera del Duero, Navarra and Penedés. Look for the label showing the wine's *denominación de origen* (guarantee of origin and quality). Recent vintages, or *cosecha* wines, are the least expensive; *crianza* and *reserva* wines are aged and more expensive. *Cava*, sparkling wines made by *méthode champenoise* are usually from Catalonia.

Tapas bars tend to serve ordinary Valdepeñas and La Mancha wines. People often dilute these with some *gaseosa*, a fizzy, slightly sweet lemonade. The resulting mixture – known as *tinto de verano* ("summer red wine") – is actually very refreshing.

Castillo de San Diego

FINO

Fino is Andalusia's signature drink. Ask for *un fino*, or *una copa de vino fino*. Depending on where you are, you may be served a dry, pale sherry from Jerez de la Frontera *(see p162)*, a dry Montilla-Moriles wine from Córdoba province, or a dry Manzanilla, a sherry from Sanlúcar de Barrameda *(see p162)*. You can also ask for *fino* by name: for instance, Tío Pepe, a sherry from the González Byass *bodega* in Jerez; Gran Barquero, which comes from Montilla *(see p147)*; or Solear, a Manzanilla from the Barbadillo *bodega* in Sanlúcar. Manzanilla is the favoured drink during the Feria de Abril in Seville *(see p38)*.

Fino wine has a higher degree of alcohol than table wines (around 15 per cent). When drunk, it should have a fresh aroma and be dry and light to the palate. It is usually served chilled, in a small-stemmed, glass with a rim narrower than its base. (Hold it by the base, not around the middle.) However, in some rustic bars, *fino* comes in a tall, straight glass known as a *copita* or a *vasito*.

Fino is most often drunk with first courses and tapas, and its dry taste is a perfect accompaniment to dishes such as *jamón serrano* *(see pp224–5)*.

BEER

Several brands of lager beers are brewed in Andalusia. These all come in bottles, though quite a few of them are available on draught, too. People often drink draught beers with tapas, especially in summer. Ask for *una caña*. One very good local beer, among the best in Spain, is Cruz Campo. Another, which may perhaps be more familiar to non-Spaniards, is San Miguel.

Una caña de cerveza

Cruz Campo in a bottle

Anise brandy (aguardiente)

Moscatel from Málaga

Lepanto coñac from Jerez

COFFEE

In the morning, the Spanish tend to drink *café con leche,* half hot milk, half coffee, often served in a glass instead of a cup. Children and insomniacs might prefer to have a *leche manchada* instead, prepared with just a "shadow" of coffee and lots of hot milk.

Café con leche

Another option is a *cortado,* which is mainly coffee, with a tiny amount of milk. After dinner, you should drink *café solo,* a black espresso-style coffee, which is served in a tiny cup, though it sometimes comes in a short glass.

Café solo

Spanish coffee is made in espresso machines from coffee beans dark-roasted *(torrefacto)* with a little sugar to give it a special flavour.

OTHER DRINKS

Herbal teas or *infusiones* can be ordered in most bars and cafés. *Poleo-menta* (mint), *manzanilla* (camomile), and *tila* (limeflower) are among the best. *Zumo de naranja natural* (freshly squeezed orange juice) is excellent but expensive and not always available. *Mosto* is grape juice. Tap water throughout Spain is safe to drink, but Andalusians are discerning about the taste of their water and buy it bottled from natural springs, such as Lanjarón *(see p189)*; it can be bought either *sin gas* (still) or *con gas* (bubbly). Fresh goat's milk is also available in most villages.

Mineral water from Lanjarón

Fresh orange juice

Camomile tea (manzanilla)

OTHER APERITIFS AND DIGESTIFS

Anise brandy, which is often called *aguardiente,* the name for any distilled spirit, can be sweet or dry. It is drunk from breakfast *(desayuno)* to late afternoon tea *(la merienda)* and is sometimes accompanied by little cakes, especially during festivities. It is also drunk after dinner as a digestif.

Tinto de verano is a summer drink of red wine with ice and *gaseosa.* *Sangría* is a red-wine punch with fruit.

With tapas, instead of *fino,* try one of the mellow aperitif wines, such as *amontillado, oloroso* or *palo cortado* *(see p31),* made in Jerez and Montilla. With your dessert try a *moscatel;* the best known of these is a Málaga wine from Pedro Ximénez or muscatel grapes. Alternatively try a sweet "cream" sherry from Jerez. After dinner, have a brandy with coffee. Spanish brandy comes mainly from the sherry *bodegas* in Jerez and is called *coñac* in bars. Most *bodegas* produce at least three labels and price ranges, often displayed on shelves whose levels correspond to quality.

A good middle-shelf brandy is Magno; top-shelf labels are Lepanto and Larios 1886.

If you are going on, say, to a nightclub, it is customary to switch to tall drinks – whisky with ice and water, gin and tonic or rum and soda. Rum is made on the south coast, where sugar cane is grown.

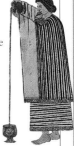

Amontillado from Jerez, an apéritif wine

HOT CHOCOLATE

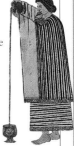

Hot chocolate

Chocolate, originally from Mexico, was imported to Europe by conquistadors. *Tchocolatl,* a bitter, peppery drink made from cocoa, was drunk by the Aztec Indians during religious celebrations.

Nuns, living in the colonies, adapted it by adding sugar to the cocoa, creating a sweeter drink more acceptable to European tastes. During the 16th century, chocolate became increasingly popular. Spain had a monopoly on the export of cocoa beans and the "formula" for chocolate was a state secret for over a century. In the 1830s, the English writer, Richard Ford, described chocolate as "for the Spanish what tea is for the English". For many Spaniards this is still the case.

Indian making tchocolatl

Choosing a Restaurant

The restaurants in this guide have been selected across a wide range of price categories for their good value, exceptional food and interesting location. The restaurants are listed by area, then alphabetically within each price category, from the least expensive to the most expensive. For map references, *see pp112–17*.

PRICE CATEGORIES
Price categories include a three course evening meal for one including a half bottle of house wine and unavoidable extras such as service and taxes.

€ under €25
€€ €25–35
€€€ €35–45
€€€€ over €45

SEVILLE

ALAMEDA Torre de los Perdigones
€€
Calle Resolana s/n, 41009 **Tel** *954 90 93 53* **Map** *1 D3*

With its tranquil setting at the foot of a historic tower and surrounded by a grassy park, this is the perfect place to relax after a day of sight-seeing. The menu is traditional Spanish cuisine with a twist; try the *arroz caldoso* (rice stew) or *magret de pato con salsa de miel y lemon* (duck breast with honey and lemon sauce). There is live music on the terrace in summer.

EL ARENAL Mesón de la Infanta
Tapas €
C/Dos de Mayo 26, 41002 **Tel** *954 56 15 54* **Map** *3 B2 (5 C5)*

Set in a restored historic building in the heart of the lively Arenal district, Mesón de la Infanta offers an excellent choice of traditional dishes, including delicious *guisos* (stews) The tapas bar is a classic on the Sevillian tapas route, with a bewildering array of fine local hams and *embutidos* (charcuterie), along with all the other usual favourites.

EL ARENAL El Cabildo
€€
Plaza del Cabildo, 41001 **Tel** *954 22 79 70* **Map** *3 C2 (5 C4)*

Part of the original ancient Arabic walls have been conserved in this classic and delightfully old-fashioned restaurant. All the traditional Andalusian favourites are on the menu, expertly cooked with fresh local ingredients. Try a platter of fresh fried fish, or Sevillian *revueltos* (scrambled eggs with different fillings), all accompanied by sturdy local wine.

EL ARENAL Enrique Becerra
Tapas €€€
C/Gamazo 2, 41001 **Tel** *954 21 30 49* **Map** *3 B1 (5 C4)*

Housed in a beautifully renovated 19th-century mansion, this plush restaurant-bar offers a fine selection of fish and meat dishes. The daily specials feature Andalusian home-style cooking. The classic aperitif is a wonderful ice-cold Manzanilla sherry, which you can follow with tapas or specialities like roast lamb with pine nuts. Closed Sun & Aug.

EL ARENAL La Isla
Tapas €€€
C/Arfe 25, 41001 **Tel** *954 21 26 31* **Map** *3 B2 (5 C4)*

This attractive, centrally located restaurant features superb seafood specialities from Galicia, including turbot, bream and delicacies such as *percebes* (sea blankets). Some Andalusian dishes, such as a meaty beef stew, also feature on the menu. There is a small tapas bar where you can enjoy fabulous prawns, oysters and a wide range of local hams.

EL ARENAL El Burladero
Tapas €€€€
Hotel Colón, C/Canalejas 1, 41001 **Tel** *954 50 55 99* **Map** *3 B1 (5 B3)*

A smart hotel-restaurant in a grand 19th-century building, El Burladero is decorated with bullfighting memorabilia. You can enjoy caviar and filet mignon, as well as local dishes such as *puchero* (meat in a pot) and, of course, a very fine version of the Andalusian classic *rabo de toro* (braised bull's tail). An upmarket tapas bar is housed upstairs.

EL ARENAL Taberna del Alabardero
Tapas €€€€
C/Zaragoza 20, 41001 **Tel** *954 50 27 21* **Map** *3 B1 (5 C3)*

Housed in a beautiful tile-lined mansion, the Taberna del Alabardero is one of the finest and loveliest restaurants in Seville. The menu offers spectacular contemporary Spanish cuisine, prepared with the freshest seasonal ingredients. There is also an inexpensive bistro for lighter fare, and a vaulted snack bar.

LA MACARENA ConTenedor
€
San Luis 50, 41003 **Tel** *954 91 63 33* **Map** *2 E4*

Directly in front of the church of San Luis, in the bohemian neighbourhood of La Macarena, ConTenedor brings market-fresh produce to the table, in an inspired medley of traditional flavours and other influences. A hip, friendly restaurant. Art exhibitions are held here on Mondays and Sundays. Closed Semana Santa, Feria de Abril; Aug.

LA MACARENA El Rinconcillo
€
Calle Gerona 42, 41003 **Tel** *954 22 31 83* **Map** *6 E2*

Said to be the oldest restaurant in Seville (built around 1670), this clings to its traditional roots, with hams and meats from the Huelva hills, vegetarian-friendly options such as spinach and chickpeas, and its speciality: the catch of the day from Cádiz. There's also a special *menú de degustación* of the day's specials, and a good range of local wines.

Key to Symbols *see back cover flap*

LA MACARENA Eslava
Tapas 📋   €€

C/Eslava 3, 41002 **Tel** *954 90 65 68*   **Map** *1 C4*

This favourite local haunt is not renowned for its decor, which is spartan at best. Instead, the emphasis is firmly on Andalusian cuisine with touches of creativity. The dining area has a full menu of seafood dishes and some excellent salads, while the bar serves up tasty, fresh tapas. Go early for a table. Closed Sun eve; Mon.

SANTA CRUZ El Rincón de Anita
Tapas 🔲 🔲 📋 🔲   €

Plaza del Cristo de Burgos 23, 41004 **Tel** *954 21 74 61*   **Map** *6 E2*

This delightful little restaurant is decorated with colourful tiles, polished wood, images of the Semana Santa processions and lots of plants. This is the perfect place to tuck into tasty Andalusian specialities. Try the *cola de toro* (bull's tail), kidneys cooked in sherry, and home-made desserts. Classic tapas can be enjoyed at the bar.

SANTA CRUZ Corral del Agua
🔲 📋   €€

Callejón del Agua 6, 41004 **Tel** *954 22 48 41*   **Map** *3 C2 (6 D/E5)*

Dine on the cool patio in a lee of the Reales Alcázares gardens, with plants trailing romantically around wrought-iron grilles and a marble fountain bubbling quietly in the background. Antique furniture and paintings adorn the dining room, and the menu emphasizes seasonal specialities, traditionally and expertly prepared. Try the sea bass in a dry sherry. Closed Sun.

SANTA CRUZ Don Raimundo
🔲 📋   €€

Argote de Molino 26, 41004 **Tel** *954 22 33 55*   **Map** *3 C2 (6 D4)*

This former 17th-century convent has stone walls and awesome chandeliers. The speciality is *langostinos*, or large prawns, and the menu veers away from the usual Andalusian tradition, with delicacies such as *costillitas* (knuckle-size ribs) of wild boar baked in a wood oven, tortilla of *camarones* (tiny shrimps), and seafood stew. Closed Sun.

SANTA CRUZ Doña Elvira
🔲 🔲 📋   €€

Plaza de Doña Elvira 6, 41004 **Tel** *954 21 54 83*   **Map** *3 C2 (6 D5)*

Another restaurant with links to the Don Juan legend, being a favourite trysting place for Tenorio and Doña Inez. Indoors or outside, at alfresco tables under trees, this offers traditionally cooked dishes: gazpacho, paella, stews, tuna, prawns and a remarkable *fritura de pescados*, or mixed fried fish. Book ahead or be sure to arrive early.

SANTA CRUZ El Giraldillo
🔲 📋   €€

Plaza Virgen de los Reyes 2, 41004 **Tel** *954 421 45 25*   **Map** *3 C2 (6 D4)*

This restaurant is so close to the Giralda, you'll feel like you're almost inside it. An upmarket variant on other eateries in the area, with a few street tables hugging its walls, El Giraldillo offers the usual typical fare (paella, mixed fish fry, braised bull's tail), as well as alternatives such as clam soup and, for dessert, a stylish chocolate cake.

SANTA CRUZ La Hosteria del Laurel
Tapas 🔲 📋   €€

Plaza de los Venerables 5, 41004 **Tel** *954 22 02 95*   **Map** *4 D2 (6 E4)*

Part of the Laurel hotel, *(see p213)* said to be where writer José Zorrilla wrote his original tale of Don Juan de Tenorio. This restaurant and tapas bar offers a good selection of mountain hams and meats from Huelva, and fish from the Cádiz coast. One of the best bets in the Santa Cruz area, La Hosteria is popular with locals and visitors alike.

SANTA CRUZ La Juderia
🔲 📋   €€

Calle Caño y Cueto 13 **Tel** *954 41 20 52*   **Map** *4 D2 (6 E4)*

Traditional restaurant tucked away in the Santa Cruz/Juderia backstreets. This broadens the typical Andalusian menu to include prime lamb from Castilla and beef from Avila. If available on the day, try other specialities such as the home-made liver pâté, smoked wild Alaska salmon or salted fish from Conil.

SANTA CRUZ Santo
🔲 📋 🔲   €€

Calle Argote de Molino 29, 41004 **Tel** *954 56 00 00*   **Map** *3 C1 (6 D4)*

Part of the five star EME fusionhotel, and located one block from Giralda Cathedral, this restaurant has a richly imaginative menu. Dishes include *sopa de mangos con vieiras* (mango soup with scallops) and *presa Iberica lacada con polenta* (lacquered Iberian pork shoulder with polenta). There is also a food and wine pairing menu.

SANTA CRUZ La Albahaca
🔲 🔲 🔲   €€€

Plaza de Santa Cruz 12, 41004 **Tel** *954 22 07 14*   **Map** *4 D2 (6 E4)*

Overlooking a charming, verdant square dominated by a wrought-iron cross, La Albahaca is one of the most authentic restaurants in the Barrio Santa Cruz. Its fine setting – in a 1920s mansion furnished with 17th-century antiques – makes it a perfect place to enjoy Basque-influenced food, along with excellent local dishes. Closed Sun.

SANTA CRUZ Becerrita
Tapas 🔲 📋 🔲   €€€

C/Recaredo 9, 41004 **Tel** *954 41 20 57*   **Map** *2 E5 (6 F3)*

Becerrita is a beautiful restaurant, warmly decorated in modern Andalusian style. Delicious regional specialities include outstanding croquettes made with bull's tail, or kid flavoured with thyme. At the bar, you can choose from a superb selection of tapas that changes daily, depending on the season. Closed Sun eve; Aug.

SANTA CRUZ Casa Imperial
Tapas 🔲 🔲 📋   €€€

Calle Imperial 29, 41003 **Tel** *954 50 03 00*   **Map** *4 D1 (6 E3)*

Part of the five-star Casa Imperial hotel but also open to non-residents, this is an excellent setting for dinner or lunch away from the hubbub of Santa Cruz. The elegant courtyards of the 16th-century palace serve as both bar and restaurant, offering a changing menu of traditional tapas and full meals from both northern and southern Spain.

SANTA CRUZ Casa Robles   ♿ 🏠   €€€

C/Álvarez Quintero 58, 41001 **Tel** *954 56 32 72*   **Map** *3 C1 (6 D3)*

Right in the heart of Seville, close to the cathedral, this elegant restaurant is decorated with oil paintings, impressive statuary and pretty tiles. Although the menu leans towards seafood, there are also plenty of local meat dishes to choose from, all expertly prepared and exquisitely presented. The desserts, in particular, are miniature works of art.

SANTA CRUZ Santa Cruz   ♿ 🏠 📋   €€€

Plaza de los Venerables, 41004 **Tel** *954 22 35 83*   **Map** *4 D2 (6 E4)*

This large, well-preserved mansion has three areas; a colonnaded interior, a large (and busy) terrace and a Salón Taurino, a small "museum" dedicated to bullfighting, with artworks inspired by the corrida. The menu embraces tradition, with braised bull's tail and a wide range of fish: fish balls, hake and cod – either fried or cooked in vinegar.

SANTA CRUZ Egaña Oriza   ♿ 🏠 📋 🍷   €€€€

C/San Fernando 41, 41004 **Tel** *954 22 72 54*   **Map** *3 C3 (6 D5)*

Tucked against the walls of the Alcázar gardens, Egaña Oriza is located in a beautiful early 20th-century mansion. The dining room is in an elegant, light-filled conservatory, and the sophisticated modern Basque cuisine leans towards fish. Meat dishes and desserts are equally delicious, though, and the wine list is superb. Closed Sat lunch; Sun.

SANTA CRUZ Salvador Rojo   ♿ 🏠 📋 🍷   €€€€

C/San Fernando 23, 41004 **Tel** *954 22 97 25*   **Map** *3 C2 (6 D5)*

A stylish, modern restaurant opposite the old Fábrica de Tabaco, Salvador Rojo offers contemporary Spanish cuisine. The freshest local produce is used with innovative twists: try the stir-fried prawns with Thai rice. Leave room for the fabulous desserts. Classic Spanish wine features, along with some excellent but lesser-known labels. Closed Sun & Aug.

TRIANA Kiosko de las Flores   ♿ 🏠   €

C/Betis (Triana), 41010 **Tel** *954 27 45 76*   **Map** *3 A2 (5 A5)*

Situated on the banks of the Guadalquivir, this restaurant has a lovely terrace with good views of the Old City. Fish is the speciality here – try a platter of mixed fried fish or make a selection from the grilled fish menu. Some meat dishes are also available.

TRIANA Casa Cuesta   *Tapas* 📋   €€

Calle Castilla 1, 41010 **Tel** *954 33 33 35*   **Map** *3 A2*

An excellent find in the streets of Triana, near the Puente Isabel II, Casa Cuesta is open until 1am daily. This café-restaurant was opened in 1880 and retains much of the original tiling and bar furniture. It prides itself on its home-made traditional Triana dishes, mountain hams and fresh fish from the coast. Tapas or restaurant menu all day.

TRIANA Abades Triana   ♿ 🏠 📋 🍷   €€€€

C/Betis 69 (Triana), 41010 **Tel** *954 28 64 59*   **Map** *3 A2 (5 A5)*

Serving excellent international and Mediterranean cuisine, this modern restaurant has a great riverside location and offers spectacular views of the city. Diners can book a spot in the windowed *El Cubo* section of the restaurant, which is a private area with a "floating" glass floor. Taster menus are available.

FURTHER AFIELD (EAST) Tribeca   ♿ 📋   €€€€

Calle Chavez Nogales 3, 41003 **Tel** *954 42 60 00*   **Map** *4 E2*

A taste of lower Manhattan in Seville, Tribeca is one of the most stylish places in town. The menu, devised by chefs Pedro and Jaime Giménez, follows the decor into the realms of modernist-minimal, but with good helpings of updated traditional dishes (lamb is a speciality) and fresh fish from the ports of the Costa de la Luz. Closed Sun.

HUELVA AND SEVILLA

ALJARAQUE Las Candelas   ♿ 📋 🍷   €€

Av de Huelva 3, 21110 **Tel** *959 31 83 01*

A long-established classic in a village 6 km (3.7 miles) from Huelva, this restaurant is decorated with maritime motifs. Seafood, unsurprisingly, dominates the Mediterranean menu, with delicacies such as monkfish in almond sauce, but there is a range of good local meat dishes as well. Traditional Spanish wines. Closed Sun; 24, 25, 31 Dec.

CARMONA Molino de la Romero   *Tapas* ♿ 🏠 📋   €€

C/Sor Angela de la Cruz 8, 41410 **Tel** *954 14 20 00*

Housed in a building dating from the 15th century, originally used by Moors for making olive oil and then as a granary, this restaurant has a large and varied menu ranging from elaborate regional plates to a large selection of tapas. There is a casual dining area and a more formal restaurant. Open for lunch and dinner.

CARMONA San Fernando   📋 🍷   €€

C/Sacramento 3, 41410 **Tel** *954 14 35 56*

An exquisite mansion built in 1700 houses this elegant restaurant, which offers fresh seasonal cuisine from the region. The *salmorejo*, a thick tomato soup garnished with boiled egg and ham, is particularly good, and the *bacalao* (salt cod) is prepared in myriad ways, including with a delectable squid ink and garlic sauce. Closed Sun eve, Mon & Aug.

Key to Price Guide *see p228* **Key to Symbols** *see back cover flap*

CARMONA Casa de Carmona   €€€

Plaza de Lasso 1, 41410 **Tel** *954 19 10 00*

This restaurant is as much about the ambience – in a grand courtyarded palace – as its unfussy modern menu. It is 30km (19 miles) east of Seville, in the beautiful village of Carmona. The restaurant is located in the former stables of the palace, and is an elegant place, though dressing up is not obligatory.

HUELVA El Portichuelo   *Tapas*   €€

Avda Vázquet López 15, 21110 **Tel** *959 24 57 68*

A simple spot in the centre of the city, El Portichuelo serves traditional Andalusian cuisine in the dining room and at the bar, where there is also a range of tapas. The excellent local hams feature prominently, as do seafood and shellfish. There are no culinary surprises, just well-cooked food made with fresh regional products. Closed Sun.

HUELVA Farqueo   *Tapas*   €€

Glorieta de las Canoas, Muelle de Levante, 21003 **Tel** *959 25 26 90*

With excellent views, Farqueo sits right on the Huelva port and has an admirable dining room upstairs, where you can enjoy modern Andalusian cuisine, including cod with a mixed shellfish sauce. There is a hugely popular bar downstairs where you can snack on tapas and enjoy the Thursday night jazz sessions. Closed Sun evening & Mon; 1–15 Sep.

HUELVA Las Meigas   €€€

Avda Guatamala 44, 21003 **Tel** *959 27 19 58*

Some of the freshest seafood can be found at this crisply decorated Galician restaurant. The Gallegos are famed throughout the country for their skill with seafood, which here is simply prepared – grilled, baked in a salt crust or served Gallego-style – in order to enhance its exquisite freshness. Fabulous home-made desserts. Closed Sun.

ISLA CRISTINA Casa Rufino   *Tapas*   €€

Av de la Playa, 21410 **Tel** *959 33 08 10*

A popular beachside place whose menu comprises eight different fish in eight different sauces, including angler fish in raisin sauce. Casa Rufino has a well-deserved reputation for outstandingly fresh seafood and shellfish, and for its excellent wine cellar, which includes all the classics. Closed evenings (except Jul–Oct); Easter, 22 Dec–2 Feb.

JABUGO Mesón 5 Jotas   *Tapas*   €€

Ctra San Juan del Puerto, 21290 **Tel** *959 12 10 71*

Fine Jabugo hams are made here, and the adjoining bar-restaurant is a good place to sample them. This is the original and best of a Spanish chain of tapas bars that have mushroomed across the country. Besides ham and sausage dishes, you can also try the fresh Iberian pork dishes, such as *presa de paletilla al mesón*.

OSUNA Dona Guadalupe   €€

Plaza de Guadalupe 6–8, 41640 **Tel** *954 81 05 58*

This traditional, family-run restaurant is located in the heart of the historic town of Osuna, with a pleasant terrace and outdoor seating. The menu leans heavily towards classic Andalusian fare: *rabo de toro* (ox tail) and a wild mountain pheasant dish cooked in seasoned rice are two of the highlights. Closed Tue; 1–15 Aug.

OSUNA Casa del Marqués   €€€

Calle San Pedro 20, 41640 **Tel** *954 81 22 23*

Part of the grand four-star Hotel de Marqués de Gomera, this is wrapped around a magnificent colonnaded interior patio. The menu is strongly fish-oriented: sole, hake, bream and cod in a variety of elaborate sauces; but also *solomillo* (sirloin) in a sweet Pedro Ximenez sherry sauce, or cooked with duck pâté. Closed Mon evening.

PALOS DE LA FRONTERA El Bodegón   *Tapas*   €€

C/Rábida 46, 21810 **Tel** *959 53 11 05*

An atmospheric former wine cellar now houses this cosy, informal restaurant, where the menu features local culinary stalwarts such as fish baked in a salt crust and meat grilled traditionally over holm oak firewood. The menu is short, but care is taken in selecting fresh local ingredients, and the results are always delicious. Closed Tue; 16–30 Sep.

SANLUCAR LA MAYOR La Alqueria   *Tapas*   €€€€

Hacienda de Benazuza, C/Virgen de las Nieves, 41800 **Tel** *955 70 33 44*

A luxurious hotel (part of the El Bulli empire) with a spectacular restaurant, where the cuisine is modelled on the culinary fireworks of celebrity chef Ferran Adriá. Expect the unexpected and prepare to be dazzled: go for the *menú de degustación*, a series of miniature marvels. Open for dinner only and closed Mon, Sun; call ahead for reservations.

CORDOBA AND JAEN

BAEZA Juanito   €€

Paseo Arca del Agua, 23440 **Tel** *953 74 00 40*

A comfortable family-run hotel and restaurant in the heart of the olive belt. The good home cooking is based on traditional recipes that feature plenty of olive oil. Try the artichokes or the *cabrito con habas*, kid with broad beans. The home-made desserts are scrumptious. Closed Sun eve; Mon.

BAEZA Vandelvira
Calle San Francisco 14, 23440 **Tel** *953 74 81 72*

Taking its name from the architect who designed most of historic Baeza, this is a converted 16th-century Dominican convent with a spacious central covered patio. The period frontage conceals a modern kitchen producing award-winning variants on specialities such as partridge pâté and beef sirlion. Closed Sun eve; Mon.

BAILEN Zodíaco Libra
Antigua Ctra Madrid-Cádiz km 294, 23710 **Tel** *953 67 10 58*

A modern hotel with a large and popular restaurant. In the summer months, the menu features a range of cold soups, such as *ajo bianco* (white garlic) with almonds. Other specialities include the scrambled eggs with ham, asparagus, prawn/shrimp and partridge. In good weather you can eat in the lovely, tree-shaded garden terrace.

CORDOBA Almudaina
Jardines de los Santos Mártires 1, 14004 **Tel** *957 47 43 42*

Once the palace of Bishop Leopold of Austria, this mansion now houses a restaurant serving typical local dishes drawing on the cuisines from distinct cultures that have shaped the city of Córdoba. The Córdoban *salmorejo* is excellent here; alternatively, try the angler fish with stewed tomatoes. Closed Sun eve.

CORDOBA El Blasón
C/José Zorrila 11, 14008 **Tel** *957 48 06 25*

A typical Andalusian mansion set around a magical tiled patio, this is a perfect place to try a wide range of Córdoban specialities, including seafood, sturdy meat stews and wonderful home-made desserts. El Blasón also has a lively and very popular tapas bar and café, and it is handily located, close to the city's main shopping district.

CORDOBA Caballo Rojo
C/Cardenal Herrero 28, 14003 **Tel** *957 47 53 75*

Right next to the Mezquita, this lovely restaurant has a central patio with wrought-iron balconies thickly hung with brightly coloured flowers. The dishes are based on ancient recipes, many adapted from Moorish and Sephardic recipes. Enjoy lamb with honey or the Sephardic salad of wild mushrooms, asparagus, roasted peppers and salt cod.

CORDOBA El Churrasco
C/Romero 16, 14008 **Tel** *957 29 08 19*

A traditional Andalusian mansion, the speciality here is charcoal-grilled meat, but vegetable dishes and soups such as *salmorejo* are also good. The dining rooms are set around two patios: in the lovely Patio del Limonero you can eat under a fragrant lemon tree. You can also sip an aperitif in the nearby wine cellars. Closed Easter, Aug & Christmas.

CORDOBA Taberna Pepe de la Judería
C/Romero 1, 14003 **Tel** *957 20 07 44*

This has been one of Córdoba's most appealing restaurants since it opened in 1928. Dine on a lovely Córdoban patio blazing with flowers, or sit in the dining rooms festooned with photos of notable customers. Try the *flamenquin* (fried rolls of veal and ham), or the unusual cherry gazpacho flavoured with mint.

JAEN Casa Vicente
C/Cristo Rey 3, 23007 **Tel** *953 23 22 22*

A classic restaurant with a bullfighting theme in an Andalusian mansion, Casa Vicente serves typical dishes from Jaén. A good *menú de degustación* features local specialities such as lamb stew, or artichokes in a delicate sauce. Have an aperitif at the bar, which also offers a handful of simple tapas. Closed Sun eve.

JAEN Casa Antonio
C/Fermin Palma 3, 23008 **Tel** *953 27 02 62*

An elegant restaurant with bold modern art and blonde wood panelling serving excellent contemporary Andalusian cuisine. Traditional recipes are reinvented with style and creativity: try the carpaccios of Huelva prawns or tuna. Casa Antonio also has an excellent *menú de degustación*. Closed Sun eve; Mon.

PALMA DEL RIO El Refectorio (Hospederia de San Francisco)
Av Pio XII 35, 14700 **Tel** *957 71 01 83*

Dine in the 15th-century refectory of this out-of-the-way former monastery, now an elegant hotel. The restaurant has an ever-changing menu that features Andalusian cuisine, with lots of typically Córdoban dishes. In autumn and winter, game features prominently. In summer dinner is served on an enchanting candle-lit patio.

UBEDA El Seco
C/Corazon de Jesús 8, 23400 **Tel** *953 79 14 52*

A delightful find in the heart of the lovely Renaissance town of Úbeda, El Seco is a charming, family-run restaurant, with a modest but immaculate dining room. On the menu: fresh and tasty home cooking, including delicious croquettes, game in season and country soups and stews. Closed evenings (except Fri & Sat); July.

UBEDA La Abadía
Calle San Juan de la Cruz 10, 23400 **Tel** *953 79 26 45*

A mix of modernist design and 16th-century architecture – casements, stone walls, arches – makes this one of the smartest places to eat in Úbeda. Starters include partridge pâté, wild mushrooms, and anchovies with grilled red peppers. There is a slim but excellent main course selection of cod and bass or chops and other prime cuts.

Key to Price Guide *see p228* **Key to Symbols** *see back cover flap*

CADIZ AND MALAGA

ARCOS DE LA FRONTERA El Convento   €€
C/Marqués de Torresoto 7, 11630 **Tel** *956 70 32 22*

A charming restaurant located in a lovely 17th-century palace, with an interior patio. They serve unusual local specialities, including the wonderful partridge in almond sauce, and a delicious local soup, *abajao*, made with wild asparagus and eggs. El Convento is linked to a delightful hotel. Closed 7–21 Jan, 1–7 Jul, 1–7 Nov.

LOS BARRIOS Mesón El Copo   €€€
Autovía Cádiz-Málaga km 111 Palmones, 11370 **Tel** *956 67 77 10*

In the village of Palmones, 9 km (5.6 miles) from Los Barrios, Mesón El Copo is one of the most reliable restaurants on this stretch of coastline. Dine on superb seafood – from fried anchovies to lobster and sea bass. Start with *coquinas* (baby clams) followed by *arroz con mariscos* (rice with shellfish). Closed Sun.

BENAHAVIS Los Abanicos   €€
C/Málaga 15, 296 79 **Tel** *952 85 51 31*

A well-known and consistently good restaurant decorated with pretty painted *abanicos* (fans) in the heart of the lovely village of Benahavis. Dine on tasty regional dishes, including the delectable house speciality, *paletilla de cordero* (shoulder of lamb). It is a favourite for Sunday lunch, so be sure to book early. Closed Tue (except Jul & Aug).

BENAOJAN Molino del Santo   €€€
Bda. Estación, 29370 **Tel** *952 16 71 51*

This converted watermill in an idyllic mountain setting, with tables set out under willows by a rushing stream, offers local and international dishes, with good vegetarian options and ingredients sourced locally (mountain hams and meats, local vegetables). It gets very busy in the evenings, so booking ahead is advised. Closed Dec–15 Feb.

CADIZ Freiduria Cerveceria Las Flores   *Tapas*   €
Plaza Topete 4, 11009 **Tel** *956 22 61 12*

The classic Andalusian dish is *pescaíto frito* (mix of fried fish), and every town has several *freidurias* (fried-fish shops). This is the best in Cádiz. Order your fish (anything from shark to squid), which is then fried on the spot and wrapped up to take away for a picnic. You can also eat it out on the terrace. Non-fish snacks include croquettes and empanadas.

CADIZ Balandro   *Tapas*   €€
C/Alameda Apodaca 22, 11004 **Tel** *956 22 09 92*

The Balandro is an elegant restaurant, and its cuisine is creative and sophisticated. The house speciality is seafood from the Bay of Cádiz, prepared with imagination, but there are also plenty of local meat dishes. Try the octopus salad or the beef medallions with port. There is also a popular, cheaper tapas bar. Closed Sun eve; Mon (except Jul & Aug); Sun (Jul & Aug).

CADIZ El Faro   *Tapas*   €€€
C/San Félix 15, 11011 **Tel** *902 21 10 68*

Located in the old fisherman's barrio of Cádiz, El Faro restaurant has a warm, cosy atmosphere. The menu, a wonderful blend of modern and traditional, changes daily but always features local seafood, such as *tortillitas de camarones* (shrimp fritters) or rice dishes flavoured with shellfish from the bay. There is a popular tapas bar, too.

CADIZ Ventorillo del Chato   €€€€
Via Augusta Julia, 11011 **Tel** *956 25 00 25*

A picturesque inn in an 18th-century staging post next to the sea, this place offers authentic Andalusian cuisine. Recipes use superbly fresh fish from the bay, local meat and fresh vegetables, often in combination. A very popular spot for Sunday lunch, when families pile off the glorious beach for a huge feast. Closed Sun evening.

ESTEPONA La Alboreda   €€
Puerto Deportivo de Estepona, 29680 **Tel** *952 80 20 47*

This quayside eatery serves excellent paella and other rice dishes, such as *arroz a la banda* (a kind of fish risotto). It also serves delicious *pescaíto frito* (mix of fried fish) and tasty home-made desserts, such as the *pudin de almendras* (creamy almond pudding). There are lovely views of the yacht-filled harbour from the terrace. Closed Wed & Nov.

ESTEPONA Lido   €€€€
Hotel Las Dunas, Urb La Boladilla Baja, 29680 **Tel** *952 80 94 00*

In the opulent surroundings of the Las Dunas Hotel, this is a stylish restaurant serving contemporary international cuisine. It has magnificent alfresco dining on a balustraded terrace overlooking the gardens, or in an elegant conservatory. Signature dishes include a foie gras mousse and seafood cannelloni. Closed Mon, Tue and evenings.

FUENGIROLA Portofino   €€
Edificio Perla 1, Paseo Maritimo 29, 29640 **Tel** *952 47 06 43*

This seafood restaurant is popular for its friendly service and good Italian food, such as the fish and shellfish brochette or delicious mussels gratinée. It also prepares traditional Andalusian dishes, all served in generous portions. The terrace has views over the glossy, yacht-filled port. Closed Mon; 1–15 Jul. Open evenings only from Jun–Oct.

GAUCIN La Fructuosa 🔲 €€
Calle Convento 67, 29480 **Tel** *617 69 27 84/952 15 10 72*

Terracotta floors, wood-beamed ceilings, white-washed walls and an antique wine press create a cosy atmosphere in this modern Mediterranean/Moroccan restaurant. Try the fresh goat's cheese drizzled with honey. Tables are on a terrace with stunning views of the African coast. Open Fri & Sat evenings; closed Nov–Jan.

GIBRALTAR The Rib Room Restaurant ♿🔲🗐 €€
Rock Hotel, Europa Road **Tel** *73000*

A Gibraltar institution, not least for Sunday lunch, the Rib Room mixes English dishes with Spanish tradition and a hint of Africa. It is more formal than its neighbours, and the menu reflects this: roast beef with cep mushrooms, pork medallions with roasted peppers, pumpkin and pancetta risotto, and Dover sole, as well as vegetarian options.

GIBRALTAR The Waterfront ♿🔲🗐 €
Queensway Quay, Marina Bay **Tel** *45666*

Overlooking Gibraltar's main leisure marina, this is the ideal spot for a light lunch or a meal at sunset. The menu is international, ranging from Cajun chicken wings to curried dishes, with a core of US (burgers, steaks) and European (pasta, steak au poivre) elements. Clement nights see an outdoor seafood barbecue on the quayside. Closed Tue.

JEREZ DE LA FRONTERA Bar Juanito *Tapas* ♿🔲🗐 €€
C/Pascaderia Vieja 8, 11403 **Tel** *956 33 48 38*

This atmospheric tapas bar and restaurant has a heady reputation for its exceptionally large portions of tapas. A fabulous array is offered, of which the local artichokes remain the star dish. You can also dine more substantially on traditional stews and casseroles and a fine *pescaíto frito* (mix of fried fish) from the bay. Closed Sun eve; Mon.

JEREZ DE LA FRONTERA La Mesa Redonda 🗐 €€
C/Manuel de la Quintana 3, 11402 **Tel** *956 34 00 69*

A charming family-run restaurant that remains a favourite with locals for the quality and excellence of its cuisine. The creative menu changes with the seasons, offering seafood, meat dishes and game. Try the *mojama* (cured tuna) as a starter, and do not miss the spectacular beef *salteado* (sautéed with black sausage). Closed Sun; 15 Jul–16 Aug.

MALAGA Antigua Casa de Guardia *Tapas* 🗐🗐 €
C/Alameda Principal 18, 29015 **Tel** *952 21 46 80*

This is Málaga's oldest bar, housed in the former guard post that gives it its name. The speciality is sherry, poured straight from one of the vast barrels stacked behind the bar. Accompany it with a few simple tapas: a plate of prawns or mussels, or silvery *boquerones* (anchovies), which bear no resemblance to their salty cousins. Closed Sun.

MALAGA Mesón Astorga *Tapas* ♿🔲🗐 €€
C/Gerona 11, 29006 **Tel** *952 34 25 63*

Using Málaga's superb local produce with flair makes this classically decorated and typically Andalusian restaurant popular. Try the fried aubergine (eggplant) drizzled with molasses, or the *lomo de cerdo con pasas y piñones* (pork loin with raisins and pine nuts). At the lively tapas bar, you can join the locals tucking into generous *raciones*. Closed Sun.

MALAGA Café de Paris ♿🗐🔣 €€€€
C/Vélez Málaga 8, 29016 **Tel** *952 22 50 43*

An unprepossessing exterior conceals this elegant, classically decorated restaurant, which serves sublime, contemporary Spanish and Mediterranean cuisine. Creative dishes are exquisitely presented, particularly in the exceptional *menú de degustación*. Excellent wine list and immaculate service. Closed Sun eve; Mon.

MANILVA Macues ♿🔲🗐 €€€
Puerto Deportivo de la Duquesa Local 13, 26961 **Tel** *952 89 03 95*

At this upmarket restaurant at the very tip of the Costa del Sol, you can dine on good international and Spanish cuisine on a shaded terrace overlooking the impressive yacht harbour below. House specialities include all kinds of fish baked in salt, and juicy local meat grilled over charcoal. Open for dinner only. Closed Mon.

MARBELLA Altamirano 🗐🔲🗐 €
Plaza Altamirano 3, 29600 **Tel** *952 82 49 32*

In the heart of Marbella's lovely, whitewashed Old Town, this is a welcoming, family-run restaurant with a pretty terrace. Tasty home-cooked dishes include plenty of local seafood, such as a platter of freshly fried fish, typical of the area. The staff are charming. This is one of the best-value options in the Old Town. Closed Wed.

MARBELLA Areté 🔲🎵🗐 €€
Calle Mediterráneo 1, 29600 **Tel** *952 77 73 34*

Set on a corner of the Paseo Maritimo seafront, this modernist hideaway offers *nueva cocina Andaluza* with an accent on healthy eating (one of the two owner-cooks is also a doctor). Recipes change monthly and specials daily, always with a light hand. Walls and floor spaces display works by local artists.

MARBELLA La Comedia 🔲🗐 €€
Plaza de la Victoria, 29600 **Tel** *952 77 64 78*

Since 1998 a fixture in Marbella's Casco Antiguo, La Comedia is now in new hands, but it still pursues the original's philosophy of "around the world in three dishes", offering a startling mix of recipes from across the globe often cross-pollinated with Andalusian classics. Overlooking one of the Old Town's prettiest squares. Closed Mon.

Key to Price Guide *see p228* **Key to Symbols** *see back cover flap*

MARBELLA Santiago
Tapas 🅱️ 📶 🗒️ 🚹 €€

C/Paseo Maritimo 5, 29600 **Tel** *952 77 00 78*

In business for over 50 years, this is probably the best place for seafood on the Costa del Sol. On any day, there might be 40 or 50 fish and shellfish dishes, all very fresh. Tapas are served at the bar, but there is also a huge variety (more than 500) on offer at the adjoining Tabernita de Santiago. Book your table at Santiago well in advance.

MARBELLA Garum
🅱️ 📶 🗒️ €€€

Paseo Maritimo 3, 29600 **Tel** *952 85 88 58*

Timo Hamalainen, formerly of La Comedia, has taken that restaurant's international mix (but not the surreal dish titles) to an airy seafront space with a large enclosed terrace. Salmon 'n' chips and burgers get an upmarket spin, alongside Andaluz classics (*rosada*, *solomillo*) and recipes from as far afield as Thailand and Mexico. Also serves breakfast.

MARBELLA Toni Dalli
🅱️ 📶 🎵 🗒️ 🚹 €€€

El Oasis, Ctra de Cádiz km 176, 29600 **Tel** *952 77 00 35*

A classic on Marbella's Golden Mile since 1981. A meal at this handsome white palace flanked by palms makes for a great night out. The Italian-influenced food includes home-made pastas, meat and fish. Live music is sometimes provided by Toni himself, formerly a popular singer with his own show in California. Closed lunch.

MARBELLA El Portalón
Tapas 🅱️ 📶 🗒️ 🚹 €€€€

Ctra Cádiz-Málaga (N340) km 178, 29600 **Tel** *952 82 78 80*

Elegantly decorated dining rooms overlook flower-filled gardens at this classic Andalusian restaurant. The highlights here are the meat and seafood, both cooked in a traditional brick oven, and you can also enjoy tapas and a glass of local wine in the attractive adjoining *vinoteca*. Closed Sun (except Aug).

MIJAS El Castillo
📶 🗒️ 🚹 €€

Plaza de la Constitución, Pasaje de los Pescadores 2, 29650 **Tel** *952 48 53 48*

This rustic-style restaurant is right on the main square of this enchanting white village. It serves both typically Andalusian and international dishes, which you can enjoy out on the breezy terrace. There is also a flamenco show on certain nights of the week (usually Tuesdays, Thursdays and Sundays, but call to confirm). Closed Fri.

EL PUERTO DE SANTA MARIA Casa Flores
Tapas 🅱️ 📶 🗒️ €€€

C/Ribera del Rio 9, 11500 **Tel** *956 54 35 12*

A traditional family-run restaurant, with a series of intimate dining rooms decorated with pretty tiles, paintings and a smattering of bullfighting memorabilia. Seafood and shellfish are the house specialities, with a spectacular array that includes everything from local sweet striped prawns to unusual delicacies such as barnacles.

EL PUERTO DE SANTA MARIA El Faro de El Puerto
🅱️ 📶 🗒️ 🚹 €€€

Ctra de Fuentebravia km 0.5, 11500 **Tel** *956 87 09 52*

Set in an elegant, low-built villa surrounded by gardens, and part of a small group that includes the El Faro and the Ventorrillo del Chato in Cádiz, this is the most refined restaurant of a remarkable trio. The menu offers sophisticated interpretations of modern dishes, and desserts are not to be missed. Finish with a select Cuban cigar.

RONDA Traga Tapas
Tapas 🅱️ 📶 🗒️ 🚹 €

Calle Neuva 4, 29400 **Tel** *952 87 72 09*

Innovative cuisine is offered as tapas, with mini-prices to match. The tapas include salmon marinated in lemon and vanilla or wild mushrooms sautéed with Spanish onions and garnished with Serrano ham. It is located in the town centre, on a busy pedestrian street. Closed Mon.

RONDA Del Escudero
🅱️ 📶 🗒️ 🚹 €€

Paseo de Blás Infante 1, 29400 **Tel** *952 87 13 67*

With an incomparable garden setting near Ronda's famous bullring, this elegant restaurant offers spectacular views over the valley to go with its traditional Andalusian cuisine. Go for the good-value fixed-price lunch menu, which you can enjoy on the panoramic garden terrace. Closed Sun eve.

RONDA Pedro Romero
🅱️ 🗒️ €€€€

C/Virgen de la Paz 18, 29400 **Tel** *952 87 11 10*

Facing Ronda's graceful bullring, this restaurant is filled with paintings and photographs of famous bullfighters, historic costumes and mounted bulls' heads. It serves well-prepared country food, including *rabo de toro* (braised bull's tail) and *perdices Estofados* (stuffed partridges) as well as traditional stews and casseroles. There is a good range of Spanish wines.

SAN FERNANDO Venta de Vargas
Tapas 🅱️ 📶 🎵 🗒️ €

Plaza de San Juan Vargas, 11100 **Tel** *956 88 16 22*

This popular small-town eaterie was immortalized by the mythical Camarón de la Isla and has lots of flamenco atmosphere. Order *raciones* of classics such as *aliñadas* (potato salad) or tuck into typical local stews and fresh fish from the bay. Finish up with *tocino de cielo*, a creamy egg custard with caramel syrup, for dessert. Closed Sun eve; Mon.

SAN ROQUE Villa Victoria (Los Remos Rest)
📶 🗒️ 🚹 €€€

Ctra San Roque-La Linea 351 km 2.8, Campamento, 11314 **Tel** *956 69 84 12*

Housed in a restored Victorian mansion with Mediterranean decor, this restaurant serves exquisite dishes. The focus is on first-rate seafood, and the *menú de degustación* includes shrimp fritters and sea nettles. There is always a good list of seasonal specialities, too, including wild mushrooms. Closed Sun eve; Mon.

SANLUCAR DE BARRAMEDA Casa Bigote   *Tapas*   €€€
C/Bajo de Guia 10, 11540 **Tel** *956 36 26 96*

At the mouth of the Guadalquivir River, this typical sailor's tavern is legendary throughout Andalusia. The tapas bar, hung with hams and piled up with wooden barrels, offers fabulous seafood tapas, or you can dine in the wooden-beamed *comedor* on *langostinos de Sanlúcar* (large, sweet prawns) and fresh fish. Closed Sun; Nov.

TARIFA Arte-Vida   €€
Ctra Nacional 340 km 79.3, 11380 **Tel** *956 68 52 46*

This is a fabulous hotel, set in dunes right on Tarifa's endless beach. Its pretty restaurant-café features a stylishly simple blue-and-white decor and serves fresh salads, pizzas and grilled seafood, along with a few more exotic dishes, such as Thai coconut soup. They also do cakes, delicious brownies and coffee. The views reach all the way to Africa.

TARIFA Mesón de Sancho   *Tapas*   €€€
Ctra Cádiz-Málaga km 94, 11380 **Tel** *956 68 49 00*

A classic inn just outside Tarifa, on the road to Algeciras. Warm and friendly, it is decorated in typical *mesón* style, and offers set menus featuring sturdy Andalusian meat dishes, such as beef with mushrooms. It also serves a range of generous *raciones* in the bar. Sancho is a popular spot for family outings, particularly Sunday lunch.

TORREMOLINOS Bar Restaurante Casa Juan   *Tapas*   €€
C/San Gines 18–24, 29620 **Tel** *952 37 35 12*

A popular beachfront restaurant with an expansive terrace offering home-cooked favourites, such as *arroz con bogavante* (rice with lobster) and *fritura Malagueña*, which are based on old family recipes (provided by Juán's mother and grand-mother). The place has been going since the tourist boom first transformed this former fishing village. Closed Mon.

TORREMOLINOS Frutos   *Tapas*   €€€€
Av de la Riviera 80, 29620 **Tel** *952 38 14 50*

The grande dame of Costa del Sol restaurants, Frutos serves superb meat and fish dishes. There is a terrace and two glassy dining areas where you can enjoy suckling pig, followed by *arroz con leche*. The remarkable wine cellar in the basement can also be visited. An informal tapas bar at the entrance serves lighter meals. Closed Sun eve.

VEJER DE LA FRONTERA Venta Pinto   *Tapas*   €€
Calle La Barca de Véjer, 11150 **Tel** *956 45 08 77*

Véjer de la Frontera is a magical, hilltop town on the Costa de la Luz, with a shadowy maze of narrow alleys that evoke its Moorish past. This pretty restaurant, in a former staging post 3 km (1.8 miles) from the town centre, serves creative versions of local dishes and has a popular tapas bar where you can also buy local specialities.

ZAHARA DE LOS ATUNES Casa Juanito   *Tapas*   €€
C/Sagasta 7, 11393 **Tel** *956 43 92 11*

In a pretty fishing village and low-key seaside resort, this is a charming, typically Andalusian restaurant with an airy, expansive terrace just steps from the beach. Seafood is the house speciality, particularly the tuna that gives the town its name. Casa Juanito also has a dining area with a tapas bar. Closed Wed (except Aug); Jan, Nov, Dec.

GRANADA AND ALMERIA

ALMERIA Club de Mar   €
Playa de la Almadrabillas 1, 04007 **Tel** *950 23 50 48*

Enjoy fresh fish and shellfish right on the seafront at the Almerían yacht club, where well-heeled locals and sailors mingle on the breezy terrace. The fresh seafood complements the views over the port, and the *bullabesa* (Spanish bouillabaisse) and *fritura* (mixed fried fish) are renowned specialities. There is also a good-value lunch menu.

ALMERIA Rincón de Juan Pedro   *Tapas*   €
C/Federico Castro 2, 04130 **Tel** *950 23 58 19*

A much-loved stalwart on Almería's busy tapas scene, this bar serves a wonderful range of tapas – included in the price of a drink. You can dine more substantially on *raciones*, as well as meat and seafood specialities and local dishes, such as *trigo a la cortijera* (a stew with wheat berries, meat and sausage). Closed Mon.

ALMERIA Casa Sevilla   *Tapas*   €€
Calle Rueda López, 04001 **Tel** *950 27 29 12*

This family restaurant has become something of a social centre: once a month, it becomes a wine club, where you can sample some of 8,000 local and national wines. At other times, you can enjoy these wines with specials from the day's catch: angler fish in a white wine and almond sauce, and tuna tartare. Closed Sun & Mon evenings.

ALMERIA Bodega Bellavista   €€€
Urbanización Bellavista, Llanos del Alquián, 04130 **Tel** *950 29 71 56*

In an unlikely location in a housing complex near the airport, this charmingly old-fashioned restaurant offers a range of classic and innovative Andalusian dishes made with top-quality local products. Fish and shellfish predominate, but you can also try good beef and kid. A huge range of wines from all around Spain is available. Closed Sun eve; Mon.

Key to Price Guide *see p228* **Key to Symbols** *see back cover flap*

ALMERIA Valentin 🗐 €€€

Calle Tenor Iribarne 19, 4001 **Tel** *950 26 44 75*

Hidden just off Almeria's central Puerta Purchena gate, this is the smartest place to sample the city's speciality: seafood. A dedicated *marisqueria* (a place specializing in shellfish), Valentin offers seafood from the tiniest white and red *gambas* (prawns) to *bogavante* (lobster), plus the day's selection from the nearby fish market. Closed Mon & Sep.

BUBION Teide *Tapas* 🛦 🎞 €

C/Carretera 70, 18412 **Tel** *958 76 30 37*

Lost in the wilderness of the Alpujarras, this is a simple stone-built restaurant surrounded by a charming, informal garden with pots of flowers and shady trees. They serve traditional dishes such as roast kid and generous salads of local vegetables. It also serves free tapas with a drink in the time-honoured Andalusian tradition. Closed Tue and 15–30 Jun.

GRANADA Antigua Bodega Castañeda *Tapas* 🛦 🗐 €

C/Almireceros 1–3, 18010 **Tel** *958 21 54 64*

With its time-worn tiles, huge wooden barrels and battered air, Bodegas Casteñeda is one of the most delightful and authentic of Granada's tapas bars. Try the melt-in-the-mouth Trevélez ham (which has its own *denominación de origen*) or the wide variety of seafood conserves. A glass of ice-cold sherry is the perfect way to begin the evening.

GRANADA Chikito *Tapas* 🎞 🗐 🍴 €

Plaza del Campillo 9, 18009 **Tel** *958 22 33 64*

Built on the site of a café where Garcia Lorca and his contemporaries used to meet, Chikito serves broad beans with ham and Sacromonte omelette (prepared with brains, but tastier than you might think) as specialities. Why not try the *piononos* (aniseed-scented cake)? You can enjoy tapas at the brick bar, inset with painted tiled scenes. Closed Wed.

GRANADA Mirador de Morayma 🎞 🎵 🗐 €€

C/Pianista Garcia Carrillo 2, 18010 **Tel** *958 22 82 90*

Situated in the Albaicín, with views of the Alhambra, this charming patio-restaurant specializes in local dishes, such as *remojón* (a salad of oranges and codfish) and kid fried with garlic. The wine list includes organic wines produced on the restaurant's own estate. Closed Sun.

GRANADA Velázquez *Tapas* 🛦 🗐 🍴 €€€

C/Profesor Emilio Orozco 1, 18010 **Tel** *958 28 01 09*

The ambience here is warm, and the food is imaginative, with modern interpretations of such Moorish dishes as *bstella*, pigeon in pastry with pine nuts and almonds, and savoury almond cream soup. Velázquez has an old-fashioned lively bar where you can enjoy tapas along with good local wines and Andalusian sherries. Closed Sun; Aug.

GRANADA Ruta del Veleta 🛦 🎞 🍴 €€€€

Ctra Sierra Nevada 136, km 5,400 Cenes de la Vega, 18190 **Tel** *958 48 61 34*

Out on the winding old road to the Sierra Nevada, on the fringes of Granada, this traditional restaurant has an excellent reputation for its hearty regional cuisine. The decoration, with typical Alpujarran textiles and ceramic jugs, goes well with dishes such as roast baby kid and good seafood. Try the game in season.

GRANADA Carmen de San Miguel 🛦 🎞 🗐 €€€€

Plaza Torres Bermejas 3, 18009 **Tel** *958 22 67 23*

The Andalusian specialities at this pretty restaurant include the *arroz caldoso con conejo y codorniz* (rabbit and Cornish hen with brothy rice) or try the menu *degustación*. Everything is fresh and imaginatively prepared by a talented team of young chefs. There are wonderful views of the Albaicín from the terrace. Closed Sun.

LOJA La Finca 🛦 🎞 🗐 🍴 €€€€

Hotel La Bobadilla, Autovia Granada-Sevilla, 18300 **Tel** *958 32 18 61*

Worth a detour off the *autovia*, this exceptional restaurant in a luxury hotel is a place for fine dining. The chef makes creative use of farm-fresh vegetables, capon and pork, game (in season) and seafood. Splash out on the wonderful *menú de degustación*, and soak up the romance of the garden terrace. Closed lunch.

MOTRIL Tropical 🗐 €€

Av Rodriguez Acosta 23, 18600 **Tel** *958 60 04 50*

A simple inn with a good restaurant serving a wide choice of typical Andalusian dishes in a classic Spanish seaside setting. Both seafood, such as *zarzuela de mariscos* (seafood casserole) and meat, such as *choto a la brasa* (roast baby kid), are specialities here. For dessert, try the sorbet made with *chirimoya* (custard apple). Closed Sun; Jun.

ORGIVA El Limonero 🛦 🎞 🗐 €

Calle Yáñez 27, 18400 **Tel** *958 78 51 57*

After 12 years, this has become an establishment in the Alpujarran capital, mixing surf and turf specials: knuckles of beef, solimillo of lamb, sea bream and steamed salmon. The emphasis is on healthy eating, with inventive salads and pastas. Open evenings (from 7pm) and Sun lunch only.

VERA Terraza Carmona *Tapas* 🛦 🎞 🗐 🍴 €€

C/Del Mar 1, 04620 **Tel** *950 39 07 60*

A simple roadside hotel with a fine restaurant that has won several local awards. The specialities here are excellent seafood and unusual regional dishes such as *gurullos con conejo* (pasta with rabbit). In season, game dishes feature prominently, including wild boar with olives and almonds. There is also a pretty tapas bar. Closed Mon; 8–21 Jan.

SHOPS AND MARKETS

Shopping in Andalusia is a highly pleasurable business, particularly if you approach it in a typically Spanish manner. Here, shopping fits in with the climate, always respects the siesta and is meant to be an unhurried, leisurely activity, punctuated with frequent coffee-breaks, tapas and afternoon tea.

Though a number of European chain stores and franchises are beginning to appear all over Spain, the towns and villages of the south are refreshingly full of shops and businesses that are unique to the area. The region is

Traditional polka-dot flamenco dress

renowned for its high-quality, traditional arts and crafts, and there is an overwhelming choice of ceramics, leather goods, marquetry, jewellery in filigree silver and sweets and biscuits.

World-famous wines can be had from the *bodegas* of Jerez, Montilla, Málaga and Sanlúcar de Barrameda. A visit to a *bodega*, an experience in itself, is the best way to become familiar with the variety of wines on offer.

Many shops still provide a charming personal service. Although few assistants speak English, most are very obliging.

Calle de las Sierpes, one of the busiest shopping streets in Seville

WHEN TO SHOP

Spanish shops tend to close during the afternoon siesta (except for department stores and touristy souvenir shops in the large towns). Most shops open at 9:30am and close at 1:30pm. They usually reopen about 4:30pm or 5pm, and stay open until around 8pm. These times will obviously vary from shop to shop; boutiques, for example, rarely open before 10am. Times also tend to vary during summer – some shops close altogether in the afternoon heat, while others will stay open later than usual, in order to take full advantage of the large numbers of visitors.

Many shops – especially if they are in small towns – close on Saturday afternoons. This practice, however, is now gradually disappearing.

Sales generally take place in January and July, though shops may also sometimes offer pre-Christmas discounts or start their sales in late December.

HOW TO PAY

It is still customary among Spaniards to pay in cash. While many shops, especially the larger stores, now accept major credit cards, few take traveller's cheques.

You are entitled to exchange goods if you can produce a receipt, although this does not apply to items bought in a sale. Large shops and department stores tend to give credit notes rather than cash refunds. It is a good idea to check the shop's policy with a sales assistant before you buy anything.

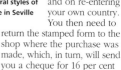

One of several styles of plate made in Seville

VAT EXEMPTION

Visitors to Spain who come from countries outside the European Union can claim a 16 per cent refund of sales tax (*IVA*, pronounced "eeva" in Spanish) on items bought at large department stores such as **Cortefiel** and **El Corte Inglés**. For each item that you purchase costing more than 90 euros, you need to collect a form from the store's central cash desk. You should have this stamped both as you leave Spain and on re-entering your own country. You then need to return the stamped form to the shop where the purchase was made, which, in turn, will send you a cheque for 16 per cent of the value of the articles.

An array of fans at Díaz, Calle de las Sierpes, Seville

Stylish hats from Sombrerería Herederos de J Russi in Córdoba

SHOPPING IN SEVILLE

Seville is a charming city in which to shop, offering the buyer a unique concoction of old-style regional crafts and good modern design.

The district that surrounds Calle Tetuán and the pedestrianized Calle de las Sierpes *(see p74)* is the place to visit for the best of Seville's old and new shops. This is a smart area of bustling streets, where you will find an eclectic range of goods.

Clothes that have a distinctly Andalusian style are displayed at the designers **Victorio & Lucchino**, while stylish **Loewe** makes exquisite luggage and leather bags, clothes and accessories in striking colours. **Purificación Garcia** sells chic clothes.

The streets around the Plaza Nueva are full of shops such as **Nuria Cobo**, **Paco Rodriguez** and **Adolfo Dominguez**, selling stylish, tailored clothes; and quaint shops that sell religious objects. For typically Andalusian items, such as elaborate fans, go to **Diaz**; for top-quality *cordobés* hats to **Maquedano** and for fabulous, hand-embroidered shawls, to **Foronda**.

Around the Barrio de Santa Cruz is a range of interesting shops. Among these are **Casa Rodríguez** and **Velasco**, which specialize in trimmings for church robes and religious images. For the most exquisite baby clothes, head for **Larrana** and for jasmine-scented eau de toilette, stop at **Agua de Sevilla**. The

Supermercado Baco is a small grocers stocking gourmet Spanish food and wines. The Calle Hernando Colón has a few curious shops for collectors of everything from old children's toys to stamps, while **El Postigo**, in the El Arenal area, is an arts and crafts centre with a good selection of hand-made items on sale. **Sevillarte**, which is close to Real Alcázar *(see pp82–3)*, and **Martián** sell attractive ceramics for both utility and decoration.

For some of Andalusia's finest ceramics, however, head for Triana *(see p102)*. Look out in particular for **Cerámica Santa Ana**, **Antonio Campos** and the many small workshops along the Calle Covadonga.

Triana is also a good area for purchasing flamboyant flamenco outfits, while at **Juan Osete** you can buy a marvellous range of *feria* accessories.

Anyone who claims to be a serious collector of antiques must make a point of calling at **Antigüedades Angel Luis Friazza**, which specializes in classic Spanish furniture.

At **La Trinidad** glass factory Seville's famous blue glass is much cheaper than that sold in the city's gift shops.

La Trinidad, makers of Seville's characteristic blue glassware

Muebles Ceballos, situated on the busy Calle de la Feria, is one of several shops in the Seville area that specializes in traditionally made wickerwork items.

CORDOBA

Córdoba presents plenty of options for the shopper. Perhaps the most fascinating shopping area is within the old narrow streets of the Judería *(see p140)*. Here the **Zoco Municipal** runs an interesting selection of craft workshops making Córdoban specialities such as filigree silver jewellery, hand-painted ceramics, leatherware and wonderful, award-winning painted masks. Ceramics, leatherware and woodwork can also be found at **Artesanos Cordobeses**. The area surrounding the Mezquita *(see p144)* is packed with souvenir shops, which apart from the expected tourist trinkets, sell a range of fine handicrafts. Of these, **Meryan** specializes in embossed leather goods.

At the guitar workshop of **Manuel Reyes Maldonado** you can purchase highest quality, custom-built guitars, many of which end up in the hands of internationally renowned musicians.

One of the most celebrated hat-makers in the whole of Spain is the **Sombrerería Herederos de J Russi**. You can purchase a typical, flat-topped *córdobes* hat here for a great deal less than the price that would be asked of you in either Madrid or Seville.

Manuel Reyes Maldonado in his guitar workshop in Córdoba

Marquetry in the making in a
Granada workshop

GRANADA

The characteristically cold
winters ensure that shops in
Granada keep a good range
of smart winter clothes and
shoes. **Julio Callejón** has an
original collection of shoes,
Zara stocks both mens-
wear and womenswear,
and **Cortefiel** is a
quality department
store specialising
in clothing. With
the Sierra Nevada
so close by, ski-
wear is sold in
most stores as
well as in many
specialist shops.

The city centre is
full of surprises,
among them the
Mercado Arabe, a long gallery
packed with shops that sell
Moroccan-inspired clothing and
accessories. **Artesania Maria
Agustia Navarro** specializes in
marquetry and mantillas.

Tienda La Victoria has a
superb selection of old prints,
curios and furniture; and in the
streets around the Gran Vía are
some grand *platerías* – smart
shops selling silverware.

Basketware from
Alhama de Granada

ANDALUSIA

In Andalusia people frequently
make special trips to towns
famed for one particular item,
such as olive oil, wine, rugs
or furniture. If you have time
to explore, the whole region
offers countless local, hand-
made specialities.

The finest virgin olive oils
come from Baena *(see p147)*
and Segura de la Sierra *(see
p156)*. Some of the best olive
oil in Sevilla province is sold
in the village of Ginés. Many
monasteries make and sell their
own sweets and biscuits, which
can be an unusual gift.

There are several *bodegas*
which are worth a visit, namely
those in Jerez *(see p162)*, in
Sanlúcar de Barrameda *(see
p162)*, in Montilla *(see
p147)* and in Málaga
town *(see p180)*.

Botijos – spouted
ceramic drinking
jugs – are a local
speciality of the
town of La Rambla,
30 km (19 miles)
south of Córdoba.
In Córdoba province,
Lucena *(see p147)* is a
good place to buy cer-
amics and wrought ironwork.
Ronda *(see p176)* has a few
shops shops selling rustic-style
furniture. In Guarromán in Jaén
province, antique furniture is
sold at **Trastos Viejos**, which
is an old *cortijo* (farmhouse).

In Granada province, the
villages of Las Alpujarras *(see
p198)* are famous for *jarapas*,
(rag rugs), basketwork and
locally grown medicinal herbs.

Fruit and vegetable market in Vélez
Blanco *(see p199)*

Just north of Granada, in the
small village of Jún, **Cerámica
Miguel Ruiz** collects and sells
some of the finest ceramics
made all over Andalusia.

Exquisite hand-embroidered
shawls are sold by **Angeles
Espinar** in Villamanrique de
Condesa, outside Seville.

MARKETS

The markets held in most
Andalusian towns offer a
wonderful opportunity to try
local food specialities, including a wide range of sausages,
cheeses and cured ham.

Most markets tend to sell a
little of everything. However,
Seville does have a few special-
ized markets. These include
an antiques and bric-a-brac
market, which is held in Calle
Feria on Thursdays.

On Sundays, Los Pájaros pet
market takes place in Plaza del
Alfalfa, and stamps and coins
are traded at Plaza del Cabildo.
All manner of bric-a-brac are
sold on Charco de la Pava
in La Cartuja, and a bigger
rastro (flea market) is held
in the Parque Alcosa, northeast of the centre.

The food markets in Plaza de
la Encarnación and El Arenal
are both very good.

Córdoba has an absorbing
flea market on Saturdays and
Sundays at the 16th-century,
arcaded Plaza de la Corredera.

On the Costa del Sol, bric-a-
brac markets and car boot sales
are popular. The best of these
is held on Saturday morning
beside the bullring at Puerto
Banús, just outside Marbella.

Pottery stall at the Plaza de la Corredera market in Córdoba

DIRECTORY

SEVILLE

Department Stores
El Corte Inglés
Pl Duque de la Victoria 10.
Map 1 C5 (5 C2).
Tel 95 459 70 00.
www.elcorteingles.es

Fashion and Accessories
Adolfo Dominguez
Calle Sierpes 2. **Map** 3 C1
(5 C2). *Tel* 95 422 65 38.
www.adolfo-
dominguez.com

Arcab
Paseo Colón 18.
Map 3 B2 (5 B5).
Tel 95 456 14 21.
www.arcab.es

Loewe
Plaza Nueva 12.
Map 3 B1 (5 C3).
Tel 95 422 52 53.
www.loewe.com

Maquedano
Calle de las Sierpes 40.
Map 3 C1 (5 C3).
Tel 95 456 47 71.

Purificación García
Plaza Nueva 8.
Map 3 B1 (5 C3).
Tel 95 450 11 29.
www.purificaciongarcia.
com

Victorio & Lucchino
Plaza Nueva 10.
Map 3 B1 (5 C3).
Tel 95 450 26 60.
www.victorioy
lucchino.com

Zara
Calle Jose de Velilla 2–4.
Map 3 B1 (5 C2).
Tel 95 456 00 96.
www.zara.es

Children's Clothes
Larrana
Calle Blanco de los Ríos 4.
Map 3 C1 (6 D3).
Tel 95 421 52 80.

Shoes
Nuria Cobo
C/Méndez Núñez esq,
Rosario 14.
Map 3 B1 (5 C3).
www.nuriacobo.com

Paco Rodriguez
C/Tetuán 5–7. **Map** 3 C1
(5 C3). *Tel* 95 421 66 06.

Flamenco
Calzados Mayo
Plaza del Alfalfa 2.
Map 3 C1 (6 D3).
Tel 95 422 55 55.

Díaz
Calle de las Sierpes 71.
Map 3 C1 (5 C3).
Tel 95 422 81 02.

Juan Foronda
Calle de las Sierpes 79.
Map 3 C1 (5 C3).
Tel 95 421 40 50
www.juanforonda.com

Juan Osete
Calle Castilla 10.
Map 3 A1.
Tel 95 434 33 31.

Perfume
Agua de Sevilla
San Fernando 3.
Map 3 C3 (6 D5).
Tel 95 450 15 38.
www.aguadesevilla.es

Religious Objects
Casa Rodríguez
Calle Francos 35.
Map 3 C1 (6 D3).
Tel 95 422 78 42.

Velasco
Calle Chapineros 4
(off Calle Francos).
Map 3 C1 (6 D3).
Tel 95 422 60 38.

Arts and Crafts
Antonio Campos
C/Alfarería 22, Triana.
Map 3 A2.
Tel 95 434 33 04.

Cerámica Santa Ana
Calle San Jorge 31,
Triana. **Map** 3 A2 (5 A4).
Tel 95 433 39 90.

Martián
Calle de las Sierpes 74.
Map 3 C1 (5 C3).
Tel 95 421 34 13.

Muebles Ceballos
Calle de la Feria 49 (near
Calle de Relator). **Map** 2
D4. *Tel* 95 490 17 54.

El Postigo
Calle Arfe s/n.
Map 3 B2 (5 C4).
Tel 95 456 00 13.

Sevillarte
Calle Vida 13. **Map** 3 C2
(6 D5). *Tel* 95 421 03 91.
www.sevillarte.com

La Trinidad
Avda de Miraflores 18–20
(off Ronda de
Capuchinos). **Map** 2 F4.
Tel 95 435 31 00.

Art and Antiques
**Antigüedades Angel
Luis Friazza**
Calle Zaragoza 48.
Map 3 B1 (5 B3).
Tel 95 422 35 67.

Food and Wine
Hornos San Bernado
Avda Menéndez Pelayo 8.
Map 4 D2 (6 E5).
Tel 95 441 90 53.

**Hornos de San
Buenaventura**
Calle Carlos Cañal 28.
Map 3 B1 (5 B3).
Tel 95 422 33 72.

Supermercado Baco
Calle Cuna 4. **Map** 3 C1
(6 D2). *Tel* 95 421 66 73.

El Torno
Plaza del Cabildo s/n.
Map 3 C2 (5 C4).
Tel 95 421 91 90.

CÓRDOBA

Fashion
Mango
Avda Gran Capitán 14–16.
Tel 957 48 53 54.
www.mango.com

Arts and Crafts
Artesanos Cordobeses
Judios, s/n (Zoco).
Tel 957 20 40 33.

**Manuel Reyes
Maldonado**
Calle Armas 4.
Tel 957 47 91 16.

Meryan
Calleja de las Flores 2.
Tel 957 47 59 02.

**Sombrerería Herederos
de J Russi**
Calle Conde, Gondomar 4.
Tel 957 47 10 88.

Zoco Municipal
Calle Judios s/n.
Tel 957 29 05 75.

GRANADA

Fashion, Shoes and Accessories
Adolfo Dominguez
Calle Alhondigas 5.
Tel 958 25 27 85.

Cortefiel
Gran Vía de Colón 1.
Tel 958 22 92 99.
www.cortofiel.es

Julio Callejón
Calle Mesones 36.
Tel 958 25 87 74.
www.juliocallejon.com

Zara
Calle Recogidas 8.
Tel 958 25 25 84.

Tienda La Victoria
Calle Estribo 6
Tel 958 22 23 47.

Arts and Crafts
Artesania Beas
Santa Rosalia 20.
Tel 958 12 00 34.

**Artesania Maria
Angustia Navarro**
Calle Alcaicería 2.
Tel 958 22 58 28.

Mercado Arabe
La Alcaicería.

Antiques and Gifts
**Antigüedades
Gonzalo Reyes**
Meson Placeta
de Cauchiles 1.
Tel 958 52 32 74.

Food and Wine
Flor y Nata
Avda Constitucion 13.
Tel 958 27 23 45.

ANDALUSIA

Angeles Espinar
Calle Pascual Márquez 8,
Villamanrique de Condesa,
Sevilla. *Tel* 95 575 56 20
(call ahead).

Cerámica Miguel Ruiz
Camino Viejo de Jún s/n,
Jún, Granada.
Tel 958 41 40 77.

Trastos Viejos
Autovía E5 km 280,
Aldea de los Rios,
Guarromán, Jaén.
Tel 953 61 51 26.

What to Buy in Andalusia

The strong and vibrant culture of Andalusia is reflected in the items available in the region's markets and shops. Andalusia has a long tradition of arts and crafts, so its towns and villages produce a surprising range of unique, often exquisite, hand-made goods. Many towns have specialities; for example, Granada is famous for marquetry and Moorish-style painted ceramics; Seville for fans and *mantillas*; Jerez, Montilla and Málaga for their renowned wines; while Córdoba specializes in filigree silver, leather work and guitars.

Traditional glazed earthenware pots from Úbeda (*see pp154–5*) in the province of Jaén

THE CERAMICS OF ANDALUSIA

The rich, terracotta soil of Andalusia has been utilized for centuries in the creation of practical and decorative ceramics. The variety encompasses simple earthenware cooking dishes *(cazuelas)*, drinking jugs *(botijos)*, pots *(tinajas)*, decorative painted tiles *(azulejos)*, and kitchen and tableware. You can buy them from workshops or, more cheaply, from local markets.

Ceramic plate painted in traditional colours

Plate from Ronda spattered in blue and green

Bowl from Córdoba in a traditional design

Replicas of 18th-century tiles from Triana (*see p100*)

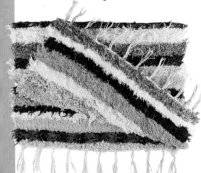

Rugs
Andalusian rug-making skills have developed over centuries. The most famous rug-making area is in the Alpujarras (see pp198–9), where rugs are made in various fibres, including cotton and wool, and in colour schemes in which earth colours and blues predominate.

Leather Goods
Leather goods such as bags and belts can be bought all over Andalusia. Embossed leather, however, is a speciality of the city of Córdoba (see pp140–46).

Inlaid Boxes
Marquetry is produced in Granada (see pp190–96). Craftsmen make furniture, boxes, and other items inlaid with ivory and coloured woods in Moorish designs.

Handmade Fans
A classic souvenir from Andalusia, a fan is useful in the searing heat. The most exclusive are wooden, carved and painted by hand.

Castanets
Castanets, a classic flamenco musical instrument, can be bought in a medley of sizes, made of wood or plastic.

Guitars
In the land of flamenco, guitars are a speciality. Workshops in Córdoba produce top-quality, custom-made guitars, many of which are destined for famous guitarists.

Mantillas
A mantilla is a headdress of lace draped over a large and ornate comb which is crafted from tortoiseshell or made in plastic.

THE FLAVOURS OF ANDALUSIA

Andalusian gastronomy reflects locally grown produce. An astonishing range of olive oils is available, and the region's grapes are made into sherry vinegars, as well as some of Spain's most distinctive wines *(see p226)*. Almonds are used to make delicious sweets, such as *turrón*, a type of nougat.

Olive oil from the provinces of Córdoba and Sevilla

Sherry wine vinegars produced by sherry *bodegas*

Yemas*, sweets produced by nuns in the Convento de San Leandro *(see p77)

Marmalade from the Convento de Santa Paula *(see p90)* in Seville

HERBS AND SPICES

Almost 800 years of Moorish occupation in Andalusia left a distinctive mark on the region's cuisine. Many dishes are flavoured with fragrant spices once imported from the East, such as cumin, coriander, paprika, and strands of saffron. Markets are the best place to buy exotic spices and locally grown herbs, which are sold loose by weight.

Saffron threads

Pimentón (paprika)

Coriander seeds

Cumin seeds

ENTERTAINMENT IN ANDALUSIA

In Andalusia there is almost always a lively buzz in the streets, and activities such as bar-hopping and people-watching can provide enough entertainment in themselves to fill up any spare moment of your holiday.

But there is also plenty more going on. Southern Spain boasts a busy programme of traditional fiestas *(see pp38–9)*, as well as a variety of annual cultural festivals

Poster for a dance festival at Itálica

(see pp34–7), bullfights *(see pp26–7)* and sporting fixtures. There's also music and dance in abundance – Andalusia is, after all, the home of flamenco.

Given the mild climate, many events take place out of doors; in summer, when daytime temperatures soar to up to 45°C (113°F), they don't start until late in the evening, when the air is cooler. Many cultural events and concerts start at around midnight.

Flamenco guitarist playing at a festival at the Teatro de la Maestranza, Seville

PRACTICAL INFORMATION

Tourist information offices are the best places to find out what is on locally, but there are also two useful listings magazines worth looking out for: *El Giraldillo* (published in Seville) and *Qué Hacer/What's On* (published in Málaga). Both appear monthly, cover all of Andalusia and are free.

Each major city has its own commercial websites offering a wealth of local information, but a number of websites covering the whole of Spain, notably **Lanetro** and **Guía del Ocio**, are also worth consulting; just choose the province in which you are interested from the drop-down menu.

BOOKING TICKETS

It is usually possible to book tickets for major sports events, operas, concerts and festivals in advance at the venue's booking office, by phone or online. Alternatively, use an agency that specializes in booking tickets for all entertainments, such as **ServiCaixa** and **Entradas.com**.

FLAMENCO

Seville and Jerez de la Frontera claim to be the birthplaces of flamenco, the traditional music and dance of Andalusia *(see pp28–9)*. Both cities have *tablaos*, bars and restaurants with floor-shows where the admission usually includes dinner or at least a drink. In Seville, it is best to look for venues in the Barrio de Santa Cruz. A good starting point is the **Museo del Baile Flamenco** *(see p75)*. Other reliable venues include **La Carbonería** and **La Casa de la Memoria de Al Andalus**.

Jerez has a **Centro Andaluz de Flamenco**, as well as several *tablaos*. In Granada, there are traditional flamenco venues in Sacromonte *(see p193)* and the Albaicín – among them, **Sala Albayzín** and **Zambra María La Canastera**. Córdoba also has a couple of flamenco bars, notably **El Cardenal** and **La Bulería**.

The two main flamenco festivals are Seville's **Bienal de Flamenco**, which is held in theatres all over the city in even-numbered years, and Córdoba's **Concurso Nacional de Arte Flamenco**, which happens every third year, the next being in 2010 and 2013.

THEATRE

Most drama staged in Andalusia is in Spanish, but there are occasional performances by visiting international companies or mime artists. The theatre season includes not only plays, but also classical music, dance and opera. Seville's main theatres are the **Teatro de la Maestranza** *(see p68)*, the **Teatro Lope de Vega** *(see p97)* and the **Teatro Central**.

In Córdoba, the place to go is the **Gran Teatro**. Granada's two main theatres are the **Teatro Alhambra** and the **Teatro Isabel La Católica**. Málaga has the **Teatro Cánovas** and the **Teatro Cervantes**.

Gran Teatro, Córdoba, one of the city's leading venues for theatre

Rosario Flores, a famous Andalusian singing star, performing at one of her concerts

CINEMA

Foreign films shown in mainstream cinemas in Andalusia are usually dubbed into Spanish. Original-version (VO for *version original*) films are shown in cinemas such as **Avenida Cines** in Seville, the **Filmoteca de Andalucía** in Córdoba and the **Complejo Cinematográfico Gran Marbella** on the Costa del Sol. From June to late August, you can also attend a *cine de verano*, an open-air "summer cinema".

OPERA AND CLASSICAL MUSIC

In Seville, most operas, including those by prestigious international companies, are performed at either the **Teatro Lope de Vega** or the **Teatro de la Maestranza** *(see p68)*. For something less high-brow, Spain has its own brand of operetta, *zarzuela*.

As for classical music, all the main cities maintain their own orchestras (such as the **Real Orquesta Sinfónica de Sevilla**). Granada is great for classical music. As well as having the **Centro Cultural Manuel de Falla** as a venue, it hosts the **Festival Internacional de Música y Danza** *(see p35)*, during which concerts are held against the backdrop of the Alhambra.

OTHER LIVE MUSIC

Touring international rock and pop stars mostly play their Spanish dates in Madrid or Barcelona, but they sometimes make it to Seville or other cities in Andalusia. Such concerts usually take place in football stadiums and bullrings. Spain has its own thriving rock-pop

scene. Andalusian musicians, in particular, have drawn on their flamenco roots to create distinctive fusions between musical genres. Two other great influences on the contemporary music of Andalusia are North Africa and Latin America. Jazz also has a devoted public in Andalusia: Seville has the **Naima Jazz Café** and Granada has the **Festival de Jazz**. To find out where the up-and-coming acts are playing, ask around or keep an eye out for flyers.

Another interesting musical tradition is represented by *la tuna*: groups of students dressed as minstrels playing lutes and mandolins and singing serenades in streets and squares.

La tuna, **traditional singers in Santa Cruz, Seville**

NIGHTLIFE

Nights out in Andalusia begin late and can easily go on until dawn. The first stop is often a *bar de copas* (also called a *pub*), which differs from a tapas bar in that no food is

served and spirits replace wine and beer for drinking. Some such bars have DJs at weekends. The next stop is a *discoteca*, which may open at midnight but not fill up for a couple of hours. There are clubs in the city centres, but many are on industrial estates or outside of town, where the noise won't bother residents.

Where to go depends on your age, your musical tastes and your sexual orientation – each city has a few gay and lesbian clubs. If you aren't concerned about being seen in the hippest places, reliably fun areas to go bar-hopping in are the Santa Cruz quarter in Seville, the Judería in Córdoba and around the Plaza del Realejo and the lower Albaicín (especially the Carrera del Darro and the Paseo de los Tristes) in Granada.

The summer nightlife of the holiday resorts on the Costa del Sol is completely different from that of the cities of Andalusia. Here you'll still find *bares de copa* and *discotecas*, but also many places geared to foreign tourists.

For a smart night out, try one of Andalusia's casinos. Don't dress too casually, and take some ID with you.

A display of flamenco dancing in a bar in Seville

Real Escuela Andaluza de Arte Ecuestre, Jerez de la Frontera

BULLFIGHTING

The **Maestranza** bullring (see p68) in Seville is mythical among bullfighting fans, and some of the most important bullfights in Spain are held here during the Feria de Abril (see p38). Ronda (see pp176–7), Córdoba and Granada also have their own bullrings and a renowned season.

The season usually runs from April to October. Booking tickets in advance is essential if the matadors are well known, and advisable if you want to sit in the shade (sombra). It may be easier to get tickets for novilladas, fights involving matadors who are not yet fully qualified. Tickets are sold at the bullring's booking office.

Tile for Seville's Betis football club

FOOTBALL

Football is the most popular spectator sport in Spain. Seville has two rival teams, FC Sevilla, based at the **Estadio Ramón Sánchez Pizjuán**, and Betis, who play at the **Estadio Manuel Ruiz de Lopera**.

Other successful teams in the region are Cádiz, Málaga and Recreativo de Huelva (the oldest football club in Spain).

The Spanish football league has three divisions, with league matches being played on Sunday (sometimes Saturday) evenings from September to June. During the season, teams also compete in an eliminatory tournament for the Copa del Rey (King's Cup) and for international trophies; such matches are usually played midweek. Important fixtures are televised, although some are only shown on pay-per-view channels. To see a live game, it is advisable to book ahead at the stadium or online.

ENTERTAINMENT FOR CHILDREN

In Spain, children go wherever adults go at just about any time of day or night. If you want to take yours for a treat, there are several options. **Isla Mágica** (see p104) in Seville is Andalusia's biggest theme park, while **Tivoli World** is the largest amusement park on the Costa del Sol. Every city and strip of coast has its water park designed specifically for older children (see p249). A cable car, the **Teleférico Benalmádena**, takes off from beside Tivoli World to the top of Mount Calamorro, 800 m (2,600 ft) above sea level. There's another good cable-car ride in Gibraltar (see pp172–3). In Seville, a boat trip down the river can be fun, as can be the trip across the Bay of Cádiz in a vaporcito (see p165). Horse and carriages travel round the streets in Marbella and Seville, and most beach resorts also have road trains.

The desert in the centre of Almería was once used as a film set for westerns (see p202), and kids love the shoot-outs staged by the small Wild West town of **Mini-Hollywood**, near Tabernas. Another good show – this time of performing horses – is put on by the **Real Escuela Andaluza de Arte Ecuestre** (see p162) in Jerez de la Frontera. Jerez also has Andalusia's best collection of exotic animals in the **Zoo Botánico**; the safari park **Selwo Aventura**, outside Estepona, is also good. There are aquariums at Roquetas del Mar (see p202) in Almería and Benalmádena, a town that also offers **Selwo Marina**, Andalusia's only dolphinarium and ice penguinarium.

The port of Gibraltar from the vantage point of a cable car

DIRECTORY

PRACTICAL INFORMATION

El Giraldillo
www.elgiraldillo.es
Guía del Ocio
www.guiadelocio.com
Lanetro
www.lanetro.com

BOOKING TICKETS

Entradas.com
Tel 902 22 16 22.
www.entradas.com
ServiCaixa
www.servicaixa.com

FLAMENCO

Seville
Bienal de Flamenco
Tel 95 42 34 46.
www.bienal-flamenco.org
La Carbonería
Calle Levies 18. **Map** 4 D1
(6 E3). *Tel* 954 21 44 60.
**Casa de la Memoria
de Al Andalus**
Calle Ximénez de Enciso
28. **Map** 4 D2 (6 E4).
Tel 954 56 06 70.

Córdoba
La Bulería
Calle Pedro López 3.
Tel 957 48 38 89.
El Cardenal
Calle Torrijos 10.
Tel 957 48 31 12.
www.tablaocardenal.com
**Concurso Nacional
de Arte Flamenco**
Tel 957 48 06 44.
www.flamencocordoba.
com

Granada
Sala Albayzín
Carretera de Murcia,
Mirador San Cristóbal.
Tel 958 80 46 46.
www.flamencoalbayzin.
com

**Zambra María
La Canastera**
Camino del Sacromonte
89. *Tel* 958 12 11 83.
www.granadainfo.com/
canastera

Jerez de la Frontera
**Centro Andaluz
de Flamenco**
Palacio Pemartin, Plaza San
Juan 1. *Tel* 956 81 41 32.
www.centroandaluz
deflamenco.es

THEATRE

Seville
Teatro Central
Avenida José Gálvez,
Isla de la Cartuja.
Map 1 C2.
Tel 955 03 72 00.
www.teatrocentral.com

Córdoba
Gran Teatro
Avenida Gran Capitán 3.
Tel 957 48 02 37.
www.teatrocordoba.com

Granada
Teatro Alhambra
Molinos 56.
Tel 958 02 80 00.
Teatro Isabel La Católica
Acera del Casino.
Tel 958 22 29 07.

Málaga
Teatro Cánovas
Plaza de El Ejido.
Tel 951 30 89 02.
Teatro Cervantes
Calle Ramos Marín.
Tel 952 22 41 00.
www.teatrocervantes.com

CINEMA

Seville
Avenida Cines
Marqués de Paradas 15.
Tel 954 29 30 25.

Córdoba
Filmoteca de Andalucía
Medina y Corella 5.
Tel 957 35 56 55.
www.filmotecade
andalucia.com

Marbella
**Complejo
Cinematográfico
Gran Marbella**
Tel 952 81 64 21.
www.cinesgranmarbella.
com

OPERA AND CLASSICAL MUSIC

Seville
Teatro de la Maestranza
Paseo de Colón 22. **Map**
3 B2 (5 C5). *Tel* 954 22
33 44. www.
teatromaestranza.com

**Real Orquesta Sinfónica
de Sevilla**
Tel 954 56 15 36.
www.rossevilla.com

Granada
**Centro Cultural
Manuel de Falla**
Paseo de los Mártires.
Tel 958 22 21 88.
www.manueldefalla.org

**Festival Internacional
de Música y Danza**
Tel 958 22 18 44.
www.granadafestival.org

OTHER LIVE MUSIC

Seville
Naima Jazz Café
Calle Trajano 47.
Map 1 C5 (5 C1).
Tel 954 38 24 85.
www.naimacafejazz.com

Granada
**Festival de Jazz
de Granada**
Casa Morisca, Horno del
Oro 14. *Tel* 958 21 59 80.
www.jazzgranada.net

NIGHTLIFE

Seville
Antique & Aqua
Calle Matematicos Rey
Pastor y Castro. *Tel* 954
46 22 07. www.
antiquetheater.com

Gran Casino Aljarafe
Avenida de la Arboleda,
Tomares. *Tel* 902 42 42
22. www.grancasino
aljarafe.com

Benalmádena
Casino Torrequebrada
Avenida del Sol. *Tel* 952
44 60 00. www.casino
torrequebrada.com

Granada
Granada 10
Cárcel Baja 10.
Tel 958 22 40 01.

Marbella
Casino Nueva Andalucía
Hotel Andalucía Plaza.
Tel 952 81 40 00.
www.casinomarbella.com

**Puerto de
Santa María**
Casino Bahía de Cádiz
Tel 956 87 10 42. www.
casinobahiadecadiz.es

BULLFIGHTING

Córdoba
Plaza de Toros
Avenida de Gran Vía
Parque.
Tel 957 45 60 81.

Granada
Plaza de Toros
Avenida Doctor Olóriz 25.
Tel 958 27 24 51.

FOOTBALL

**Estadio Manuel Ruiz
de Lopera (Real Betis)**
Avenida Heliópolis, Seville.
Tel 902 19 19 07.
www.realbetis
balompie.es

**Estadio Ramón Sánchez
Pizjuán (Sevilla FC)**
Avenida Eduardo Dato,
Seville. **Map** 4 F2.
Tel 902 51 00 11.
www.sevillafc.es

ENTERTAINMENT FOR CHILDREN

Benalmádena
Selwo Marina
Parque de la Paloma.
Tel 902 19 04 82.
www.selwomarina.com

Teleférico Benalmádena
Explanada de Tivoli. *Tel*
902 19 04 82. www.
telefericobenalmadena.
com

Tivoli World
Arroyo de la Miel.
Tel 952 57 70 16.
www.tivoli.es

Estepona
Selwo Aventura
Autovía Costa del Sol,
Las Lomas del Monte.
Tel 902 19 04 82.
www.selwo.es

Jerez de la Frontera
Zoo Botánico
Calle Taxdirt.
Tel 956 15 31 64.
www.zoobotanico
jerez.com

Tabernas
Mini-Hollywood
Tabernas, Almería.
Tel 950 36 52 36.

OUTDOOR ACTIVITIES AND SPECIALIST HOLIDAYS

Andalusia has a perfect climate for enjoying a range of outdoor activities, with comparatively few cold or wet days, and reliable sunshine most of the year. Its coastline offers a great variety of watersports – from windsurfing on the Atlantic coast, to scuba diving in the clear, calm waters of the Mediterranean. Away from the seashore, there are many golf courses and some great countryside – mostly hilly or mountainous – suitable for hiking and horse riding. In winter, skiers head for Europe's southernmost winter-sport resort on the slopes of the Sierra Nevada.

Hot-air ballooning in Andalusia

WALKING AND TREKKING

Andalusia has a huge variety of landscapes suitable for walking: from coastal fringes, through forests, to mountain ranges. Spring is the best time to be outdoors: temperatures are mild, and the landscape blossoms with wildflowers. Mid-summer is best avoided because of the extreme heat and the risk of dehydration.

Two popular areas for hiking are the Alpujarras (see pp198–9) and the Sierra de Grazalema (see p174), but all of the region's nature reserves have marked footpaths.

Always carry a good map. The Spanish army (Servicio Geográfico del Ejercito) produces a useful series of 1:50,000 maps, but the best are the 1:25,000-series maps published by the Centro Nacional de Información Geográfica (CNIG). Wear good walking shoes, preferably boots, and long trousers to avoid lacerations from spiky Mediterranean shrubs. Bring a hat and, if you are going to be gaining altitude, a warm jacket. Always carry drinking water.

For more advice, contact the **Federación Andaluza de Montañismo** . Companies such as **Andalucian Adventures** (see Specialist Holidays) and **Spanish Steps** offer guided walks through the region.

CYCLING

Andalusia's terrain is mainly mountainous, which discourages all but the hardiest cyclist. Added to this, there are few quiet backroads to use as alternatives to busy main roads. However, the trend of converting disused railway lines into "green ways" (vias verdes) has created 12 traffic-free cycling routes, such as the 55-km (34-mile) Via Verde del Aceite (Olive Oil Green Way) between Jaén and Alcaudete. To locate green ways, see the **Fundación de los Ferrocarriles Españoles** website. If you want to go on an organized cycling holiday with accommodation arranged for you, try **Biking Andalucia**.

Fishing at a beach on Andalusia's Mediterranean coast

FISHING

Andalusia offers good sea-fishing off its coasts as well as rather more limited opportunities for freshwater fishing in its scattered reservoirs and rivers, such as in the Cazorla Nature Reserve (see p156) . For information about where to go and permits needed, contact the regional fishing association, the **Federación Andaluza de Pesca Deportiva**.

WILDLIFE AND BIRDWATCHING

The best place to get close to Andalusia's wildlife is the Doñana National Park (see pp130–31), but other nature reserves in the region also offer good opportunities for wildflower- and bird-spotting. Contact **Iberian Wildlife** for tours. Several companies run whale-watching trips out of Tarifa harbour (see p170); among them is the **Foundation for Information and Research on Marine Mammals**.

Hiking down from the Sierra Nevada through the Alpujarras

EQUESTRIAN SPORTS

The horse forms a proud part of Andalusia's traditions, as can be seen during Seville's April Fair (*see p38*), the pilgrimage to El Rocío (*see p38*) and many other fiestas. The undisputed equestrian capital of Andalusia is Jerez de la Frontera (*see p162*), home of the Real Escuela Andaluza de Arte Ecuestre, which stages regular shows featuring dancing horses.

A day's trek on horseback can be a splendid way to get to know the countryside of Andalusia. There are stables everywhere that will organize anything from a brief outing to an extended riding holiday. Two of them are **Dallas Love** in the Alpujarras and **Los Alamos** on the Costa de la Luz. For all things to do with horses, the organization to contact is the **Federación Andaluza de Hípica**.

The stunning golf course at La Cala de Mijas, near the beaches of Málaga

GOLF

Andalusia boasts more than 90 golf courses, mainly concentrated on the Costa del Sol (also known as the "Costa Golf") and around the major cities. Most have 18 holes and are open to non-members on payment of a green fee; advance booking is recommended.

The largest golf club is **La Cala de Mijas**, which has three 18-hole courses and one six-hole course. Another outstanding course can be found at **Montecastillo**, in Jerez de la Frontera, which is used for the Volvo Masters and other important tournaments. To find your nearest golf course, consult the **Federación Andaluza de Golf**.

Horse riding on the deserted Atlantic beach of Zahara, near Cádiz

TENNIS

Tennis is extremely popular in Andalusia. To find out where to play, ask around locally. Many large hotels have courts available for the use of guests, and there are also private clubs you can join. An inexpensive option is to book a court at the local sports centre. For more information, contact the **Federación Andaluza de Tenis**.

WATERSPORTS

Watersports such as kayaking and waterskiing are available at all major resorts along the coast. Sea-going boats can be hired at most of the marinas. For information about sailing in the waters off Andalusia, contact the **Real Federación Española de Vela**.

Tarifa (*see p173*) has ideal conditions for wind- and kite-surfing; Hotel Hurricane (*see p218*) will point you towards lessons and equipment rental. The headlands at La Herradura, on the coast of Granada province, and around the Cabo de Gata in Almería are known for their scuba diving. The **Federación Española de Actividades Subacuáticas** will direct you to the nearest dive school, where you can try an introductory dive or sign up for an intensive course.

Andalusia also has ten water parks (*parques acuáticos*) especially aimed at children, with slides and wave pools. They are at Torre del Mar, Torremolinos, Granada, Mijas, Córdoba, Seville, Almuñecar (on the coast of Granada), Puerto de Santa Maria, Huelva and Vera (in Almería).

AIR SPORTS

To find out where and how to hang-glide, balloon or parachute over Andalusia, contact the **Federación Andaluza de los Deportes Aéreos**.

Because of its normally reliable weather conditions, Andalusia is considered a good place for parachuting: **Skydive Spain** has its own drop zone near Seville and runs beginners' courses as well as taking clients on tandem jumps. **Glovento Sur** flies one-hour balloon trips over Granada.

SKIING

The **Sierra Nevada** (*see p197*) is Europe's southernmost skiing resort. Its base station is at 2,100 m (6,890 ft), and its highest run starts from 3,300 m (10,800 ft). The resort has 80 pistes, with a longest continual run of almost 6 km (4 miles) down the Pista del Águila.

Kite-surfing, a popular activity on the beaches of windy Tarifa

The impressive and atmospheric Turkish baths in Granada

NATURISM

Topless bathing is tacitly accepted at all resorts, most of which have one or more discreet, officially recognized naturist beaches in a cove away from the main beach. **Vera Playa Club** in Almería is a hotel specifically for nudists, and **Costa Natura** near Estepona is a residential "village" also dedicated to naturism. For further information about naturism, contact the **Asociación Naturista-Nudista de Andalucía**.

SPAS AND ARAB BATHS

Andalusia's traditional spas are mainly small, out-of-the-way towns where springs of thermal or medicinal waters supply hotels-cum-sanatoriums that treat patients with a range of ailments. The main ones are Alhama de Almería, Sierra Alhamilla (Almería), Alhama de Granada, Alicun de las Torres (Granada), Graena (near Guadix), Lanjarón (in the Alpujarras), San Andrés (Jaén), Carratraca (Málaga), Fuente Armaga at Tolox (Málaga) and Fuente Amarga at Chiclana in Cádiz. Contact the **Asociación Nacional de Estaciones Termales** for further details.

Spa hotels have seen a huge growth in popularity over the past few years. These hotels tend to be larger, luxury properties and are often beachside or complemented with a golf course. The spa facilities are normally reserved for the use of hotel guests and tend to focus more on pampering and beauty treatments rather than providing health-enhancing therapy.

The spa at **Gran Hotel Guadalpin Byblos** (Mijas Costa) specializes natural therapies using sea water. Signature treatments include a caviar firming facial using La Prairie products. Guests at the **Hotel La Fuente de la Higuera**, in Ronda, can choose from a range of facials, wraps and massages or have a soak in the Turkish baths. **Incosol Hotel** in Marbella focuses more on well-being, offering slimming and anti-stress treatments. The serenity spa at **Las Dunas**, in Estepona, uses Ligne St Barth products from the French Caribbean in all of its pampering treatments. The **Marbella Club Hotel** (see p217) has a beachfront spa that offers 99 thalasso, body and beauty treatments, including the seashell facial massage. The Elysium Spa at **NH Sotogrande** (Sotogrande) offers treatments such as hydromassage and a colour-therapy relaxation room.

When Andalusia was under the sway of the Moors, it had many public bathhouses – the equivalent to Turkish baths. The last one closed in the 17th century, however private companies have been recreating their own "Arab baths", with hot and cold rooms and massages available, in the cities of Seville, Córdoba, Málaga and Granada. Sessions need to be reserved – and, in some cases, paid for – in advance.

SPECIALIST HOLIDAYS

A good way to spend a week or two in Andalusia while learning something useful at the same time is to go on a special-interest holiday. If you want to get deep into the heart of Andalusia, you could try a residential flamenco dancing workshop at **Cortijo del Caño** in Granada, for example.

Cooking is another way to learn something about your surroundings. **Alhambra Travel** runs residential courses in Mediterranean cooking, while at **L'Atelier** in the Alpujarras you'll be taught vegan and vegetarian cuisine.

Learning to speak Spanish is another obvious way to make a holiday yield tangible benefits, but be warned: you may pick up an Andaluz accent rather than the more neutral pronunciation of central Spain. Many private companies run courses in Spanish lasting from a week to several months, but a safe option is to make arrangements with the organization in charge of promoting the Spanish language, the **Instituto Cervantes**.

Other subjects on offer are not directly related to Andalusia. **Andalucian Adventures** will teach you painting, photography and yoga, as well as taking you for guided walks, and the **Complejo Turístico Salitre** in the mountains behind Estepona will introduce you to the delights of the night sky from its observatory.

An artist painting the coastal scene at Nerja, on the Costa del Sol

DIRECTORY

WALKING AND TREKKING

Federación Andaluza de Montañismo
Calle Santa Paula 23,
2º Planta, Granada.
Tel 958 29 13 40.
www.fedamon.com

Spanish Steps
Calle Carreteria 6,
Cómpeta (Málaga).
Tel 952 55 32 70.
www.spanish-steps.com

CYCLING

Biking Andalucia
Apartado de Correos 124,
Orgiva (Granada).
Tel 676 00 25 46.
www.bikingandalucia.com

Fundación de los Ferrocarriles Españoles
www.ffe.es/viasverdes

FISHING

Federación Andaluza de Pesca Deportiva
Calle Leon Felipe 2,
Almería.
Tel 950 15 17 46.
www.fapd.org

WILDLIFE AND BIRDWATCHING

Foundation for Information and Research on Marine Mammals
Pedro Cortés 4, Tarifa.
Tel 956 62 70 08.
www.firmm.org

Iberian Wildlife
Apartado de Correos 59,
Potes (Cantabria).
Tel 942 73 51 54.
www.iberianwildlife.com

EQUESTRIAN SPORTS

Los Alamos
Apartado 56, Barbate
(Cádiz).
Tel 956 43 10 47.
www.losalamosriding.co.uk

Dallas Love Stables
Bubión (Alpujarras).
Tel 958 76 30 38.
www.spain-horse-riding.com

Federación Andaluza de Hípica
Tel 954 21 81 46.
www.fah.es

GOLF

La Cala Resort
La Cala de Mijas,
Mijas Costa.
Tel 952 669 033.
www.lacala.com

Federación Andaluza de Golf
Tel 952 22 55 90.
www.fga.org

Montecastillo Barceló Golf Resort
Carretera de Arcos,
Jerez de La Frontera.
Tel 956 15 12 00.
www.barcelomontecastillo.com

TENNIS

Federación Andaluza de Tenis
Tel 954 44 44 33.
www.fatenis.com

WATERSPORTS

Federación Española de Actividades Subacuáticas
Tel 932 00 67 69.
www.fedas.es

Real Federación Española de Vela
Tel 915 19 50 08.
www.rfev.es

AIR SPORTS

Federación Andaluza de los Deportes Aéreos
Estadio de la Cartuja,
Seville.
Tel 954 32 54 38.
www.feada.org

Glovento Sur
Placeta Nevot 4, Granada.
Tel 958 29 03 16.
www.gloventosur.com

Skydive Spain
Apartado de Correos 66,
Bolullos de la Mitación.
Tel 687 72 63 03.
www.skydivespain.com

SKIING

Sierra Nevada
Tel 902 70 80 90.
www.sierranevadaski.com

NATURISM

Asociación Naturista-Nudista de Andalucía
Tel 628 80 62 50.
www.naturismo.org/anna

Costa Natura
Carretera de Cádiz
km 151, Estepona.
Tel 952 80 80 65.
www.costanatura.com

Vera Playa Club
Carretera de Garrucha a
Villaricos, Vera (Almería).
Tel 950 62 70 10.
www.playahoteles.com

SPAS AND SPA HOTELS

Asociación Nacional de Estaciones Termales
Tel 902 11 76 22.
www.balnearios.org

Las Dunas Beach Hotel & Spa
Urb. La Boladilla Baja,
Ctra de Cadiz km 163.5,
29689 Estepona, Marbella.
Tel 952 80 94 00.
www.las-dunas.com

Gran Hotel Guadalpin Byblos
Urbanización Mijas Golf,
29650 Mijas Costa,
Málaga.
Tel 952 47 30 50.
www.guadalpinbybloshotel.com

Hotel La Fuente de la Higuera
Partido de los Frontones,
29400 Ronda, Málaga.
Tel 952 11 43 55.
www.hotellafuente.com

Incosol Hotel
Urbanización Golf Rio
Real, 29603 Marbella,
Málaga.

Tel 952 86 09 09.
www.incosol.net

NH Sotogrande
Autovía A-7, Salida 130,
11310 Cádiz.
Tel 956 69 54 44.
www.nh-hotels.com

ARAB BATHS

Córdoba
Calle Corregidor
Luis de la Cerda 51.
Tel 957 48 47 46.
www.hammamspain.com

Granada
Calle Santa Ana 16.
Tel 958 22 99 78.
www.hammamspain.com

Málaga
Calle Martires 21.
Tel 958 80 54 81.
www.medinanazari.com

Seville
Calle Aire 15.
Tel 955 01 00 25.
www.airedesevilla.com

SPECIALIST HOLIDAYS

Alhambra Travel
Casa Azahar, Calle
San Luis 12, Granada.
Tel 958 20 15 57.
www.alhambratravel.com

Andalucian Adventures
Tel 01453 834 137 (in the UK).
www.andalucian-adventures.co.uk

L'Atelier
Calle Alberca 21,
Mecina Fondales
(Alpujarras).
Tel 958 85 75 01.
www.ivu.org/atelier

Complejo Turístico Salitre
Tel 952 11 70 05.
www.turismosalitre.com

Cortijo del Caño
Lanjarón (Alpujarras).
Tel 958 77 12 44.
www.alpujarrasinfo.com/dance

Instituto Cervantes
Tel 91 436 76 00.
www.cervantes.es

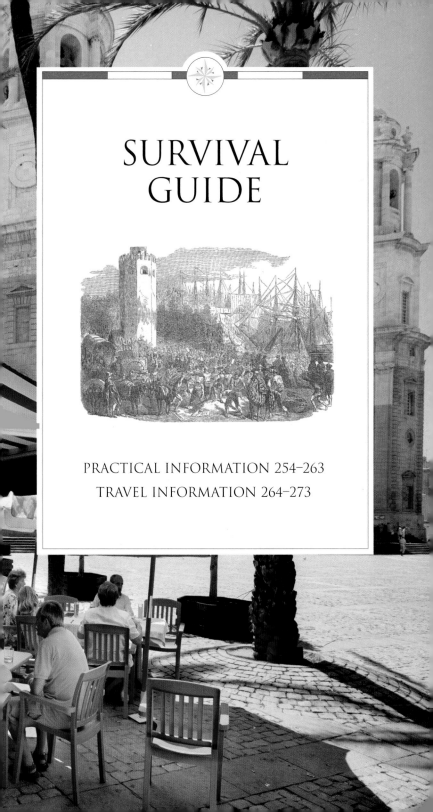

SURVIVAL
GUIDE

PRACTICAL INFORMATION

The economy of Andalusia is heavily dependent on tourism. The rich variety of natural attractions and its cultural heritage draw visitors to the area throughout the year. Many have even settled in this evocative region, home of all things quintessentially Spanish: rich terracotta landscapes, olive groves, flamenco dancing, and *corridas* (bullfights).

Junta de Andalucía tourist office logo

Events such as Expo '92 in Seville, the 500th anniversary of Columbus, the Sierra Nevada Ski Championships, and the cultural tours created for the Legado Andalusi in 1995 have led to an increase in the number of tourist facilities and an improved infrastructure. The Junta de Andalucía has tourist offices across the region, offering a wealth of helpful brochures, maps and leaflets.

Try not to do too much at once, but savour the particular delights of one or two places. Adjust to the slower pace and, in summer, do your sightseeing early in the day before the heat becomes unbearable.

able to direct you to a number of multilingual agencies.

El Legado Andalusi ("The Legacy of Andalus"), a project organized in 1995, highlights Andalusia's Moorish heritage through exhibitions and self-guided cultural tours. These are accompanied by leaflets and a guidebook.

Tickets for Hospital de los Venerables, Seville *(see p81)*

ADMISSION CHARGES

Some monuments and museums offer free entry to Spanish residents and members of the European Union. Others charge a moderate fee (children up to 12 years pay half price). Large groups may be offered a 50 per cent discount on tickets. Payments must be made in cash and not by credit card.

Leaflets on Andalusian culture, published by Junta de Andalucía

TOURIST INFORMATION

Most of the major cities of Andalusia have several Oficinas de Turismo (tourist offices). Turespaña provides tourist information on Spain at a national level, while offices run by the Junta de Andalucía cover Andalusia as a region. Local tourist offices, found also in small towns, usually have details only of their environs.

Most tourist offices are well organized, offering brochures covering monuments, trips, emergency services and places to stay, among other services. They have a range of leaflets listing local festivals and can also offer suggestions on nightlife, theatres and flamenco shows. If you require more detailed information on sports, exhibitions, and concerts, check the listings in local papers *(see p263)*.

If you wish to hire a tour guide while staying in a major city, the tourist office will be

OPENING HOURS

Hours kept by monuments and museums can vary considerably, so it is always best to check them before your visit. From October until March, most museums open between 9:30 and 10am and close for the siesta at 1:30 or 2pm. They open again from

Foreign visitors on a guided tour of Seville

◁ **Cafe Bar and Cathedral Plaza de Pio XII, Old Town Cadiz**

Flamenco street performers entertaining visitors outside a bar

around 4:30pm and then close at 6 or 8pm. Most close on Sunday afternoons. However, during the tourist season many museums stay open all day.

Most churches open only for Mass, but in small towns a caretaker will often let visitors in between religious services.

VISITING CHURCHES

Mass is held every hour on Sundays, and at about 7–9pm on weekdays. In most churches, tourists are welcome in the church during a service as long as they are quiet.

Dress codes are not as strict as in other Catholic countries, but avoid skimpy shorts and bare arms. There is usually no admission charge, although a donation may be expected.

ETIQUETTE

The open, friendly character of the Spanish means that strangers usually greet each other with a *¡Hola!, ¡Buenos días!,* or *¡Buenas tardes!* on meeting in doorways or lifts – and even when passing on the street in small towns. It is also considered polite for people who know each other to shake hands each time they meet, and for women to kiss each other on both cheeks.

Smoking is not allowed in cinemas, lifts or on public transport, but elsewhere non-smoking areas are rare.

Spaniards rarely drink alcohol without nibbles until after dinner. It is not thought polite to share the price of a round of drinks except with people you know very well.

While totally accepted on the Costa del Sol, topless sunbathing is frowned upon in many small coastal places.

TIPPING

Owing to the rising cost of living, tipping tends to be an issue of discretion in Spain. A service charge *(servicio)* tends to be included *(see p221)* in checks, but it is common to tip five to 10 per cent in addition and to give small change to taxi drivers.

COMPLAINTS BOOK

If you are not happy with a service, particularly in a restaurant or hotel, you are entitled to ask for the *Libro de Reclamaciones*. This is an official complaints book at the disposal of customers, which

Sign indicating the establishment has a *Libro de Reclamaciones*

DIRECTORY

TOURIST INFORMATION

Oficinas de Turismo
Avenida de la Constitución 21, Seville. **Map** 3 C2 (5 C4).
Tel 95 478 75 78.
Costurero de la Reina, Paseo de las Delicias 9, Seville.
Map 3 C4.
Tel 95 423 44 65.
Calle Torrijos 10, Córdoba.
Tel 957 35 51 79.
Calle Santa Ana 4, Granada.
Tel 958 57 52 02.
www.andalucia.org

Tourist Office of Spain UK
23 Manchester Square, London, W1M 5AP.
Tel (020) 7486 8077.
www.spain.info
www.okspain.org

RELIGIOUS SERVICES

Catholic in English
Iglesia del Señor San José
Calle San José 17, Seville.
Map 4 D1 (6 E4).
Tel 95 422 03 19.

Jewish
Sinagoga Beth El
Urbanización el Real km 184, Marbella.
Tel 95 277 40 74.

Muslim
Mezquita Del Rey Abdulaziz CN340 km 178, Marbella.
Tel 95 277 41 43.

is inspected periodically by the local authorities. Only use it for very unsatisfactory affairs, or threaten to use it if you suspect you are being cheated.

TOILETS

Public toilets are scarce. However, there is a bar on virtually every corner which is legally bound to allow you to use their toilets. Nevertheless some bars do so reluctantly, if no purchase has been made. A "D" on the door stands for *Damas* (ladies), and a "C" indicates *Caballeros* (men).

Keep small change handy – some toilets are coin-operated. Also, bring a pack of tissues as often you will find there is no toilet paper.

Foreign student relaxing by a fountain in Seville

IMMIGRATION AND CUSTOMS

Visitors from the US, Canada, Australia and New Zealand do not need a visa for stays of up to 90 days. If your visit is for longer than this, you will need to apply to your Spanish Consulate for a permit *(visado)*. Visa requirements are liable to change at short notice, so always check before travelling.

Visitors from the EU can stay indefinitely.

On arrival, it is not necessary to register with the local police, but hotels will take your passport details. Vaccinations are not needed.

A sales tax *(IVA)* refund system is available in large department stores *(see p238)*, applicable to all except members of the EU.

EMBASSIES AND CONSULATES

In the event of losing your passport or needing legal advice or other help, contact your national embassy or con-sulate. Most towns have volun-teer interpreters, found at local police stations *(see p258)*. On the Costa del Sol, the Foreigners' Department of the Ayuntamiento (Departamento de Extranjeros) can help.

USEFUL ADDRESSES

Australian Embassy

Torre Espacio, Paseo de la Castellana, 259D, Planta 24, 28046 Madrid. *Tel* 91 353 66 00.

British Consulate

Edificio Eurocom, Calle Mauricio Moro Pareto, 29006 Malaga. *Tel* 95 235 23 00. www.ukinspain.fco.gov.uk

Canadian Consulate

Edificio Horizonte, Plaza de la Malagueta 2, 1st floor, 29016 Malaga. *Tel* 95 223 33 46. www.international.gc.ca

US Consulate

Plaza Nueva, 8-8 dupl, 2nd floor, Seville. *Tel* 95 421 85 71. www.embusa.es

DISABLED TRAVELLERS

Modern buildings generally have adequate provision for the disabled, with lifts, ramps and special toilet facilities. However, owing to their construction, entry to certain historical monuments may be restricted. Local tourist offices, or the monument staff, can provide information about wheelchair access.

Two UK charities, **RADAR** and **Accessible Tourism** provide travel information for the disabled. **Servi-COCEMFE** in Madrid advises on hotels that are suitably equipped for disabled travellers *(see p209)*.

STUDENT INFORMATION

Seville, Granada and Córdoba attract large numbers of students, many of whom come to Andalusia to learn Spanish. Most large towns have a **Centro de Documentación e Información Juvenil** which provides information for students and young people. A valid International Student Identi-fication Card (ISIC card) entitles you to some price reductions, including museum entrance fees and travel.

TAX-FREE SHOPPING

If you reside in a country outside the European Union, you can reclaim the VAT *(IVA* in Spanish) you pay on goods bought in any shop in Spain that is authorized to carry out such transactions. In order to claim a refund, you must spend a minimum of €90.15

Horse-riding in the Granada countryside

STREET SIGNS IN ANDALUSIA

Many of the streets of Andalusia's towns are adorned with beautiful street signs. They are usually made of white tiles with a painted border, often displaying the emblem of the town or province. For example, the Calle Barrio Alto sign features a pomegranate *(granada)*, the historical emblem of the city of Granada.

Colourful street signs, found all over Andalusia

in the same shop on the same day. At the time of purchase, show your passport (as proof of your residency) and ask for a tax-free receipt. Show the goods you have bought to the customs officer at the airport you are departing from and get him or her to stamp the receipt. Then go to the desk at the airport that issues refunds, and you will be refunded the amount of VAT you have paid – either as cash or credited to your credit card.

ELECTRICAL ADAPTORS

The current in Spain is 220V-AC with two-pin, round-pronged plugs. Adaptors can be found in many supermarkets, supermarkets and also some electrical stores. If you can, take one with you to be on the safe side. Most hotels and *pensiones* have electric points for hair dryers and shavers in all the bedrooms. Many now use the key/card system for switching on the electricity supply in rooms.

ADDRESSES

In speech, on maps and in written information, the Spaniards often drop the *Calle* in street names, so that Calle Mateos Gago becomes Mateos Gago. Other terms, such as *Plaza, Callejón, Carretera* and *Avenida*, do not change.

In addresses, a *s/n (sin número)* after the street name indicates that the building has

no number. Outside towns, an address may say "Carretera Córdoba–Málaga km 47" – the sight is on the highway near to the kilometre sign.

SPANISH TIME

Spain is one hour ahead of Greenwich Mean Time (GMT) and British Summer Time. The time difference between Seville and other cities is: London -1 hour, New York -6, Perth +7, Auckland +12, Tokyo +8. These figures may vary for brief periods in spring and autumn when clock changes are not synchronized.

The 24-hour clock is used in listings and for official purposes but not in speech. The morning (am) is referred to as *por la mañana* and the afternoon (pm), *por la tarde*. Afternoon does not start at midday, but rather after siesta time, at around 4 or 5pm.

CONVERSION CHART

Imperial to Metric
1 inch = 2.54 centimetres
1 foot = 30 centimetres
1 mile = 1.6 kilometres
1 ounce = 28 grams
1 pound = 454 grams
1 pint = 0.6 litres
1 gallon = 4.6 litres

Metric to Imperial
1 centimetre = 0.4 inches
1 metre = 3 feet, 3 inches
1 kilometre = 0.6 miles
1 gram = 0.04 ounces
1 kilogram = 2.2 pounds
1 litre = 1.8 pints

Personal Security and Health

Andalusia is, by and large, a safe place for visitors. Women travelling alone tend not to be hassled, but may have to put up with so-called compliments from men of all ages. Pickpockets and bag-snatchers, however, are very common, especially in Seville, so it is best to be cautious around popular tourist spots and on crowded buses. Try to avoid carrying valuable items and, if possible, wear a money belt. If you become ill during your stay, go to the nearest pharmacy, where someone should be able to advise you. Organize your travel insurance before leaving for Spain as it is difficult to obtain and more expensive once there.

Officer of the *Policía Nacional*

Mounted police officers from the *Policía Nacional*

PROTECTING YOUR PROPERTY

Pickpockets are common in crowded areas, especially outside monuments and at markets. Be particularly wary of people asking you the time, as they are probably trying to distract you while someone else attempts to snatch your bag or wallet. Wear bags and cameras across your body and not on your shoulder. If you have a scooter, make sure that it is securely chained, especially in bigger cities.

Travellers' cheques can be replaced if they are stolen. It is worth taking a photocopy of your passport and leaving the original in the hotel safe. If you have a car, do not leave valuables in view and try to leave it in a secure car park.

Try to report any incident to the police (*poner una denuncia*) as soon as possible (at least within 24 hours). This is extremely important if you wish to obtain a statement (*denuncia*) to make an insurance claim.

Holiday insurance is there to protect you financially from loss or theft, but be sure to take sensible precautions.

PERSONAL SAFETY

The abundance of street-life means that you will rarely find yourself alone or in a position to be harassed. However, women may be intimidated by men passing comment as they walk by, or even following them. This pastime, known as *piropo*, is common and not meant as a serious threat.

There are no particularly notorious areas of Seville to be avoided. Just act street-wise: do not use maps late at night and try to look like you know where you're going.

When visiting the Sacromonte caves in Granada to see gypsy families perform flamenco (*see p193*), it is a good idea to go in a group and keep an eye on your belongings.

Make sure that you take official taxis displaying a licence number and avoid public transport late at night if alone. Any cab driver touting for business is likely to be illegal.

Marked car of the *Policía Nacional*

***Policía Local* patrol car, mainly seen in small towns**

POLICE

There are basically three types of police in Spain – the *Guardia Civil*, the *Policía Nacional* and the *Policía Local*. When approaching the police remember that it is illegal to be without ID.

Out of the main towns you will usually encounter the green-uniformed *Guardia Civil*. They patrol the country highways and, although they have a mean reputation, they will help if your car breaks down (*see p271*).

The *Policía Nacional*, who wear a dark blue uniform, are the best to turn to, especially when reporting a crime. They have many different responsibilities, including dealing with visitors' permits and documentation. In the bigger cities the *Policía Nacional* also guard many important establishments, such as government buildings, embassies and barracks.

The *Policía Local* take care of the day-to-day traffic policing of towns and cities.

EMERGENCY NUMBERS

First Aid
Seville *Tel 112*.
Córdoba *Tel 112*.
Granada *Tel 112*.

Police
Tel 112.

Traffic Police
Seville *Tel 95 462 11 11*.
Córdoba *Tel 957 20 30 33*.
Granada *Tel 958 15 69 11*.

PHARMACIES

For minor complaints, visit a pharmacy *(farmacia)*, where pharmacists are highly trained. They dispense a wide range of medication over the counter, including antibiotics.

Farmacias have a green or red neon cross outside, usually flashing, and are found in most villages and towns. They keep the same hours as most other shops (9:30am–1:30pm and 4–8pm). At least one will be *de guardia*

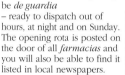

Spanish pharmacy signs

– ready to dispatch out of hours, at night and on Sunday. The opening rota is posted on the door of all *farmacias* and you will also be able to find it listed in local newspapers.

MEDICAL TREATMENT

If in need of urgent medical assistance, go to the nearest *Urgencias* – the emergency ward of a hospital or clinic.

All the cities have several hospitals each, while the Costa del Sol has a hospital situated on the main coastal highway (N340) just east of Marbella. Most hospitals have volunteer interpreters who speak English and occasionally also other languages.

The Cruz Roja (Red Cross) has an extensive network throughout Spain and runs an ambulance service.

All EU nationals are entitled to Spanish social security cover. To claim, you must obtain the European Health Insurance Card from a post office or online (see www.ehic.org.uk) before you travel. The card comes with a booklet, *Health Advice for Travellers*, which explains exactly what health care you are entitled to, and where and how to claim. Give the card to anyone who treats you. You may find that you have to pay and claim the money back later. Not all treat-

ments are covered, and some are costly, so arrange for medical cover before you travel. If you want private medical care, ask at your hotel or embassy for the name and number of a doctor.

If you have private travel insurance, make sure you have your policy on you when requesting medical assistance. Depending on the insurance company, you may be expected to pay for treatment and be reimbursed at a later date.

HEALTH PRECAUTIONS

Beware of the sun, particularly from May to October when temperatures can reach up to 45° C (113° F). Try to avoid walking in the midday sun and stay in the shade whenever possible. Drink plenty of bottled mineral water.

It is advisable to wear sunglasses and a hat when you are out sightseeing. When in the countryside, you may see signs showing a bull or saying *Toro bravo* (fighting bull). These signs should be taken seriously as these bulls are extremely dangerous animals

A Red Cross ambulance

and by no means should be approached.

LEGAL ASSISTANCE

If you are involved in an incident which requires a lawyer, ask your Embassy or Consulate *(see p256)* for the name of a reputable one. However, do not expect all lawyers to speak English. Police stations can sometimes provide volunteer interpreters *(intérpretes)* to help visitors from other countries. Otherwise it may be necessary to hire an interpreter to state your case clearly. *Traductores Oficiales* or *Jurados* are qualified to undertake most types of legal or official work.

Banking and Local Currency

Changing money in Spain can often be quite time-consuming. Finding exchange facilities is not a problem, however. There are usually one or two banks even in small towns (but not necessarily in villages). Other options for changing traveller's cheques and currency include *casas de cambio*, hotels and travel agents. Alternatively, credit cards and Eurocheques are widely accepted in larger shops, hotels and restaurants.

You can take any amount of foreign currency into Spain, but sums worth over €6,000 should be declared at customs when you enter the country.

CHANGING MONEY

You can change money and cash traveller's cheques at *casas de cambio* (bureaux de change), banks and *cajas de ahorros* (building societies). Travel agents and hotels also change money. Málaga airport has 24-hour exchange facilities and Seville airport has a bank open at the usual times.

It is better to take enough euros for your initial needs before travelling, and to shop around for the best rates at your leisure after you arrive. Hotels and travel agents do not give good exchange rates and commissions charged on foreign currency transactions also vary. They are higher than average at the airports.

It is compulsory to show your passport or driver's licence when changing money or traveller's cheques.

Debit cards are also a good way to go, since they are widely accepted and cash machines – which take both debit and credit cards – are numerous.

USING BANKS

It usually requires a lot of patience when using banks in Andalusia, since queues can be endless. In larger banks you may find that some staff speak English, but only a few words.

In some banks you must fill in a few forms at the *cambio* (exchange desk) before going to the *caja* (cash desk) to queue up for your money. It is best to choose one of the bigger banks, such as the BBVA (Banco Bilbao Vizcaya Argentaria) or the Banco Central Hispano. These banks will have branches throughout Andalusia and you often have to queue just once to receive your money.

To enter a bank you will have to ring a bell, then the teller will open the door for you from behind the counter.

BBVA

Logo for BBVA, the Banco Bilbao Vizcaya Argentaria

Alternatively, many banks now have electronically operated double doors. First you must press the button to open the outer door. Once inside, wait until you see the green light (which comes on when the outer door closes) and the second door will then open automatically.

BANKING HOURS

Banks in Andalusia are open for business from 8:30am to 2pm Monday to Friday. Only some banks open on Saturdays, and if they do they do so only in the mornings in wintertime.

Banks are never open on public holidays *(see p37)* and during a town's annual *feria* week *(see pp38–9)* the banks will open for just three hours from 9am to noon. This is to allow the staff to join in the general merrymaking.

CREDIT CARDS

Credit cards such as VISA, American Express and Mastercard (Access) are widely accepted all over Spain. Some establishments may require identification such as a passport or driving licence before accepting the transaction. Major banks will give cash on credit cards, and if your card is linked to your home bank account, you can also use it with your PIN number to withdraw money straight from cash machines. Instructions are given on the display in several languages.

Standard bank cards that bear the Cirrus and Maestro logos can also be used widely across Andalusia to withdraw money from cash machines or, as at home, as swipe cards to purchase goods.

TRAVELLER'S CHEQUES

Most types of traveller's cheques are accepted in Spanish banks. It is probably best to choose US dollars or pounds sterling, but most currencies are acceptable. All banks charge a commission for cashing traveller's cheques. However, American Express offices do not charge any commission on their own cheques.

If you wish to cash cheques larger than €3,000, you must give the bank 24 hours' notice. Also if you draw more than €600 on traveller's cheques, you will probably be asked to produce the purchase certificate.

THE EURO

The Euro (€) is the common currency of the European Union. It went into general circulation on 1 January 2002, initially for twelve participating countries. Spain was one of those countries, and the peseta was phased out by March 2002.

EU members using the Euro as sole official currency are known as the Eurozone. Several EU members have opted out of joining.

Euro notes are identical thoughout the Eurozone countries, each one including designs of fictional architectural structures and monuments. The coins, however, have one side identical (the value side) and one side with an image unique to each country. Both notes and coins are exchangeable in each of the participating countries.

Bank Notes

Euro bank notes have seven denominations. The €5 note (grey in colour) is the smallest, followed by the €10 note (pink), €20 note (blue), €50 note (orange), €100 note (green), €200 note (yellow) and €500 note (purple). All notes show the 12 stars of the European Union.

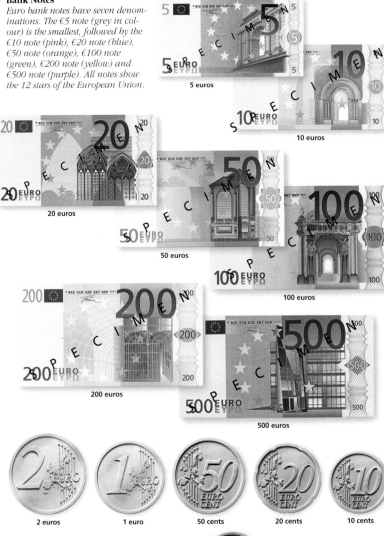

5 euros

10 euros

20 euros

50 euros

100 euros

200 euros

500 euros

2 euros

1 euro

50 cents

20 cents

10 cents

Coins

The euro has eight coin denominations: €1 and €2; 50 cents, 20 cents, 10 cents, 5 cents, 2 cents and 1 cent. The €2 and €1 coins are both silver and gold in colour. The 50-, 20- and 10-cent coins are gold. The 5-, 2- and 1-cent coins are bronze.

5 cents

2 cents

1 cent

Communications

Post office (correos) sign

The telephone system in Spain is run by Telefónica. It is efficient, but one of the most expensive in Europe. Most lines abroad are good and there are plenty of public telephones. In recent years, Spain has also built up internet and electronic communications.

Spain's postal service is notoriously inefficient but letters posted at central post offices will not take too long. Radio and television are very popular and there are many local radio stations. Regional newspapers have also gained popularity in Andalusia.

Telefónica's modern, blue and green-coloured public telephones

TELEPHONING IN ANDALUSIA

Spaniards love to talk, so there are plenty of phone booths (*cabinas telefónicas*) on the streets, and most bars have public phones. There are also public telephone offices (*locutorios*), where you make a call and pay for it afterwards, and also private bureaux with both phone and fax facilities.

Public phones use coins and phonecards (*tarjetas telefónicas*). *Cabinas* are often positioned in pairs on the streets, one accepting coins

Logo of Spanish telecom system, Telefónica

and one phonecards. You can buy phonecards from all tobacconists (*estancos*) and newsstands. They are priced according to their value in call units.

It is easiest to make long-distance calls (*conferencias interurbanas*) at *locutorios*. A

call made from a *cabina telefónica* or *locutorio* costs 35 per cent more than from a private phone. In a bar the cost can be prohibitive, since many bars install phone meters and some charge very high rates. Calls from hotel telephones are also more expensive. Calling abroad is cheapest between 10pm and 8am daily.

USING A COIN AND CARD TELEPHONE

1 Lift the receiver, wait for dialling tone and for the display to show "*Inserte monedas o tarjeta*".

2 Insert either coins (*monedas*), pressing the button to the right of the slot if there is one, or a card (*tarjeta*).

3 Key in the number (Spanish-phones prefer you to pause between digits).

4 As you press the digits, the number you are dialling will show on the display. You will also be able to see how much money or units are left and when to insert more coins.

5 When your call is finished, replace the receiver. A phonecard then re-emerges automatically. Any excess coins inserted will also be returned.

Spanish phonecard

USING A PUBLIC TELEPHONE

Most of the new public phone booths have a visual display to guide users. Illustrated instructions on how to use the phone, and lists of local and national dialling codes, are posted up in most booths in cities and centres of tourism. Some phones are designed so that users may change the language of the instructions by pressing a button with a flag symbol.

Expect some public phones in streets to be out of order. If you call from an open booth, watch your purse, wallet and bags as you are an obvious target for pickpockets.

SENDING LETTERS

The Spanish postal service is rightly known as slow and unreliable. Services between major cities are fairly efficient,

Distinctive yellow Spanish postbox *(buzón)*

but mail to or from smaller towns can be very slow. Postcards sent abroad can take more than a month to arrive, particularly in the summer. Letters posted at a central post office will usually arrive in reasonable time, but be aware that post-boxes *(buzones)* may not be emptied for days, even in large towns and cities.

If you need to send important or urgent mail use the *certificado* (registered) and *urgente* (express) mail. It should arrive anywhere in Spain on the following day and in towns elsewhere in Europe in three to five days.

Buy stamps *(sellos)* at post offices and *estancos* (state-run tobacconists), displaying a distinctive yellow and red sign. Main post offices open 8am–9pm Monday to Friday, 9am–7pm Saturday; local post offices 9am–2pm Monday to Friday, 9am–1pm Saturday.

POSTE RESTANTE

In most large towns a *poste restante* service is available. A letter should be addressed to the relevant person, *"Lista de Correos"*, the town name and region. Letters are kept at the town's main post office from where they can be collected. A passport or other form of identification is needed but there is no collection fee.

TV AND RADIO

There are two state channels in Spain, TVE1 and TVE2, plus stations Antena 3 and Telecinco (5). In addition, Andalusia has its own TV channels: Canal Sur and Canal 2 Andalucia. Canal Plus is a cable television company showing films, sport and documentaries. Subtitled foreign films are listed in TV listings by the letters V.O. *(Versión Original).*

The best radio news programmes are broadcast on Radio Nacional de España. BBC World Service frequencies and listings can be found in its monthly *Worldwide* magazine for English language listening.

Canal Sur, the local broadcasting station

A selection of national and regional Spanish newspapers

NEWSPAPERS AND MAGAZINES

The most important national papers are *El País* (which prints an Andalusian version daily and is linked to the

Socialist Government), *ABC* (conservative), and *El Mundo* (independent). Local papers such as *Ideal* in Granada, the Córdoba *Diario* or the Málaga *Sur,* have more extensive listings of local cultural and sporting activities. An English version of *Sur* is distributed free in Málaga on Fridays. The local listings magazines are the *Giraldillo* in Seville and the *Guía del Ocio* in Granada *(see p230)*. *La Tribuna*, Córdoba's weekly free sheet, publishes useful practical information.

Travelling by Train

Logo for AVE high-speed trains

Owing to the natural bottleneck of the Pyrenees, train connections between Spain and the rest of Europe are a little restricted. However, a subsidiary of Spain's national network, RENFE, runs a service that links Madrid and Barcelona to France, Italy, Austria and Switzerland. **RENFE** offers routes throughout the country, on a variety of trains, and at a high level of service. The high-speed AVE *(Tren de Alta Velocidad Española)* linking Seville, Córdoba and Madrid and Málaga to Madrid (via Córdoba) has cut down journey times by almost half, and is extremely efficient.

AVE high-speed trains at Estación de Santa Justa, Seville

ARRIVING BY TRAIN

Trains coming from other European countries to Spain terminate in either Madrid or Barcelona. From Barcelona it is about five and a half hours to Seville by AVE; from Madrid it takes around three hours travelling by AVE.

Andalusia's most important station is Santa Justa *(see p268)* in Seville. It has connections with major Andalusian towns and with Barcelona and Madrid (including 21 AVE high-speed trains running daily).

European and American rail passes, including EurRail and Inter-Rail, are accepted on the RENFE network, subject to the usual conditions. However, on certain trains you may find a supplement is payable.

TRAIN TRAVEL IN SPAIN

The train network in Spain is very extensive and there are services designed to suit every pocket. Travelling on the AVE is expensive, but

fast. There is also a money-back guarantee that the train will reach its destination no more than five minutes late.

Other long distance services, known as *largo recorrido*, are divided into *diurnos* (daytime) and *nocturnos* (night-time). *Intercity* is the name given to standard daytime trains. *Talgos* are slightly more luxurious and more expensive. Night trains include *Expresos* and *Talgo cama (cama* means bed). *Regionales* run daytime from city to city within a limited area. *Cercanías* are commuter trains running from large

towns to their surrounding suburbs, towns and villages.

BOOKINGS AND RESERVATIONS

It is advisable to book long-distance journeys in advance, essential if you travel on public holidays *(días festivos)* or long weekends *(puentes)*. You can book a ticket up to 60 days in advance and to collect it up to 24 hours before travelling. It can also be sent to your hotel *(servicio a domicilio)*.

Tickets for *regionales* cannot be booked in advance. Few staff speak English, so RENFE agents in travel agencies are often more helpful.

Tickets can now be booked online and discounts are usually given if bookings are made in advance, at the last minute or for round trips.

TICKETS

Train travel in Spain is fairly reasonably priced. *Largo recorrido* and *regionales* have first and second class *(primera/segunda clase)*. The pricing for AVE trains and the Talgo 200 from Málaga to Madrid is worked out on a class system – *turista* (low), *preferente* (medium) and *club* (high) – and also by how busy trains are at certain times – *valle* (low), *plano* (middle) and *punta* (high). Thus, the most expensive tickets are *club punta* and the cheapest are *turista valle*. The tickets on Spanish trains always show a number for your seat (or bed on sleepers). Tickets for long journeys are sold at main line stations,

The railway station at El Chorro, Andalusia

SPAIN'S PRINCIPAL RENFE NETWORK

Spain's Rail Network operates a wide variety of services. Study a RENFE brochure or train time-table before you buy your ticket.

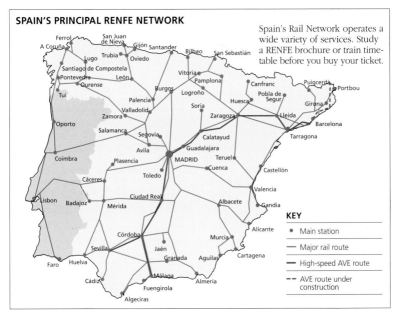

KEY

●   Main station

—   Major rail route

—   High-speed AVE route

--   AVE route under construction

at the RENFE offices and some *cercanías* stations. Credit cards are accepted at the main stations, but not at the smaller or *cercanías* stations. You can change the date of a ticket twice, but you pay an extra 10–15 per cent. If further changes are then required, the ticket is reissued at full fare.

TICKETS FOR CERCANIAS AND REGIONAL TRAINS

On regional lines and on *cercanías* you can buy a ticket, or *bono*, covering ten journeys, which offers a saving of about 40 per cent of the standard price. When entering a station, you pass the *bono* through a slot in the automatic barrier leading to the platform.

TIMETABLES

The punctuality rating of trains in Andalusia is quite high, particularly for the AVE. Brochures with prices and timetables are distributed free and are easy to follow. Information for *laborables* (week-days) and *sábados, domingos y festivos* (Saturdays, Sundays and public holidays) is at the bottom of the timetable.

USEFUL NUMBERS

Booking Agents for RENFE
Tel 90 224 02 02.
www.renfe.es

Seville
Viajes Távora,
Calle Zaragoza 1.
Map 5 C2.
Tel 95 422 61 60.

Córdoba
Córdoba Tours,
Ronda de los Tejares 11.
Tel 957 47 78 35.

Granada
Bonanza Viajes,
Reyes Católicos 30.
Tel 958 22 97 77.

Málaga
Solceuta,
Calle Trinidad Grund 2.
Tel 95 221 81 91.

USING A TICKET MACHINE

Ticket machines for *cercanías* and regional lines are easy to use. Use the button on the bottom left of the screen to select your language. The machine will guide you through step by step until your ticket is dispatched.

1 Select your destination from panel on left.

2 Select ticket type; *sencillo* (single), *ida y vuelta* (return) or *tarjeta dorada* (for pensioners).

3 Insert money (notes or coins). The machine will return your change.

4 Or insert credit card.

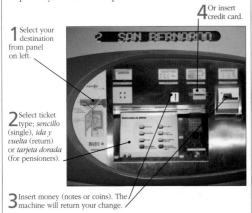

The façade of Seville's Santa Justa railway station

SEVILLE, SANTA JUSTA

Modern and user-friendly, Santa Justa is one of Andalusia's more modern landmarks. Even when busy, it seems spacious and safe, though visitors should look out for pickpockets during the summer months.

It is an easy station to use and all trains and platforms are visible through huge windows in the centre of the building.

Near the ticket office there are large notices featuring timetables for AVE and other long-distance train services. Self-service ticket machines are available for regional journeys and journeys by *cercanías (see pp266–7)*. The station has a large self-

Electronic departures board at Santa Justa railway station

Ticket counter at Santa Justa railway station

service restaurant-cum-café, gift shops, newsstands, cash-point machines and money-changing facilities. For lost property, ask at the office marked *Atención al Cliente*.

renfe

RENFE logo

At the front of the station you will find a large taxi rank and a spacious car park. The station is open from 4am to midnight and, though it is located in a slightly drab suburb, it is only about five minutes by car or bus from the city centre.

CORDOBA

Córdoba has a grand, modern station. Located in the north-west of the city, it is just a few minutes by car or taxi to the city centre. Like Santa Justa it is large, efficiently run and easy to find one's way around. Trains run to Madrid, Málaga, Barcelona, Seville, Jaén and Bilbao. The AVE to Madrid takes just 2 hours; to Seville 45 minutes. The station is well served with cafés, shops and ticket offices. Lockers for storing luggage are available.

GRANADA

Small and provincial, the station in Granada is housed in an old building and has few amenities. There is a small café-cum-restaurant and a taxi rank outside. Most trains that pass through are regional or

cercanías but long-distance trains do run to Madrid, Seville, the Costa Blanca, Barcelona, Almería, Córdoba and Málaga. Storage lockers are available.

Exterior of Granada station

MALAGA

Málaga station was renovated and expanded when the AVE line was added. There is a direct daily train to Barcelona and a connection to Madrid (via Córdoba). Lines to Seville are under construction. The station has a taxi rank outside and luggage storage facilities, and a train connection to Málaga airport.

TRAIN STATIONS

Seville, Santa Justa
Avenida Kansas City. **Map** 2 F5 & 4 F1.

Granada
Avenida Andalusia s/n.

Córdoba
Glorieta de las Tres Culturas.

Málaga
Explanada de la Estación s/n.

Rail Enquiries
Tel 902 24 02 02
www.renfe.es

Travelling by Coach

The major coach links between Andalusia and the rest of Europe are with France, Holland, Belgium, Switzerland and Austria. Within the region itself, coach travel is very popular and has improved enormously in recent years. Most coaches now have air-conditioning, a video, bar and WC. Travelling by coach in Andalusia is very economical and thanks to the improvement in roads, it can be quick and enjoyable. However, around the many holidays in the Spanish festive calendar, travelling can be difficult: coach stations tend to be over-crowded, coaches slow to depart and the roads busy.

Regional coach operated by the Alsina Graells company

ARRIVING BY COACH

The major coach stations in Andalusia are in Seville, Granada, Córdoba and Málaga. However, some individual companies have a policy of avoiding central coach stations for departures and arrivals, particularly in Granada where there are a number of different companies in operation.

Coaches run frequently between major cities and towns and can sometimes provide the only way of getting to and from small villages. Travelling on these routes will certainly give you an experience of the region's local colour.

SEVILLE

Seville's main coach station is in the centre of town at the Plaza de Armas. From here the Alsa coach company operates routes to international destinations, as well as Madrid, Huelva, Badajoz and Extremadura. For all other destinations, head to the coach station in Prado de San Sebastian.

CORDOBA

The main coach station in Córdoba is run by the Alsina Graells coach company. It is small and basic, comprising just a small waiting area with a café and a newsstand. Coaches depart regularly from this point for Granada, Murcia, Almería, Málaga, Algeciras, Cádiz and Seville.

GRANADA

In Granada, coach travellers may be confused by the choice of coach companies, each of which deals with a variety of different destinations. The largest is Alsina Graells Sur, and its station is what is normally referred to as the central coach station. Dirty and overcrowded, it is not an attractive place to linger, and it is advisable to buy your ticket in advance and turn up at the coach station a few minutes before departure. This coach station offers routes all over Murcia and Andalusia. Coaches for Madrid leave from outside the main train station in Avenida Andaluces.

MALAGA

Málaga coach station is located in the centre of town. From here you can take coaches daily to a variety of locations all over Spain including Madrid, Barcelona, Valencia and Alicante, as well as the eight provincial capitals of Andalusia. Julia Tours and Lineabus operate coaches to Belgium, Holland, Switzerland and Germany from Málaga. Eurolines and Iberbus operate lines to the United Kingdom via Madrid and Paris.

COACH STATIONS

Seville
Estación Plaza de Armas
Plaza de Armas. **Map** 1 B5 & 5 A2.
Tel 95 490 80 40.
Prado de San Sebastian Estación
Map 4 D3. *Tel 95 441 71 11.*

Córdoba
Terminal Alsina Graells
Glorieta de las Tres Culturas.
Tel 957 40 40 40.

Granada
Terminal Alsina Graells Sur
Carretera de Jaen, Granada.
Tel 958 18 54 80.

Málaga
Estación de Autobuses
Paseo de los Tilos.
Tel 95 235 00 61.

The main departure hall of Plaza de Armas coach station in Seville

Driving in Andalusia

Logo of a leading chain of petrol stations

Many of the main roads and motorways in Andalusia are new and in very good condition. However, as a result of the rapid expansion of the road network in recent years, some road maps are out of date, so be sure to buy one that was published recently. You should also bear in mind that the number of accidents on Spanish roads is the second highest in Europe. Always drive with caution, but particularly in July and August when the roads are packed with holiday-makers who do not know the area. When visiting towns and villages, it is generally best to park away from the centre and then walk in.

Typically narrow Andalusian street blocked by a parked car

ARRIVING BY CAR

Visitors driving vehicles from other countries need no special documentation in Spain. You should just make sure you have all the relevant papers from your country of origin: your driving licence, vehicle registration document and insurance. Your insurance company should be able to arrange an overseas extension of your car insurance. To hire a car in Spain you need show only a current driving licence.

When driving from Britain, if you have an old-style green licence you will also need to purchase an International Driving Permit. Obtain these from the RAC or the AA.

Most Spanish motorways are well equipped with an SOS network of telephones, which provide instant access to the emergency services. Ask for *auxilio en carretera*.

RULES OF THE ROAD

In Spain people drive on the right, so you must give way to the right. At roundabouts, you should give way to cars already on the roundabout – but be extremely careful when on a roundabout yourself: some oncoming cars may disregard you and drive straight on.

The speed limits are 50 kmh (30mph) in built-up areas; 90–100 kmh (55– 60 mph) outside them and 120 kph (75 mph) on motorways. Seat belts are compulsory both in the back and front; motor cyclists must

wear crash helmets. Drivers must always carry a warning triangle and a reflective vest, and they can be fined by the traffic police for not being equipped with a first-aid kit.

ROAD SIGNS

The standard European road signs are used on the roads in Andalusia. However, sign-posting is often confusing and inconsistent, so you need to be especially attentive when navigating in or out of cities. When leaving a town, scan the road for direction signs to other towns. Some are rather small and easily missed.

If you find yourself on the wrong road so that you need to change direction, look for signs which say *Cambio de Sentido*. They generally lead to bridges or underpasses where you can turn round.

LOCAL DRIVERS

Many drivers in Andalusia ignore road signs and most speed up at amber traffic lights instead of stopping.

It is common for drivers to close right up to the tail of the

ROAD SIGNS IN ANDALUSIA

Look out for the following road signs: *Peligro*, indicating danger, *Obras*, meaning roadworks ahead, *Ceda el Paso*, showing that you should give way and *Cuidado*, advising caution.

A road sign showing major routes at a crossroads

Be alert to the fact that bulls may be on the road

Overhead sign indicating the road is a motorway

Warning of the likelihood of snow or ice

car in front to signal that they want to overtake. Vehicles overtaking may signal with an arm for you to let them pass.

Indicators are not necessarily used by Spanish drivers, so be alert and try to anticipate the movements of nearby vehicles.

MOTORWAYS

In Andalusia almost all the motorways are toll-free; they are called *autovías* and they are often revamped pre-existing routes. An *autopista* (toll motorway), the A4 (*Autopista Mare Nostrum*) connects Seville and Cádiz.

As you approach the *autopista,* drive into one of the lanes to the booths, move up when a green light shows, and take the ticket which is given. You pay when you leave the *autopista* for the distance you have travelled, so take care not to lose your ticket.

DRIVING IN THE COUNTRYSIDE

Only head off the major "N" roads (*rutas nacionales*) if you are not in any hurry. The "N" roads are usually very good, but some of the minor roads in Andalusia wind and climb, and their surfaces will often be in poor condition. In addition, although diversions may be marked, when you take them you may find they are inadequately or confusingly signposted. You could add hours to a journey by taking a minor road.

BUYING PETROL

More than half of the petrol stations in Andalusia still have attendants, although this is changing. There are many petrol stations out of town, and the larger ones tend to remain open 24 hours a day.

At self-service stations you generally have to pay for the petrol before it is dispatched. S*uper* (four-star), *gasoil* (diesel), and *sin plomo* (unleaded) are usually available. Credit cards are widely accepted.

DRIVING IN TOWN

Driving in the towns and cities of Andalusia can be difficult. The centres of Seville (in particular around Santa Cruz) and Córdoba (near the Mezquita) have streets that are narrow, labyrinthine and hard to negotiate in a car.

When this is coupled with the fast, often inconsiderate driving of the residents, it can be stressful to drive in town. If you arrive by car, you are advised to garage it and use public transport until you are familiar with the area.

PARKING

It's not easy to find street parking in Seville. There are no official areas with parking meters (known as *zonas azules* in other parts of Spain), but a few convenient underground car parks.

In some streets, there are parking attendants. They are not official but most of them are honest. For a tip they will help you into a space and then watch your car until you return.

Self-styled parking attendant

It is very difficult to park in Córdoba centre, but you may find space in the underground car park beside the Mezquita.

Granada is reasonably well provided with parking spaces and with indoor car parks. The charge for parking is around €1.50 an hour.

CYCLING

Although there are now cycle lanes in Córdoba and Granada, cars tend to treat cyclists as a nuisance. A certain amount of sexual harassment also tends to afflict female cyclists. The traffic in these cities is usually too fast and chaotic to make for enjoyable or safe cycling, so it is best to stick to excursions into the country on mountain bikes.

Seville has pedestrianized two of its main roads in the centre, and these are wide promenades which allow bikes.

DIRECTORY

BREAKDOWN SERVICES

ADA
Tel 900 10 01 42.
www.ada.es

Europ Assistance
Tel 91 597 21 25.

RACE
(affiliated to the RAC in the UK)
Tel 91 593 33 33.

CITY CAR HIRE

Avis
Seville *Tel 954 44 91 21.*
Córdoba *Tel 957 40 14 45.*
Granada *Tel 958 44 64 55.*

Hertz
Seville *Tel 954 51 47 20.*
Córdoba *Tel 957 40 20 61.*
Granada *Tel 958 20 44 54.*
Malaga *Tel 952 23 30 86.*

Driving in the Sierra Nevada along one of the highest roads in Europe

Getting Around on Foot and by Bus

Many of Andalusia's towns and villages have small, historic centres, characterized by narrow streets and tiny squares. Walking is an excellent and practical way of getting around the sights, especially as entry by car is restricted to residents only in parts of many towns. For the same reason, city buses are generally not much good for travelling between monuments, but they are useful to get to shopping areas or from your hotel into the centre of town. Buses are very cheap, clean and safe, and generally only crowded at rush hours.

Route numbers   Bus routes, with
for *circulares*   stops shown

An autobus urbano, operating in Seville

WALKING

In many Andalusian towns, major sights are often only a short walk from where you are likely to be staying – at most just a short bus or taxi ride away.

In Seville, the tourist offices have a brochure, *Paseando por Sevilla* (strolling around Seville), which lists the city's interesting walks. However, one of the joys of Andalusia's cities is to lose yourself in their narrow streets and to stumble upon the sights as you go.

There are plenty of organized walking groups which make excursions to the countryside. Look them up in the listings magazine *Giraldillo (see p263)* under *Deportes* (Sports).

The evening *paseo*, or stroll, is an institution. Groups of friends, couples and families dress up and take to the streets to shop, drink coffee, and see and be seen, before stopping off for dinner at around 10pm.

CROSSING ROADS

Drivers in Spain tend not to respect pedestrians, even where pedestrians have the right of way. It is very rare for a driver to stop at zebra crossings. Crossings with pedestrian signals often have only a flashing amber light showing to oncoming drivers, even when the signal pedestrians see shows a green man; it is advisable to be very cautious when crossing if you can see any traffic approaching.

Red signal for wait; green for walk with care

CITY BUSES

Buses in Spain are all single-decker. Get on at the front and either pay the driver, show your travel card or punch your *bonobus* (ticket) in the machine at the front of the bus. When alighting, press the button to request your stop and, if the bus is crowded, remember to give yourself plenty of time to get off at the side exit.

Seville's air-conditioned buses are controlled mainly by **Autobuses Urbanos Tussam** and are red-and-black. The useful lines for visitors are the *circulares*, numbered C1 to C5, which run around the city centre. Buses run from 6am on weekdays and Saturdays (from 7am on Sundays and public holidays), until 11:30pm in winter and 12:30am in summer. After these times, night buses take over, running on the hour until 2am.

A great way to see the major sights in Seville is by **Sevirama City Tour**, an open-topped double-decker bus. It goes from the Torre del Oro *(see p69)* or Plaza de España *(see p98)*.

Buses are less useful in Granada, as most of the sights are in pedestrian areas. Bus No. 31 runs from the centre of the city to Albaicín, No. 32 from the centre to Albaicín and Alhambra, and No. 34 from the centre to Alhambra and Sacromonte.

In Córdoba the centre of town is again geared towards pedestrians. The Nos. 3 and 16 take passengers from the historic area to the newer, commercial centre of the city.

CITY BUS COMPANIES

Autobuses Urbanos Tussam
Avda de Andalucia II, Seville. **Map** 4 D3.
Tel 902 45 99 54. **www**.tussam.es

Sevirama City Tour
Paseo de Colón 18, Seville.
Map 3 B2. **Tel** 954 56 06 93.

Sevillanos enjoying the Spanish national institution of the *paseo*

HORSE-DRAWN CARRIAGES

There is no better way to soak up the ambience of Andalusia's fine cities than from the seat of an old-fashioned, horse-drawn carriage. The official tariffs are usually posted by the places where the drivers wait in line with their carriages; for example near the Giralda *(see p78)* in Seville or the Mezquita *(see pp144–5)* in Córdoba. The price is usually 40 euros for a 40-minute ride for four people, although drivers are sometimes willing to negotiate a cheaper fare. The carriages can seat up to four passengers.

Horse-drawn carriage by the cathedral in Seville

TICKETS AND TRAVEL CARDS

In Seville, a *billete sencillo* or *univiaje* (single ticket) can be purchased on the buses. Make sure, however, that you have enough small change, as a driver who cannot change a large note may ask you to get off at the next stop.

A *bonobus* ticket, valid for ten journeys, is good value at half of the price of ten single tickets. A *bonobus con derecho a transbordo* is similar, but it allows you to switch buses to continue a journey, as long as you do so within an hour. It is slightly more expensive.

Also good value, if you make more than five bus journeys in a day, is a *tarjeta turística* (a three- or seven-day tourist bus pass), which gives you unlimited bus travel. This can

be bought from Tussam kiosks, newsstands and tobacconists.

For visitors staying longer in Seville, a *bono mensual* (a one-month pass) is good value. To buy one you need a photo-card, which you can get made up at the Tussam central office.

TAXIS

Spanish towns and cities are generously supplied with taxis, so there is not usually a problem finding one, day or night. Taxis are always white and have a logo on the doors, which diplays their official number. Drivers rarely speak any English, so learn enough Spanish to explain where you are going and to negotiate the fare. The meter marks up the basic fare; however, supplements may be added for *tarifa nocturna* (night-time driving), *maletas*

(luggage), or *días festivos* (public holidays). If in doubt of the correct price, ask for the *tarifas* (tariff list).

Standard, white Seville taxi, with its logo and official number

TAXI BOOKING NUMBERS

Seville
Tel 95 458 00 00.
Córdoba
Tel 957 76 44 44.
Granada
Tel 958 28 06 54.
Málaga
Tel 952 33 33 33.

METRO

Seville's metro system was designed to aid transport between the outer areas of Seville and the city centre. It consists of four metro lines. The first, Line 1, opened in early 2009. The lines provide easy access to bus and train stations and include a line to the airport (Line 4).

The Metro-Centro tram began service in early 2008 in Seville city centre. It provides rapid transport between Prado de San Sebastian and Plaza Nueva. Other lines will be added over the next few years, extending the network to Puerta Osario and Santa Justa train station.

USING A TICKET STAMPING MACHINE

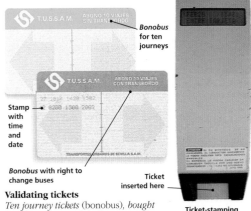

Bonobus for ten journeys

Stamp with time and date

Bonobus with right to change buses

Ticket inserted here

Ticket-stamping machine

Validating tickets

Ten journey tickets (bonobus), bought in advance, are valid when stamped.

General Index

Acknowledgments

Dorling Kindersley would like to thank the following people whose contributions and assistance have made this book possible.

Main Contributors
David Baird, resident in Andalusia from 1971 to 1995, has written many articles and books on Spain, including *Inside Andalusia*.
Martin Symington is a travel journalist and author who has written extensively on Spain. He is a regular contributor to *The Daily Telegraph* and also worked on the *Eyewitness Travel Guide to Great Britain*.
Nigel Tisdall, contributor to the *Eyewitness Travel Guide to France*, is the author of many travel publications, including the *Insight Pocket Guide to Seville*.

Additional Contributors
Louise Cook, Josefina Fernández, Adam Hopkins, Nick Inman, Janet Mendel, Steve Miller, Javier Gómez Morata, Clara Villanueva, John Gill, Mari Nicholson.
Additional Illustrations
Richard Bonson, Louise Boulton, Brian Cracker, Roy Flooks, Jared Gilbey, Paul Guest, Christian Hook, Mike Lake, Maltings Partnership, John Woodcock.
Additional Cartography
James Anderson, DK Cartography, Uma Bhattacharya, Mohammed Hassan, Jasneet Kaur.
DTP, Design and Editorial Assistance
Claire Baranowski, Francisco Bastida Cabaña, Eugenia Blandino, Greta Britton, Maggie Crowley, Cathy Day, Vinod Harish, Tim Hollis, Claire Jones, Vincent Kurien, Colin Loughrey, Francesca Machiavelli, Nicola Malone, Lynnette McCurdy, Susan Mennell, Michael Osborne, Ellen Root, Olivia Shepherd, Azeem Siddiqui, Sylvia Tombesi-Walton, Conrad Van Dyk, Word on Spain.

Index
Helen Peters.

Additional Photography
Patrick Llewelyn-Davies, Lynnette McCurdy, David Murray, Martin Norris, Ian O'Leary, Rough Guides/ Demetrio Carasco, Clive Streeter.

Photographic and Artwork Reference
Concha Moreno at Aeropuerto Málaga; Fanny de Carranza at the Area de Cultura del Ayuntamiento, Málaga; Tere González at Oficina de Turismo, Ayuntamiento, Cádiz; and staff at Castillo San Marcos, El Puerto de Santa María, Itálica, Seville cathedral and the Museo Bellas Artes, Seville.

Special Assistance
Dorling Kindersley would like to thank all the regional and local tourist offices, *ayuntamientos* and *diputaciones* in Andalusia for their valuable help, and especially the Oficina de Turismo de Sevilla de Junta de Andalucía and other departments of the Junta de Andalucía. Particular thanks also to: Javier Morata, Jose Luis de Andrés de Colsa and Isidoro González-Adalid Cabezas at Acanto Arquitectura y Urbanismo, Madrid; Juan Fernández at Aguilar for his helpful comments; Robert op de Beek at Alvear, Montilla; Francisco Benavent at Fundación Andaluza de Flamenco, Jerez de la Frontera; staff at the Locutorio, Granada; Paul Montegrifo; Amanda Corbett at Patronato Provincial de Turismo de Sevilla; José Pérez de Ayala at the Parque Nacional de Doñana; Gabinete de Prensa, RENFE, Sevilla; Graham Hines and Rachel Taylor at the Sherry Institute of Spain, London; Dr David Stone; Joaquín Sendra at Turismo Andaluz SA; *6 Toros 6* magazine, Madrid.

Photography Permissions
The publisher would like to thank all those who gave permission to photograph at various *ayuntamientos*, cathedrals, churches, galleries, hotels, museums, restaurants, shops, transport services and other establishments too numerous to thank individually.

Picture Credits
t = top; tl = top left; tc = top centre; tr = top right; cla = centre left above; ca = centre above; cra = centre right above; cl = centre left; c = centre; cr = centre right; clb = centre left below; cb = centre below; crb = centre right below; bl = bottom left; b = bottom; bc = bottom centre; br = bottom right; d = detail.

Every effort has been made to trace the copyright holders and we apologize in advance for any unintentional omissions. We would be pleased to insert the appropriate acknowledgments in any subsequent edition of this publication.
Works of art have been reproduced with the permission of the following copyright holders: (c) Suceesion Picasso/ DACS, London 2006 52clb; DACS, London 2006 53cb; © PATRIMONIO NACIONAL MADRID: 43br, 46cl, 46cb, 47ca, 50bl.
Photos taken with the assistance of AL-ANDALUS, IBERRAIL SA, Madrid: 266b; CASA-MUSEO FG LORCA, Fuentevaqueros, Granada: 195b; TEATRO DE LA MAESTRANZA, Seville: 230t; CANAL SUR, Sevilla: 245cr.
The publisher would like to thank the following individuals, companies and picture libraries for permission to reproduce their photographs:
AISA ARCHIVO ICONOGRÁFICO, Barcelona: 4t, 23b, 23cr, *Juanita Cruz*, A Beltrane (1934) 27bl (d); Biblioteca Nacional Madrid/Museo Universal, *La Spange de C Davillier*, Gustavo Doré 28cl (d); 41t, 42tl, 42c, 42br, 43cr, 44ca; Cathedral, Seville, *San Isidoro y San Leandro*, Ignacio de Ries (17th century) 45crb; Universidad de Barcelona, *La Corte de Abderramán*, Dionisio Baixeres (1885) 46cr–47cl; 47tc, 47bl, 48bl, 48br, 49bl, 50bl; Museo Naval Madrid, *Retrato de Magallanes*, 50br; 52cl; Casón del Buen Retiro, *La Rendición de Bailén*, J Casado del Alisal (1864) 53t; Greenwich Museum, *Battle of Trafalgar*, G Chamberg 53ca (d); 52cr–53cl, 55br, 121bl; Museo-Casa de los Tiros, *Gitanos Bailando el Vito*, Anonymous 193bc (d); Algar 44bl, 46clb; Servicio Histórico Nacional, *Alfonso XII*, R de Madrazo 53br (d); 55ca; © DACS 1996 Museo Nacional d el Teatro, Almagro, Ciudad Real, poster "Yerma" (FG Lorca) by José Caballero y Juan Antonio Morales (1934) 55cb; D Baird 36b, 39c; Bevilacqua 45bl, 49c; JD Dallet 42clb; Dulevant 50clb; J Lorman 33tc; M Ángeles Sánchez 38t; Sevillano 39t; ALAMY IMAGES: Authors Image/ Mickael David 11tr; Bildarchiv Monheim GmbH/ Markus Bassler 11tl; blickwinkel 249br; Stuart Crump 266br; Danita Delimont/ Alan Klehr 171tr; David Sanger Photography/ Sam Bloomberg-Rissman 169tl; Susan E. Degginger 10tc; Kathy deWitt 107cr; Mark Eveleigh 166tr; Kevin George 106tl; Eric James 252-253; Jose

Antonio Jimenez 169crb; Jon Arnold Images/ Jon Arnold 106cla; Chris Knapton 248bl; Lightworks Media 249tr; Melvyn Longhurst 167tc; Barry Mason 10cla, 250br; Geoffrey Morgan 246br; Robert Harding Picture Library Ltd/ Michael Jenner 223cl; Felipe Rodriguez 10br; SAS 178tc; Carmen Sedano 249cl; Alex Segre 225tr; Gordon Sinclair 166bl; 166cla; Nicholas Stubbs 11br; Renaud Visage 222cl; Ben Welsh 248cr; Ken Welsh 140cl; Peter M. Wilson 167br, 168bl.
ARENAS FOTOGRAFÍA ARTÍSTICA, Seville: 49cr, 116cl, Monasterio de la Rábida, Huelva, *Partida de Colón*, Manuel Cabral Bejarano 127b (d).
LLA BELLE AURORE, Steve Davey & Juliet Coombe: 15c, 230clb; BRIDGEMAN ART LIBRARY/INDEX: *The Life and Times of Don Quixote y Saavedra* (1608), Biblioteca Universidad Barcelona 51bl.
CEPHAS: Mick Rock 20tr, 30tr, 30cl, 31cr, 31br, 159; Roy Stedall 27tr; CNES, 1987 DISTRIBUTION SPOT IMAGE: 11t; BRUCE COLEMAN: Hans Reinhard 21crb; Konrad Wothe 149crb; DEE CONWAY: 25ca, 25cr; CORBIS: Owen Franken 223tl; Robbie Jack 29ca; GIANCARLO COSTA, MILAN: 27bc (d), 41b.
JD DALLET, MÁLAGA: 18bl, 32tl, 32clb, 32br, 35b, 36t, 122tl, 146cr, 158, 190t.
AGENCIA EFE, MADRID: 52clb, 56b, 57b, 57crb; EMPRESA PÚBLICA DE EMERGENCIAS SANITARIAS: 259cb; EQUIPO 30, SEVILLE: 29tl; EUROPA PRESS REPORTAJES: 57br; MARY EVANS PICTURE LIBRARY: 9 (inset), 28tl, 59 (inset), 70b, 92b, 111 (inset), 177b (d), 253 (inset); EL VAPOR DE EL PUERTO: 165br.
FRS IBERIA S.L.L:265cr.
GETTY IMAGES: AFP 27cr; GLOVENTO SUR S.L.: 248tc; THE ROLAND GRANT ARCHIVE: *"For a Few Dollars More"*, United Artists 202t; GIRAUDON, PARIS: 42cr; Flammarion-Giraudon 43c; JOSÉ M GUTIERREZ GUILLÉN, SEVILLE: 84; ROBERT HARDING PICTURE LIBRARY: Sheila Terry 49br, 58–59; HEMISPHERES IMAGES:Jean du Boisberranger 107tl; Patrick Frilet 250tl; Bertrand Gardel 107bl; Hervé Hughes 107cb; Stefano Torrione 168cra; HULTON DEUTSCH: 54cr–55cl, AM/Keystone 57tl, 171b.
IBERIA ARCHIVES: 264t; INCAFO ARCHIVO FOTOGRÁFICO, MADRID: 157t, 157ca; A Camoyán 157cra, 157cb; JL Glez Grande 157cla; Candy Lopesino/Juan Hidalgo 157clb; JL Muñoz 157b; INDEX, BARCELONA: 43cb, 44br, 46cla, 46bl, 46br, 47cb, 52tl, 52br, 53crb, 53clb (d), 53bl, 179cra; Image/Index 54tl, Private Collection, *Sucesos de Casaviejas*, Saenz Tejada 55tl, 205 (inset); Iranzo 44clb; THE IMAGE BANK: © Chasan 61b; Stockphotos inc © Terry Williams 184; IMAGES: 4b, 17, 20b, 21tl, 21bl, 32tr, 34b; AGE Fotostock, 13b, 17t, 26tr, 26clb, 27c, 28br, 31cl, 37t, 37b, 39b, 137t, 157c, 226tr, 246t; Horizon/ Michele Paggetta 27c–29c; courtesy ISLA MAGICA: 104tl, 106b.
PABLO JULIÁ, SEVILLE: 245b.
ANTHONY KING: 21tr.
LIFE FILE PHOTOGRAPHIC LIBRARY/Emma Lee 30tl, 148bl; JOSÉ LUCAS, SEVILLE: 82crb, 165tc, 244c, 246c, 258clb,

272cra; NEIL LUKAS: 130cb, 130b.
ARXIU MAS, BARCELONA: 26br; Museo Taurino, Madrid, poster for a bullfight featuring Rodolfo Gaona, H Colmenero 27bl; 45tc, 46tl, 48tl, 48c, 48cr–50cl; Museo América, Madrid, *View of Seville*, Sánchez Coello 50cr–51cl; © Patrimonio Nacional Madrid 45br, 48cl, 48cb, 49ca; MAGNUM/Jean Gaumy 57cb.
NHPA: Vicente Garcia Canseco 131 ca; NATURPRESS, MADRID: Jose Luis G Grande 131b; Francisco Márquez 21br; NETWORK PHOTOGRAPHERS: 31tl; Rapho/Hans Silvester 34c.
ORONOZ ARCHIVO FOTOGRÁFICO, MADRID: Private Collection, *La Feria* (Seville), J Domínguez Bécquer (1855) 8–9; 26ca, Private Collection *Reyes Presidiendo a una Corrida de Toros* (1862), Anonymous 27br, Banco Urquijo *Cartel Anunciador Feria de Sevilla* (1903), J Aranda 34t, 38c, 42b, 43tl, 43tc, 43cl, 43crb, 43br, 43tl, 45tl; María Novella Church, Florence, *Detail of Averroes*, Andrea Bonainti 47tl; 47crb, 47br, 49tl, Diputación de Granada, *Salida de Boabdil de la Alhambra*, Manuel Gómez Moreno 49clb; 50tl, 50cla; Museo del Prado, *Cristo Crucificado*, Diego Velázquez 51c (d); Museo de Prado, *Expulsión de los Moriscos*, Vicent Carducho 51cb (d); Musée du Louvre, Paris, *Joven Mendigo*, Bartolomé Murillo 51br (d); © Patrimonio Nacional Madrid, Palacio Real, Riofrio, Segovia, *Carlos III Vestido de Cazador*, F Liani 52bl; © DACS London 1996, Sternberg Palace, Prague, *Self-Portrait*, Pablo Picasso 54clb; Private Collection, Madrid, *Soldados del Ejército Español en la Guerra de Cuba* 54br; 55crb, 55bl, 56tl, 57tc, 72bl, 83b, 143t, 142c; 84t; Private Collection, Madrid, *Patio Andaluz*, Garcia Rodríguez 138cl; 156tl; Museo de Bellas Artes, Cádiz, *San Bruno en Éxtasis*, Zurbarán 193r; 193bl; 227br.
EDUARDO PAEZ, GRANADA: *Porte de la Justice*, Baron de Taylor 40; PAISAJES ESPAÑOLES, MADRID: 89t; JOSE M PEREZ DE AYALA, DOÑANA: 130tr, 130cl, 129t, 129ca; PICTURES: 39b; PRISMA, BARCELONA: 51tl, 135b; Museo Lázaro Galdiano, Madrid, *Lope de Vega*, F Pacheco 136b; 139t; *Vista desde el Puerto* Nicolás Chapny (1884) 183t; 245t, 264b; Ferreras 256b, Hans Lohr 161b; Anna N 174c; Sonsoles Prada 43bl.
RENFE: 268c.
M ÁNGELES SÁNCHEZ, MADRID: 242tr, 242tc; TONY STONE IMAGES: Robert Everts 82cla. VISIONS OF ANDALUCÍA SLIDE LIBRARY, MÁLAGA: M Almarza 21cr; Michelle Chaplow 19br; 28cr–29cl, 162b, 267b; A Navarro 36cl; SOL.COM: 106bl.
PETER WILSON: 1, 2–3, 35t, 61cb, 144t, 174t, 174b, 179t.
Front endpaper: all commissioned photography except JD DALLET, MÁLAGA: bc; The IMAGE BANK: Stockphotos inc © Terry Williams br; JOSE M GUTIERREZ GUILLÉN, SEVILLE: tc.
JACKET: Front - DK IMAGES: Linda Whitwham clb; SUPERSTOCK: Age fotostock main image. BACK - CEPHAS PICTURE LIBRARY: Mick Rock clb; DK IMAGES:Neil Lukas tl, bl; ORONOZ ARCHIVO FOTOGRAPHICO: J. Aranda cla. SPINE: DK IMAGES: b; SUPERSTOCK: age fotostock t.

Phrase Book

In Emergency

Help!	¡Socorro!	soh-**koh**-roh
Stop!	¡Pare!	**pah**-reh
Call a doctor!	¡Llame a un médico!	**yah**-meh ah **oon** **meh**-dee-koh
Call an ambulance!	¡Llame a una ambulancia!	**yah**-meh ah **oonah** ahm-boo-**lahn**-thee-ah
Call the police!	¡Llame a la policía!	**yah**-meh ah lah poh-lee-**thee**-ah
Call the fire brigade!	¡Llame a los bomberos!	**yah**-meh ah lohs bohm-**beh**-rohs
Where is the nearest telephone?	¿Dónde está el teléfono más próximo?	**dohn**-deh ehs-**tah** ehl teh-**leh**-foh-noh mahs **prohx**-ee-moh
Where is the nearest hospital?	¿Dónde está el hospital más próximo?	**dohn**-deh ehs-**tah** ehl ohs-pee-**tahl** mahs **prohx**-ee-moh

Communication Essentials

Yes	Sí	see
No	No	noh
Please	Por favor	pohr fah-**vohr**
Thank you	Gracias	**grah**-thee-ahs
Excuse me	Perdone	pehr-**doh**-neh
Hello	Hola	**oh**-lah
Goodbye	Adiós	ah-dee-**ohs**
Good night	Buenas noches	**bweh**-nahs **noh**-chehs
Morning	La mañana	lah mah-**nyah**-nah
Afternoon	La tarde	lah **tahr**-deh
Evening	La tarde	lah **tahr**-deh
Yesterday	Ayer	ah-**yehr**
Today	Hoy	oy
Tomorrow	Mañana	mah-**nya**-nah
Here	Aquí	ah-**kee**
There	Allí	ah-**yee**
What?	¿Qué?	keh
When?	¿Cuándo?	**kwahn**-doh
Why?	¿Por qué?	pohr-**keh**
Where?	¿Dónde?	**dohn**-deh

Useful Phrases

How are you?	¿Cómo está usted?	**koh**-moh ehs-**tah** oos-**tehd**
Very well, thank you.	Muy bien, gracias.	mwee bee-**yehn** **grah**-thee-ahs
Pleased to meet you.	Encantado de conocerle.	ehn-kahn-**tah**- doh deh koh-noh-**thehr**-leh
See you soon.	Hasta pronto.	ahs-tah **prohn**-toh
That's fine.	Está bien.	ehs-**tah** bee-**yehn**
Where is/are ...?	¿Dónde está/están ...?	**dohn**-deh ehs-**tah**/ehs-**tahn**
How far is it to ...?	¿Cuántos metros/kilómetros hay de aquí a ...?	**kwahn**-tohs **meh**-trohs/kee-**loh**-meh-trohs **eye** deh ah-**kee** ah
Which way to ...?	¿Por dónde se va a ...?	pohr **dohn**-deh seh vah ah
Do you speak English?	¿Habla inglés?	ah-blah een-**glehs**
I don't understand	No comprendo	noh kohm-**prehn**-doh
Could you speak slowly please?	¿Puede hablar más despacio por favor?	pweh-deh ah-**blahr** mahs dehs-pah-thee-oh pohr fah-**vohr**
I'm sorry.	Lo siento.	loh see-**ehn**-toh

Useful Words

big	grande	**grahn**-deh
small	pequeño	peh-**keh**-nyoh
hot	caliente	kah-lee-**ehn**-teh
cold	frío	**free**-oh
good	bueno	**bweh**-noh
bad	malo	**mah**-loh
enough	bastante	bahs-**tahn**-teh
well	bien	bee-**yehn**
open	abierto	ah-bee-**ehr**-toh
closed	cerrado	thehr-**rah**-doh
left	izquierda	eeth-key-**ehr**-dah
right	derecha	deh-**reh**-chah
straight on	todo recto	toh-doh **rehk**-toh
near	cerca	**thehr**-kah
far	lejos	**leh**-hohs
up	arriba	ah-**ree**-bah
down	abajo	ah-**bah**-hoh
early	temprano	tehm-**prah**-noh

late	tarde	**tahr**-deh
entrance	entrada	ehn-**trah**-dah
exit	salida	sah-**lee**-dah
toilet	lavabos, servicios	lah-**vah**-bohs sehr-vee-**thee**-ohs
more	más	mahs
less	menos	meh-nohs

Shopping

How much does this cost?	¿Cuánto cuesta esto?	kwahn-toh **kwehs**-tah ehs-toh
I would like ...	Me gustaría ...	meh goos-tah-**ree**-ah
Do you have?	¿Tienen?	tee-**yeh**-nehn
I'm just looking.	Sólo estoy mirando, gracias.	soh-loh ehs-**toy** mee-**rahn**-doh **grah**-thee-ahs
Do you take credit cards?	¿Aceptan tarjetas de crédito?	ah-**thehp**-tahn tahr-**heh**-tahs deh **kreh**-dee-toh
What time do you open?	¿A qué hora abren?	ah keh oh-rah **ah**-brehn
What time do you close?	¿A qué hora cierran?	ah keh oh-rah thee-**yehr**-rahn
This one.	Este	ehs-teh
That one.	Ese	eh-seh
expensive	caro	kahr-oh
cheap	barato	bah-**rah**-toh
size, clothes	talla	**tah**-yah
size, shoes	número	noo-mehr-oh
white	blanco	**blahn**-koh
black	negro	neh-groh
red	rojo	roh-hoh
yellow	amarillo	ah-mah-**ree**-yoh
green	verde	vehr-deh
blue	azul	ah-**thool**
antique shop	la tienda de antigüedades	lah tee-**yehn**-dah deh ahn-tee-gweh-**dah**-dehs
bakery	la panadería	lah pah-nah-deh-**ree**-ah
bank	el banco	ehl **bahn**-koh
book shop	la librería	lah lee-breh-**ree**-ah
butcher	la carnicería	lah kahr-nee-theh-**ree**-ah
cake shop	la pastelería	lah pahs-teh-leh-**ree**-ah
chemist	la farmacia	lah fahr-**mah**-thee-ah
fishmonger	la pescadería	lah pehs-kah-deh-**ree**-ah
greengrocer	la frutería	lah froo-teh-**ree**-ah
grocery	la tienda de comestibles	lah tee-**yehn**-dah deh koh-mehs-tee-blehs
hairdresser	la peluquería	lah peh-loo-keh-**ree**-ah
market	el mercado	ehl mehr-**kah**-doh
newsagent	el kiosko de prensa	ehl kee-**yohs**-koh deh **prehn**-sah
post office	la oficina de correos	lah oh-fee-**thee**-nah deh kohr-**reh**-ohs
shoe shop	la zapatería	lah thah-pah-teh-**ree**-ah
supermarket	el supermercado	ehl soo-pehr-mehr-**kah**-doh
tobacconist	el estanco	ehl ehs-**tahn**-koh
travel agent	la agencia de viajes	lah ah-**hehn**-thee-ah deh vee-**ah**-hehs

Sightseeing

art gallery	el museo de arte	ehl moo-**seh**-oh deh **ahr**-teh
cathedral	la catedral	lah kah-teh-**drahl**
church	la iglesia la basílica	lah ee-**gleh**-see-yah lah bah-**see**-lee-kah
garden	el jardín	ehl hahr-**deen**
library	la biblioteca	lah bee-blee-yoh-**teh**-kah
museum	el museo	ehl moo-**seh**-oh
tourist information office	la oficina de información turística	lah oh-fee-**thee**-nah deh een-fohr-mah-thee-**yohn** too-**rees**-tee-kah
town hall	el ayuntamiento	ehl ah-yoon-tah-mee-**yehn**-toh
closed for holiday	cerrado por vacaciones	thehr-**rah**-doh pohr vah-kah-thee-**yoh**-nehs
bus station	la estación de autobuses	lah ehs-tah-thee-**yohn** deh owtoh-**boo**-sehs
railway station	la estación de trenes	lah ehs-tah-thee-**yohn** deh **treh**-nehs

Staying in a Hotel

Do you have a vacant room?	¿Tiene una habitación libre?	tee-**yeh**-neh **oo**-nah ah-bee-tah-thee-**yohn lee**-breh
double room	habitación doble	ah-bee-tah-thee-**yohn doh**-bleh
with double bed	con cama de matrimonio	kohn **kah**-mah deh mah-tree-**moh**-nee-oh
twin room	habitación con dos camas	ah-bee-tah-thee-**yohn** kohn dohs **kah**-mahs
single room	habitación individual	ah-bee-tah-thee-**yohn** een-dee-vee-doo-**ahl**
room with a bath	habitación con baño,	ah-bee-tah-thee-**yohn** kohn bah-nyoh
shower	ducha	**doo**-chah
porter	el botones	ehl boh-**toh**-nehs
key	la llave	lah **yah**-veh
I have a reservation.	Tengo una habitación reservada.	tehn-goh **oo**-na ah-bee-tah-thee-**yohn** reh-sehr-**vah**-dah

Eating Out

Have you got a table for …?	¿Tienen mesa para …?	tee-**yeh**-nehn meh-sah pah-**rah**
I want to reserve a table.	Quiero reservar una mesa.	kee-yeh-roh reh-sehr-**vahr oo**-nah **meh**-sah
The bill please.	La cuenta por favor.	lah **kwehn**-tah pohr fah-**vohr**
I am a vegetarian	Soy vegetariano/a	soy beh-heh-tah-ree-**yah**-no/na
Waitress/ waiter	Camarera/ camarero	kah-mah-**reh**-rah kah-mah-**reh**-roh
menu	la carta	lah **kahr**-tah
fixed-price menu	menú del día	meh-**noo** dehl **dee**-ah
wine list	la carta de vinos	lah **kahr**-tah deh **bee**-nohs
glass	un vaso	oon **vah**-soh
bottle	una botella	oo-nah boh-**teh**-yah
knife	un cuchillo	oon koo-**chee**-yoh
fork	un tenedor	oon teh-neh-**dohr**
spoon	una cuchara	oo-nah koo-**chah**-rah
breakfast	el desayuno	ehl deh-sah-**yoo**-noh
lunch	la comida el almuerzo	lah koh-**mee**-dah ehl ahl-**mwehr**-thoh
dinner	la cena	lah **theh**-nah
main course	el primer plato	ehl pree-**mehr plah**-toh
starters	los entremeses	lohs ehn-treh-**meh**-sehs
dish of the day	el plato del día	ehl **plah**-toh dehl **dee**-ah
coffee	el café	ehl kah-**feh**
rare	poco hecho	**poh**-koh **eh**-choh
medium	medio hecho	**meh**-dee-yoh **eh**-choh
well done	muy hecho	mwee **eh**-choh

Menu Decoder

al horno	ahl **ohr**-noh	baked
asado	ah-**sah**-doh	roast
el aceite	ah-**theh**-ee-teh	oil
las aceitunas	ah-theh-**toon**-ahs	olives
el agua mineral	ah-gwa mee-neh-**rahl**	mineral water
el ajo	**ah**-hoh	garlic
el arroz	ahr-**rohth**	rice
el azúcar	ah-**thoo**-kahr	sugar
la carne	**kahr**-neh	meat
la cebolla	theh-**boh**-yah	onion
la cerveza	thehr-**veh**-thah	beer
el cerdo	**therh**-doh	pork
el chocolate	choh-koh-**lah**-teh	chocolate
el chorizo	choh-**ree**-thoh	red sausage
el cordero	kohr-**deh**-roh	lamb
el fiambre	fee-**ahm**-breh	cold meat
frito	**free**-toh	fried
la fruta	**froo**-tah	fruit
los frutos secos	**froo**-tohs seh-kohs	nuts
las gambas	**gahm**-bahs	prawns
el helado	eh-**lah**-doh	ice cream
el huevo	oo-**eh**-voh	egg
el jamón serrano	hah-**mohn** sehr-**rah**-noh	cured ham

el jerez	heh-**rehz**	sherry
la langosta	lahn-**gohs**-tah	lobster
la leche	**leh**-cheh	milk
el limón	lee-**mohn**	lemon
la limonada	lee-moh-**nah**-dah	lemonade
la mantequilla	mahn-teh-**kee**-yah	butter
la manzana	mahn-**thah**-nah	apple
los mariscos	mah-**rees**-kohs	seafood
la menestra	meh-**nehs**-trah	vegetable stew
la naranja	nah-**rahn**-hah	orange
el pan	pahn	bread
el pastel	pahs-**tehl**	cake
las patatas	pah-**tah**-tahs	potatoes
el pescado	pehs-**kah**-doh	fish
la pimienta	pee-mee-**yehn**-tah	pepper
el plátano	**plah**-tah-noh	banana
el pollo	**poh**-yoh	chicken
el postre	**pohs**-treh	dessert
el queso	**keh**-soh	cheese
la sal	sahl	salt
las salchichas	sahl-**chee**-chahs	sausages
la salsa	**sahl**-sah	sauce
seco	seh-koh	dry
el solomillo	soh-loh-**mee**-yoh	sirloin
la sopa	**soh**-pah	soup
la tarta	**tahr**-tah	pie/cake
el té	teh	tea
la ternera	tehr-**neh**-rah	beef
las tostadas	tohs-**tah**-dahs	toast
el vinagre	bee-**nah**-greh	vinegar
el vino blanco	**bee**-noh **blahn**-koh	white wine
el vino rosado	**bee**-noh roh-**sah**-doh	rosé wine
el vino tinto	**bee**-noh **teen**-toh	red wine

Numbers

0	cero	**theh**-roh
1	uno	**oo**-noh
2	dos	dohs
3	tres	trehs
4	cuatro	**kwa**-troh
5	cinco	**theen**-koh
6	seis	says
7	siete	see-**yeh**-teh
8	ocho	**oh**-choh
9	nueve	**nweh**-veh
10	diez	dee-**yehz**
11	once	**ohn**-theh
12	doce	**doh**-theh
13	trece	**treh**-theh
14	catorce	kah-**tohr**-theh
15	quince	**keen**-theh
16	dieciséis	dee-eh-thee-**seh-ees**
17	diecisiete	dee-eh-thee-see-**yeh**-teh
18	dieciocho	dee-eh-thee-**oh**-choh
19	diecinueve	dee-eh-thee-**nweh**-veh
20	veinte	**beh**-yeen-teh
21	veintiuno	beh-yeen-tee-**oo**-noh
22	veintidós	beh-yeen-tee-**dohs**
30	treinta	**treh**-yeen-tah
31	treinta y uno	treh-yeen-tah ee **oo**-noh
40	cuarenta	kwah-**rehn**-tah
50	cincuenta	theen-**kwehn**-tah
60	sesenta	seh-**sehn**-tah
70	setenta	seh-**tehn**-tah
80	ochenta	oh-**chehn**-tah
90	noventa	noh-**behn**-tah
100	cien	thee-**yehn**
101	ciento uno	thee-**yehn**-toh **oo**-noh
102	ciento dos	thee-**yehn**-toh **dohs**
200	doscientos	dohs-thee-**yehn**-tohs
500	quinientos	khee-nee-**yehn**-tohs
700	setecientos	seh-teh-thee-**yehn**-tohs
900	novecientos	noh-veh-thee-**yehn**-tohs
1,000	mil	meel
1,001	mil uno	meel oo-*noh*

Time

one minute	un minuto	oon mee-**noo**-toh
one hour	una hora	**oo**-na **oh**-rah
half an hour	media hora	meh-**dee**-a **oh**-rah
Monday	lunes	**loo**-nehs
Tuesday	martes	**mahr**-tehs
Wednesday	miércoles	mee-**ehr**-koh-lehs
Thursday	jueves	**hweh**-vehs
Friday	viernes	bee-**yehr**-nehs
Saturday	sábado	**sah**-bah-doh
Sunday	domingo	doh-**meen**-goh

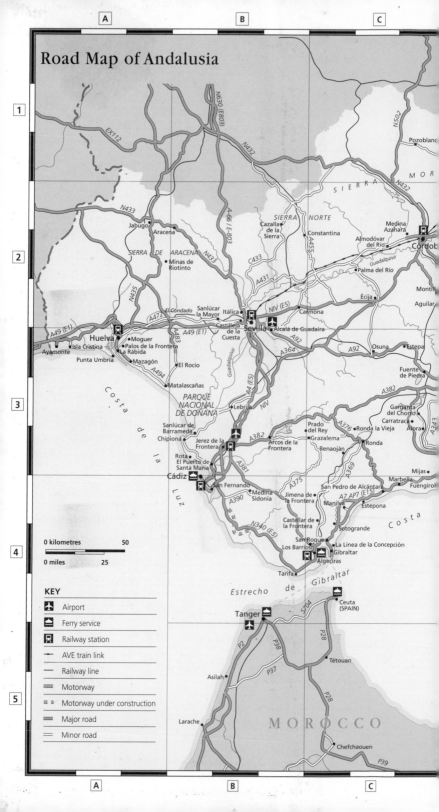